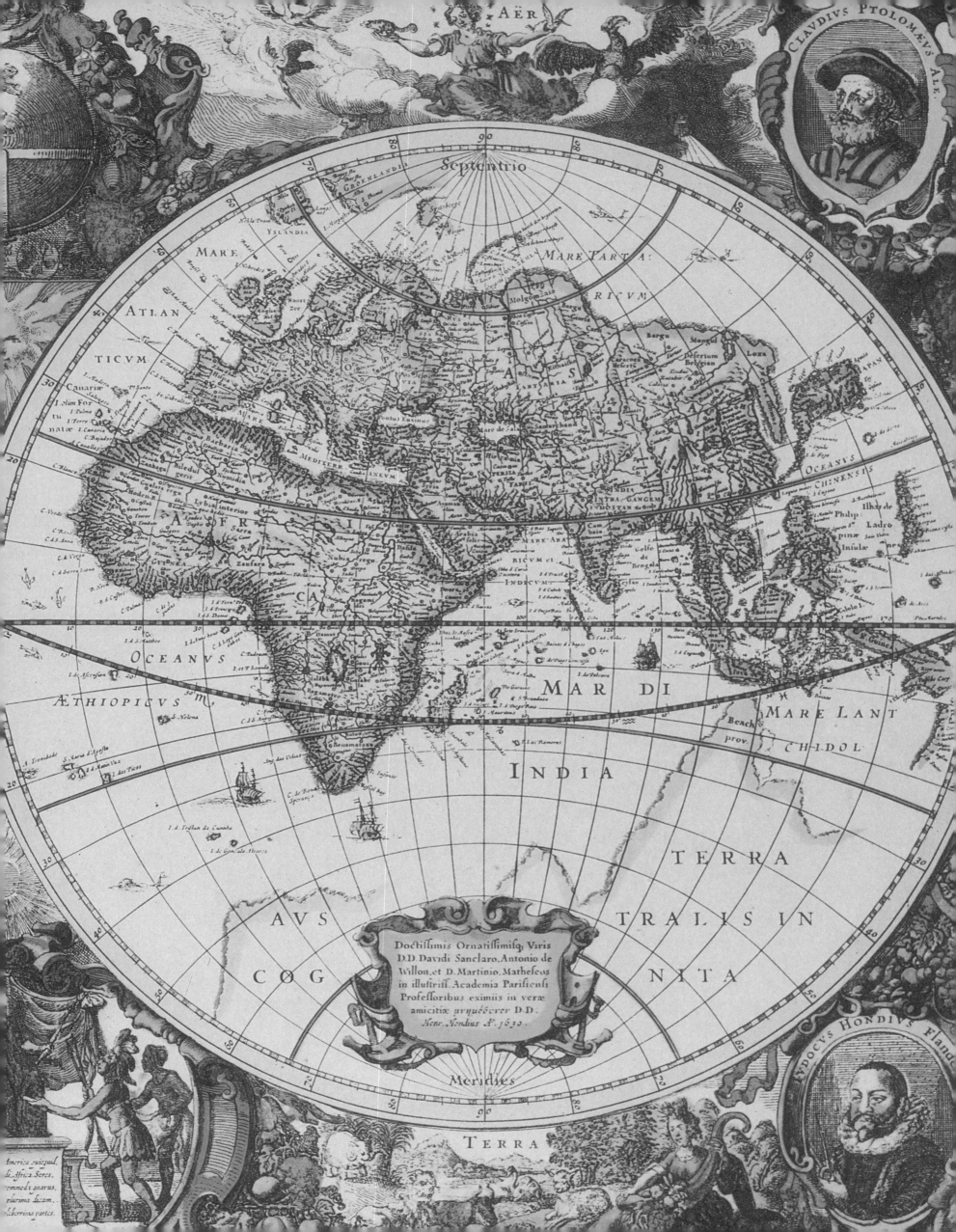

World Atlas of the Oceans

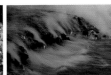

The harbor of Rotterdam – the world's largest port

A buoy-layer off the North Sea coast. On the horizon stands the lighthouse "Roter Sand"

A scene in the Antarctic: penguins on a drifting iceberg

Coral reefs – here off Tasmania in the Pacific – are known for their wonderful colors

A volcanic eruption on Hawaii: red-hot magnum flowing from Kilauea into the sea

An oilrig in the North Sea during a thunderstorm

A rich harvest from the sea: Japanese fishermen hauling in the nets in Tokyo Bay

World Atlas of the Oceans

A FIREFLY BOOK

Published by Firefly Books (U.S.) Inc. 2001
Copyright © 2001 English translation RM Buch und Medien Vertrieb GmbH/ HVK Hamburger Verlagskontor GmbH

Copyright © 2001 by RM Buch und Medien Vertrieb GmbH / HVK Hamburger Verlagskontor GmbH (Germany)

First published in 2000 in the German language by Der Club Bertelsmann. Published in the English language in Canada in 2001 by Key Porter Books

Translation from the German language into English:
Barbara Ann Klingmann, Birgit Lamerz-Beckschäfer

First Printing

U.S. Cataloging in Publication Data
World atlas of the oceans: more than 200 maps and charts of the ocean floor. – 1st American ed.
Originally published "Weltatlas der Ozeane", Ger.: Club Premiere, 2000 [264]p.: col. ill.: maps; cm.
Includes bibliographic sources and index.
Illustrations are from the General Bathymetric Chart of the Oceans.
Summary: Includes ocean cartography, geology, topography, volcanic and seismic activity; commercial use, currents, meteorology, animal and plant life, shipping, the Panama Canal, treasure hunting and shipwrecks, fishing (commercial and subsistence), oil exploration and extraction, polar oceans activity, coral reefs, recreational use and pollution.

ISBN: 1-55209-585-1
1. Oceans – Maps. 2. Ocean bottom – Maps. I. Title.
912 21 2001

Published in the United States in 2001 by Firefly Books (U.S.) Inc.
P.O. Box 1338, Ellicott Station
Buffalo, New York, USA
14205

Published in Canada in 2001 by Key Porter Books Limited.

Printed and bound in Spain

Idea and editor:
Dr. Manfred Leier

Art Director and graphic design:
Detlef Schlottmann, Red. Teamwork, Hamburg

Texts:
Jörg-Uwe Kerstein, 60–69
Dr. Erwin Lausch, 22–29, 70–71, 116–119
Hanns-J. Neubert (ScienceCom), 32–43, 56–59, 92–95, 112–115, 122–259
Monika Rößinger, 54–55
Dr. Gerd Schriever (BIOLAB), 48–53
Dr. Beatrix Stoepel, 108–109
Gerhard Thomssen, 72–91, 96–107, 110–111

Art editor: Rudolf Gillmann
Editors and readers: Gisela Merz-Busch
Documentation: Dr. Onno Groß (Oceanography)
Sebastian Kimstedt (Economics)
Axel Grychta (Arctic)
Cartographic consultants: Bernhard Winters
Lithography: W&Co MediaServices GmbH & Co. KG, Hamburg
Production: HVK Hamburger Verlagskontor GmbH

Cartography:
Relief map of the world's oceans (pp. 30–31):© Marie Tharp/Library of Congress
Relief maps of the individual oceans (pp. 32–43 and in extracts p. 122ff): © Heinrich C. Berann/National Geographic Society

Bathymetric Charts of the Oceans (pp. 120–225, 242–243) GEBCO:
© Her Majesty in Right of Canada, Department of Fisheries and Oceans 2000, Ottawa, Canada
© Sa Majesté du Chef du Canada, Ministère des Pêches et Océans, 2000, Ottawa, Canada
International Bathymetric Chart of the Mediterranean Sea and its Geological-Geophysical Series, IBCM pp. 226–241):
© Head Department of Navigation and Oceanography, St. Petersburg, Russia
Bathymetric Charts of the North Sea and the Baltic Sea (pp. 244–249, 252–259)
© Günther Edelmann

Thematic charts of individual oceans and seas:
© Edition Hölzel, Vienna (pp. 60–61, 66–67, 70–71, 72–73, 76–77, 78–79, 80–81, 82–83, 84–85, 86–87, 94, 95, 98–99, 100–101, 104–105, 108–109)

Informative graphics: Harald Blanck, Rainer Droste, Günther Edelmann, Stefanie Peters, Melanie Wolter
Cartographic retouching: Rainer Droste, Stefanie Peters

GEBCO charts: Mercator projection
Scale: 1 : 10,000,000 at Equator
World map: 1 : 35,000,000 at Equator
Pole charts: stereographic projection 1 : 25,000,000 at Equator
IBCM chart Mediterranean Sea: Mercator projection scale 1 : 10,000,000

The CEBCO charts are also available in a digitalized edition

GEBCO CHARTS NOT TO BE USED FOR NAVIGATION
Reproduction of information from the General Bathymetric Chart of the Oceans (GEBCO) originally produced by Canadian Hydrographic Service are for illustrative purposes only.

Scientific coordination of CEBCO charts:
Agapova, Galina, Institute of Physics of the Earth, U.S.S.R.
Brenner, Carl, Lamont-Doherty Geological Observatory, U.S.A.
Cande, S., Lamont-Doherty Geological Observatory, U.S.A.
Drewry, D. J., Scott Polar Research Institute, U.K.
Falconer, R. H. K., N.Z. Oceanographic Institute, N.Z.
Fisher, Robert L., Scripps Institution of Oceanography, U.S.A.
Groenlie, G., Universitetet i Oslo, Norway
Hayes, Dennis E., Lamont-Doherty Geological Observatory, U.S.A.
Heezen, Bruce C., Lamont-Doherty Geological Oberservatory, U.S.A.
Iwabuchi, Y., Hydrographic Department, Japan
Johnson, G. L., Office of Naval Research, U.S.A.
LaBrecque, John, Lamont-Doherty Geological Observatory, U.S.A.
Laughton, A. S., Institute of Oceanographic Sciences, U.K.
Mammerickx, J., Scripps Institution of Oceanography, U.S.A.
Monahan, David, Canadian Hydrographic Service, Canada
Rabinowitz, P.D., Lamont-Doherty Geological Observatory, U.S.A.
Robin, Gordon de Q., Scott Polar Research Institute, U.K.
Searle, R. C., Institute of Oceanographic Sciences, U.K.
Smith, S. M., Scripps Institution of Oceanography, U.S.A.
Sobczak, L., Earth Physics Branch EMR, Canada
Tharp, Marie, Lamont-Doherty Geological Observatory, U.S.A.
Turko, Natali, Institute of the Physics of the Earth, U.S.S.R.
Udintsev, Gleb B., Institute of the Physics of the Earth, U.S.S.R.
Ulrich, J., Institut für Meereskunde an der Universität Kiel, Germany (Fed.Rep)
Vanney, Jean-René, Université Pierre et Marie Curie, France
Vogel, Michael, Lamont-Doherty Geological Observatory, U.S.A.

Common Commission of the International Hydrographic Organisation (IHO) and the Intergovernmental Oceangraphic Commision (IOC) for the edition of GEBCO charts:
Agapova, G. V., U.S.S.R.
Bettac, W., Germany
Calder, M., Australia
Ewing, Gerald N., Canada
Fisher, Robert L., U.S.A.
Heezen, Bruce C., U.S.A.
Iwabuchi, Y., Japan
Kapoor, D. C., I.H.B., Monaco
Langeraar, W., Netherlands
Laughton, Anthony S., U.K.
Lonardi, A., Argentina
Mouzo, Félix H., Argentina
Osborn, J. H. S., Australia
Prakash, Satya, India
Rombach, Henri, Netherlands
Roubertou, André, France
Sato, T., Japan
Scott, D. P., U.K.
Simpson, Eric S. W., South Africa
Udintsev, Gleb B., U.S.S.R.

Acknowledgment:
A work such as this "World Atlas of the Oceans" would not have been possible without the commitment and cooperation of the following persons all over the globe. The publisher would like to take the opportunity here to convey expressive gratitude to all those who with their knowledge, commitment, and willingness to accept the difficult production conditions, made this publication possible. Particular mention is made of:

• Michael Casey, Director of the Marine Cartography at the Canadian Hydrographic Service in Ottawa, through whose mediation the GEBCO charts were placed at our disposal for publication in an atlas of the oceans for the first time
• Admiral Anatoliy Komaritsyn, Director of the Head Department of Navigation and Oceanography at the Russian Federation Ministry of Defence in St. Petersburg who enabled us to publish the IBCM charts of the Mediterranean
• In cooperation with Dr. Dimitry Travin (Intergovernmental Oceanographic Commission, UNESCO)
• Horst Hecht from the Federal Office of Shipping and Oceanography in Hamburg who placed his connections to the International Hydrographic Organisation and the Canadian Hydrographic Service at our disposal in the implementation of this work
• Bernhard Winters from the Federal Office for Shipping and Oceanography in Hamburg who gave freely of his amazing knowledge and support with the many cartographical problems
• Olaf Knoche, Thorsten Schumann, Axel Krebber and Stephanie Haase from the W&Co Media Services in Hamburg who helped us with their technical expertise in overcoming the, at times, apparently sheer insoluble lithographical problems and creating perfect reproductions of the GEBCO charts and
• Renate Troyer Berann who, together with the National Geographic Society, placed at our disposal the relief charts of the oceans made almost thirty years ago by her father, Prof. Heinrich C. Berann who died last year. Without her enthusiasm for oceanography and without her personal commitment in implementing "World Atlas of the Oceans" this publication would not have been possible.

World Atlas of the Oceans

With the General Bathymetric Chart
of the Oceans (GEBCO) published by the Canadian
Hydrographic Service

Published by
Dr. Manfred Leier

FIREFLY BOOKS

A thorough exploration of our waters did not begin until four centuries after the discovery of new maritime routes and the New World

A drifting iceberg in the Antarctic (pages 68-69)

Fishing for herring in the Baltic Sea (pages 94-95)

Relief map of the North Atlantic

THE OCEANS

HISTORICAL MAPS OF THE WORLD

THE OCEAN AS A HABITAT AND A COMMERCIAL AREA

How crude oil is exploited: gigantic oil rigs far out at sea (pages 96-97)

Sea lions hunting for prey (pages 52-53)

For whom the bell tolls: naval disasters in the 20th century (pages 90-91)

In the Garden of Eden: a zebra fish in a coral reef (pages 108-109)

BATHYMETRIC CHARTS

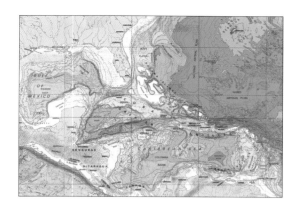

Bathymetric chart of the Caribbean

THE ATLANTIC OCEAN

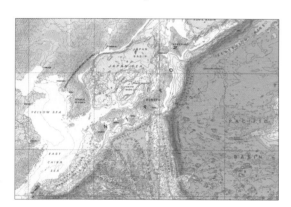

The Pacific: Yellow Sea and the Sea of Japan

THE PACIFIC OCEAN

THE INDIAN OCEAN

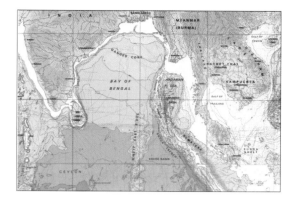

The Gulf of Bengal in the Indian Ocean

Mountains at the North Pole: the Arctic

THE ARCTIC AND ANTARCTIC

THE MEDITERRANEAN

THE NORTH SEA AND THE BALTIC

Dear Reader,

You hold in your hands an atlas covering a part of the world hitherto unknown to us. For the first time, all the important discoveries of modern marine exploration and oceanography have been assembled in this *World Atlas of the Oceans*, together with data on topographical features of the oceans of the world, exact details regarding the depths of all ocean trenches, as well as detailed information on the many "sea mounts" and underwater mountain ranges which play such an important role for marine life. The volume provides authoritative yet easily understandable information for the scientifically minded individual.

Interest in oceanography was first aroused 150 years ago, but it was not until the second half of the 20th century that a coordinated research effort was made on an international level, allowing knowledge to be meticulously and systematically gathered. From then on, major seafaring nations such as the United States, the former USSR, Great Britain, France, the Netherlands, Spain, Portugal, Germany, Canada, Australia, New Zealand, Japan, India, South Africa, Argentina, and Brazil worked together; each participating country sharing in the enormous costs but, at the same time, able to concentrate on its own, unique research area. United under the International Hydrographic Organization (IHO) in Monaco and the Intergovernmental Oceanographic Commission (IOC) of the United Nations, the results of the world-wide marine research operation were finally published by the Canadian Hydrographic Service in an unprecedented collection of charts — the General Bathymetric Chart of the Oceans (GEBCO).

This collection of ocean charts was published at the beginning of the 1980s in a small edition for collectors; there were few copies available and the charts were only known to specialists and experts. The *World Atlas of the Oceans* puts an end to this exclusivity by providing the GEBCO charts for the first time in an atlas format. For this purpose, the original GEBCO charts have been divided into segments, and these chart segments are published in their original format. In cases where the legends on the bathymetric charts have made it necessary, we have repositioned the text to make the cartographical representation of the ocean bed more comprehensible and to identify heights and depths. The depth lines of the ocean bed are given in meters, the color and varying intensity of the blues illustrate the differences in depth, and the faint brown lines mark the passage of each of the exploratory voyages of the surveying vessels.

To illustrate the topography of the ocean bed, a second atlas of panoramic drawings of the world oceans has been used. It was created by the Austrian artist Heinrich C. Berann (1915–99) at the end of the 1960s and the beginning of the '70s for the National Geographic Society. These panoramic drawings still remain the most impressive representations of the ocean bed. Even if some of the details in Berann's illustrations are in need of correction – they could not take into account the results of recent research – they continue to impart, as no other atlas does, a picture of the steep drops of the continental shelves, the vast expanses of ocean basins, the deep trenches, and the mighty mountain ranges which stretch for 60,000 kilometers (37,284 mi.) through the seas.

At the same time, Berann's drawings are such an exact representation of the ocean bed that it was decided to illustrate each of the ocean regions on the segments of the GEBCO charts with a corresponding section from the relief charts. Occasional inaccuracies are more than compensated for by the graphic

quality with which Heinrich C. Berann visualized the mysteries of the ocean bed beneath the waves.

The maps published in this atlas are labeled in a variety of ways. While place names on the relief maps are provided in English, those on the bathymetric charts provided by GEBCO follow a different principal – guided by the United Nation's naming conventions, and the two official languages of the IHO, English and French. Readers will thus find that water names are generally given in English, while land names appear in the national spelling. Exceptions were only made when these conventions would cause confusion for western readers. In these instances, the common English names and spellings were used.

This atlas would never have been made possible without the support, advice, and generous sponsorship of the Canadian Hydrographic Service in Ottawa, the German Federal Maritime and Hydrographics Office in Hamburg, the Russian Head Department of Navigation and Oceanography in St. Petersburg, as well as Mrs. Troyer-Berann and the National Geographic Society, who placed these panoramic charts at our disposal. We express our gratitude for their enormous commitment and involvement in the creation of this book.

The Publisher

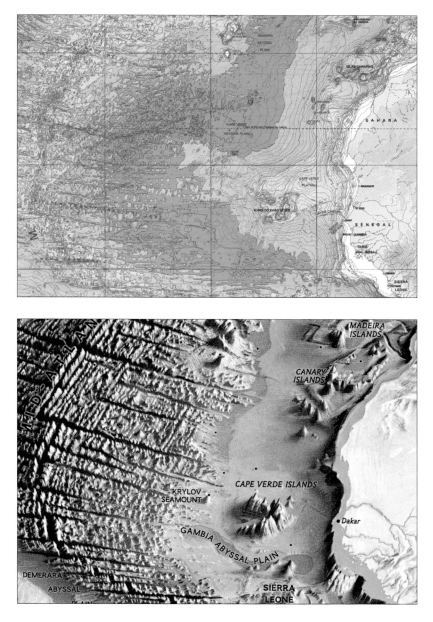

A look into the Atlantic: The deep sea basin off the coast of West Africa and the mountain range of the Mid Atlantic Ridge are easily recognizable both on the GEBCO chart (top) and on the relief chart drawn by Heinrich C. Berann.

How the oceans were formed

Although the Earth is dominated by seas and oceans, a thorough exploration of our waters did not begin until four centuries after the discovery of new maritime routes and the New World.

● ● ● The name of our planet – the Earth – is rather misleading. Just over one-quarter of the surface is actually "earth," while the remaining 71 per cent is covered by seas and oceans. And it is the oceans, not the landmasses, which make us different from the other known planets. Viewed from space, the Earth was given another name – the Blue Planet. "The Earth looks like a blue gem resting on black velvet," said Frank Bormann during the first manned space flight to the Moon in December 1968.

"Ocean" or "Sea" would be a more fitting name for the planet on which we live. Not only does the actual expanse of water exceed that of the continents, but the ocean's heights and depths also exceed those that exist on land. The deepest continental abyss is the Grand Canyon in the USA, but its depth of 1,800 meters (5,900 ft.) seems modest compared with deep sea trenches which exceed this figure several times over – for example, the Mariana Trench, which is 11,034 meters (36,200 ft.) deep. Mauna Kea and Mauna Loa on Hawaii – which measure more than 5,000 meters (16,400 ft.) from the sea bed to sea level and from there another 4,205 meters (13,796 ft.) and 4,169 meters (13,678 ft.) respectively – surpass even the highest mountain on land, Mount Everest (8,848 meters/29,029 ft.). Even the greatest mountain chain on the planet is not on land but under water, stretching under all three oceans, over 60,000 kilometers (37,284 mi.) in length and up to 4,000 kilometers (2,486 mi.) in width.

Those who named our planet in the past knew little, of course, of the seas' dimensions and influence. They believed that the flat

Fernão de Magalhães (Ferdinand Magellan) was the first to circumnavigate the world.

disc we lived on was mostly land, even though it could accommodate the Mediterranean, the Black Sea, and the Red Sea. Surrounding the Earth was a river that the Ancient Greeks called Oceanus, which flowed all around the world, and to the west of which was the entrance to the Underworld.

Although Pythagoras and his followers realized in the 6th century that the Earth was

round, it was a long time before the belief that the earth was dominated by landmasses began to change. The extent of the gigantic expanses of sea remained undiscovered for another 2,000 years.

Egyptians and Phoenicians, Carthaginians and Greeks, undertook sea voyages of discovery into unknown territory but always stayed close to the coast. The Vikings did likewise, setting off from Scandinavia on expeditions to the north and west. Even when Portugal's Prince Henry the Seafarer – the initiator of planned and sponsored maritime expeditions – sent ships to the south, his captains still made their way gradually along the west coast of Africa, keeping close to land.

Early settlement of the Pacific Islands

Those seafaring peoples who undertook incredible and daring voyages from South East Asia and New Guinea, taking possession of the widely dispersed islands of the oceans, naturally had a different picture of the world than the Europeans. From the 1st and 2nd centuries BC up to the end of the 1st century AD they settled on practically all of the habitable islands between the Philippines and the Easter Islands, between New Zealand and Hawaii.

It is hard to imagine how they simply sailed off into the blue taking their families and livestock with them. It is certain that they explored the enormous stretches of water beforehand, could navigate their way through them, and were sufficiently confident of being

The discoverer of the New World: Christopher Columbus, a Genoese seafarer in the service of the Spanish monarch, crossed the Atlantic in 1492, landing on the island of San Salvador (Guanahani). Later, he traveled along the coasts of Central and South America. This copper engraving from 1596 shows Columbus setting foot on land in the New World for the first time.

The water of life:
All life on our planet has its origins in the oceans. Only 29 per cent of the Earth's surface is land; 71 per cent is covered by water.

able to find their way back to their point of departure.

From the European point of view, the discovery of the seas and oceans began to occur more rapidly at the end of the 15th century, with one discovery following another.

In 1488, the Portuguese seafarer Bartolomeu Diaz sailed around the southern tip of Africa, but then turned back when there was a mutiny by his crew. Ten years later, his fellow countryman, Vasca da Gama, reached the coast of Kenya after having rounded the Cape of Good Hope. From Malindi he crossed the Arabian Sea with the monsoon behind him on well-established Arabian trading routes and reached Calicut, which in those days was the most important trading center in India.

In the meantime, Christopher Columbus, a Genoese seafarer in the employ of the Spanish, crossed the Atlantic in 1492 and discovered America, firmly believing that he had found a sea route to Asia. In 1513, after crossing the Panama isthmus, conquistador Vasco Núñez de Balboa became the first person to see that there was another ocean to the west of the newly discovered world. He claimed the land immediately for Spain by wading ceremoniously into the water dressed in full armor. He could not possibly have conceived the extent of the area he had just claimed. This was left to Ferdinand Magellan who, along with his men on the first circumnavigation of the world, made the discovery.

The first circumnavigation of the world

Having fallen into disgrace in his native Portugal, Magellan set sail with five ships under the Spanish flag in 1519 for the Moluccas – at that time, the highly valued Spice Islands. Portugal had already discovered and secured (by means of a kind of monopoly agreement) the sea route from the west around the southern tip of Africa. Magellan now planned to secure a new route to the Spice Islands for Spain from the east. He entered the passage he had been seeking – known today as the Magellan Strait – and finally reached the Pacific Ocean. His fleet had by then been reduced to three ships, but the real challenge was yet to come.

James Cook explored the seas of the southern hemisphere, crossing the southern Polar Circle three times between 1772 and 1775. This copper engraving from 1780 shows his fleet landing in "Christmas Harbor Bay" on the Kerguelen Islands.

The waters they now crossed were seemingly unending and the crew was tortured by thirst, hunger, and scurvy. Their first landing was at Guam, the largest of the Mariana Islands, after having spent a grueling 99 days at sea. Later Magellan and 30 of his crew were killed in a fight with natives in the Philippines. The rest of the expedition did reach the Moluccas but only one ship was fortunate enough to return home to Spain, along a route that was fraught with danger from the Portuguese. Out of a crew of 270 men who had set off three years before, just 18 returned.

After this terrible voyage, it became obvious that the scholars were wrong about the world's land-to-sea ratio. And the maps still showed a gigantic continent in the southern hemisphere which no-one had ever seen. According to general conviction, there simply had to be a large landmass acting as a counterbalance – the Terra Australis Incognita, the

unknown territory in the south. Dutch ships discovered Australia and New Zealand, but everyone imagined the unknown continent to be much larger.

In order to answer the question once and for all, the British naval officer James Cook was commissioned to make a second long voyage from 1772 to 1775, and to sail around the world as far south as possible. Maneuvering through icebergs, and steering between blizzards and sleet, Cook kept watch for land – to no avail. Three times he crossed the southern Polar Circle. Even if the landmasses of the Antarctic were discovered later, one fact became quite certain: Wherever this unknown land in the south was supposed to be, there was nothing but water. There was no longer any doubt that the Earth was dominated by the oceans and seas.

Ocean "boundaries"

In literature, the world's oceans are often referred to poetically as the "Seven Seas." If boundaries are to be set, however, today's oceanographers speak of three principal oceans – the Pacific, the Atlantic, and the Indian – and their adjacent seas, which are referred to as either being "marginal" or "mediterranean." A mediterranean sea, like the European Mediterranean Sea or the Baltic Sea, is almost entirely surrounded by land, whereas marginal seas, such as the North Sea or the Bering Sea, have a greater exchange of water with the open ocean. It is not possible to distinguish sharply between them.

As there are no natural boundaries between the oceans in the southern hemisphere,

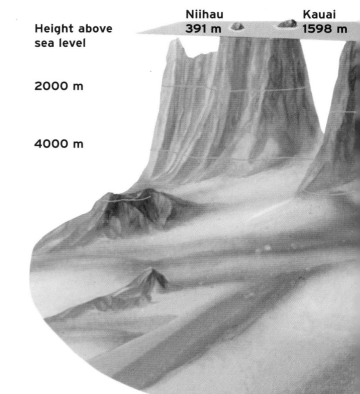

Height above sea level

Niihau 391 m Kauai 1598 m

2000 m

4000 m

The highest mountains in the world are the Mauna Kea and the Mauna Loa of Hawaii, which rise directly from the sea bed to reach a height of 9,000 meters (29,530 ft.). Their peaks are 4,205 meters (13,796 ft.) and 4,169 meters (13,678 ft.) above sea level, respectively. The highest mountain on land, Mount Everest, is 8,848 meters (29,029 ft.).

three dividing lines have been drawn. The shortest connection from Cape Horn to the Antarctic Peninsula is seen as the boundary between the Atlantic Ocean and Pacific Ocean. The meridian 20° east that runs from the southern tip of Africa to the Antarctic separates the Atlantic Ocean from the Indian Ocean. And, lastly, the meridian 147° east that cuts across the southern cap of Tasmania serves as a dividing line between the Indian Ocean and Pacific Ocean.

As a result of this division, half of the overall 362 million square kilometers (139 mill. sq. mi.) of ocean are in the Pacific, giving it a larger expanse than all the landmasses of the Earth put together. The entire continent of Europe, for instance, would easily fit into the Pacific Ocean about 17 times.

What lay beneath these enormous water-covered areas remained unknown to man for a long period of time. It was not until the 18th century that hydrographic services began

to systematically chart information about the seas (beginning in France in 1720) with the aim to make shipping quicker and safer.

From the results of these hydrographic surveys, and from observing currents and winds, the occurrence of ice, and the frequency of mist and fog, these service departments created nautical charts, nautical manuals, and tide tables. These endeavors were carried out with modest means.

Soon individual scientists became curious and wanted to know more about the unexplored world of seas and oceans. What was the composition of sea water? Precisely how deep were the oceans? What was the sea bed like? What was the temperature down there? Was there any life at all in the darkest depths? If there was, what kind of creatures lived there? To answer these questions, gradually the science of the sea, now known as oceanography, began to grow.

Its development was slow compared with other branches of research, where imaginative experimenters and conscientious observers could work alone or in small teams to make important discoveries with few resources. However, for oceanographic investigations, ships were needed along with numerous assistants. To express it in modern terms, oceanography was a large-scale research operation right from the beginning.

In 1872, five British scientists set off to complete an inventory of the oceans during which they were to set standards for future oceanographic expeditions. With the research ship

The Grand Canyon is the deepest abyss on any continent. Compared with the ocean trenches however the US monument is only of very modest dimensions - a mere 1,800 meters (5,900 ft.).

Mauna Kea
4205 m

Oahu
2025 m

Molokai
1515 m

Lanai
1027 m

Maui
3055 m

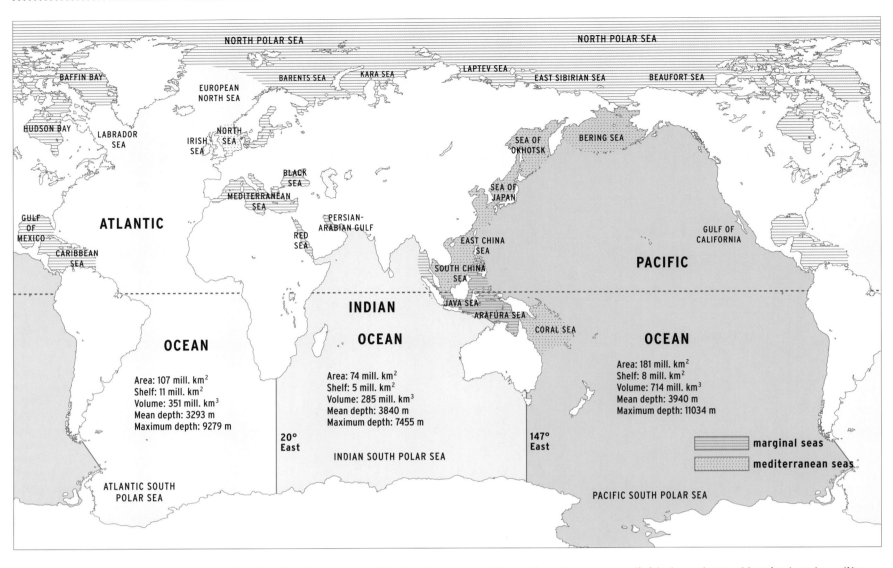

The world's three principal oceans – the Pacific Ocean, the Atlantic Ocean, and the Indian Ocean – are divided as shown. Marginal and mediterranean seas lie in the continental areas.

Challenger – a revamped, steam-driven corvette – they spent three years in the three great oceans carrying out biological, chemical, physical, and geological observations. After a voyage of 127,000 kilometers (79,000 mi.) they returned home in 1876 with rich findings which, when evaluated, gave us the first comprehensive information about the nature of the oceans.

Searching for answers: Challenger and Meteor

Led by Charles Wyville Thomson, Professor of Natural History at the University of Edinburgh, the scientists on board the *Challenger* planned to investigate the sea and sea bed in as many places as possible according to a standardized program. While the steam engines held the vessel in position, the scientists and the crew carried out deep soundings, measured the temperature of the water at various depths, and took water samples at each spot. Then the ship pulled dragnets through the water and a dredge along the bottom of the sea to fetch up living organisms and samples of the sea bed.

The investigations were carried out in 362 locations and 4,417 living organisms were found. On board the *Challenger* it was proved that a variety of living creatures exist in the greatest depths, even though the temperatures there were near a constant 0° C (32° F). The scientists observed ocean currents and collected an incredible amount of meteorological data. For the first time, an

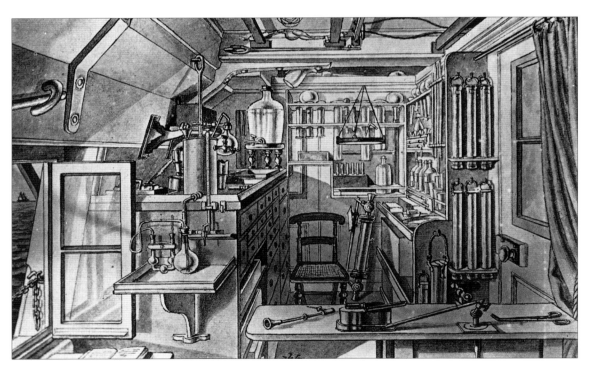

The laboratory aboard the Challenger: Animals and plants that had been fished out of the sea were investigated and chemical and biological tests were undertaken.

impression of the world-wide sea bed was beginning to take shape. Marine scientists were given an idea of what depths they could reckon with: in the Pacific, an astounding 8,168 meters (26,798 ft.) was sounded off the Mariana Islands.

Between 1876 and the First Word War, about a dozen research vessels followed in the

tracks of the *Challenger*, extending the inventory that, in view of the vastness of the world's oceans, still remained a collection of random samples. A second phase of oceanography was undertaken by the German *Meteor* between 1925 and 1927 with a lengthy voyage to the South Atlantic. Ten marine scientists set about systematically investigating and surveying the ocean.

dedication and resources, oceanography continues to be carried out on a mostly international scale.

In view of the vastness of the oceans and their enormous volumes of water, even an oceanographer who had an entire fleet of research vessels at his or her disposal would find it difficult to gather enough data to measure conditions and to continuously follow their development. Oceanographers are therefore beginning to increasingly rely on instruments to carry out their measuring programs automatically.

Oceanograph's mechanical assistants

"Subsurface drifting sondes" are set at different depths and are left to drift for months, or even years, with the currents. Emitting acoustic signals that can be heard a long distance off, they regularly submit their "reports" on where a current has brought them as well as at what speed.

So-called "gliders," which are equipped with a small rotor driven by batteries, float along prescribed depths and regions measuring the directions of currents and their speed, as well as temperatures, salt content, diverse trace substances, oxygen, and carbon dioxide in the water. At defined intervals they resurface, transfer their data to satellites, and disappear once more under the water.

"Observatories" and "moorings" are set down on an ocean bed in order to make continuous measurements of the currents or the water/solid exchange with sediment. These, too, are often left alone for weeks or months. Other meters, attached to long cables, are anchored into the sea bed and held at a desired depth until a ship retrieves them and collects their stored data.

Today's oceanographers are also aided by satellites, which provide a world-wide picture of what is happening on the surface of the oceans. These space lookouts measure water temperature and register even the finest differences in color, which gives an indication of how quickly plankton is growing. Radar satellites that scan the ocean with microwaves can register the "roughness" of the water's surface, thus providing extensive details of wind conditions. It is even possible to measure the depth of the sea today from outer space.

Oceans and climate

Before serious exploration of the oceans began, these extensive basins on the Earth's surface, filled with vast expanses of water, didn't seem to be the most interesting subjects of inquiry. Scientists soon discovered that the oceans were indeed fascinating – and there certainly was a lot to be explored!

The world's oceans make up 71 per cent of the Earth's surface. Compare this with the landmasses: The entire continent of Australia only comprises 1.5 per cent of the surface, and Antarctica only 2.8 per cent. As well, the oceans contain about 97 per cent (1,370 million cubic kilometers [328 mill. cu. mi.]) of all the water on the Earth – a crucial factor since water is essential for life. The remaining 3 per cent of the Earth's water is in the ice masses

The German research vessel Meteor cruised the South Atlantic from 1925 to 1927, making the first systematic survey of the ocean.

The scientists on the *Meteor* performed deep soundings, measured temperatures, studied a variety of living organisms brought up by the nets and dredgers, and released balloons carrying meteorological instruments into the air. The most important subject of investigation was the water itself. Numerous measurements were made on temperature, the salt content of sea water, and the speeds of currents, ultimately proving the theory that these mighty volumes of water did not remain motionless in their basins.

Water as the object of scientific investigation

It has been known for a long time that currents do not just flow on the sea surface but down in the depths. At different levels the water flows in varying directions, and this pattern incessantly changes with the seasons as well as during shorter or longer scales of time.

With the movements of the currents, all is in constant motion. The scientists on the *Meteor* were the first to observe these movements – the dynamics of the sea.

Soon after the *Meteor*'s successful voyage, many marine scientists realized what was necessary in order to gain a more precise picture: Measurements would have to be taken at different places simultaneously. And that ultimately meant international cooperation.

Such a grand scale of cooperation did not occur until after the Second World War. In the International Geophysical Year 1957/58, 23 vessels from eight European nations set sail for a mutual investigation of the Atlantic Polar Front. This long and narrow zone, stretching from the banks of Newfoundland to the Sea of Norway, forms the boundary between the warm and very salty water from the south and the cold, less saline waters from the north. Conditions frequently change very quickly here, having an influence on the weather in the North Atlantic and, thus, in Western Europe, too.

With the success of the Atlantic Polar Front exploration, further cooperative projects soon followed. And due to world-wide of the Arctic and the Antarctic, ground water to a depth of up to 4,000 meters (13,123 ft.), lakes and rivers (which, in all, total 0.01 to 0.02 per cent), as well as the humidity in the atmosphere.

Weather and climate are determined decisively by the world's oceans. With nearly three-quarters of the Earth's surface covered by ocean, these bodies of water pick up most of the Sun's energy that reaches our planet. Once heated by solar energy, the water begins to evaporate, and this steam rises up from the surface of the water into the atmosphere, eventually returning to Earth's surface in the form of rain or snow. Every year, 350,000 cubic kilometers (83,965 cu. mi.) of water evaporates from the oceans – enough water to submerge the whole of Germany by over half a mile. If it were not for the oceans, the fertile regions of our world would very soon become deserts.

The oceans are excellent heat accumulators, as water can absorb a great amount of heat without causing erratic changes in temperature to the world as a whole. If the Earth's surface was only comprised of landmasses, conditions would be very different. There would be unbearable heat during the day and Arctic cold at night. So the oceans act as a world-wide air-conditioner of sorts, moderating extremes in temperature, and thus making the Earth inhabitable.

Oceans also dissipate the solar energy that falls in ample quantities in the Tropics, but less and less so towards the north and south. Warm ocean currents transport large masses of energy towards the poles; without the Gulf Stream, for instance, Europe would be a rather inhospitable place. Still, twice as much energy is distributed through the atmosphere as is through the ocean currents.

The fundamental impact of our oceans on the climate is the main reason why oceanographers chase after data on currents, tempe-

The first-ever deep sea drilling operations were carried out from the "Glomar Challenger."

ratures, and salinity (the measure of how heavy the water is and, therefore, its tendency to either sink to the bottom or rise to the top). Such data is continuously required in order for scientists to be able to make forecasts of future climatic changes, or to report on our current society's contribution to the threatening greenhouse effect.

The impact of the oceans on human life

Water has always been the true cradle of life – not the land. Although it is not yet clear where life began, it is certain that it developed from simple beginnings in the seas, where it remained for more than three billion years before the first plants and animals appeared on land approximately 400 million years ago. Photosynthesis, the basis of existence for practically all living things, developed in the sea; and oxygen, a waste product of the photosynthesis process (and a crucial element for life on our planet) then bubbled out of the water.

As a reminder of our marine origins, human embryos still have gill arches and gill slits which undergo an astonishing metamorphosis before birth. The gill arches develop into the auditory ossicles, i.e., the hammer (malleus), anvil (incus), and stirrup (stapes), the hyoid bone and the thyroid cartilage on the epiglottis. The gill slits develop into the eustachian tube and tympanic cavity, the lymphatic nodes in the neck, the thymus gland, the parathyroid gland, and the tonsillar crypt.

Not only do the oceans make life hospitable for us, sustain us, and even feed us, but they also provide humans with resources – from sand and gravel for building materials to crude oil, natural gas, and ores. In recent years, methane hydrate has caught the attention of oceanographers; it is an ice-like and curiously flammable compound of water and methane – a gas rich in energy that can be found in enormous quantities at the bottom of the sea bed. Rough estimates suggest that marine methane hydrate contains twice as much carbon as that in all known sources of natural gas, crude oil, and coal in the world, making it a potentially huge source of energy.

A new understanding of the Earth

It was beneath the waters that geoscientists finally discovered the key to a completely new concept of the Earth – a concept which turned out to be even more dramatic than previous generations of researchers could possibly have imagined.

Up until the 1960s, it was generally believed that the great oceans had remained unchanged over millions of years. On the continents, there was no denying the traces of profound changes in the past. Smaller and larger continents had risen or sunk, mighty mountains formed only to disappear again through erosion, and huge heaps of rocks buckled and twisted before breaking up. The flat shelf seas at the edge of the oceans also shared the same destiny as the continents. Only the extensive deep sea and ocean regions appeared to have remained unaffected by the tremors on land.

However, in the 1950s, scientists began to report on findings which seemed to have no

place in this peaceful image of the oceans. Seismic investigations showed that only a relatively thin layer of sediment covered the ocean bed – a layer much too thin to have existed unchanged over billions of years. More and more sections of the Mid-Ocean Ridge were discovered and finally recognized as parts of a distinctive system – mountain chains of volcanic rock, rising 2,000 meters (6,500 ft.) to 3,000 meters (9,800 ft.) from the floor of the ocean, and sometimes more. In the ridge regions, a chasm, known as a "transform fault," more or less follows the line of the mountain range. In this ocean area, otherwise not prone to earthquakes, there is a high concentration of numerous earthquake centers, and heat from the interior of the Earth flows here much more intensively than anywhere else in the ocean.

In addition to the high mountain ranges, there are also deep sea trenches. Their location near the continents or island chains was surprising enough, but detailed investigations brought even more astonishing information to light – the side nearest to the land is steeper than the one facing the ocean. Scientists began to ask themselves more ques-

The Blue Planet: From outer space, it is easy to see how the oceans have given our planet its name.

Ridge. Magma is forced up from the transform fault and fills the gaps left behind. In this way, the sea builds up a new bed foot-by-foot, and where continents are bordered by trench systems, it re-enters and dissolves into the Earth's mantle from which it originated.

According to Hess (putting into words the then outrageous consequences of his theory): "The ocean basins are inconstant phenomena on Earth and the continents are constant ..." Hess wrote that every 300 to 400 million years the whole of the ocean was swept clean. We now know that the ocean bed actually only reaches half that age before a new bed is created.

Hess's explanation soon found its followers and became known as the "seafloor spreading" theory. It was additionally supported by further investigations of the magnetic stripes, called parallel anomalies. It had been known for some time that certain minerals in solidifying magma were directed towards the Earth's magnetic fields and, like frozen compass needles, preserved the dominating magnetic field of the moment. It was also known that the magnetic field reverses its direction by 180° every few hundred thousand to several million years, i. e., the North Pole becomes the South Pole and vice versa.

Detailed investigations of magnetic parallel anomalies near transform faults showed that the width of each stripe corresponded to the time interval to the next reversal of the magnetic fields. Within a short phase, only a narrow band of sea floor is produced, during a longer phase correspondingly more. It is always developed on both sides of the transform fault, mirror-inverted.

Definitive proof of how young the oceans are, as compared with the landmasses, was provided by the ocean drilling vessel *Glomar Challenger* in the South Atlantic at the end of 1968. The ship had recently been put into service carrying out the first drilling operations in the ocean by sinking a shaft through the sediments down to the basalt magma. Fossils from the lowest sedimentary layer left no doubts as to the age of the deposits; the closer the *Glomar Challenger* drilled to the transform fault, the more recent were the deposits directly above the basalt – the youngest of them being only a few million years old.

Based on the theory of seafloor spreading, plate tectonics – "the theory to explain everything" as it is called in a contemporary and widely-used textbook on geology – was developed. The idea of drifting plates forming the outer crust of the Earth explained the formation of the oceans and continents, the location of earthquake zones and volcanic chains, and why the mountains are where they are and not anywhere else. Many hitherto unexplained findings from the Earth's past, such as indications of a tropical climate in areas which today lie outside of the Tropics, were suddenly clear. The answer was that everything is constantly moving. The ocean floor is not only constantly changing, but complete oceans between continents disappear while new ones are born elsewhere.

With their constant renewal, then, the oceans are an active element in the dynamics between the plates which have formed the face of our planet through the ages. The landmasses, on the other hand, have remained rather passive.

set off in the same way as the mountain ridges and the transform fault, with fracture zones separating what was once obviously a whole.

All of these curiosities were convincingly explained at the beginning of the 1960s by the American geophysicist Harry Hess. At the time, his ideas seemed daring in view of the old and still upheld dogma of ancient and unchanging oceans. Initially, he carefully distanced himself from them by speaking merely of his "attempt at geo-poetry."

The seafloor spreading theory

According to Hess's new and truly radical picture of the oceans, the ocean bed is constantly moving, driven by convection currents in the Earth's crust. Circulating hot viscous rocks rise from the Earth's interior, spread out parallel to the Earth's surface, and finally sink back again and cool. These convection currents rise up under the Mid-Ocean Ridges, returning to earth in the ocean trenches.

The ocean bed is moving at a speed of a few inches a year sideways from the Mid-Ocean

tions. How did these deep depressions occur? And, considering how close they are to land, why have they not filled up with sediment?

Also puzzling were the results of investigations that measured rock magnetism in the ocean. The ocean bed was discovered to contain "stripes" of magnetism, with alternating weak and strong magnetic zones. These stripes were on average 20 kilometers (12.5 mi.) wide, running parallel to the nearest mid-ocean ridge and displaying considerable differences.

These magnetic anomalies, with their characteristic sequences of stripes in varying widths, can be followed over hundreds of miles, but not without some difficulty; they have been repeated laterally but are abruptly

The Oceans
The sea floor in relief

Open borders in the north

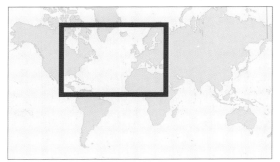

●●● No one knows exactly where the Atlantic Ocean ends in the north – some people even regard the Arctic Ocean as a part of the Atlantic. For the sake of simplicity, however, many are simply guided by the latitudes. In most cases, the 65. latitude or the Polar circle at 66° 30' is considered as the northern border of the Atlantic.

Attempts have also been made, however, to define a natural border running from east Greenland along the Iceland-Greenland Rise over Iceland and the Iceland–Faeroes Rise to the Faeroe Islands. There it turns off towards Norway, past the Voring Plateau jutting out off the west coast of Norway, and meets up with the coast again in the north of Norway. This would make the east side of the southern tip of the European Polar Sea a part of the Atlantic as the warm Norwegian current, a branch of the Gulf Stream, flows here to the north.

Oceanographers do not have to keep to landmarks. They count the warm waters of the Sea of Norway as part of the Atlantic Ocean. In contrast, they see the cold waters of the Greenland Sea opposite as belonging to the Arctic.

The Atlantic was formed about 180 million years ago when the northern primeval continents began to break apart. The western and the eastern continents separated and the ocean basin opened.

The most conspicuous landmark in the Atlantic Ocean is the Mid-Atlantic Ridge. Running almost exactly through the middle of the ocean, it makes up about one-third of the sea floor. In some places it is 1,600 kilometers (1,000 mi.) wide – for example, between the Cape Verde Islands and the Bermudas. On the restless volcanic island of Iceland, it rises almost 1,500 meters (5,000 ft.) above sea level. Magma from the Earth's interior flows from the central split of the ridge, forming a new sea bed and driving the continents on both sides apart.

The northern end of the Atlantic and the Sea of Labrador are considered the "lungs" of the oceans. There, gigantic masses of oxygen-enriched surface water plunge into the ocean, and drift into the Antarctic, before spreading into all the other oceans. In many places the water rises to the surface again and flows back into the North Atlantic. It can take a thousand years to complete one cycle.

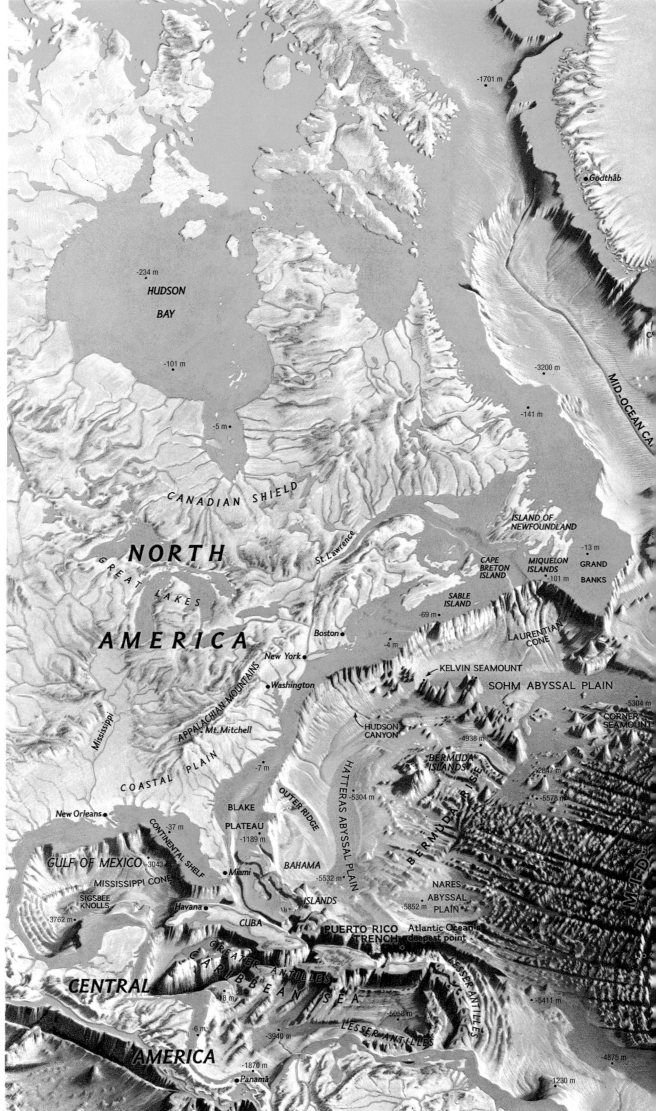

EENLAND

-212 m

ICELAND

• Reykjavík

SURTSEY

-2743 m

JAN MAYEN RIDGE

SCANDINAVIA

-2377 m

REYKJANES RIDGE

-1240 m

FAEROE ISLANDS

-161 m

-101 m

LOUSY
BANK

-1966 m

-181 m

ROCKALL

-530 m

NORTH

-238 m

DEVILS HOLE

SEA

-558 m

Stockholm

-91 m

BALTIC SEA

BRITISH

ISLES

• Hamburg

-2899 m

London

• Le Havre

EUROPE

-93 m

-4694 m

BISCAY ABYSSAL PLAIN

-4694 m

ALPS

-4499 m

-4700 m

-5267 m

Danube

MILNE
SEAMOUNT

RIFT VALLEY

-4663 m

AZORES

-5395 m

IBERIAN

Marseille

ADRIATIC SEA

CORSICA

PENINSULA

Rome

SARDINIA

-5084 m

Lisbon

-3420 m

BALEARIC IS.

SICILY

Athens

AEGEAN

GRAPHER FRACTURE ZONE

-265 m

-40 m

AMPERE
SEAMOUNT

-2597 m

-1472 m

SEA

CRETE

MEDITERRANEAN RIDGE

RIDGE

-3658 m

-3868 m

-3291 m

ATLANTIC

-293 m

MADEIRA
ISLANDS

ATLAS MOUNTAINS

-448 m

-5432 m

-4572 m

CANARY
ISLANDS

-3840 m

S A H A R A

-5677 m

Nile

-5200 m

-4115 m

CAPE VERDE ISLANDS

KRYLOV
SEAMOUNT

-1298 m

Niger

A F R I C A

• Dakar

GAMBIA ABYSSAL PLAIN

-4800 m

Rises in the South Atlantic

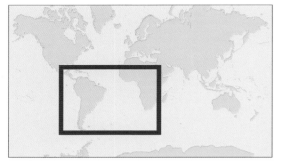

●●● The boundaries of the South Atlantic are not disputed in the way the northern boundaries are – the waters around the Antarctic are usually referred to today as the "Southern Ocean" or the "Antarctic Ocean".

The line of separation from the Southern Ocean runs approximately along 40° latitude; there, currents of cold water from the Antarctic meet up with warmer waters from the north. Although the "border" between these currents is wide, it is relatively stationary. The division between the Atlantic and Indian Oceans is at 20° latitude, between Cape Agulhas (the southernmost tip of Africa) and the Antarctic.

In comparison with the North Atlantic, the southern part of the ocean has few islands and no marginal seas. The coasts, too, are less varied than they are in the north.

The mighty Mid-Atlantic Ridge, which divides the ocean from north to south into two large basins, is traversed by numerous trenches and rifts, some of which are 500 kilometers (310 mi.) long, 25 kilometers (15.5 mi.) wide, and 3 kilometers (2 mi.) deep. At the most narrow point – between Cape São Roque in Brazil and Cape Palmas in Liberia – the Atlantic is a mere 2,850 kilometers (1,770 mi.) wide. Just south of the Equator, a deep trench – the Romanche Fracture Zone – divides the Mid-Atlantic Ridge into a northern and a southern part.

The great basins on either side of the Mid-Atlantic Ridge are themselves divided into smaller basins separated by underwater thresholds. In the east is the Walvis Ridge, between Cape Angola and the Cape Basin; in the west is the Rio Grande Rise, between the Argentine and the Brazilian Basins.

The rises were formed about 80 million years ago from a chain of volcanoes which were then active along the Mid-Atlantic Ridge. After the volcanoes became extinct, they slid with the sea floor – which was constantly flowing from the central rift – along the ridge, down the slope to the bottom of the plain, and then sank. The rises prevent the spread of ocean currents. For instance, bottom water flowing from the Antarctic to the north cannot overcome the Walvis Ridge. In comparison, the Rio Grande Rise has two deep saddles through which the bottom water can go further north and still reach the Angola Abyssal Plain through the Romanche Fracture Zone.

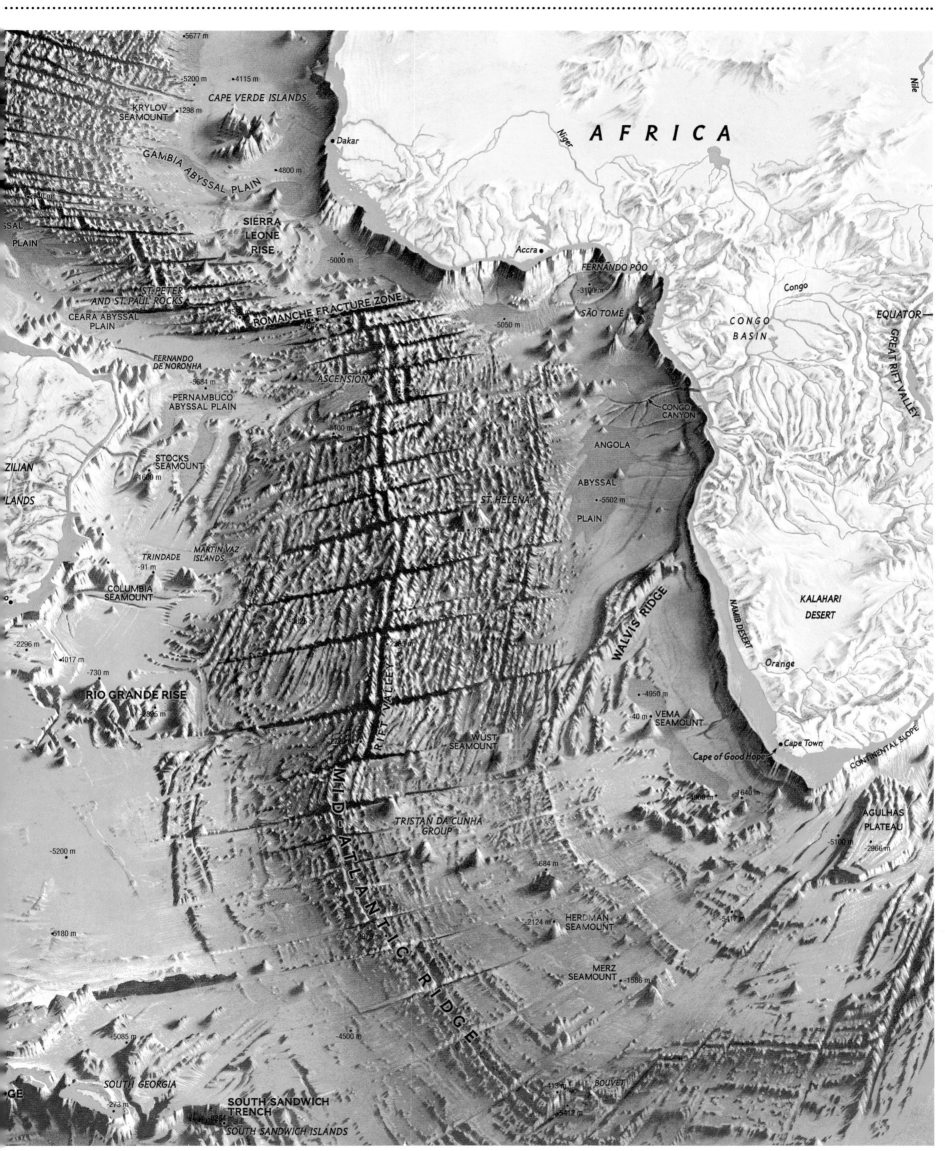

•5677 m

KRYLOV
SEAMOUNT •1298 m

CAPE VERDE ISLANDS

•5200 m •4115 m

GAMBIA ABYSSAL PLAIN

•4800 m

Niger

A F R I C A

Nile

•Dakar

SSAL

PLAIN

SIERRA
LEONE
RISE

Accra•

•5000 m

FERNANDO PÔO

Congo

CONGO
BASIN

EQUATOR

ST. PETER
AND ST. PAUL ROCKS

ROMANCHE FRACTURE ZONE

SÃO TOMÉ

•3100 m

CEARA ABYSSAL
PLAIN

•5050 m

GREAT RIFT VALLEY

FERNANDO
DE NORONHA

•5684 m

ASCENSION

•98 m

CONGO
CANYON

ZILIAN

LANDS

PERNAMBUCO
ABYSSAL PLAIN

•8400 m

ANGOLA

STOCKS
SEAMOUNT
•1600 m

ST. HELENA

ABYSSAL

•5502 m

•1348 m

PLAIN

•°

TRINDADE
•91 m

MARTIN VAZ
ISLANDS

•2296 m

COLUMBIA
SEAMOUNT

•4017 m

•826 m

KALAHARI
DESERT

NAMIB DESERT

•730 m

•2855 m

WALVIS RIDGE

Orange

RIO GRANDE RISE

•2895 m

RIFT VALLEY

•4950 m

•40 m VEMA
SEAMOUNT

•Cape Town

WUST
SEAMOUNT

CONTINENTAL SLOPE

•5200 m

Cape of Good Hope

•1960 m •1640 m

AGULHAS
PLATEAU

TRISTAN DA CUNHA
GROUP

MID-ATLANTIC RIDGE

•684 m

•5180 m •2966 m

•5180 m

•2124 m HERDMAN
SEAMOUNT

•5417 m

MERZ
SEAMOUNT •1586 m

•5085 m

•3975 m

•4500 m

SOUTH GEORGIA

•413 m BOUVET

GE

•273 m

SOUTH SANDWICH
TRENCH

•5412 m

SOUTH SANDWICH ISLANDS

The Big Blue

●●● The Pacific is the largest of all the world's oceans. Its area is equivalent to that of all the other oceans combined, and it contains half of the ocean water on our planet. The Pacific Ocean is also home to a variety of geological wonders. Particularly conspicuous are the deep trenches along its edges, its island arcs, and the high mountains that have risen up on the eastern side. The Pacific "Ring of Fire" consists of numerous volcanoes which are active both on the island arcs adjacent to the trenches and on the mountain chains.

Trenches, islands, and mountain chains owe their existence to the movements of the continents and the sea bed. The island arcs in the north, such as the Aleutians, were formed by these movements when the plates of the Pacific collided with the plate of the Asian continent. In the west, the Pacific floor collided with parts of the Indian Plate on which the Indian Ocean, Australia, and the islands of South East Asia lie. When such a collision takes place, the sea floor pushes its way beneath the continent and bends under, thereby forming the trenches. At the same time, the island arcs – as a part of the continental plate – are pushed upwards. When the layers of earth rub together, the rock softens, and numerous volcanoes are formed.

On the east side of the Pacific, the South American and the North American continental plates are advancing to the west over the Pacific floor, causing the sea bed to be pushed downwards. On land, fracture zones – such as the San Andreas Fault in California – have formed, along with volcanic zones in the coastal mountain ranges of North America, Central America, and South America.

In the Pacific there are a conspicuous number of "guyots" – flat-topped, submarine mountains (seamounts) and islands. In the central and western regions, submerged volcanoes form long chains, and some of their peaks jut out of the water as islands – one example being the cluster of islands that make up Hawaii.

In the warmer climatic belts of the Tropics, coral rings formed around the peaks of volcanoes and jutted out of the water. As the peak gradually sank into the sea bed, the coral reefs grew higher and higher, remaining as ring islands, or atolls, even when the volcano itself had already sunk below the water line. Outside of the Tropic belt many volcanoes have simply submerged, such as the Emperor seamount chain – the extension of the Hawaiian Ridge which deflects to the south.

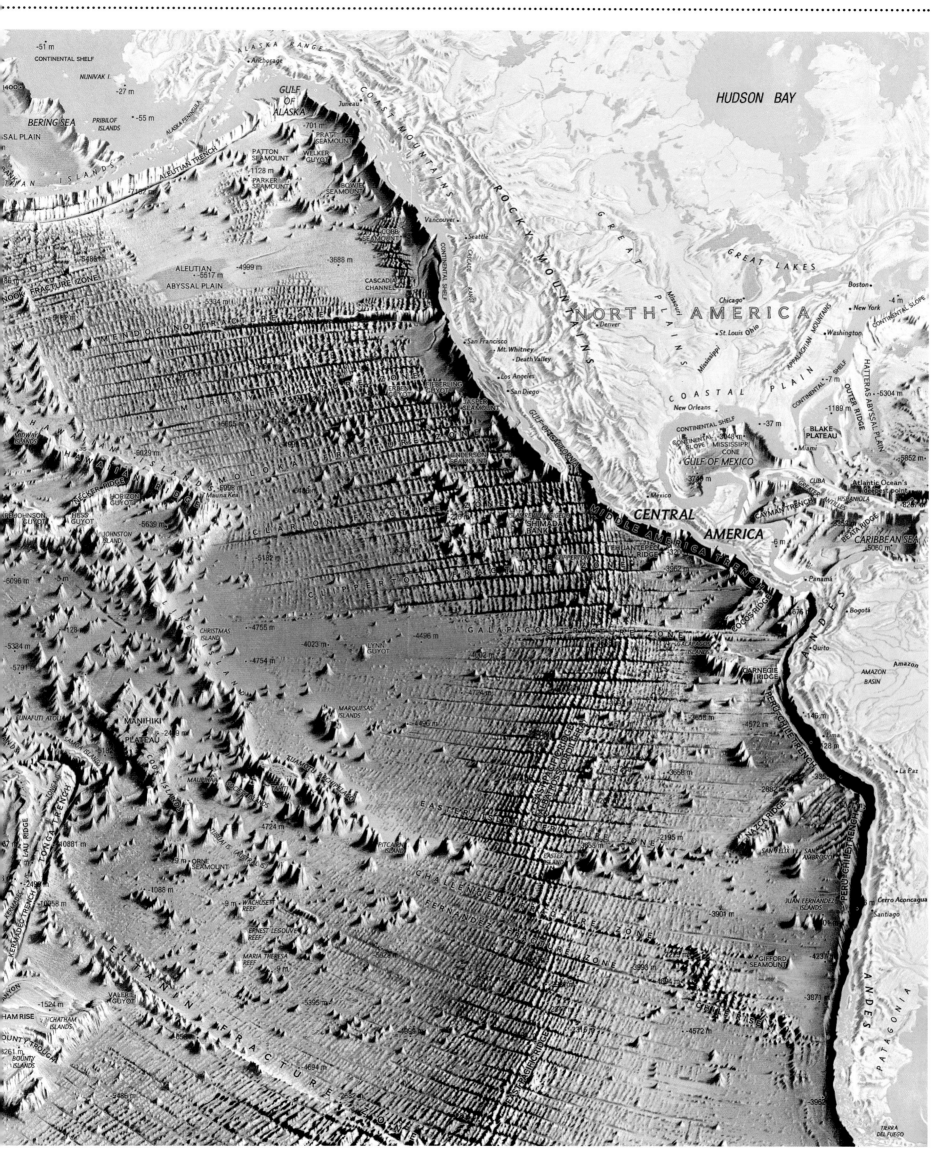

The youngest ocean

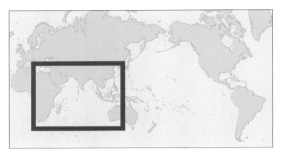

● ● ● The Indian Ocean is the youngest of the oceans on our planet. However, its comparative youth makes it no less complex. Although its current shape stabilized about 36 million years ago, the history of its development is much more complicated than that of the other oceans.

When Gondwana (the Southern Continent) broke apart 150 million years ago, room was made for a new ocean that was constantly exposed to far-reaching changes – for example, when India set off on its way to Asia 125 million years ago, arriving 75 million years later. The shape of the Indian Ocean also changed once Africa had drifted to the west and Australia had separated from the Antarctic.

The Indian Ocean's boundaries are still the subject of dispute. The separation lines to the Atlantic and the South Pacific are the clearest. One runs from Cape Agulhas – the southernmost point of Africa – at 20° latitude to the Antarctic; the other from the East Cape of Tasmania along 147° latitude to the Antarctic. However, there has been no consensus as to whether the Bass Strait between Australia and Tasmania belongs to the Indian Ocean or the Pacific.

All in all, though, it is the Indian Ocean's northeast boundary that dominates most of the arguments. The most generally accepted boundary runs from Cape Londonderry in Australia via the Sunda Strait to Sumatra. Between Sumatra and the Thai Pensinsula, the Sunda Strait separates the Indian Ocean from the Pacific.

The Indian Ocean is unusual in some respects. Since the northern part is surrounded by land, it has no Arctic waters as the Pacific and the Atlantic Oceans do. As well, the continental shield is, on average, 120 kilometers (75 mi.) wide, making it relatively narrow. Only off Bombay and North West Australia does it reach a width of 300 kilometers (186 mi.).

The Indian Ocean is home to few islands. Of them, Madagascar is the world's fourth largest. The occurence of trenches in this ocean is also small, but the Java Trench, which is only 80 kilometers (50 mi.) wide, stretches 2,500 kilometers (1,550 mi.), making it the second longest trench on Earth.

Ninety East Ridge (the Bengal Ridge) was discovered in 1962. It is noticeably free of earthquakes and follows an absolutely straight course along the 90° latitude line (after which it was named). It is still detectable even under the thick layers of sediment in the Bay of Bengal.

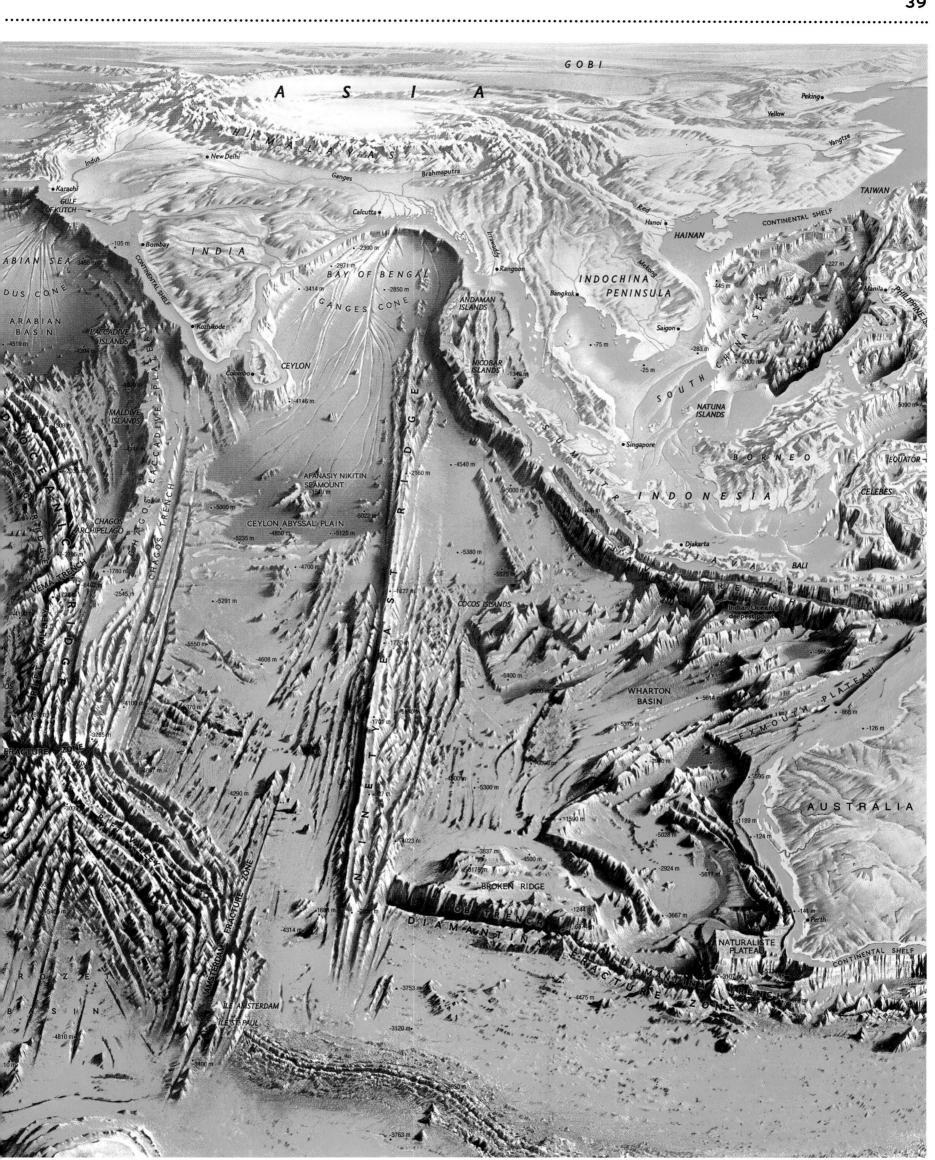

GOBI

A S I A

Peking

Yellow

H I M A L A Y A S

Yangtze

Indus

New Delhi

TAIWAN

Ganges

Brahmaputra

Karachi

Red

CONTINENTAL SHELF

GULF
OF KUTCH

Hanoi

HAINAN

Calcutta

Irrawaddy

-105 m   Bombay

INDIA

-2390 m

Rangoon

INDOCHINA
PENINSULA

-445 m

Manila

ABIAN SEA

-3460 m

-2971 m

BAY OF BENGAL

ANDAMAN
ISLANDS

-227 m

DUS CONE

-3414 m

-2850 m

GANGES CONE

Bangkok

Saigon

-283 m

PHILIPPINE

ARABIAN
BASIN

Kozhikode

CEYLON

NICOBAR
ISLANDS

-75 m

SOUTH CHINA SEA

-2000 m

-4519 m

-4394 m

Colombo

-1349 m

-25 m

NATUNA
ISLANDS

-5090 m

-508 m

-4840 m

-4146 m

Singapore

B O R N E O

EQUATOR

MALDIVE
ISLANDS

-1746 m

AFANASIY NIKITIN
SEAMOUNT

-2160 m

-4540 m

SUMATRA

INDONESIA

CELEBES

-2055 m

-1549 m

-5000 m

-5380 m

Djakarta

J A V A

BALI

CHAGOS
ARCHIPELAGO

-5000 m

CEYLON ABYSSAL PLAIN

-5022 m

-5575 m

-1806 m

-2196 m

-1780 m

-5235 m

-4850 m

-5125 m

COCOS ISLANDS

-5663 m

VEMA TRENCH

-6402 m

-4700 m

-1627 m

-2545 m

-5291 m

-5400 m

WHARTON
BASIN

-5614 m

EXMOUTH PLATEAU

-868 m

-5550 m

-1770 m

-5860 m

-5375 m

-126 m

-4608 m

-1701 m

-5098 m

-2990 m

FRACTURE ZONE

-4100 m

-5370 m

-595 m

-3285 m

-4290 m

-827 m

-4600 m

-5300 m

AUSTRALIA

-3093

-4867 m

-1590 m

-5028 m

-1189 m

RIFT VALLEY

-4023 m

-3837 m

-124 m

-5617 m

-5900

-4500 m

-2924 m

-540 m

-1688 m

-2860 m

BROKEN RIDGE

-3178 m

-141 m

NATURALISTE
PLATEAU

Perth

-4314 m

OB TRENCH

-1244 m

-3667 m

-4810 m

ÎLE AMSTERDAM

-3753 m

DIAMANTINA

-4475 m

-3107 m

CONTINENTAL SHELF

10 m

ÎLE ST PAUL

-3120 m

-3400 m

-3650 m

-3763 m

The seas around the North Pole

●●● The Arctic is the smallest of the Earth's oceans. It is comprised of the marginal seas: the Chukchi Sea, the East Siberian Sea, the Laptev Sea, the Kara Sea, the Barents Sea, the Greenland Sea, the Beaufort Sea, and the White Sea. Some oceanographers would also add the Bering Sea and the Norwegian Sea to this list.

Compared with other seas, there has been little exploration of the Polar Sea and, therefore, little is known of its formation and history. For instance, it was not discovered that there was no land under the ice until the end of the 19th century. Scientists only have a rough idea of the Sea's development in the past 66.4 million years.

At that time, the Mid-Oceanic Ridge – the Nansen Cordillera – still lay beneath a corner of the Eurasian continent. Magma flowed from its central rift, spreading to both sides. The magma blasted off a splinter of the continent (today called the Lomonosov Ridge) thus exposing the Nansen Cordillera.

The magma formed new sea beds with which the Mid-Oceanic Ridge pushed itself away from the continent. Simultaneously, the flowing magma bed pushed the Lomonosov Ridge away from the Nansen Cordillera to its current location.

Almost exactly in the middle of the Lomonosov Ridge is a depression in which the geographical North Pole lies.

The whole of the Arctic Ocean lies below 75° latitude, beneath an almost unbroken and compact layer of ice that prevents the wind from whipping up the water and the water from heating up and evaporating. Furthermore, the ice reflects most of the sunlight in the summer months back into space.

On the other hand, the wind keeps the ice moving, causing numerous wide cracks to occur. This opens salt water lakes – called "polynyas" – and piles up ice floes to several feet high. The open water in the cracks and polynyas make up 10 per cent of the ice-covered areas.

These open regions are utilized, particularly in the summer, by commercial ice-breakers through the North East Passage off Siberia; here they conduct convoys of freight ships that wish to avoid any unnecessary contact with the ice.

Research ice-breakers try to follow the commercial ones in order to save fuel and time in their efforts to reach the North Pole. The colossal ice-breakers are supported by their own fleet of helicopters, which fly off in advance of the vessel, acting as scouts to find the most favorable passage since the cracks and polynyas can change by the hour.

N LOWLAND

TAYMYR PENINSULA

-9 m

-42 m

KARA SEA

-390 m

-115 m

BOL'SHEVIK I. -44 m

NORTH LAND

KOMSOMOLETS ISLAND

-49 m

-2469 m

-3292 m

GRAHAM BELL I.

-2701 m

SVYATAYA ANNA CONE

-3840 m

BARENTS ABYSSAL PLAIN

ARCTIC MID-OCEAN RIDGE

NANSEN CORDILLERA

-2399 m

LOMONOSOV

POLE ABYSSAL PLAIN

-1000 m

RIDGE

-4511 m

+ NORTH POLE

TCHER ABYSSAL PLAIN

-1756 m

-3993 m

MARVIN RIDGE

-1399 m

-4206 m

OLDER

IS

OUNT

RARY SEAMOUNT

OSTENSO SEAMOUNT

-3901 m

-1899 m

-79 m

-13 m

Archangel

-332 m

NOVAYA ZEMLYA

-27 m

-140 m

FRANZ JOSEF LAND

GEORGE LAND

ALEXANDRA LAND

-46 m

-121 m

-146 m

-18 m

SVALBARD

-33 m

NORTH EAST LAND

SPITSBERGEN

-148 m

YERMAK PLATEAU

-2185 m

NANSEN FRACTURE ZONE

GREENLAND FRACTURE ZONE

-3414 m

-3536 m

-37 m

-282 m

-141 m

CONTINENTAL SHELF

-179 m

KANIN PENINSULA

-150 m

-80 m

-64 m

North Cape

-177 m

LAKE ONEGA

-33 m

WHITE SEA

-256 m

KOLA PENINSULA

Murmansk

ARCTIC CIRCLE

LAKE LADOGA

-84 m

LAKE REGION

SCANDINAVIA

Tromso

Narvik

-183 m

-387 m

-344 m

NORWEGIAN

-1420 m

VORING PLATEAU

DUMSHAF ABYSSAL PLAIN

-3231 m

-1893 m

-1686 m

-3008 m

-2740 m

-2271 m

-3078 m

SEA

JAN MAYEN

-792 m

-1387 m

JAN MAYEN RIDGE

-811 m

-2076 m

-16 m

-274 m

PEARY LAND

LINCOLN SEA

-135 m

G R E E N L A N D

KING FREDERIK VIII LAND

KING WILHELMS LAND

-82 m

KNUD RASMUSSEN LAND

ELLESMERE ISLAND

AXEL HEIBERG ISLAND

-707 m

ELLEF RINGNES I.

SVERDRUP ISLANDS

-628 m

-183 m

RDEN I.

N ELIZABETH ISLANDS

RRY ISLANDS

E ISLAND

BATHURST I.

-179 m

T MELVILLE SOUND

-576 m

CORNWALLIS I.

Resolute

BARROW STRAIT

SOMERSET ISLAND

PRINCE OF WALES ISLAND

-135 m

-123 m

BOOTHIA PENINSULA

MCLINTOCK CHANNEL

PRINCE REGENT INLET

BRODEUR PENINSULA

GULF OF BOOTH

DEVON ISLAND

LANCASTER SOUND

-741 m

BYLOT I.

BORDEN PENINSULA

BAFFIN ISLAND

HAYES PENINSULA

Thule

KING CHRISTIAN X LAND

GREENLAND

-130 m

-436 m

-460 m

BAFFIN

-2469 m

BAY

-37 m

DISKO

-11 m

-1701 m

-146 m

DENMARK STRAIT

-176 m

-124 m

ICELAND

Reykjavik

-71 m

Angmagssalik

KING CHRISTIAN IX LAND

-9 m

ARCTIC CIRCLE

-2377 m

ATLANTIC OCEAN

KING FREDERIK VI COAST

-18 m

The south's icy ocean

●●● The Antarctic Ocean, better known as the Southern Ocean, comprises the southern portion of the Pacific, Atlantic, and Indian Oceans. It is unbroken by landmasses with the exception of the Drake Passage – the 1,000-kilometer-wide (620-mi.) strait between the southern tip of South America and the northern branch of the Antarctic Peninsula.

The sea around the Antarctic was compared in the past to a moat around a castle. The stormy west winds of the "Furious Fifties" and the "Screaming Sixties" – so named after the latitudes in which they rampage – made it difficult for early explorers to reach the continent.

Intense storms drive a voluminous circulation of water around the Antarctic – the Circumpolar Current – which, on one hand, drags along other currents coming from the north and, on the other, allows cold currents to branch off and spread back to the north again.

Since the water masses south of 40° latitude have so much in common, oceanographers have determined the northern boundary of the ocean along this line. (It runs, in one area, right through the middle of the Bass Strait between Australia and Tasmania, and between the two islands which make up New Zealand.) At this latitude the Sub-Antarctic Convergence is found, where the warm surface water of tropical and sub-tropical regions meet up with colder sub-Antarctic waters.

The political boundary laid down by the Antarctic states is at 60° latitude. It runs just north of the tip of the Antarctic Peninsula and the South Orkney Islands; the Antarctic Convergence lies within.

It is here – beneath the gigantic, permanent ice cover in two great bays that cut into the continent, and beneath the ring of ice that surrounds the Antarctic, building up every winter – that the coldest and heaviest water masses on the planet are formed. They sink and spread along the beds of the three principal oceans beyond the Equator.

The winter ice ring stretches from the coast of the continent over an area of 20 million square kilometers (7.72 mill. sq. mi.). In summer, only 3 million square kilometers (1.16 mill. sq. mi.) remain. Even then, the layer of ice covering the Antarctic continent is on average 2,000 meters (6,561 ft.) thick, winter or summer. These permanent fields of ice make up 90 percent of the world's ice masses. Without these ice masses, the continent would certainly be very much smaller as large parts of it would be flooded.

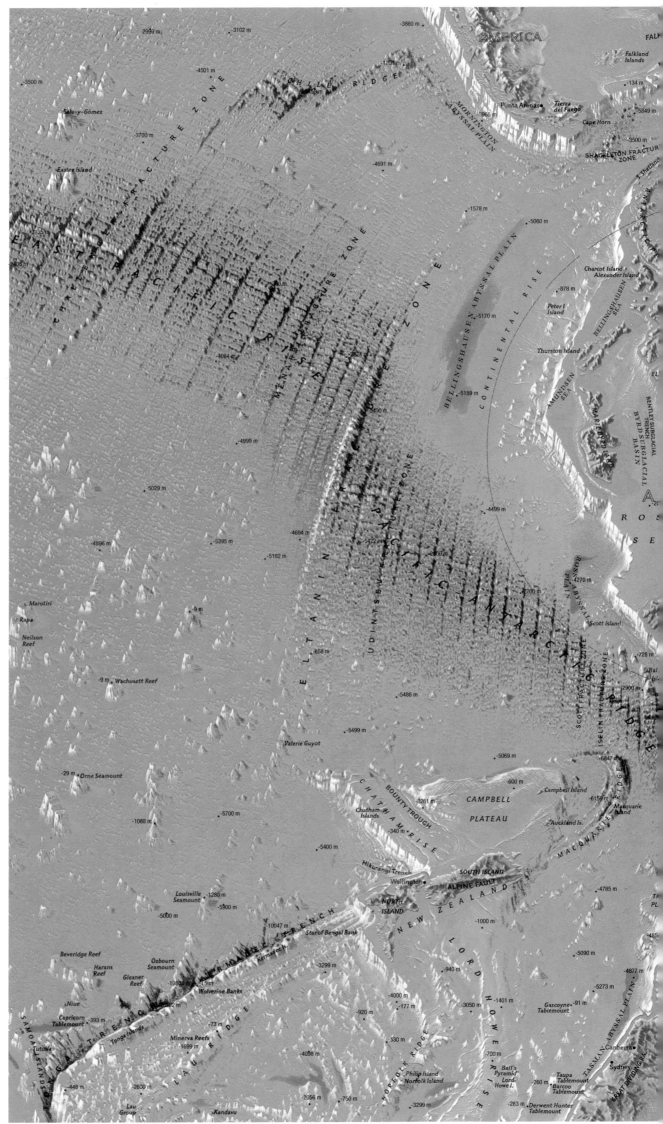

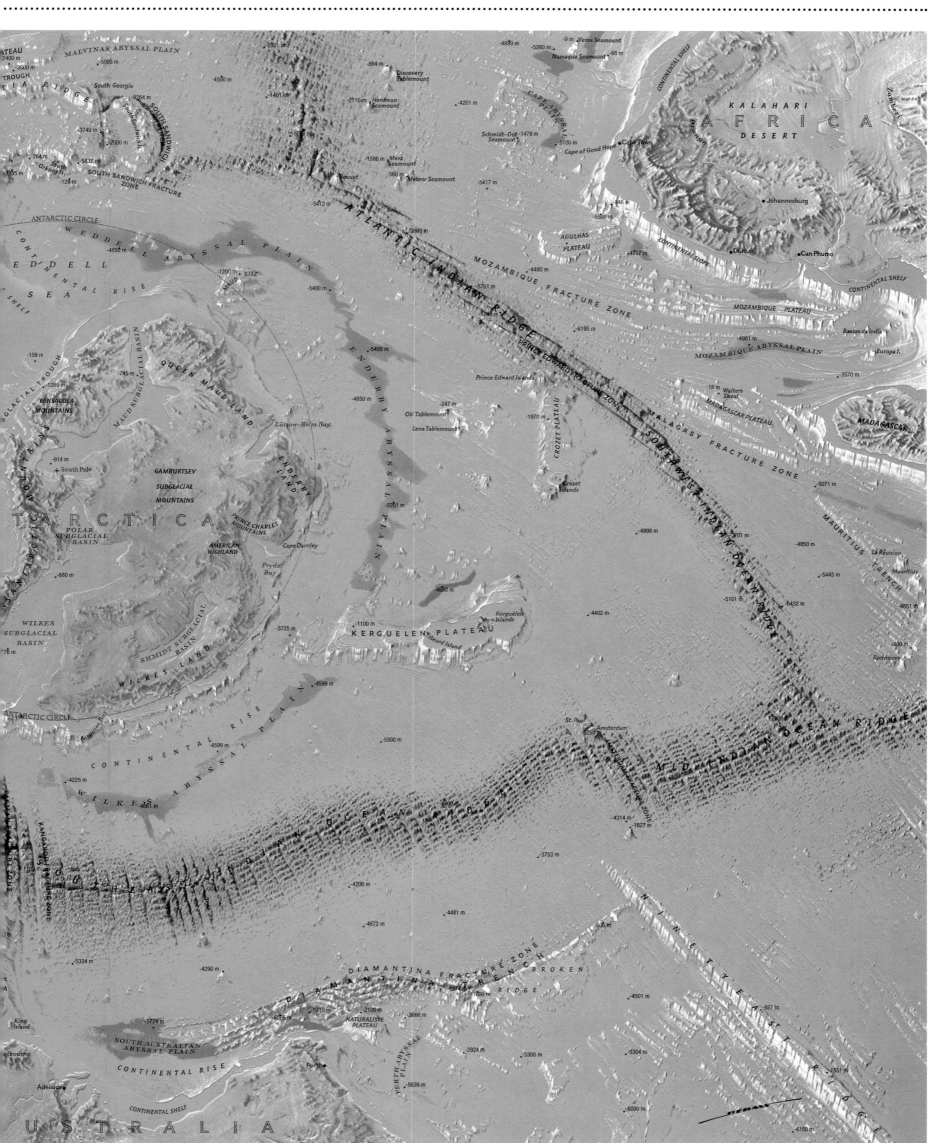

TEAU
2400 m
-3500 m
MALVINAS ABYSSAL PLAIN
-5085 m
-9 m Vema Seamount
-5260 m
-4809 m
-2301 m
Namaqua Seamount
-68 m
CONTINENTAL SHELF
ZAMBEZI
RIA RIDGE
TROUGH
South Georgia
-8264 m
-684 m
Discovery
Tablemount
KALAHARI
AFRICA
DESERT
-4500 m
South Sandwich Is.
-1401 m
-2110 m Herdman
Seamount
-4201 m
Schmidt-Ott -1479 m
Seamount
-5100 m
-3749 m
-2500 m
-264 m
-5637 m
SOUTH SANDWICH
CAPE ABYSSAL PLAIN
-5417 m
Cape of Good Hope Cape Town
-846 m
Johannesburg
South
Orkney Is.
-1586 m Merz
Seamount
-560 m Meteor Seamount
-5500 m
-125 m
SOUTH SANDWICH FRACTURE
ZONE
Bouvet
-5412 m
AGULHAS
PLATEAU
Durban Can Phumo
ANTARCTIC CIRCLE
WEDDELL ABYSSAL PLAIN
ATLANTIC-INDIAN RIDGE
MOZAMBIQUE FRACTURE ZONE
-4717 m
CONTINENTAL SLOPE
CONTINENTAL SHELF
CONTINENTAL RISE
-4850 m
-2899 m
-4480 m
MOZAMBIQUE PLATEAU
WEDDELL
SEA
-1200 m MAUD RISE
-5400 m
-5761 m
-6195 m
MOZAMBIQUE ABYSSAL PLAIN
-4981 m
Bassas da India
CONTINENTAL SHELF
SHELF
-159 m
QUEEN MAUD LAND
MAUD SUBGLACIAL BASIN
-5400 m
-1249 m
PRINCE EDWARD FRACTURE ZONE
-18 m Walters
Shoal
Europa I.
-3570 m
-1289 m
-745 m
ENDERBY ABYSSAL PLAIN
Prince Edward Islands
MADAGASCAR PLATEAU
MADAGASCAR
PENSACOLA
MOUNTAINS
-4850 m
-247 m
Ob Tablemount
MALAGASY FRACTURE ZONE
-5071 m
Lützow-Holm Bay
GAMBURTSEV
SUBGLACIAL
MOUNTAINS
CROZET PLATEAU
-1970 m
-914 m
+ South Pole
ENDERBY LAND
-5201 m
SOUTH-WEST INDIAN OCEAN RIDGE
-501 m
MAURITIUS TRENCH
TARCTICA
PRINCE CHARLES
MOUNTAINS
Crozet
Islands
-4998 m
-4850 m
La Réunion
POLAR
SUBGLACIAL
BASIN
AMERICAN
HIGHLAND
Cape Darnley
-4402 m
-5101 m
-6432 m
-5445 m
Mauritius
SAN ARCTIC MOUNTAINS
-680 m
Prydz
Bay
-4650 m
-4651 m
WILKES
SUBGLACIAL
BASIN
SHMIDT SUBGLACIAL
BASIN
-3725 m
-1100 m
Kerguélen
Islands
-800 m
Rodríguez
-78 m
WILKES LAND
KERGUELEN PLATEAU
Heard Island
MID-INDIAN OCEAN RIDGE
ANTARCTIC CIRCLE
-4599 m
St. Paul Amsterdam
-3250 m
CONTINENTAL RISE
-4599 m
-5300 m
-4225 m
WILKES ABYSSAL PLAIN
SOUTH-EAST INDIAN OCEAN RIDGE
-4661 m
-1686 m
-4314 m
-1627 m
KANGAROO FRACTURE ZONE
-3753 m
100 m
-3543 m
-4206 m
-5334 m
-4481 m
NINETYEAST RIDGE
-4290 m
-4572 m
-506 m
-4501 m
-927 m
DIAMANTINA FRACTURE ZONE
BROKEN RIDGE
DIAMANTINA TRENCH
-884 m
-1000 m
King
Island
-5774 m
-6055 m
-5515 m
NATURALISTE
PLATEAU
-3666 m
-2100 m
-5300 m
-5304 m
-1551 m
elbourne
SOUTH AUSTRALIAN
ABYSSAL PLAIN
-2924 m
PERTH ABYSSAL PLAIN
-5639 m
Adelaide
CONTINENTAL RISE
Perth
-6000 m
CONTINENTAL SHELF
-6150 m
USTRALIA

Historical maps of the world

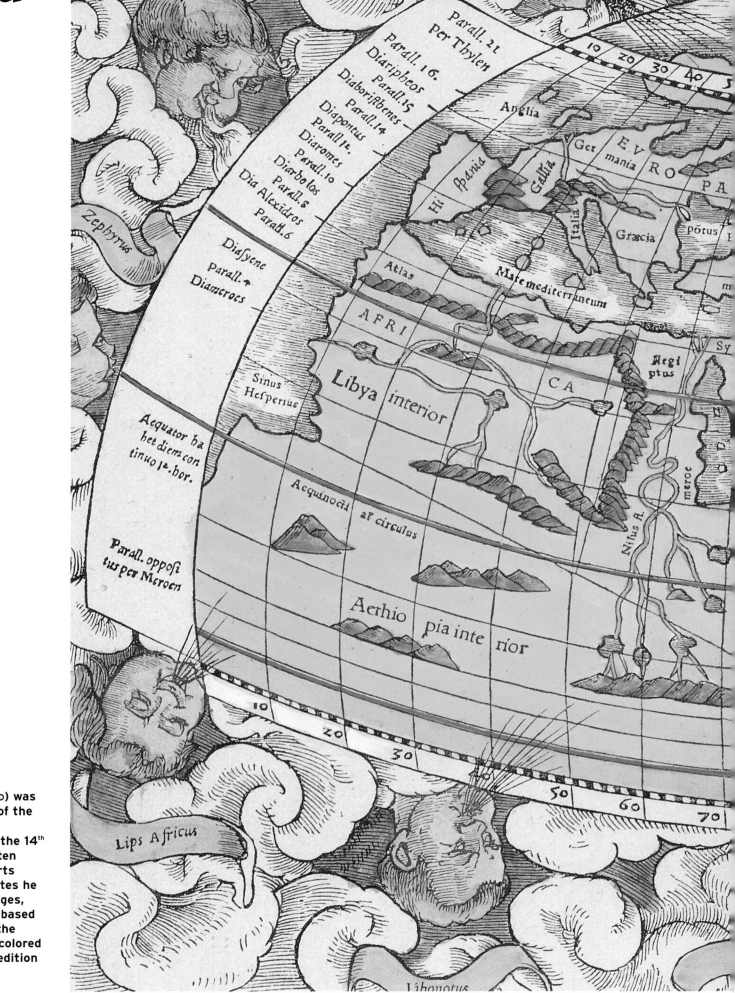

Claudius Ptolemaeus (90-168 AD) was the most renowned geographer of the Ancient World. His "Guide to Geography", passed down since the 14th century in the form of handwritten documents, is comprised of charts drawn according to the coordinates he determined. In the late Middle Ages, numerous other maps appeared based on Ptolemaeus's description of the Earth. The chart seen here is a colored wood engraving from the Basle edition of the Ptolemaeus "Guide to Geography" from 1545.

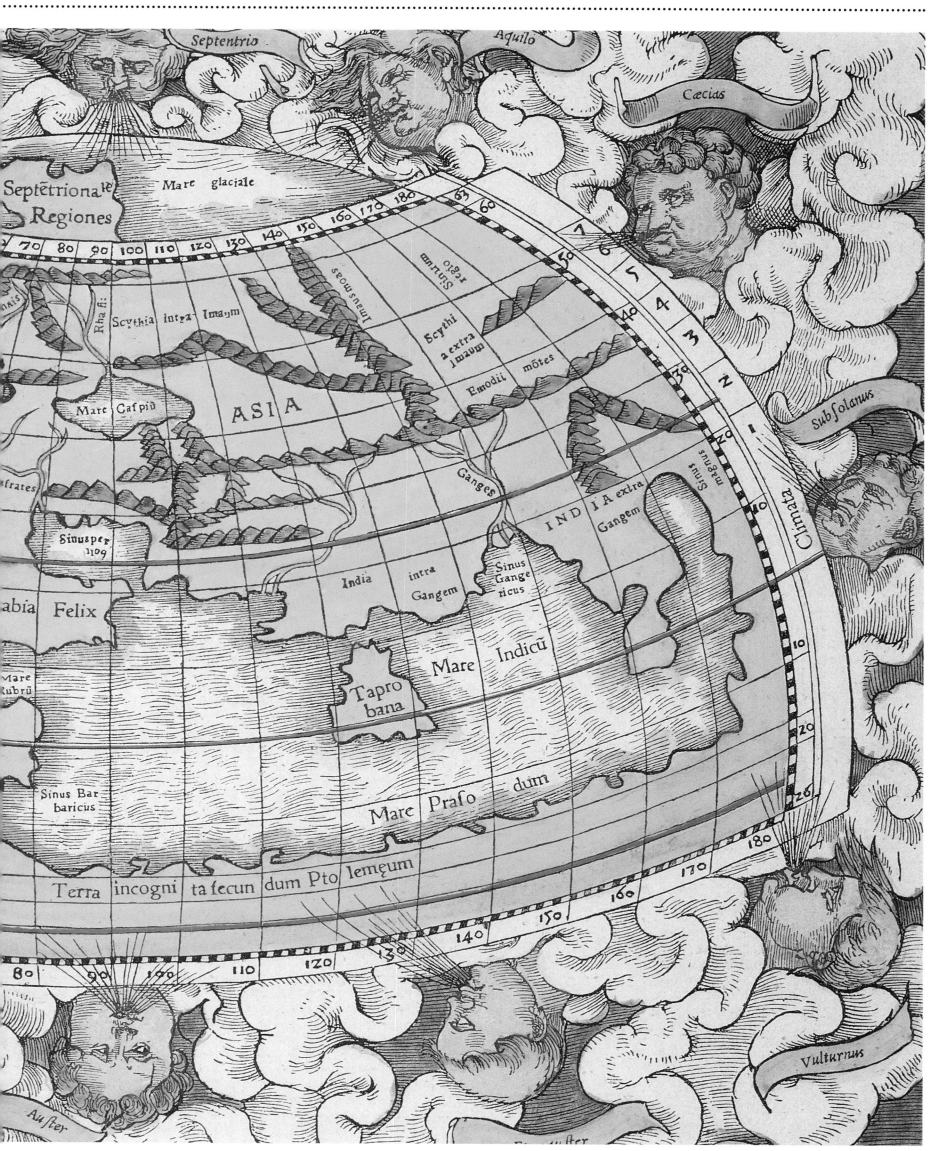

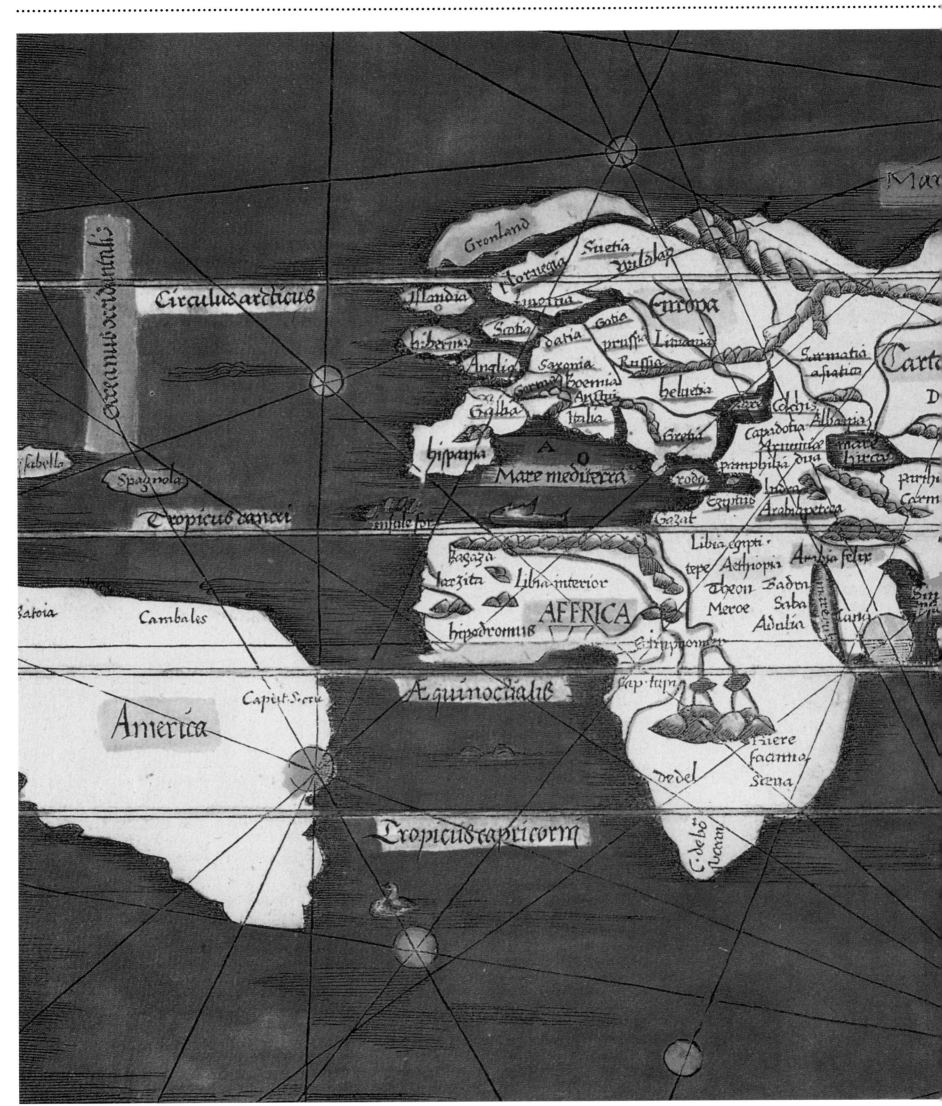

After explorers searched out the route to America and the East Indies from Spain and Portugal, cartographers drew maps of the world, including the "new" oceans that had just been discovered. This colored wood engraving by Laurentius Frisius (circa 1490-1532) is from the Martin Waldseemüller Third Edition of 1541.

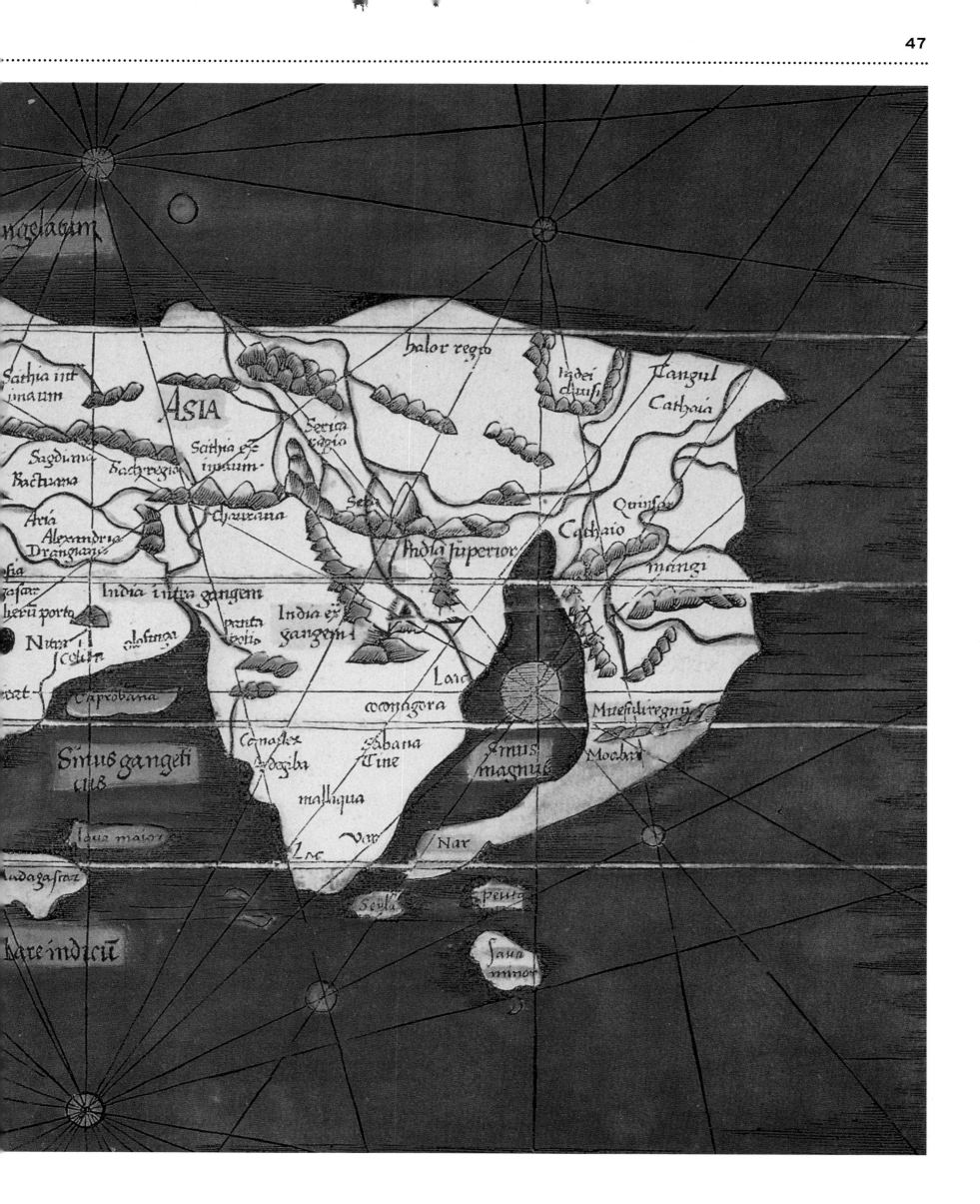

Home to remarkable creatures

Wherever hot mineral springs bubble out of the sea bed, there live a varied symbiosis of animals that can exist without light and have developed their own unique food chain.

●●● For a long time it was assumed that organisms could only survive up to a depth of 600 meters (1,970 ft.), and the greatest depths of the sea were considered to be almost devoid of life. The *Challenger* expedition of 1872 to 1876 was the first to bring back proof that there was life even at a depth of up to 3,800 meters (12,460 ft.). No specimens of any new animal family were hauled on board but numerous species of sea stars, sea cucumbers, and sponges usually associated with shallow waters (and previously not known to the scientists) were found.

In the 1950s, deep sea research was given a fresh start when what was then the Soviet Union, along with the USA, France, and Great Britain, began new investigations. Germany joined in 1963 with its new research vessel *Meteor II*. Sonic depth finding systems were now able to provide rapid information regarding water depth and the character of the sea bed, while new types of nets and grabbing devices – so-called "snappers" – made it easier to take samples.

The first investigations of the creatures found revealed that they were mostly new species of animals they were already familiar with, such as sea stars, crustaceans, sponges, and sea anemones. Despite this, there were still a few surprises. For example, a Neopilina limpet – a living fossil – was discovered in the Pacific at 4,000 meters (13,000 ft.). Up until that point, it had only been seen in a fossilized form and was thought to be a long extinct link in the evolutionary history of invertebrates.

Modern grabbing devices were able to bring samples on board the research vessels. To the surprise of the scientists, although the number of creatures living in the sediments was definitely smaller than in shallow waters, there was an astonishing variety of species. Even today, it is not clear how this variety originates and how many species are spread throughout the oceans.

A refuge undisturbed?

Until a few years ago, the oceans – the largest ecological systems in the world – were referred to as the last undisturbed refuge. Today, this is no longer true. Humans have now invaded this habitat, using it to dispose of industrial and atomic waste. The oil industry utilizes the oceans for its natural resources, and has recently penetrated down as far as 2,000 meters (6,600 ft.).

It is absolutely essential that we know the most common species in each area of exploration in order to be able to judge the effects of future commercial use of the ocean. Deep-sea submersibles – equipped with the means to film at the sea

Ocean fish food: three varieties of shrimp

bed and to transmit the pictures directly onboard the research vessels – have provided scientists with a greater knowledge of the quantity of ocean creatures living on the sea floor. The variety of species is impressive. About 350 to 500 different sea stars, sea cucumbers, sponges, sea anemones and crustaceans live at a depth of 4,100 meters (13,450 ft.) off the coast of Peru. These are joined by guests from the water column, such as the rat-tailed fish and flea-like creatures called amphipods and octopi, which only remain at the level of the sea bed for a short period of time.

At such incredible ocean depths, what do these creatures live on? A primary source of food is that which descends from the surface – organisms of all sizes, from microscopic algae to fish and whales that sink to the sea bed after their demise.

For a long time it was thought that food at the bottom of the ocean had been digested several times on its way down, making deep sea animals specialists in using minute quantities of organic substances to their greatest potential.

However, in 1982, English scientists discovered that the food supply in the ocean was more ample than had been previously supposed. Once algae has finished blossoming on the water's surface, it dies and sinks in large masses down 4,000 meters (13,450 ft.), to serve as food for the bottom-dwelling organisms.

Bacteria, worms, and small crustaceans consume the foodstuffs from the upper water levels. They breed, and then become a source of food themselves for their predatory enemies.

The scavengers

The blossoming of plankton on the water surface depends on the time of year, and this differs from region to region. Thus food supply in the oceans differs in quantity depending on the season and region.

A particular feast for scavengers such as crabs, fish, octopi, and amphipods is the corpse of a dolphin or whale. Investigations made by English scientists have shown that crabs, fish, and sea stars are able to perceive and reach a food source within a 20 square kilometer area (8 sq. mi.). A dead dolphin will be devoured within about seven days, right down to the bones, while one that weighs several tons will take about 15 months. Ocean animals have adapted optimally to such food sources. Amphipods, for example, can eat up to four times their own body weight in a very short time, and then starve for up to 14 months.

In 1977, a further sensation was reported from the deep seas. While working with the biologist Robert Hessler, American scientists made a discovery in one of the fracture zones in an area of hot springs (called hydrothermal vents) near the Galapagos Islands in the Pacific. Using the deep-diving submarine *Alvin*, they discovered large concourses of a hitherto unknown species. Not only was the combination of species new, but the density of such animal life in the ocean was completely unknown up till that time. Thousands of pogonophora (a deep-sea worm), crustaceans, and sea anemones were living there as if in an oasis in the middle of a desert – not far from hot, sulfurous waters that streamed out of the sea bed at temperatures up to 380° C (716° F).

Research into this new animal community revealed astonishing facts. The sulfur compounds in the hot water – which are normally fatal to living things – serve as food for bacteria inside the pogonophora, crustaceans, and sea anemones; the bacteria then convert these sulfur compounds into organic material, on which the pogonophora and other organisms in their environment live. This example of specialization had never been seen before. Similar hot springs have now been discovered in numerous regions of the Atlantic and the Pacific.

A variety of creatures live in the vicinity of "black smokers" - hydrothermal vents, or hot springs which spew out minerals from the interior of the Earth onto the sea bed. This illustration shows some of these inhabitants. The animals on the page 48 were discovered near Atlantic and West Pacific vents; those on this page were found near the Galapagos islands. The Latin names have been added to assist in their identification:

1. Alvinella worm "Feather dusters" (Alvinocaris lusca, 6 cm/2.4 in.)
2. Vent sea anemone (appr. 1 m/3.3 ft., undescribed)
3. Blind Atlantic vent shrimp (Rimicaris exoculata, 5 cm/2 in.)
4. Deep-sea boarfish (Neocyttus helgae, 22 cm/8.7 in.)
5. Rock crab (Paralomis jamsteci, 7 cm/2.8 in.)
6. Spider crab (Colossendeis colossea, 50 cm/20 in.)
7. Vent mussels (Bathymodiolus brevior, 14 cm/5.5 in.)
8. Cut throat eel (Thermobiotes mytilogeiton, 25 cm/10 in.)
9. Vent spiked snail (Alviniconcha hessleri, 9 cm/3.5 in.)
10. Vent mollusk (Ifremeria nautilei, 10 cm/4 in.)
11. Vent squat lobster (Munidopsis marianica, 12 cm/4.7 in.)
12. Scaled polychaetes (Thermiphione fijiensis, 2 cm/0.8 in.)
13. Deep-sea vent barnacle (Neolepas zevinae, 6 cm/2.4 in.)
14. Vent barnacle (Eochionelasmus ohtai, 3 cm/1.2 in.)
15. Vent whelk (Eosipho desbruyeresi, 7 cm/2.8 in.)
16. Spiral vent tubeworm (Alaysia spiralis, 30 cm/12 in.)
17. Sea cucumber (Benthogone rosea, 15 cm/5.9 in.)
18. Scale worm (Thermopolynoe branchiata, 5 cm/2 in.)
19. Vent crab (Bythograea thermydron, 6 cm/2.4 in.)
20. Chaetopoda (Paralvinella grasslei, 8 cm/3.2 in.)
21. Tube worm (Laminatubus alvini, 10 cm/4 in.)
22. Caterpillar worm (Hesiolyra bergi, 10 cm/4 in.)
23. Vent viviparous blenny (Thermarces cerberus, 27 cm/33.5 in.)
24. Limpet (Rhynchopelta cencentrica, 1 cm/0.4 in.)
25. Vent mussel (Bathymodiolus thermophilus, 18 cm/7 in.)
26. Vent squat lobster (Munidopsis subsquamosa, 5 cm/2 in.)
27. Giant vent tubeworm (Riftia pachyptila, 1.5 m/4.5 ft.)
28. Jericho worm (Tevnia jerichonana, 35 cm/14 in.)
29. Pompeii worm (Alvmella pompejana, 15 cm/5.9 in.)

Predatory fish in the deep seas

A plethora of fauna have adapted to life at astonishing depths.

●●● The English sent the first research vessel, *Challenger*, on an expedition around the world from 1872 to 1876 to explore the depths of the oceans. They brought back proof from all the oceans of the world that the waters were rich in living things even at a depth of about 3,800 meters (12,470 ft.) – the deepest point they were able to reach at that time. The scientists also made a major discovery. Due to the lack of light at these depths, no plants, or "flora", were able to survive. Indeed, only animals, or "fauna", were found.

Over a century has passed since the *Challenger* expedition. What have we learned about the oceans since then? In spite of intensive research activities, we still know more about the hidden side of the moon than we do about the largest habitat on our own planet.

What sort of creatures are able to live in the waters of the deep sea, and how must they adapt to their environment? Besides plankton organisms, we have found fish, crustaceans, thaliacea, octopi, and whales that either use this deep sea habitat temporarily or firmly settle down there.

Some creatures never leave the depth

Whales are able to dive deep down for a short time to search for food. Some fish, thaliacea, octopi, and much plankton never leave the depths but move between various depth zones – their behavior controlled by the movement of the organisms on which they prey. These organisms search for food at certain times in certain deep zones, controlled, for example, by the day-night rhythm of the upper layers. They play an important role in transporting organic material formed near the surface of the water into the depths of the sea. If there were no formation of organic substances in the light-flooded upper water column and no natural transport down to the depths, no life would exist there.

It is known that fish follow the movement of plankton to the surface at twilight and then return to the depths at dawn. Other animals come up from depths of more than 1,000 meters (3,300 ft.) to the boundaries of the surface waters (200 meter/ 660 ft. below sea level) during the day to search for food.

Practically all known major animal groups from shallow waters have found their way to the deep seas – whether they are fish, whales, crustaceans, mollusks, or worms. We know that the sperm whale can dive down to at least 1,200 meters (4,000 ft.) – probably even to 3,000 meters (10,000 ft.) – achieving durations of 90 minutes. As mammals, they must return at regular intervals to the surface to breathe.

It is quite a different situation with the giant octopi and giant squids, the largest known invertebrates. They can reach lengths of 20 meters (66 ft.) and live exclusively at great depths, where the octopus hunts for prey. Scars from their suckers have been found on the bodies of captured sperm whales, giving an indication of their enormous size.

Octopi and squids do not belong to the fish family; they are mollusks, making them related, therefore, to snails and mussels. They are the most highly developed of the invertebrates, with a well-developed nervous system, a rudimentary brain, and eyes with lenses that allow them to see as well as many mammals.

Both drifting plankton and actively swimming creatures have been found at very great depths. These bizarrely shaped fauna have never been described by biologists or given scientific names; but they are considered to belong to known families such as the copepods. Many of these creatures form an approximately 50 meter (160 ft.) plankton layer near the sea bed. They most likely play a major role in transporting material between free water and the sediment on the ocean floor.

Flashes of light in the eternal darkness

When the crews of deep-sea submersibles reach seemingly unending depths they have often

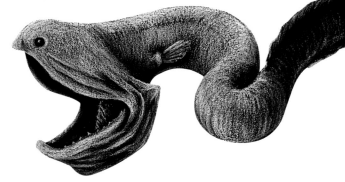

reported seeing flares in the water. Only in some cases were they able to determine how this flare – or bio-luminescence – was generated. It is known that many fish, octopi, and crustaceans are equipped with luminescent organs.

Scientists have long been puzzled by the origins and purpose of the luminescence. The first puzzle – its origin – has been solved: a brief light is generated by the interplay of two enzymes which are released in certain parts of the body during movement.

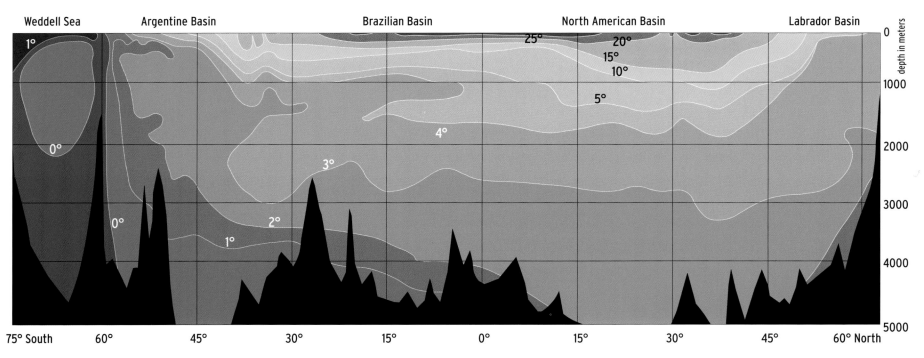

Water temperatures in the Atlantic down to a depth of 5,000 meters (16,400 ft.): the mountains on the sea bottom rise from the polar Labrador Basin to the Antarctic Weddell Sea. The chart shows the Atlantic Basin from south to north.

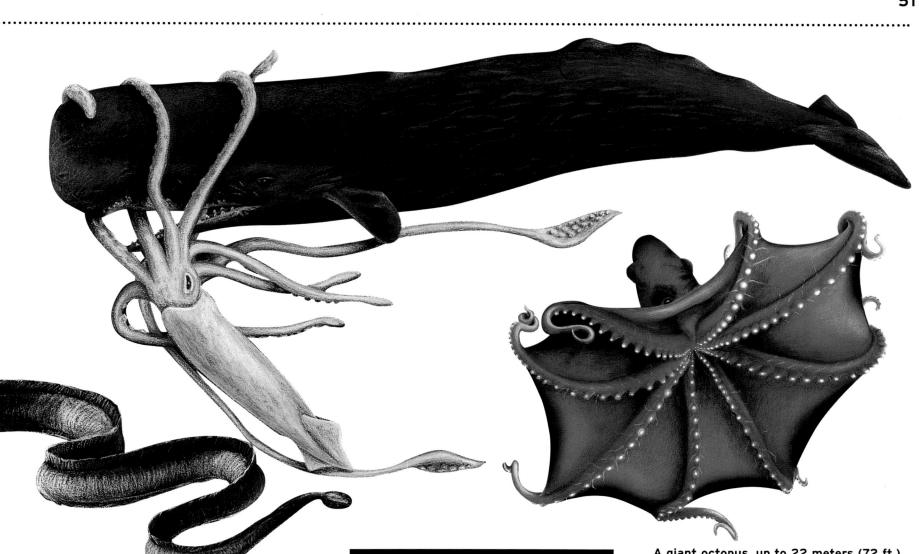

The second question regarding the purpose can only be partly answered. In the case of octopi and crustaceans, the purpose is still unknown. In regards to fish, however, scientists have made several discoveries. Some fish use luminescence to find their mate in the darkness, while others use it to send a warning signal to an enemy.

In the deep-sea anglerfish, the foremost spine of its dorsal fin is modified into a "fishing rod" tipped with a luminous "bait." When hunting for prey, it moves the "rod" up and down in front of its mouth, generating a light which attracts other fish, small octopi, amphipods (tiny flea-like creatures), or shrimp. When they stray close enough, the anglerfish swallows them.

Most small, deep-sea fish have a conspicuously large mouth and extremely long, pointed teeth, enabling them to catch and eat prey that is frequently much bigger than they are themselves. As well, considering the scarcity of food, it is essential to hang on to prey once it has been caught.

Unanswered questions

Due to the extreme conditions of their habitat, there is still very little information available about deep-sea animals. At a depth of more than 1,000 meters (3,300 ft.), it is not the darkness which presents an obstacle for scientists but the low temperatures and extreme underwater pressure that they encounter. Deep-sea creatures have rarely been brought to the surface alive – and only with the help of deep-diving submarines or sample-taking devices.

The deep-sea anglerfish attracts his prey with a "luminous bait".

Usually, the animals do not survive their travels through the warm water levels near the surface. In Arctic and Antarctic waters where living animals were successfully brought to the surface, they died after a very short time in the aquarium, even though the conditions of their habitat were a simulation of their natural environment. It is not yet clear how important pressure actually is for their survival; they could also be lacking a necessary food.

Due to all of these factors, the life cycle of these deep-sea creatures remains a mystery. Perhaps, one day, it will be possible to construct an aquarium in which creatures from great depths can be maintained. Only then might it be possible to find some answers to the last mysteries of the oceans.

A giant octopus, up to 22 meters (72 ft.) long, attacks a sperm whale with its tentacles. The pelican eel, also called the umbrella-mouthed gulper (left), is 60 cm (23 in.) long and has an abnormally large mouth. The tiny, red vent shrimp (right) only reaches a size of 9 cm (3.5 in.).

FACTS AND FIGURES

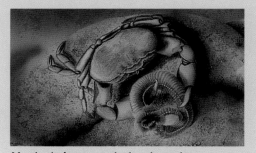

Vent shrimps and chaetopoda

Small creatures from the depths

Many very small creatures live in the oceans. The table lists those that are able to live around the hot hydrothermal vents:

Limpet	1 cm (0.4 in.)
Scale worm	2 cm (0.8 in.)
Deep-sea clam	2 cm (0.8 in.)
Deep-sea vent barnacle	3 cm (1.2 in.)
Sea anemone	3 cm (1.2 in.)
Vent shrimp	5 cm (2.0 in.)
Vent squat lobster	5 cm (2.0 in.)
Vent crab	6 cm (2.4 in.)
Vent mussel	6 cm (2.4 in.)
Sea urchin	7 cm (2.7 in.)
Rock crab	7 cm (2.7 in.)
Chaetopoda	8 cm (3.1 in.)
Brittle star	10 cm (3.9 in.)

Sea lions, fish, and crustaceans

The sea is home to a variety of creatures, large and small, that are all contributors to their unique ecosystem.

● ● ● Everybody recognizes them: the sea elephants are one of the most conspicuous inhabitants of the Polar coastal waters. They are frequently up to 6 meters (20 ft.) in length and can weigh several thousand kilograms. Since their bodies have adapted to the water, moving across land often proves very difficult for them. However, these colossal creatures travel elegantly through the water, where they spend most of the year hunting for fish and cuttlefish, only taking to land in large groups to mate. Generally, they do not fear humans and cannot sense the danger that hunters can bring.

Their relatives in the tropical seas – the dugongs – are members of the sea cow, or sirenian, family. They never leave the water and are pure vegetarians, feeding only on sea grass. These sea mammals are not only excellent swimmers but brilliant divers. Of all the seals, the sea elephant holds the record for diving. It has been proven that they can reach depths of 1,580 meters (5,200 ft.), diving for 80 minutes.

Other species of seal hunt along the coasts of temperate zones, looking for the great schools of herring, mackerel, and cod – their preferred foods. In the story of evolution, sea lions, sea elephants, and seals are, astonishingly enough, close relatives to the dog and the bear. The sea cow, however, is closer to an elephant than it is to a whale.

Whales and sharks

Baleen whales, the largest living creatures on the planet, normally stay far away from coastal areas. In the warm parts of the year they can be found in Polar regions, filtering small crustaceans from the sea. In the spring, however, they turn up in the Tropics. What makes these giants of the ocean leave their home waters and move thousands of kilometers away to the north or the south – to the Caribbean Sea or the Gulf of California? This long journey benefits their young. The whale calf needs a warm nursery – it would have no chance of survival in cold waters. Unfortunately, the mating grounds of the baleen whales in the Tropics is frequently disturbed by human beings.

Humans have considerably more respect for sharks, although most shark species present no danger to us. The largest fish of all – the whale shark – weighs several tons, reaches a length of 14 meters (46 ft.), and is completely harmless; like the baleen whale it feeds mainly on small crustaceans. Sharks that live in the North Sea, like the haddock and cat sharks, hunt small fish, crustaceans, and invertebrates. But they, too, have enemies – the fishermen. In Germany, the belly of the haddock is smoked and lands on the dinner plate as a ringlet-shaped delicacy called "Schillerlocken."

Less benign to humans, however, is the white shark. It belongs to the group of deep-sea sharks, that can reach up to 8 meters

(26 ft.) in length, and may weigh over a ton. It roams the waters looking for prey – mainly swarms of fish – but it will not turn down a young seal or dolphin. And if it has hunted for some time without success, it will attack people near coastal regions. It is particularly attracted to the smell of blood and can detect and find a blood source across great distances. Survivors from ship catastrophes have reported shark attacks – many injured people

Belonging to the family of toothed whales, dolphins are known for their playful manner.

who are drifting and bleeding in the sea have become victims of hungry sharks although, as a rule, sharks feeds on what is found in their own habitat.

The food chain

A complex food chain is necessary in order for there to be sufficient food for the "big" animals. At the bottom of this food chain, we find microscopically small algae that produce organic substances from light and nutrients in the water. These algae belong to the plankton organisms floating in the water.

The name plankton – which means "wandering or drifting life" – was given to them in the second half of the 19th century by the German marine explorer Victor Hensen. Plankton consists of vegetable and animal organisms that float in the water – too weak to swim against the currents and waves. Usually, they are minute creatures only a few millimeters in size which spend their whole life in the water.

Small crustaceans, so-called cyclopids, specialize in eating other plankton. In addition to minute jellyfish or plankton worms, they often feed on their own kind, engaging in cannibalism. The cyclopids themselves are eaten by the larger fish larvae or the larvae of chaetopods. When they die, they sink to the bottom of the sea where they either rot or are consumed by other creatures.

Shore crabs, snails, and sea stars search for usable foodstuffs on the sea bed. A sandy or sludgy sea floor, grown over with algae or sea grass, provides some protection for many animals.

Two sea lions hunting: Since their extremities have evolved into fins, these rather clumsy land creatures are very elegant swimmers.

Sharks are the ocean's most feared creatures. They only attack people in exceptional cases and normally feed on what is found in their own habitat. This photo shows a group of Caribbean reef sharks and small black-nosed sharks.

Most marine creatures, with a few exceptions such as the seals and whales, go through a larval stage. Sometimes bizarre forms of larvae develop from the fertilized eggs of sea urchins, crustaceans, mussels, snails, worms, and fish. They live temporarily as plankton, feeding on algae. They go through several larval stages and, after a certain time, become a small sea urchin or sea star, a minute mussel, a crustacean, or a fish.

Larval development

The greatest danger during the larva stage is that of being eaten. As most of these animals do not take care of their young, the loss of offspring is particularly great during the first stage of life. The fact that they have not all become extinct is due to the enormous number of eggs that are fertilized. The lobster, which is the largest crustacean in northern waters, lays about 35,000 to 40,000 eggs. Greatly reduced numbers of these eggs develop into larvae and, of these, only about 0.5 percent to 0.1 percent actually reach the adult stage. The statistics for mussels and fish are often even lower.

When the larva has become a fully-developed animal – a mussel, crab, or sea star – both, its habitat and feeding habits, change. Mussels, barnacles, and sea anemones remain firmly fixed to the sea floor; they attach themselves to stones or colonize the large algae in shallow waters. The "leaves" of

some algae serve as nurseries for the common mussel that is found along the coasts. The "baby" mussels, only a few centimeters in size, attach themselves to the algae and filter their food from the water. They feed on minute plants and organisms that float nearly invisibly in their millions as plankton in the water.

When the mussels have grown for three to four months, they leave the algae and travel down to deeper waters where they look for a firmer base on which to attach themselves. The mussels continue to play a major role by filtering water and, thus, keeping it clean.

All animals have a function in the ecological system of the seas, either as a link in the food chain or as scavengers – both contributing to keeping their habitat clean.

Rock crab

Krill (luminescent shrimp)

Sea urchin

Sea star

Migratory movements of the whales

The world's largest mammal visits warmer waters to bear its young – and then sets off again to the Polar ice.

●●● Whales are divided into two groups according to their differing anatomy – the toothed cetaceans (odontoceti) and the baleen whales (mysticeti). The latter have no teeth but hundreds of long, triangular horny plates, or baleens, that hang down from the roof of the mouth; they filter the water, using the fringe of the baleens as a strainer to catch small crustaceans and fish, or to search through the sea bed for a type of worm called Sabellaria spinulosa, as well as other tiny sea life. Toothed cetaceans, including dolphins, porpoises, and sperm whales, feed on fish, octopi, and – like some other orcas (killer whales) – on other sea mammals.

The different feeding habits of each group lead to differences in behavior that can be seen in regards to migration. Most of the cetaceans remain relatively true to one location, moving around only a little depending on food availability. (The one exception among the cetaceans is the sperm whale, which undertakes north-to-south and south-to-north migrations in relation to the seasons.) In contrast, most of the baleen whales commute regularly between feeding grounds in the Polar zones and the mating grounds and nurseries for their offspring that are in warmer waters towards the Equator.

The 11 species of baleen whales include the lesser rorqual (9 meters [30 ft.] long), the humpback whale, the Bryde's whale, the right whale, the gray whale, and the blue whale – which at almost 30 meters (100 ft.) in length, is the world's largest animal. The Bryde's whale remains in tropical and subtropical waters throughout the year, commuting only between the two Tropics.

The migration of the Pacific gray whales and the humpback whales are well documented. The gray whale spends its summer in the Arctic seas, which are the most nutrient-rich in the world. For the whales this is a "land of milk and honey" – a paradise full of copepods (a flea-like creature) and shrimp, where the gray giants can (and must) tuck away as much as possible in order to develop a thick layer of fat. During their migration, these 14-meter (45 ft.) long creatures that weigh up to 35 tons must live from their reserves. It is assumed that hormones – which likely depend on the number of daylight hours as a cue – are responsible for the time of departure. The gray whale's journey takes it through three seas – from the Chukchi Sea at the edge of the pack ice through the Bering Sea to the Pacific.

The whale's internal provisions

The colder it is in the north, the further south these sea mammals travel. They winter in the warm, subtropical waters off Mexico. Here the whales mate and bear their young 12 months later. The baby whale is about 4,5 meters (15 ft.) long at birth and weighs about 600 kilograms (1,320 lb.). Each day, it suckles about 200 liter (52 gal.) of its mother's rich, fatty milk, converting it into a layer of fat. At the tender age of just two-and-a-half to three months the baby whale follows its mother on the long trek back to the Arctic.

The gray whales usually travel in small groups or in mother-and-child formations. They swim just under the surface of the water with blowholes closed. Every few minutes they come up for air, but only to a point where the blowhole is just above the surface of the water. Gray whales communicate with underwater barking, whistling, and clicking sounds, and since sound waves travel better in water than on land, acoustic orientation is more important than visual orientation – an important factor when waters are churned up and cloudy, and visibility is less than one-and-a-half feet.

Coastal patrol

Above the water, however, whales see very well. Whale watchers recognize the typical scouting position – when the whale sticks its head out of the water and looks around. It is assumed that these animals can recognize and note characteristic landmarks, as their migratory routes are often just a few miles off the coast. They can also orientate themselves by means of underwater noises – for example, the surf – or the "taste" of the river delta they are passing.

The humpback whale is one of the "cosmopolitans" among the baleens – it is found in all the oceans of the world. The male is known for his "singing" during the mating season. Just like the gray whale, the humpback spends the winter in warm tropical waters where it reproduces. In the summer, it travels back to the poles. Although it spends summer and winter in shallow waters off the coast or near

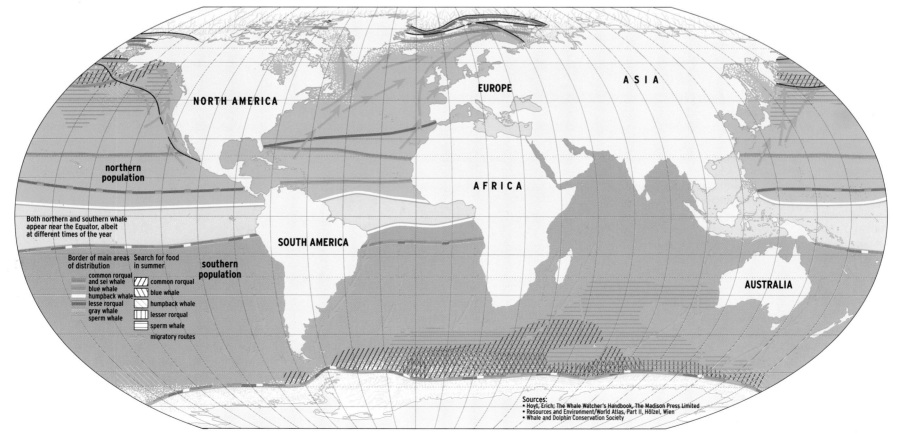

Ocean habitats: No other creature is as widely distributed as the whale. The graphics show which of the populations, separated between the northern and southern hemisphere, migrate between cold and warm oceans.

This baby humpback is one week old. It was born after a gestation period of 11 to 12 months in the warmer waters of the South Pacific.

islands, its migratory routes are across the open sea. Humpback whales move at a speed of about 5 kilometers (3 mi.) an hour – a little more slowly than the gray whales (at about 7 kilometers [4 mi.] an hour). There are at least 10 geographical populations. Some mixing occurs, unless they live in different hemispheres. While the northern populations leave the Arctic winters to spend time in the Tropics, their southern cousins are enjoying the southern summer in the Antarctic. As they probably never meet, no genetic exchange takes place between these populations.

The humpback whale in the North Atlantic bring up their young in the Caribbean; those in the North Pacific raise them off Hawaii, Mexico, or California. A small population still migrates back and forth between Norway and Cape

Verde. In the southern hemisphere, the humpbacks spend the southern winter (from June to October) off the coast of Australia, South Africa, or the South Sea Islands of New Caledonia and Tonga. The longest migration of humpbacks ever observed was of whales that lived south of Cape Horn in the summer and wintered off the coasts of Columbia and Costa Rica, where their young are born.

The blue whale also undertakes long migrations between lower latitudes in winter and higher latitudes in the summer, differentiating between at least three populations: those in the North Atlantic, those in the North Pacific, and those in the southern hemisphere. There are blue whales living in the Indian Ocean that probably never leave their habitat. In the North Atlantic only a few hundred blue whales remain. This species has been almost entirely wiped out due to the whale fishing industry.

In past times, whale fishers were predominantly seeking whale oil and whalebone (the baleens), but today the whole of the animal is used, particularly since whale meat is considered a delicacy. In order to increase protection for the whales, an area of 18 million sq. kilometers (7 mill. sq. mi.) in the Atlantic was declared as a whale sanctuary in December 1994.

Population of migratory whales
GRAY WHALE 22,000, extinct in the Atlantic
HUMPBACK WHALE 20,000
LESSER RORQUAL 1 million
BLUE WHALE less than 5,000
SPERM WHALE 2 million
ATLANTIC RIGHT WHALE 3,500
SEI WHALE 60,000
BRYDE WHALE 60,000
COMMON RORQUAL 75,000
BOWHEAD WHALE 8,000

FACTS AND FIGURES

The migratory routes
SPERM WHALE: Widely distributed. Migrates in the summer in the direction of the poles – older male species right to the edge of the Polar ice, females and young animals seldom past 45° north and 42° south latitudes. Spend the winter in temperate and tropical waters.

RIGHT WHALE: Atlantic right whales live in the North Atlantic and North Pacific, off the coasts of North America, Japan, China, and Russia. The Southern Antarctic right whale lives around the Antarctic, off the coasts of South America, South Africa, South Australia, and New Zealand.

LESSER RORQUAL: Worldwide, but more frequently in colder waters. In the summer, large congregations gather in higher latitudes; in winter, in lower latitudes.

COMMON RORQUAL: After the blue whale, the second largest animal in the world (18-26 meters [59-85 ft.] long). Distributed throughout the world (also in the Mediterranean) they are found most frequently on the southern hemisphere and in temperate latitudes.

Ocean currents

The waters of the oceans are constantly in motion, and these powerful currents have a great deal of influence on our climate.

●●● The currents of the ocean make up an almost unbroken circulatory system which moves clockwise (anti-cyclonically) in the Northern Hemisphere and counterclockwise (cyclonically) in the Southern Hemisphere. On the whole, the currents correspond roughly to the great wind systems – but not quite, as they only follow the prevailing wind movements and do not react to the frequent changes in wind direction.

The Coriolis effect – a force exerted by the Earth's rotation – is another factor which influences the currents. It is strongest at the poles and no longer measurable at the equator. The Coriolis deflects wind-generated currents and to the right in the Northern Hemisphere and to the left in the Southern Hemisphere.

On each half of the Earth there are three wind zones: the region near the Equator, with the trade wind coming from the east; further towards the poles is the zone of the west winds, known as the "westerlies"; and, near the poles, the zone of polar east winds.

These three wind systems generate three ocean current systems in each hemisphere – the equatorial currents, and the subtropical gyres and the subpolar gyres – two large spirals spanning the oceans. Then, finally, there is the circumpolar current that circulates around the Antarctic.

The Equatorial Counter Current

Particularly spectacular are the equatorial currents. Pushed along by the trade winds, they flow in a constant westerly direction and are the main force behind the surface circulation of the oceans. Between them, the narrow and very fast Equatorial Counter Current flows in the opposite direction. The wind-driven currents push along great volumes of water off the eastern sides of continents, raising the sea level there to a higher level than on the west side of the oceans.

In the Atlantic, the Equatorial Counter Current flows north of the equator throughout the whole year. It develops over the Mid-Atlantic Ridge and rolls onwards as far as the Bay of Guinea.

The Equatorial Counter Current is at its most impressive, however, in the North Pacific. It is 500 to 700 kilometers (300 to 430 mi.) wide and flows 15,000 kilometers (9,300 mi.) – from the Philippines in the west to as far as the Gulf of Panama in the east. On the way it gradually loses speed, with only a weakened version of the current reaching Central America.

The waters of the equatorial currents come from the eastern sides of the oceanic basins where the trade winds blow more strongly towards the equator. Source currents are the Canary Current and the Benguela Current off Africa, and the California and Humboldt Currents in the Pacific off the two Americas. The Indian South Equatorial Current is fed by the relatively weak West Australian Current.

Since they originate in cold regions, the temperature of these eastern fringe currents is relatively low. The warm air in these latitudes cannot heat up, as winds from the land cause a cross-circulation; therefore, on their way to the equator they turn on their own longitudinal axis, bringing additional cold waters from depths of 100 to 300 meteres (330 to 1,000 ft.) to the surface – which then sink down again 150 to 300 meters (500 to 1,000 ft.) off the coasts.

These deep-water masses bring nutrients to the surface that accelerate plankton growth, thus providing food for the rich fish population off the west coasts of the continents.

Fringe currents

On the west side of the oceans, the equatorial currents flow towards the poles, forming strongly concentrated fringe currents such as the Gulf Stream off North America, the Kuroshio Current off Japan, the Brazilian Current off South America, and the Agulhas Current off southeast Africa.

The western fringe currents vary in strength. The Gulf Stream Current is the strongest. Forming part of the larger Gulf Stream system, it begins at the convergence of the Yucatan Current, which comes as the Florida Current from the Gulf of Mexico, and the Antilles Current, a branch of the North Equatorial Current, flowing closely by the continental slope between the exit of the Florida Straits and Cape Hatteras.

Southeast of the Newfoundland bank it is joined by the cold Labrador Current from

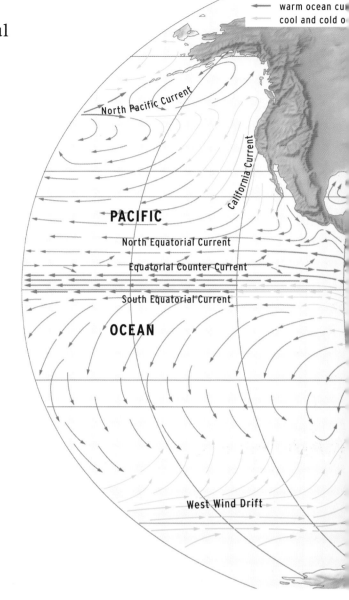

Powerful systems of ocean currents push massive vo
counter currents to where they began.

The different colors of the water show the convergence of rising cold water and warmer surface water.

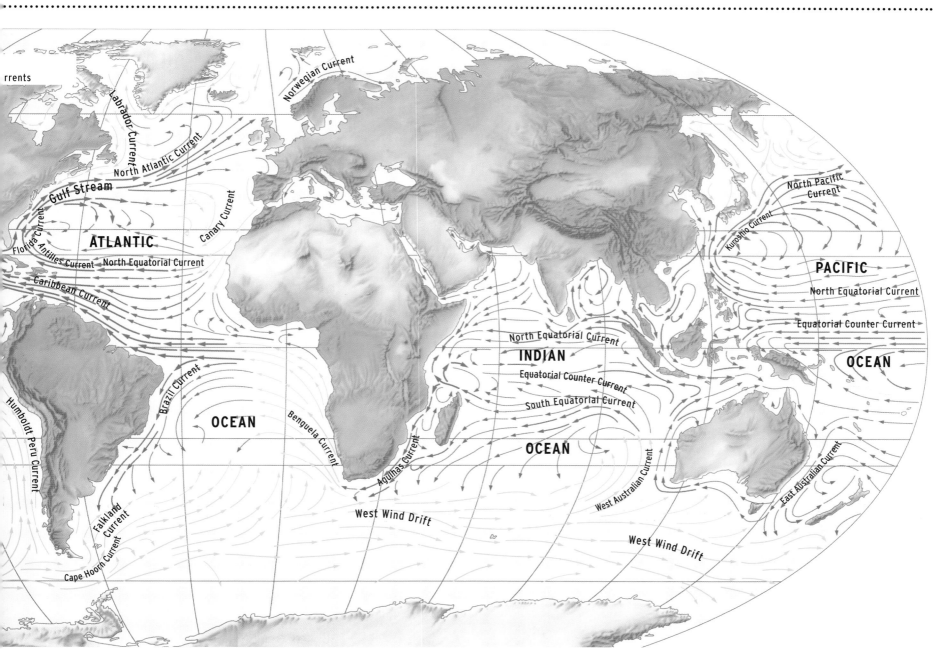

of water to the west, driven by the constant winds along the surface. On the east coasts of the landmasses, they flow north and south, returning as

the north, which causes great meanders in the Gulf Stream to break up.

The swirls break off and form eddies, some of which drift a long way into the Labrador Sea. Most of them, however, move north and east as the North Atlantic Drift.

Cascading water masses

On their way into the region between northern Norway and Greenland, Arctic winds cool the strongly saline waters, which become so heavy that they sink down through lighter waters to the bed of the Arctic North Atlantic. On average, about 17 million square kilometers (4 mill. cu. mi.) of water per second plunge into the depths – an estimated 20 times more water than the volume of all the rivers in the world combined. This massive deep bottom current is the reason why the waters of the Gulf Stream are able to reach as far north as they do.

A similar system is impossible in the Indian Ocean, due to its extended northern landmasses. In the Indian Ocean, it is the alternating monsoon winds that influence the currents.

The northwestern Pacific Ocean also lies within the influence of monsoons, but here it has a different effect than in the north-

ern Indian Ocean. The offshore winter monsoon drives cold Asian air from the mainland over the sea, whereas the onshore summer monsoon brings back warm oceanic air. Thus, the surface temperature changes with the alternating monsoons by, on average, 10° C (50° F) off North Korea, and in Manchuria by up to 20° C (68° F).

Ice develops in the northern marginal seas of the Pacific. Even Vladivostok, which lies on the same latitude as Florence, is not completely free of ice in winter. In summer, the oceanic air masses saturated with vapor break over the cold seas, forming persistent fog. Large parts of the Sea of Okhotsk and the Bering Sea make up some of the most inhospitable waters in the world.

Between the trade wind region and the West Wind Drift region lie the Horse Latitudes. Near to the Equator these currents take on the characteristics of the trade wind in summer. In winter the parts toward the Pole take on the characteristics of the West Wind Drift. Trade wind current and West Wind Drift circulate around the interior regions of the Horse Latitudes, leading to an accumulation of light surface water in the heart of the whirl which is saline. At this latitude, more water evaporates than can be replaced by rain.

FACTS AND FIGURES

Wind force and wave size

Heavy seas at wind force 10

WIND FORCE 4: waves up to 1 m (3 ft.), a few white caps
WIND FORCE 6: waves up to 3 m (10 ft.), extensive white foam crests
WIND FORCE 8: waves up to 7 m (23 ft.), long crests, "rolling" sea
WIND FORCE 9: waves up to 9 m (30 ft.), very high wave crests, visibility is impaired by spray
WIND FORCE 10: waves 10 m (33 ft.) and more, the surface of the sea takes on a white appearance; medium-size ships "disappear" in the trough of the waves

The layers of the oceans

Deep sea currents have their own circulatory system, and transport nutrients from the depths of the water as they make their way to the surface.

● ● ● Massive sea currents roll along at different levels in the oceans like gigantic conveyor belts. They are all linked by one circulatory system which flows through all of the seas. Each cycle takes a thousand years to complete.

The mechanism that drives the deep sea currents is called thermohaline circulation. It is created when water on the surface evaporates or freezes, leaving salt behind. Depending on the temperature, it forms layers between light and dense water or sinks to the bed. If a vast amount of rain or river water reaches the sea, it remains on the surface as long as it is warm. As soon as cools off, however, it will also sink down to deeper levels.

The varying densities of water make up three main ocean layers that are more or less stable. The surface layer contains the warmest and, therefore, lightest water. It is only about 100 to 500 meters (330 to 1,600 ft.) thick and covers the surface to as far as 45° latitude. The masses of surface water are blown about and mixed up by the wind.

Below this layer is the so-called pycnocline, an interim layer between the surface and the bed, just about one kilometer (0.6 mi.) thick. Here, the salt content (i.e., density), increases with depth, while the temperature decreases.

Eighty per cent of all ocean water collects in the cool, deep layer. Compared with the wind-driven currents at the surface. The Gulf Stream, for example, reaches speeds of up to 9 kilometers (6 mi.) an hour, the deep waters move at only 0.36 kilometers (0.2 mi.) per hour. Salt content is relatively uniform and is between 34 and 35 parts per thousand, with temperatures between 0° C (32° F) and 5° C (41° F).

The low temperature is an indication that deep waters come from the subpolar and polar regions of the Earth. Here the water cools and becomes denser than waters at a higher latitude that are warmed by the Sun. The cool water drops through lighter water levels until it reaches a depth where the density of the water corresponds to its own.

Water "pumps"

As colder water sinks from the surface, it is inevitably replaced. The convection currents provide the driving power behind deep water circulation.

The largest of the "pumps" lies between Norway and Greenland where waters originating in the southern Gulf Stream arrive with the North Atlantic Drift. The water is relatively saline, since much of the water has evaporated in the warmer latitudes. As it is warm, it remains on the surface, flowing

Dense waters, rich in salt, cool off and drop to the depths where they converge with bottom currents circulating in the deep waters.

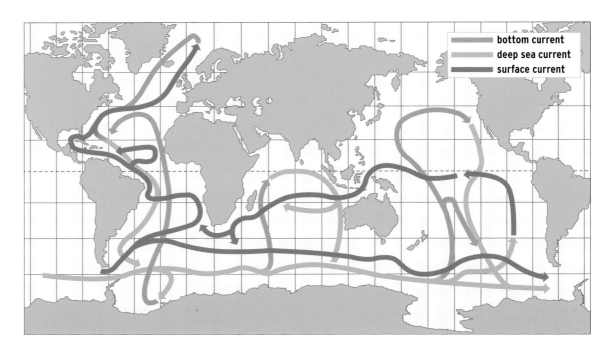

At different levels, the oceans circulate completely different currents. The map illustrates the interaction of these layers, called thermohaline circulation.

far to the north where it gradually cools off and becomes denser. When it reaches the latitude of Iceland it begins to sink slowly, and once it reaches the Greenland Sea it is so dense that it falls through all the other water levels right down to the ocean floor to a depth of 3,000 meters (9,840 ft.), initiating the thermohaline circulation.

Down below, it moves as North Atlantic deep water back to the south, flows over the Faeroe–Iceland Rise, and slowly rolls along into the west basin of the Atlantic to the South Pole. On reaching the Antarctic Circumpolar Current, it widens out into the Indian and Pacific oceans.

Occasionally, batches of colder water from the Arctic Ocean reach the Greenland Sea in the North Atlantic via the Nansen Cordillera between Greenland and Svalbard. When ice is formed, only fresh water freezes, leaving salt behind. Therefore this water, too, is very saline. It forms a layer – the Arctic Bottom Water – below the North Atlantic Deep Water, and spreads along the

bottom until it is stopped by the Newfoundland Rise. The Arctic Bottom Water is the densest of all sea waters.

Bottom water also develops in the Antarctic, forming on the continental shelf of the southern continent, mainly off the Weddell Sea. In winter, the temperature of the water under the ice is −1.9° C (28.6 °F). It is the densest of all waters in the Southern Ocean and drops to the floor of the Atlantic-Indian Ocean.

The water column

The wind-driven Antarctic water ring generates a deep, circumpolar current that involves the whole of the water column. The bottom water follows the current around the Antarctic and, because it mixes with the warmer waters above, warms up during its passage around the continent from −1° C

The parting of the ways for the deep currents of the Southern Ocean is also a popular tourist viewpoint. Coming around the Cape of Good Hope, a current traveling from the the Indian Ocean will find its way into the Atlantic.

(30,2° F) in the Weddell Sea to 0.4° C (32,7° F) in the Drake Passage between the Antarctic Peninsula and the southern tip of South America.

The Antarctic Bottom Water spreads into all the other oceans from the Antarctic Circumpolar Current. In the Atlantic it crawls along the bottom, particularly along the west side as far as the foot of the Newfoundland Banks. Then it pushes its way under the North Atlantic Deep Water, which flows on the same side down to the south. In the eastern Atlantic basin, it is prevented from continuing to the equator by the Walvis Ridge. However, it does find a way to the east side by escaping through a hole in the middle of the Atlantic Ridge, known as the Romanche Gap.

The water cycle

The Antarctic Bottom Water gradually rises on its way north and mixes with the less dense waters above it, retuning with deep water to the Southern Ocean. Atlantic Bottom Water can be found in the Pacific Ocean as far north as the Aleutians.

Some Atlantic Deep Water mixes with that of the Southern Ocean and spreads out in the Pacific to the north as Atlantic Bottom Water. It becomes less saline – and less dense – and rises up to 1,000 to 2,000 meters (3,300 to 6,600 ft.), returning

as North Pacific Deep Water to the Southern Ocean, and joining up again with the Antarctic Circumpolar Current. Other mixtures of North Pacific Deep Water reach the northwest Pacific, where they are thoroughly mixed up by storms. These water masses also return to the Antarctic as interval waters between the surface and deep waters.

Heavy deep water is also formed in other parts of the world. For example, in the Labrador Sea cold waters cascade at 10 centimeters (4 in.) per second into vents at 2,000 to 3,000 meters (6,600 to 9,900 ft.).

Small amounts of dense water also come from warmer regions, where the water is very salty due to high rates of evaporation – for example, the Red Sea or the Persian Gulf. At the bottom of the Straits of Gibraltar, salt-rich waters of the Mediterranean Sea flow into the Atlantic, mixing at 1,000 to 2,000 meters (3,300 to 6,600 ft.) and forming the upper level of the North Atlantic Deep Water.

The North Atlantic Deep Water that lies submerged between Greenland and Norway is slowly replaced by rising, older deep waters, especially in the Southern Ocean. Deep water leaves the Atlantic by means of the Antarctic Circumpolar Current, being ripped along by the swirl, returning through the Drake Passage as cold, low-salt Pacific water. It stays as subantarctic interval water between the surface water of the warm water spheres and the deep waters.

A further, minor in-current from the Indian Ocean also finds its way back to the Atlantic around the Cape of Good Hope and the cycle begins anew.

Until 1980, about 0.5 million cubic meters (17.5 mill. cu. ft.) per second of deep water was formed in the Greenland Sea, but since then deep water formation has declined by 20 percent. If less deep water is formed, then less warm water will flow to the north on the sea surface and, therefore, long-distance heating from the ocean will become weaker.

Whether this is a long-term trend caused by general global warming remains to be seen.

FACTS AND FIGURES

Currents and water volumes

Water transported in the ocean currents is measured in Sverdrup units; 1 Sverdrup (Sv) = 1 million cubic meters (35 mill. cu. ft.) of water per second. The greatest currents on Earth:

Gulf Stream	14 Sv
Atlantic South Equatorial Current	14 Sv
North Atlantic deep water mixed with Antarctic Bottom Water	18 Sv
Atlantic-Antarctic Bottom Water	4 Sv
Agulhas Current	4 Sv
Benguela Current	10 Sv
Indian South Equatorial Current	14 Sv
Indian Circumpolar deep water	24 Sv
Deep water Indian Ocean	10 Sv
Pacific South Equatorial Current	4 Sv
Pacific Circumpolar deep water	20 Sv

The driving force of the Sun

Our climate depends on the interplay between the oceans and the sun; heat distribution is the key.

● ● ● Although sunshine and rain come from above, weather is not created solely in the skies. Our climate depends on the close interchange between the atmosphere and the oceans, which is ultimately controlled by the Sun.

At the equator, the Sun's rays strike the earth almost perpendicularly, heating up the surface waters. Towards the poles, the Sun's warming energy is distributed over larger areas due to the Earth's curvature. Irradiation decreases in winter, as half of the Earth is temporarily turned away from the Sun. And since our planet emits heat into cold space at the poles, heat loss greatly exceeds irradiation.

Gigantic masses of heat

If there were no redistribution of heat energy, the seas at the equator would boil and the ice plates in the north and south would stretch into the low latitudes. However, air and sea currents transport gigantic masses of heat towards the poles; and at the equator, warm, moist air masses rise up to 18 kilometers (11 mi.). Theoretically, they could then travel directly north and south, since in the lower layers, cold air masses would move in the opposite direction (i.e., towards the Equator). However, the Earth's rotation prevents this simple heat exchange. Instead, cold and warm air masses move separately in great spirals around the Earth, not converging until they reach temperate latitudes where they form powerful cyclones.

Warm air rises in depressions and the air pressure over the sea drops. The resulting updrift draws in fresh air, which becomes warmer and lifts moisture from the sea. During the ascent it cools, and the water condenses to form clouds and precipitation. On their way from west to east, such depressions bring large volumes of rain, from which Europe and North America benefit.

There are several climatic belts around the Earth in which winds of a particular direction prevail. The direction is determined by the Coriolis effect, in which particles accelerated by the Earth's rotation are deflected sideways (clockwise in the Northern Hemisphere and counterclockwise in the Southern Hemisphere). The further from the equator, the greater its effect.

Depressions and "doldrums"

The first climatic belt comprises a cloud-covered zone from latitude 10° north to 10° south, with little wind and much precipitation (the "doldrums"). This includes the trade winds up to latitude 25° north and 25° south. They blow up to 25 kilometers (16 mi.) an hour from a northeasterly direction in the Northern Hemisphere and a southeasterly direction in the Southern Hemisphere.

On both sides of the Equator, around 30° latitude, lie the horse latitudes; with little wind and very dry air, they are one rea-

As there are practically no landmasses in the Southern Hemisphere to obstruct the winds, storms are much more frequent than in the Northern Hemisphere.

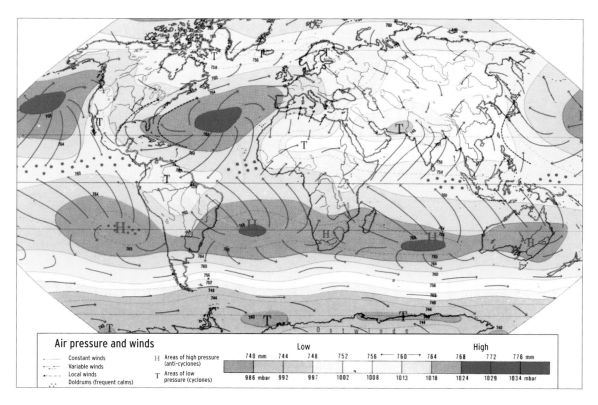

Air pressure and winds

		Low							High		
⎯⎯ Constant winds	H Areas of high pressure (anti-cyclones)	740 mm	744	748	752	756 ⟵ 760 ⟶	764	768	772	776 mm
– – Variable winds										
–·–·– Local winds	T Areas of low pressure (cyclones)	986 mbar	992	997	1002	1008	1013	1018	1024	1029	1034 mbar
··· Doldrums (frequent calms)										

The trade winds develop between the equator and the tropics. They blow uniformly, moving westward and influencing the climate above the seas.

son why the desert regions of Africa and Asia are expanding.

In the temperate latitudes, strong winds drive the depressions previously mentioned to the east. Since they meet with little obstruction from landmasses in the Southern Hemisphere, the winds can reach velocities of up to 160 kilometers (100 mi.) an hour. Seamen refer to these stormy regions as the "roaring forties" or the "screaming sixties." Around latitude 60° north and 60° south, the

polar fronts spread as belts of low pressure, and further towards the poles, the west winds dominate.

While climatic belts in the Southern Hemisphere follow one upon the other in a relatively undisturbed fashion, circulation of the atmosphere in the Northern Hemisphere is interrupted by the great landmasses of Eurasia and North America. In summer, the landmasses of Asia heat up and warm air rises over the Himalayas.

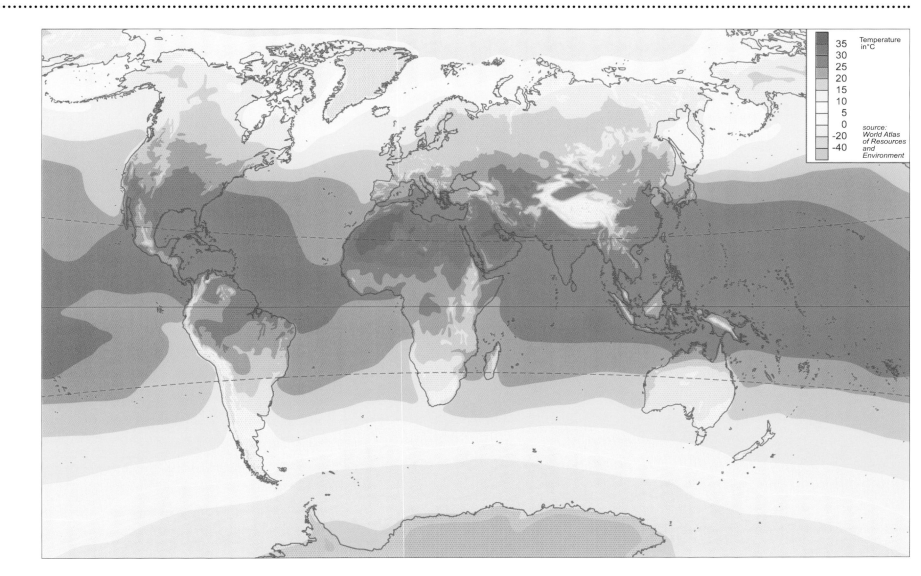

Average July temperatures: Due to the larger landmasses, the warm zones in the Northern Hemisphere shift much more than those in the Southern Hemisphere. Temperatures over the sea change less than those over the continents.

Through the uplift, southerly winds from the Indian Ocean bring rain to India (the southwest monsoon). In the winter, when the land masses cool down again, the wind direction changes by 180° (northeast monsoon).

Like the atmosphere, the oceans also carry heat from the equator to the north and the south. The wind-driven surface currents are deflected by the Coriolis effect and detoured by landmasses, causing the development of complex currents, including the Gulf Stream (in the North Atlantic) and the Kuroshio (in the North Pacific).

A popular symbolic act : the "crossing of the line" ceremony at the equator.

Both are nourished by the trade winds and run within narrow lanes towards the poles. The Gulf Stream transports about one billion megawatts of heat to the north; its branches are responsible for palms growing on the west coast of Ireland and the southern Barents Sea remaining free of ice the whole year through.

Cascades of water

In the Greenland Sea in winter, about 17 million cubic meters (600 mill. cu. ft.) of surface water per second cools off and then plunges down in columns only 15 kilometers (9 mi.) wide. With the loss in heat, the water becomes not only denser, but gas solubility also increases, so the cascades of water fill up with copious quantities of oxygen and carbon dioxide before plunging down like waterfalls. At depths of 2,000 to 3,000 meters (6,400 to 9,600 ft.) they move off in the direction of the Antarctic as the North Atlantic Deep Water and further on into the Indian Ocean and the Pacific. Around the coasts of Peru and California, sea waters that sank a few centuries ago will surface once more, thus completing the circle over the wind-driven surface currents.

Deep water, rich in oxygen, also forms in the south polar Weddell Sea. It pushes its way in the Atlantic under the approaching Atlantic Deep Water as Antarctic Bottom Water, transporting, as if on a gigantic conveyor belt, oxygen to the deep sea – and so creating conditions for life in the darkness.

FACTS AND FIGURES

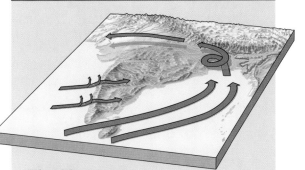

The Monsoon

The uneven distribution of the landmasses causes a climatic event that is, above all, significant for the Indian subcontinent – the monsoon. In summer, the Eurasian landmasses heat up more quickly than the Indian Ocean. Warm air rises over the Himalayas and the Tibetan highlands, thus attracting fresh masses of air from the south. The air masses fill up with moisture over the Arabian Sea and the Indian Ocean and release it over the continent as very heavy rain. Because of its prevailing wind direction, the monsoon in Asia that lasts from June to September is known as the southwest monsoon. In winter, when the landmasses of Europe and Asia have cooled down, the winds change direction.

When air and sea clash

A water temperature of more than 27° Celsius is a prerequisite for a cyclonic storm, regardless of where it comes from or where it goes.

A cyclonic storm races across the Caribbean towards Florida. This satellite picture shows the enormous area covered by one such hurricane.

● ● ● In the delicate balance between ocean and atmosphere, irregularities are more or less pre-programmed. In moderate latitudes, cold air masses from the south and north converge with warm air masses from the equator to form deep pressure cyclones that drift eastwards. However, in winter, extremely cold Arctic air masses flow across the Northern Hemisphere. If they meet up with humid and warm air over the Gulf Stream or the Kuroshio Current, sudden and violent storms can develop. Tropical cyclones over the Atlantic – hurricanes – reach typical speeds of more than 200 kilometers (125 mi.) an hour, and their destructive force is correspondingly great.

The devastating force of natural disasters

On 23 August 1992, Hurricane Andrew was approaching land at Turkey Point, south of Miami. In its center, winds were raging at a speed of up to 220 kilometers (137 mi.) an hour. Its birth had already been registered by satellite on 17 August, but not until 21 August did it become apparent that it would probably develop into a serious hurricane. Andrew wreaked havoc and devastation on a terrifying scale. Damage was assessed at more than $25 billion US, 14 people were killed and yet it was only the third strongest hurricane of the 20th century to reach the coast of the United States. The greatest natural disaster in the history of the United States occurred on 8 September 1900 near Galveston, Texas, when a hurricane claimed the lives of more than 8,000 people.

But it's not only the winds and rains that cause devastation. In 1928, a hurricane

them. In 1944 in the North Pacific, a US marine convoy was caught in a typhoon. Three destroyers sank, nine ships were severely damaged, and a further 19 suffered light damage.

Every year up to 20 hurricanes occur in the tropical North Atlantic, particularly in the Caribbean. More than 30 typhoons – south Asiatic cyclones – tear across the Philippines to China or Japan each year. Cyclones also occur in the Indian Ocean and off Australia.

Storms of summertime

All cyclones originate in oceanic areas where the water temperature is at least 27° C (80° F) – mostly in late summer. Initially deflected by the Coriolis effect far from the equator, their beginnings are limited to a narrow path running north of the 5° latitude line in the Atlantic and south of 5° latitude in the Pacific. From here they move in an arc either northwards or southwards.

In the center of a cyclone – the so-called "eye" of the storm, which measures between 10 and 100 kilometers (6 to 60 mi.) across – low pressure sucks up warm, humid

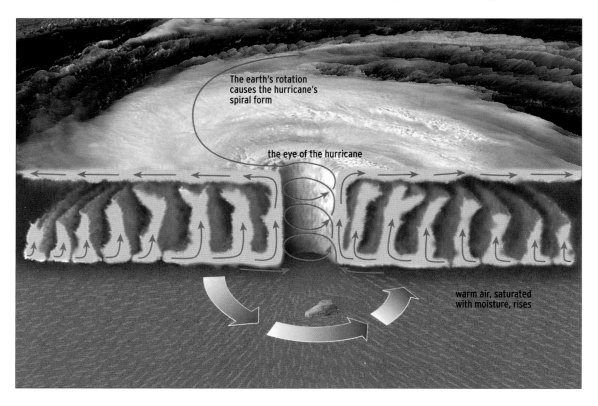

The earth's rotation causes the hurricane's spiral form

the eye of the hurricane

warm air, saturated with moisture, rises

Cyclonic storms are formed when the temperature of the water reaches 27° C (80° F). Humid air masses then rise up, which can develop into mighty rotating winds.

south of Lake Okeechobee, Florida, triggered a tidal wave that drowned 1,800 people. Such waves are also a danger on the high seas. In 1995, the luxury liner *Queen Elizabeth II* was hit by a 70-foot tidal wave that had been triggered by Hurricane Luis.

A vessel caught in a cyclone faces extreme danger. With winds constantly changing direction and waves coming from all sides, it is impossible to steer against

sea air from all directions. In the eye, it travels upwards, releasing rain and conversion energy, whereby it heats up further, rises even higher, and spreads out in the upper levels. The uplift current lowers the pressure of the air over the sea and the storm gains in strength.

At sea level, the winds circle more and more rapidly around the eye. The tropical seas provide additional water through evap-

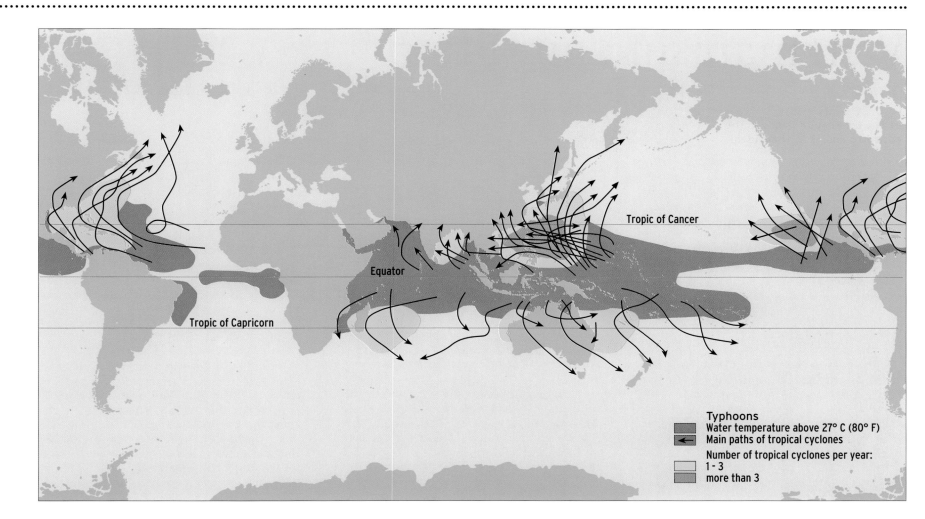

Cyclones are formed over the seas in a narrow zone near the equator. The prerequisite for their formation is a high water temperature. In the Northern Hemisphere, the winds are deflected to the north; and in the Southern Hemisphere, to the south.

A waterspout over the Caribbean sea.

oration, and when this falls as rain, further energy is set free.

A storm will slacken off when the water mixes to the point where cold water begins to well up. Storms also lose force once they reach the mainland. Usually, such hurricanes only last a few days.

Other climatic events have a much longer duration, such as when the winds force the ocean currents to change direction.

In the Indian Ocean, this is called the monsoon, and in the Pacific, the El Niño phenomenon.

El Niño

Normally, the trade winds force the warm surface waters of the Pacific westwards, so the sea level off New Guinea and the Philippines is 40 centimeters (16 in.) higher than off Peru. Every three to seven years, however, the east winds drop so drastically that the water masses slosh back, preventing the ascent of cold, nutrient-rich deep sea water – a catastrophe for marine life. With their food supplies interrupted, even the smallest algae or plankton cannot thrive in the warmer surface waters. Fish move on to cooler regions, and the sea birds and mammals remain behind – hungry. As the coastal waters were always warmer at Christmas time, fishermen christened the event El Niño – the "Christ child."

The upheaval is not restricted to the coast. Moisture rises over the warm sea, forming thick columns of cloud, which move to the land interior. While parts of South America experience torrential rains, Australia and Indonesia suffer droughts. The summer monsoon over Asia is weakened and typhoons and cyclones pile up over the Pacific instead. In addition, the changed Pacific currents seem to influence the occurrence of winter storms over California and the southern parts of the USA.

The consequences are immense. In regions of drought, farmers experience dramatic drops in yield, and in the rain-soaked areas, flooding and landslides are common.

In addition to monitoring via satellite, meteorologists have installed a network of sensors over the Pacific. Host computers create simulation models using the data measured, allowing relatively accurate forecasts to be made.

Almost half a century ago, scientists were able to warn of the "El Niño of the century" in 1997/98, which reached hitherto unknown dimensions – even off California, where the warm surface waters prevented colder deep sea waters from ascending.

FACTS AND FIGURES

Catastrophic hurricanes
The worst cyclones to devastate the USA in the 20th century

Place	Year	Victims
Texas	1900	8000
Florida	1928	1836
Florida	1919	600
New England	1938	600
Florida	1935	408
Audrey	1957	390
New England	1944	390
Grand Isle	1909	350
New Orleans	1915	275
Galveston	1915	275
Mississippi	1969	256
Florida	1926	243
New England	1955	184
Florida	1906	164
Florida	1906	134
New England	1972	122
South Carolina	1954	95
Florida	1965	75

Source: National Hurricane Center/Florida international University

Legend:
Typhoons
Water temperature above 27° C (80° F)
Main paths of tropical cyclones
Number of tropical cyclones per year:
1 - 3
more than 3

What causes the tides

Oceans react to the forces of the Moon and the Sun. On coasts with particularly high tides, these forces can be used to generate energy by means of tidal power stations.

●●● Visitors to the coasts of Brittany can witness a wonderful natural spectacle. The sea ebbs slowly, almost hesitatingly, exposing wide areas of sand to the inclemency of the weather. Then comes the powerful return, when even mighty rocks disappear beneath the waves rolling in to the shore. The tidal rise in the Bay of St. Malo is more than 11 meters (36 ft.) – so certain safety aspects must be considered for shipping and the harbor.

Centrifugal versus gravitational forces

It is extremely difficult to forecast the tides, even though their cause has more or less been clarified. Just imagine the Earth as a ball covered with a uniform layer of water. The Moon rotates around this blue planet at an unchanging distance. In turn, both the Earth and the Moon rotate around a common center of gravity that lies in the interior of the Earth, and whose mass is greater than that of the Moon.

During rotation, centrifugal forces are created. This force is of the same strength and direction all over the planet – parallel to the connecting axes of the two planets and averted from the Moon. In contrast to that, the gravitational forces are directed to the mass center of the Moon and dependent on the distance of a position on Earth to the Moon. It is only in the center of the Earth that the gravitational pull and the centrifugal forces are neutralized; in the water layer, however, the sum of both forces affects each molecule. The result is that the gravitational pull is greatest on the side of the Earth facing the Moon, so that the water layer there bulges.

A similar bulge is created on the side away from the Moon where the centrifugal force is greater than the gravitational pull. Both water bulges circulate around the Earth at the same time as the Moon, i.e., once every 24 hours and 50 minutes. However, the frictional resistance of the Earth to the water masses causes a time delay.

Spring tides and neap tides

The Sun, too, exerts a force on the Earth that generates tides, although it is only half as strong as that of the Moon. Depending on the position of Sun and Moon in relation to one another, this tide-generating force grows or diminishes. So when the Moon is new or full, or when Sun, Moon, and Earth are all on one orbit, the tidal forces are at their strongest. They are at their weakest when the forces of Sun and Moon are at a right angle to one another (quarter Moon and three-quarter Moon). These tidal phenomena are known as spring tides (when tidal forces are greatest), and neap tides (when they are lowest), and occur one or two days after the relevant constellation has been observed.

The greatest tidal rise is in Canada's Bay of Fundy. The photo shows the Hopewell Rocks, where the difference between high tide and low tide is 16 meters (53 ft.).

Spring and neap tides occur at intervals of about 14.77 days, a phenomena called the "half-monthly irregularity." A "monthly irregularity" period of 27.55 days is the result of the Moon not following a circular, but rather an elliptical, orbit. When the Moon is nearest the Earth, the tidal rise is greatest, and when it is at its furthest from Earth, the tidal rise is at its lowest.

The complicated pattern of force distribution resulting from the movements of Sun. Moon. and Earth generates a series of partial tides of varying strength and times. Depending on the characteristic of the irregularity, various forms of tides are created.

On the one hand, there are semidiurnal and mixed tides. The former can be seen on the English North Sea coast when there are two high waters and two low waters of almost the same amplitude within a span of 25 hours.

Mixed tides occur on the Californian coast near San Francisco, where two high waters and two low waters can be seen daily, although the water levels of the subsequent high or low waters can be rather different.

On the other hand, there are one-day tides and mixed, mostly one-day tides. In the Gulf of Tonkin (near Do-Son, Vietnam) the one-day tides bring high water only once a day. Mixed, mostly one-day tides, as can be seen off Manila, are characterized by one single high water per day after a high moon declination, and two high waters varying in character after passing the equator.

The influence of ground topography

But the appearance of tides is even more complex than all of this suggests. The interplay of forces between the planets is not always the critical factor for tides. In addition to tides caused by astronomical forces, oscillations due to ground topography, especially in areas where the sea is not so deep, can cause so-called shallow water tides.

In many places on Earth, meteorological tides are also important. They are caused by the strength and direction of the wind and the flow from the mainland, which fluctuates with the seasons and plays a considerable role in the observed water levels.

Finally, the tides are deflected by the Coriolis effect, and the backwards and forwards movement of the oceans are modified by a dissimilar distribution of land and sea, so the tidal rise can vary strongly from place to place. In ocean regions it is hardly more than three feet, at the coasts it is considerably higher; for example, at the German North Sea coast it is approximately 3 meters (9 ft.).

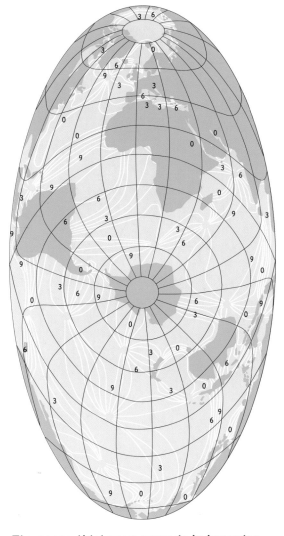

The ocean tidal wave spreads in irregular wavy lines, and there are strong variations in tidal rise.

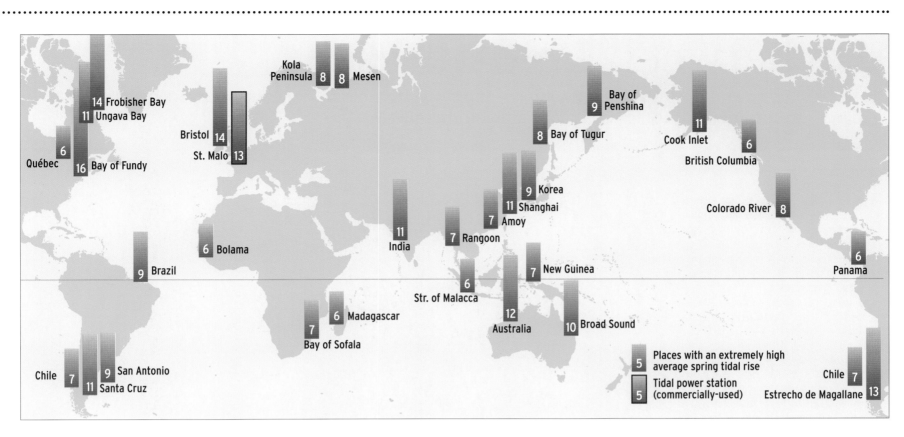

The map shows various tidal rise locations with the following values:

- 14 Frobisher Bay
- 11 Ungava Bay
- 6 Québec
- 16 Bay of Fundy
- Bristol 14
- St. Malo 13
- Kola Peninsula 8
- 8 Mesen
- 9 Bay of Penshina
- 8 Bay of Tugur
- 11 Cook Inlet
- 6 British Columbia
- 9 Korea
- 11 Shanghai
- 7 Amoy
- 8 Colorado River
- 6 Bolama
- 11 India
- 7 Rangoon
- 9 Brazil
- 7 New Guinea
- 6 Str. of Malacca
- 6 Panama
- 6 Madagascar
- 12 Australia
- 10 Broad Sound
- 7 Bay of Sofala
- Chile 7
- 9 San Antonio
- 11 Santa Cruz
- Chile 7
- Estrecho de Magallane 13

| 5 | Places with an extremely high average spring tidal rise |
| 5 | Tidal power station (commercially-used) |

Whereas the tidal rise on the Canadian coast is 16 meters (52 ft.), the tidal wave on the oceans is only about 1 meter (3 ft.) high. The difference in height increases in bays where access is narrow. The map shows medium tidal rise at prominent coastal locations.

The largest tidal power station in the world: In the French town of Saint-Malo, the delta of the Rance River was closed off by a tidal barrage. The powerful turbines – driven by the rising and falling water in and out of the bay – generate electricity.

The greatest tidal rise in the world – up to 16 meters (52 ft.) – takes place in the Bay of Fundy on Canada´s east coast.

In enclosed marginal seas, such as the Baltic and the Mediterranean, tides are often hardly noticeable as the wind, which could force the waters into narrow bays and fjords, is much more temperate.

It is not unusual for tides to continue for kilometers inland, as they do along the River Elbe, even 100 kilometers (62 mi.) upriver to the Port of Hamburg. In the case of spring tides, even very large waves, known as bores, can move up river from the delta as on the River Gironde and the River Seine. In the delta regions of the Amazon, such waves can reach a height of up to 8 meters (26 ft.) and a speed of 25 kilometers (15 mi.) an hour.

Coastal tides are of major importance for man and nature. Each year, storm floods are caused by the usual local water level being greatly increased by the force of the wind, thus endangering the lives of coastal inhabitants.

FACTS AND FIGURES

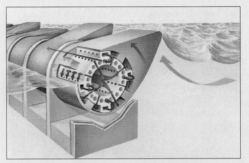

A model of a wave power station

Tidal power stations

The principle is very simple: A tidal barrage is built across a bay or a river delta. When the flow reaches its highest level, the locks are closed. The waters flow back on the ebb tide, driving the turbines. A tidal power station can only function efficiently on a coast with a tidal rise of more than 6 meters (20 ft.). There are more than 30 potential locations worldwide but, up to now, only few tidal power stations have been built. In Canada, the Annapolis Plant in the Bay of Fundy has been generating 20 megawatts since 1983, and a Russian pilot plant at the Barents Sea has been generating 2 megawatts since 1968. In China, nine plants have been built, of which the largest generate 5, 3, 2, and 1.3 megawatts. The only tidal power station built for commercial use is in the Rance delta near Saint-Malo on the French Atlantic coast. Twenty-four turbines, each with a maximum 10 megawatt capacity, are built into the dam, which is 750 meters (2,460 ft.) long and 32 meters (104 ft.) wide at the top. The station came into operation supplying the electricity network in 1967.

Life between land and sea

Mangrove forests and mud flats are among the most sensitive oceanic regions. They make heavy demands on the adaptability of both plant and animal life.

● ● ● Animals and plants living directly on the coast where they are under constant exposure to the seas have had to develop their own strong resistance to the inrush and back-draft of the waves. As if that was not enough, there is still the problem of heat and cold, rain and drought, from land weather when the flood tide has withdrawn.

The boundary zones between sea and land are particularly extensive where the coast is flat and the tides are strong. In the mud flats that extend from Denmark to the Netherlands, miles of mud and sand can dry up. The creatures living there are able to seek protection in the soft underground.

Rocky tidal zones, on the other hand, provide little shelter. Where the coast is rocky, only a few meters of the sea floor is exposed at ebb tide to reveal a great variety of living things huddled together according to a strict order. First there is a narrow belt of land vegetation, which is moistened now and then by spray water. Only very few land plants are found here, and then only those that are resistant to salt and are able to store water in their thickened leaves or stems. These halophytes – such as the sea fennel, a native plant of the limestone rocks of the Mediterranean – are accompanied by a variety of insects.

Challenging tides

Limestone remains pretty much uninhabited and is therefore particularly enhanced by the Sun – the reason why this belt is referred to as the "white zone." The neighboring "gray zone" is kept moist by recurrent spray. The darker coloring of this zone is caused by blue algae which bore their way one millimeter (0.04 in.) into the limestone; it is also home to the first of the marine

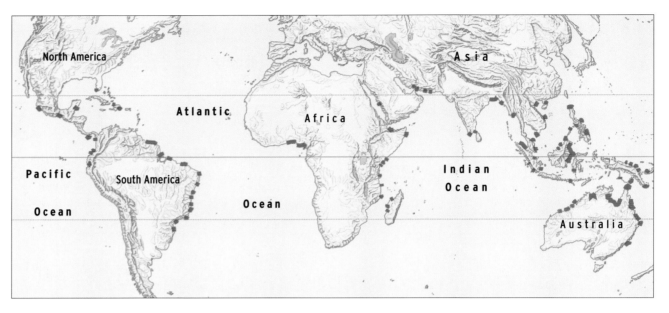

In tropical and subtropical coastal waters, mangrove forests are widespread (on the map, they are marked in green). They have adapted perfectly to the ebb and flow of the tides.

animals, such as the common winkle, which can sit out dry periods in the shade of cool crevices and graze later on the covering of algae when there is sufficient moisture.

In the "black zone," the borders of which are reached by lapping waves, the tangle of blue algae is particularly thick.

The true tidal zone – the eulittoral zone – extends between medium-high water and low water (see illustration below). The number of marine organisms increases dramatically in the lighter colored areas. Crowded colonies of white limpets sit huddled together on rocks and boulders. When the flow tide comes, they fervently try to catch food using their cirri – feathery retractable organs formed by a metamorphosis of some of their legs. The common mussel also finds

Plants and animals of the mud flats: the barnacle and the common mussel, winkles and limpets have their habitat here, as do the bladder wrack and sugar kelp

protection here among its equals. Red algae form thick crusts on the limestone at the medium water line where the algae felts are rasped off by trochoiea and placophora snails and limpets.

The flood pools of the tidal zones are home to many animals and plants that need to be permanently covered by water. Sea anemones look for food here and hermit crabs drag themselves and their snail house slowly along the pool bottom. The transparent rock shrimps are well camouflaged, and the apparently motionless gudgeons also remain unnoticeable. But the colorful marbled blebby is always ready to retreat in great haste.

Survival pools

When the tidal pools are cut off from the sea, life in the pools diminishes as the salt content and temperature increase mercilessly. Below the medium water line Arctic rock borer and sponges bore into the limestone, and the channels they leave behind are visited by black, spiky sea urchins.

A graduated change from land to marine life can be observed on any rocky coastline – only the variety of creatures and plants differs from place to place. Mud flats and sand flats also have distinct zones, as do salt marshes inhabited by grasses and herbs which have become tolerant to the salt. Even the mangrove swamps follow the pattern.

Mangrove forests develop on wind-protected

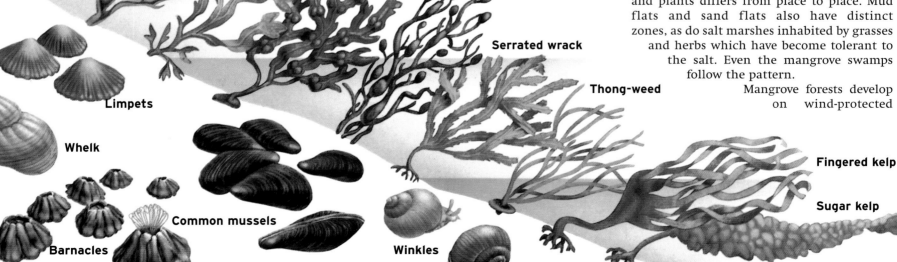

Channelled wrack
Spiralled wrack
Bladder wrack
Knotted wrack
Serrated wrack
Thong-weed
Limpets
Whelk
Fingered kelp
Sugar kelp
Common mussels
Barnacles
Winkles

In order to survive in the swampy regions of tidal zones, the mangrove tree has developed a special root form. Mangrove swamps serve as a nursery to many animals and are of major importance for coastal protection.

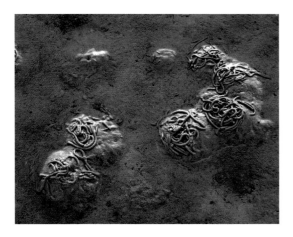

When the Waddensea in the North Sea dries out, traces of animal life become visible – like these sandy feaces piles of the lug worm.

coastal strips in the tropical and subtropical seas. In temperate and cold ocean regions they are replaced by salt meadows. At the Atlantic coasts, three to four dominating tree types form a loosely knit thicket, whereas in the Indo-Pacific, the coasts are fringed with woods more than 30 meters (98 ft.) high and comprising more than 40 species, the most important of which are the Rhizophora (the red mangrove), Sonneratia, and Avicennia (the black mangrove).

The mangrove trees themselves display a range of adaptations to their living conditions. Just a few centimeters down in the swampy ground, there is not only a lack of oxygen but copious amounts of toxic hydrogen sulfide. Instead of sinking its roots down deep into the ground, the tree produces adventitious roots to gain stability.

The lateral roots of Sonneratia produce new roots that come out of the ground almost vertically – like asparagus. They serve to absorb oxygen when the waters are low. The whole root system is kept together by deeper anchor roots.

Mangrove forests: the coast's stronghold

Marine animals that normally inhabit hard bedrock, such as sponges, coraloids, and ascidia, penetrate into the flooded forest areas. Barnacles and mussels, usually seen in rocky mud flats, sit on dried out tree trunks. Numerous types of birds nests, including those of the cormorant, heron, and ibis, sit in the treetops, neighbors to apes and raccoons. And the deep channels provide a dwelling for sea cows and crocodiles.

The mangroves stand in close exchange with neighboring habitats; for example, coral fish spawn in the prop roots, the baby fish remaining well-sheltered until they set out for the offshore reefs.

Humans, however, have caused much destruction in the mangrove forests by eroding vast areas to make room for aqua-cultural farming. Not only is a natural paradise disappearing but also a stronghold that helps to check coastal erosion.

FACTS AND FIGURES

The destruction of the mangrove forests

Although the forests are rich in mangrove species, the areas are still considered to be nothing more than a swampy desert. Worldwide these regions have been continually declining in size worldwide in the past few decades. If we look at the situation in individual countries, the picture is disturbing. For example, the coasts of Indonesia have lost more than half of their mangrove forests since the 1970s. Hotel parks were built for the tourists, Japanese and Indonesian companies received concessions to clear the forests for the paper industry, and last, but not least, the development of aqua-culture farming had a harmful effect on the mangroves.

The mighty roots of mangrove trees.

The long travels of an iceberg

More than 7,000 icebergs are formed each year in the north polar region alone. They are driven by currents into the North Atlantic and have been seen as far south as the Bermudas.

●●● "Cape Horn – Danger! Iceberg!" This was the warning transmitted to all ships between the Antarctic and the southern tip of South America by the National Ice Center in Suitland, Maryland, in July 1999. The US authorities had been following the icy giant since 1992 via a weather satellite. After it had broken off the Thwaites Glacier, it drifted about off the coast before breaking in two. The largest chunk moved in a great curve through the Amundsen Sea, then through the Bellingshausen Sea, past the tip of the Antarctic Peninsula up to 60° into the Antarctic Circumpolar Current.

Iceberg graveyard

Every year, several thousand icebergs, large and small, break off the Antarctic ice plate – although the plate itself shows no signs of being exhausted. The ice layer is up to 3 kilometers (2 mi.) thick and highland snow continually replenishes it with fresh ice. Due to the pressure of its own weight, it begins to thaw on the underside. The melted water acts like a lubricant on which the inland ice slides a few hundred meters every year towards the coast. Most of the ice rivers, which are up to 150 kilometers (90 mi.) wide, flow into the Weddell Sea and the Ross Sea, losing contact with the ground and then drifting as shelf ice on the sea.

Four percent of the South Polar Sea is covered with shelf ice up to 300 meters (1,000 ft.) thick – the edge of which lies in the Weddell Sea, more than 500 kilometers

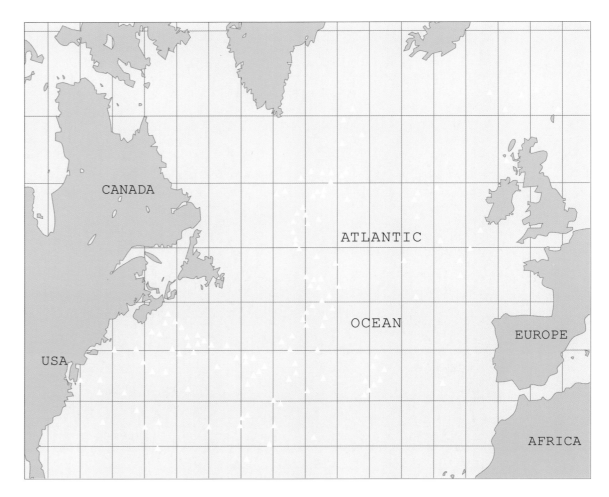

The North Atlantic is a fearsome place for sailors due to the hazards of drifting icebergs. This map shows the positions where ships warned of icebergs during the 20th century.

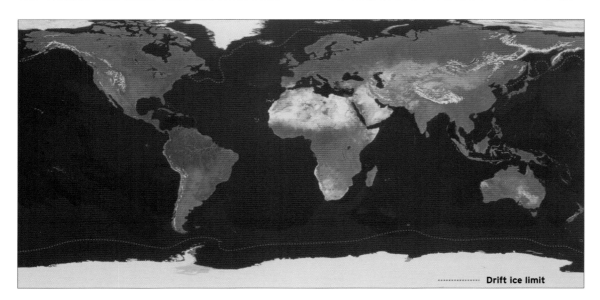

Drift ice limit

Gigantic icebergs break away from ice masses and glaciers in the north and south of the polar seas. The map shows where ships may expect to meet up with icebergs.

(300 mi.) off the coast. Due to the movement of the sea, cracks and crevices in the ice increase until a fresh piece breaks off. If the iceberg is big enough, it can cross the Circumpolar Current and drift up to 25° northwards.

During their journey, these ice giants drive long scratches into the ground, even at a depth of more than 450 meters (1,500 ft.). In iceberg graveyards – underwater elevations – the icebergs are stranded, often by the dozens.

It is estimated that the sea bed is ploughed over once every 35 years in this way (in comparison to the Continental Shelf at every 230 years). Approximately five percent of the seabed's surface is constantly "scarred" and it takes decades for the devastated habitat to recover.

In the polar regions, Disko Bay on the west coast of Greenland is held to be the main iceberg production area. Here, the six fastest glaciers in the world advance up to 30 meters

(100 ft.) per day through narrow valleys into the fjords. At their head, bizar-rely shaped blocks of ice break off, crashing noisily into the cold waters, often causing tidal waves. This so-called "calving" process produces about 5,000 icebergs per year.

At first, these icebergs drift through the Baffin Sea then via the Davis Straits into the Labrador Sea. From there, they drift with the Labrador Current, which transports up to 7,500 icebergs a year as far as the Newfoundland Bank. On average, 400 icebergs advance up to 48° north, and a southerly sighting has even been made near the Bermudas.

Fields of ice at the North Pole

Since the North Polar Sea has no contact with glacier regions, it is practically free of icebergs. However, icebergs do distribute themselves right around the Antarctic, including in the South Polar Sea where additional sea ice is formed in winter. This icy mush is jostled around into curved discs (called "ice paddies") by wind and waves. When this pancake ice is pressed, floes are formed and then pushed together to become an unbroken field of ice that is only compact near the coast.

Further out at sea, ice-free areas quickly increase until they make up to more than 20 percent of the overall area. In the Weddell Sea, the edge of the pack ice can lie up to more than 2,000 kilometers (1,200 mi.) off the coast;

The Biscoe Islands off the Antarctic Peninsula: Penguins watch as an iceberg drifts past. If it were possible to maneuver icebergs like this one through the seas, their volume of fresh water could be used to irrigate large areas of land.

otherwise it is usually only 300 kilometers (200 mi.) wide. In the summer, the sea ice melts down to an area of 3 million square kilometers (1.2 mill. sq. mi.) and the pack ice only survives the warm season in the western Weddell Sea.

Huge blocks of pack ice

The North Polar Sea lies at higher latitudes than the South Polar ring ocean and is enclosed by landmasses and wide shelf seas. In the summer, the sea ice withstands the wind-driven surface circulation without any trouble. The average duration in the Beaufort Vortex is five to eight years – compared to three to four years in the Transpolar Drift. The ice fields spread over the central North Polar Sea and are up to 6 meters (20 ft.) thick. At the edge of the pack ice, floes piled up to 20 meters (65 ft.) high pack ice ridges.

In winter, the sea ice covers an area of 16 million square kilometers (6.2 mill. sq. mi.), about 90 percent of the Arctic Ocean. Only in the summer, when the ice retreats from the marginal seas for two months, is the Northeast Passage from the Barents Sea to the Bering Straits navigable.

Instead of melting, the ice leaves the North Polar Sea via the Transpolar Drift. The current transports about 2,800 cubic kilometers (700 cu. mi.) of frozen water via the Fram Straits into the east Greenland Current – about

90 percent of the total volume of ice transported and 10 percent of the total amount of ice in the Arctic.

About 99 percent of global ice, or 90 percent of global fresh water, is bound up in the polar ice caps, which have always reacted sensitively to climatic changes in the Earth's history. In theory, if all the ice caps melted, the sea level would rise by almost 60 meters (200 ft.). The ice plates in Greenland and the East Antarctic are currently believed to be stable; in comparison, the margins of the ice rivers in the West Antarctic are slowly retreating. Scientists blame this on a belated reaction to the change over from the last Ice Age to the current warm period, which took place 10,000 years ago.

In the Antarctic Peninsula, however, there are signs of dramatic disintegration. Two centuries ago, the northern part of the Larsen Shelf Ice was approximately 90,000 square kilometers (35,000 sq. mi.). Today it is only 2,500 square kilometers (950 sq. mi.). In January 1995 alone, 4,200 square kilometers (1,600 sq. mi.) of shelf ice broke up. Shortly after an iceberg of 1,500 square kilometers (580 sq. mi.) and another one of 200 square kilometers (77 sq. mi.) separated from the southern portion of the shelf. Local warming seems to be responsible for this; since the 1940s, the average yearly temperature of the peninsula – which reaches far into the north – has risen by 2.5° C (4,5° F).

Earth plates and volcanic chains

The seas are tectonically the most active parts of the planet: On the Mid-Ocean Ridge, new crustal plates are constantly being formed, while in the deep-sea trenches, the sea bed is descending into the Earth's interior.

● ● ● In 1912, the German meteorologist and polar explorer Alfred Wegener published his hotly contested theory of continental displacement or drift. When Wegener lost his life in 1930 during an expedition to Greenland, this theory was not yet recognised. The idea that the continents were sliding around the world like icebergs in the water – put forward by an outsider, no less – was simply too daring for the experts: the geologists.

Proof in fossils

Since the 17th century scholars had pointed out the similarities between the coastlines of eastern South America and western Africa. In the meantime, numerous other indications of a common past had been found. Not only did Wegener determine that the contours were a perfect match, but even the age of the rocks and geological structures, mountain chains, traces of prehistoric icing, and fossilized remains of extinct animals and plants were the same on both sides of the South Atlantic.

According to Wegener's theory of continental displacement, 200 million years ago all of the Earth's landmasses formed one single large mass or super-continent. The mighty mass then broke up, and the parts drifted around over millions of years, until they reached their present positions. However, Wegener was unable to explain convincingly how all this had happened – at that time it was not possible to provide any evidence. All of Wegener's evidence came from the land. The proof to support his dynamic picture of the Earth could only be found in the deep sea, and this required technical means for exploring the ocean floor which were still decades away.

The discovery of the seafloor spreading, the production of new ocean bed in the Mid-Ocean Ridge, and its drift to both sides of the mountain chain was a decisive step towards the science of plate tectonics – a comprehensive theory as to how the Earth functions. According to this theory, the apparently solid outer shell of our planet is in reality a mosaic of plates which are continuously pushing against one another.

The plates, which vary in thickness from only a few kilometers to about 200 kilometers (120 mi.), consist of not only the Earth's crust but also the topmost layer of the Earth's mantle. Both form the

Where one plate slides under a neighboring plate and descends deep down into the Earth's interior, a deep-sea trench is formed. The subduction zone is mostly close to land.

lithosphere (meaning stone layer); below this is the upper part of the mantle, the soft, presumably molten layer called the asthenosphere (meaning weak layer).

Heavy plates

Whilst the plates are sliding on to the asthenosphere at an average speed of 1 to 17 centimeters (0.4 to 6 in.) per year, in the Mid-Ocean Ridge they are increasing in size through new layers of molten lava. This is how the Earth's crust has formed in the oceans. In the words of Hans-Ulrich Schminke, a volcanologist from Kiel, it is "a gigantic puzzle with hundreds and thousands of pieces of volcanic complexes all interlocked with one another as well as solidified magma chambers and influx channels."

Most of the volcanic outbreaks take place at the Mid-Ocean Ridge, mostly invisible to and seldom even noticed by scientists under the great water masses.

The plates at the Mid-Ocean Ridge are only a few miles thick. The cold ocean waters cool the rock whilst it slides sideways from the ridge, slowly and gradually into deeper regions. On cooling, it contracts and, at the same time, more solidified lava settles down on the plate. In the course of millions of years the plates have become

A fascinating natural phenomenon occurs when red-hot lava – here pictured in Hawaii – flows into the sea. However, there are many more volcanic outbreaks under the sea than there are above it.

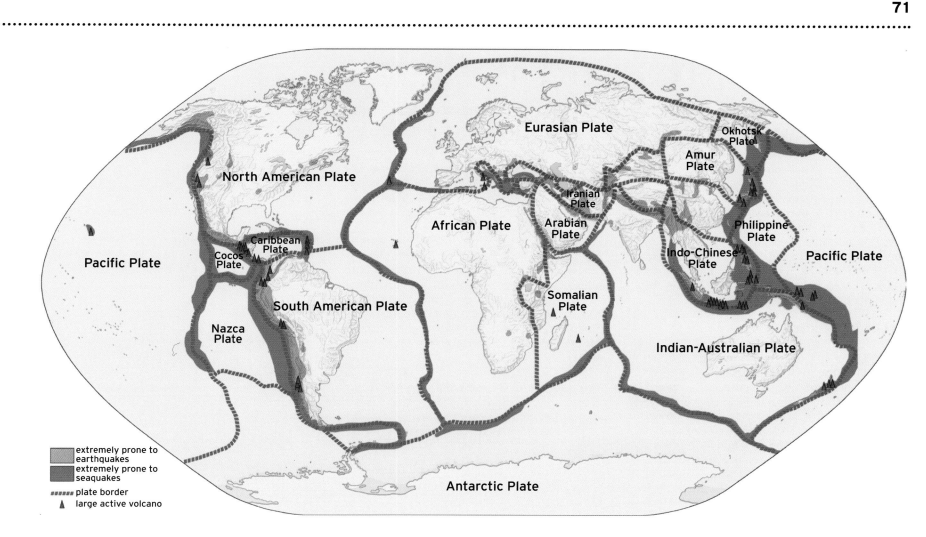

Eurasian Plate

Okhotsk Plate

North American Plate

Amur Plate

Iranian Plate

African Plate

Arabian Plate

Philippine Plate

Caribbean Plate

Cocos Plate

Indo-Chinese Plate

Pacific Plate

Pacific Plate

South American Plate

Somalian Plate

Nazca Plate

Indian-Australian Plate

extremely prone to earthquakes
extremely prone to seaquakes
••••• plate border
▲ large active volcano

Antarctic Plate

The outer crust of the Earth is made up of a mosaic of plates which are continually pushing against one other. New crust is constantly being formed under the sea in a system of mountain ranges that span the oceans over 60,000 kilometers (37,000 mi.). The plates return to the Earth's interior in the deep-sea trenches. The resulting melting process gives rise to chains of volcanoes which form along the deep-sea trenches.

Fossilized corals prove that we are on the former ocean bed.

thicker and heavier and have sunken deeper into the Earth's crust.

In this way, the sea bed slowly sinks from approximately 2.5 kilometers (1.5 mi.) in depth over the mountain ridge to 6 kilometers (3.7 mi.) in depth in the wide basins. At the end of this displacement, after 150 to 200 million years, the plate slides down at an incline over a neighboring plate. This so-called subduction leads to the formation of a deep-sea trench. New information has shown that at least a part of the plate sinks through the Earth's mantle to the edge of the Earth's iron core at a depth of 2,900 kilometers (1,800 mi.).

The genesis of volcanoes

Since the slide into the depths is not a smooth process, the subduction zones are areas known to be prone to earthquakes. Also, the most dangerous volcanoes on Earth are

connected to the sinking plates. At a depth of about 100 kilometers (60 mi.), magma forms and rises to the Earth's surface. Parallel to the deep-sea trench, about 200 to 300 kilometers (120 to 190 mi.) away, a chain of highly explosive volcanoes arise. This volcanic chain, which can stretch for thousands of kilometers, comes up either on land or in the sea as an island arc depending on whether the ocean floor disappears under a continent or under a neighboring plate on the sea floor.

If it is a continent, or if two continents collide with one another, mountains are formed. Such was the case with the Alps, which formed the crushed section between the African and the Eurasian plates. Continents are made of a lighter rock than the volcanic substratum of the sea and so they do not sink but play piggyback with the plates. While the deep seas are constantly renewed, the continents have lasted for billions of years, albeit in an ever-changing form.

A new ocean is born when basaltic lava rises from the Earth's mantle in a trench on the mainland and an oceanic crust forms between two landmasses drifting apart. This is what is currently happening in the Red Sea and the Gulf of California.

Presently, seven very large and dozens of smaller plates, are drifting around the world. Over 200 million years ago, all the continents were one single landmass, as Alfred Wegener claimed. Cores taken from the deep sea have shown how the supercontinent (Pangaea) broke apart and how the parts drifted to their present-day positions, thus giving the oceans their appearance that is so familiar to us today.

FACTS AND FIGURES

Summit trenches in the Atlantic Ridge.

The formation of plates in the Mid-Ocean Ridge

The Mid-Ocean Ridge, a part of which is shown on this map, separates the African and the American Plates. The gaps left by the separation process are continually filled with rising magma. This happens in the deep clefts in the ridge region, the peak trench (shown in blue). It stretches the length of the mountains, i. e. from north to south, but is repeatedly displaced to the side by faults, as is the whole mountain chain.

Sea freight

While container traffic has made distribution channels quicker, the movement of goods is becoming concentrated on major port terminals.

The Danish vessel "Svendborg Maersk" is currently the largest in the world for containerized freight.

●●● The former US Secretary of State, John M. Hay, must have been a prophet. He is reputed to have said at the beginning of the 20th century: "The Mediterranean was the sea of the past, the Atlantic is the sea of the present, and the Pacific will be the sea of the future."

Hardly 100 years on, it is clear just how right he was. Six of the 10 largest container terminals are Pacific. Sixteen of 25 ports through which more than 50 million tons of freight are moved per year are situated around the Pacific and the Indian Ocean. Almost a quarter of the world's trade is dealt with in the Pacific-Asian area. As well, 40 years ago goods worth only $8.8 billion US were exchanged via the Pacific. Today, the figure is more than $500 billion. The value of goods on the Atlantic rose in the same period from $23.7 billion to $385 billion.

Japan: the world's largest exporting country

The Pacific-Asian area began to boom after the Second World War, and the Japanese soon became the largest exporting nation in the world. Vehicles, cameras, and electronics were all produced in the Land of the Rising Sun. The sales markets for the goods in demand in Europe, the USA, and the rest of the world could only be reached by sea from the island archipelago.

It was in the middle of the 1980s, when the economies of the so-called "tiger states" began to copy the boom of the Japanese, that an increased need for free freight capacities on the high seas developed.

Most of the ships travel over the North Pacific between China, Japan, and the USA, or they head for the Panama Canal in Central America. The growing importance of the ports of Hong Kong and Shanghai

has meant that the South China Sea is increasingly becoming a turntable for shipping and is today one of the busiest waters in the world, besides the North Sea.

Safe European seas

Still, even today, the region is popular amongst pirates. The rugged coasts of the Philippines, Indonesia and the surrounding islands provide numerous opportunities for pirates to beat a retreat after seizing a ship.

Not even the major shipping lanes are safe from these heavily armed gangsters. The slow and cumbersome freighters are often no match for pirates in their small, maneuverable speedboats.

In comparison, the Mediterranean, the North Sea, and the Baltic Sea are much safer. Due to their geographical position around the most important countries of Europe, all three are of great significance for world trade and can boast four of the world's largest ports.

Trade on the North Sea and the Baltic was already brisk at the time of the Hanseatic League. In ancient times, the Greeks, the Egyptians, and the Romans used the Mediterranean for trading and as a theatre of war.

The main oceanic shipping routes: After the Second World War, the exchange of goods among the continents grew dramatically. Japan and Southeast Asia became the new centers of goods movement.

very heavily frequented shipping routes
heavily frequented routes
moderately used routes

Source: World Atlas and Environment

A view of the second largest container terminal in the world: Goods from China are shipped to all parts of the world through Hong Kong.

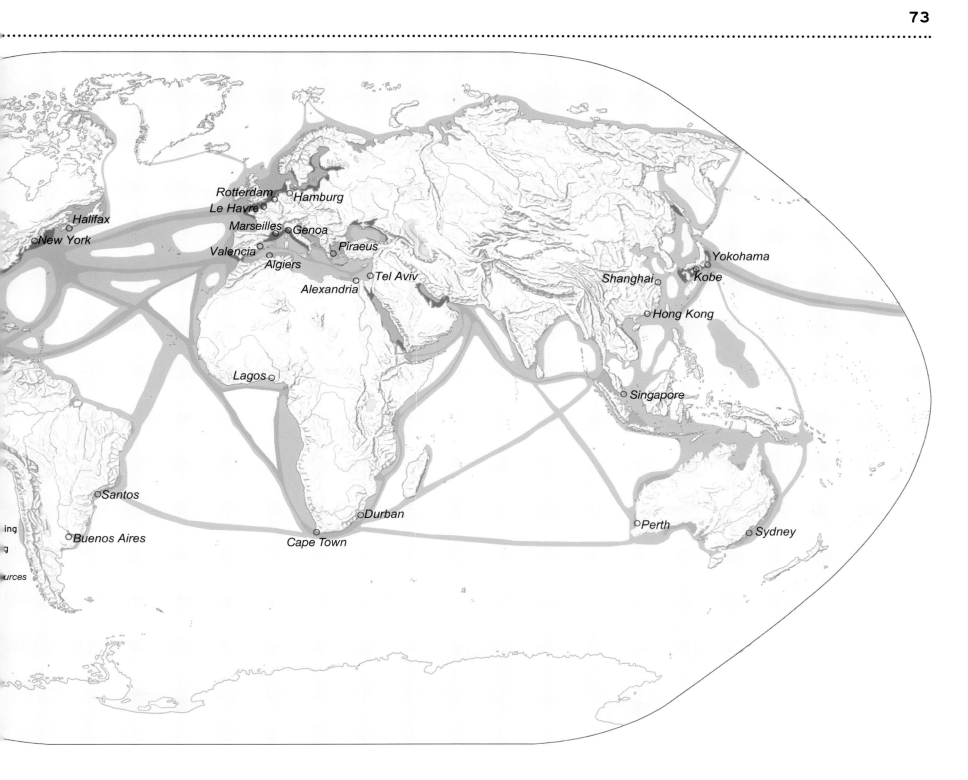

Today, ships from all over the world come into port at Valencia or Marseilles. In addition to the regional shipping lanes, the sea route from the North American east coast through the Suez Canal to Southeast Asia also runs through the Mediterranean.

The canal from Port Said to Suez saves most trading vessels the long and hazardous sea route around the tip of South Africa, shortening the voyage by well over 5,000 sea miles. However, many supertankers with freight from the Persian Gulf, or container ships destined for South America or the North American east coast, can no longer take the route through the narrow Red Sea and the even narrower Suez Canal, but have to use the ancient trading routes of the East Indies seamen once again.

Raw materials for the North's industry

The decisive factor for the shipping routes connecting continents is the distribution of transported goods. As a rule, raw materials are brought to the north. Over distances of up to 11,000 sea miles to Europe

and Japan come bauxite from Australia, oil from Kuwait, and iron ore from South America – everything needed to make cars, electrical appliances, and machines in Stuttgart, Detroit, Paris, or Tokyo. These products are later transported in huge container ships or Roll-on, Roll-off ships back to Australia, Kuwait, or South America.

Passenger ships, however, have declined in importance. Short ferry crossings fulfill regional and tourist functions, but the plane has replaced the ship for long-distance traveling.

This is particularly true in the North Atlantic. Up until the 1960s, proud ocean liners were still taking the traditional and much-frequented routes from Europe to America and back. Again and again, the captains of these ocean giants tried to set new records for the North Atlantic passage in order to win the so-called Blue Ribbon for their shipping company.

This award was given to the ship which completed the trip from New York to the British Scilly Isles in the shortest time. Today, the luxury liner *Queen Elizabeth II* is the only one left that regularly makes the voyage.

FACTS AND FIGURES

Modern pirates
Even today piracy is still a threat to shipping on some of the seas. Armed pirates in their speedboats hunt down freighters on the South China Sea, the Malacca Straits, and off the coasts of Brazil and Nigeria. Even supertankers are seized with utmost brutality. Smaller boats are kidnapped and occasionally the crew is murdered. Every year there are about 230 incidents involving the deaths of about 50 seamen.

A particular game of today's pirates is official despotism: ships at anchor waiting for their freight to be discharged are laid in chains under some flimsy excuse and are not released until a "fee" has been paid.

Straits – the eye of the needle

Growing trade among the continents is leading to increasingly denser traffic in the straits off the world's major ports.

●●● "I believe Captain Nemo would turn around now in order not to have to pass into the narrow passage of the Red Sea ... the only way out of this narrow passage for the Nautilus was the Straits of Bab al-Mandab," wrote Jules Verne in 1870 in his famous novel *20,000 Leagues under the Sea.*

Bab al-Mandab – the Wailing Gate – is the only natural sea route to the Red Sea. It takes its name from the days of slave trading, when thousands of Africans were shipped from here as cheap labor from Djibouti to Arabia. The 30 kilometers-wide (19 mi.) sea route was then insignificant for world trade.

Strategic importance of Bab al-Mandab

Things changed with the opening of the Suez Canal in 1869. Today, 14 percent of world trade passes through the Canal between the Red Sea and the Mediterranean. Most of the almost 17,000 vessels which take this route through the desert each year take course for Bab al-Mandab.

The strategic location of Bab al-Mandab makes it important for the transport of oil.

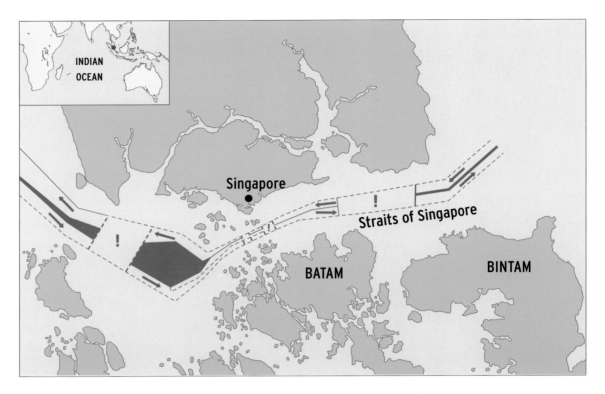

The Malacca Straits are part of the sea route from Europe to Southeast Asia and Japan. The port of Singapore can only be reached through this narrow passage.

The sea route in the Mediterranean passes through the Straits of Gibraltar. The volume of traffic is so great that the ships occasionally have to pass through in close range of one another.

Every day, almost 3.5 million barrels of "black gold" are shipped through the straits to the USA and Europe, mainly from the Arabian oil-exporting countries.

The Wailing Gate is just one of almost 200 maritime bottlenecks worldwide. Many of them lie on international routes, providing welcome short cuts; they are therefore important and, because of their strategic positions, sometimes dangerous passages for shipping. This is particularly true

of the Straits of Gibraltar – only 14 kilometers (9 mi.) wide and the only sea route to the Mediterranean.

The Straits of Gibraltar, separating the continents of Europe and Africa, were formed in the same way as Bab al-Mandab – through the Continental Drift. They take their name from a distinctive rock at the southern tip of the Iberian Peninsula. Since 1704, the strategically important enclave has been a British crown colony and, still today,

the presence of the British on the peninsula (which is only 5.8 square kilometers [2.24 sq. mi.] in area) is a thorn in the side of the Spanish – with the Spanish government demanding the return of Gibraltar in a diplomatic dispute.

The Straits of Gibraltar compete with the Straits of Malacca in Southeast Asia for the title of most frequented shipping route in the world. Currently, the Straits of Malacca are leading with, on average, 600 large tankers and freight ships passing through each day. Some days there are up to 2,000 ships going through the 400 kilometers (250 mi.) of water between Malaysia and Sumatra, which at the narrowest point is only 27 kilometers (17 mi.) wide. It has a depth of at least 25 meters (82 ft.) and thus provides enough water under the keel of even supertankers.

However, navigation is hampered by drifting sandbanks, so the Indonesian and Malaysian governments require tanker captains to make the voyage further south through the Straits of Lombok – something the captains do unwillingly as it means an extra 1,500 kilometers (930 mi.) from the oil fields at the Persian Gulf to Japan or China.

The price of war

According to calculations made by the military, 15 percent of the world's trade passes through the Straits of Malacca and other major bottlenecks in the South China Sea. The United States looks on in concern at the rattling of swords between China and Vietnam over the Spratly Islands, which lie right in the middle of the most important shipping lanes in the world.

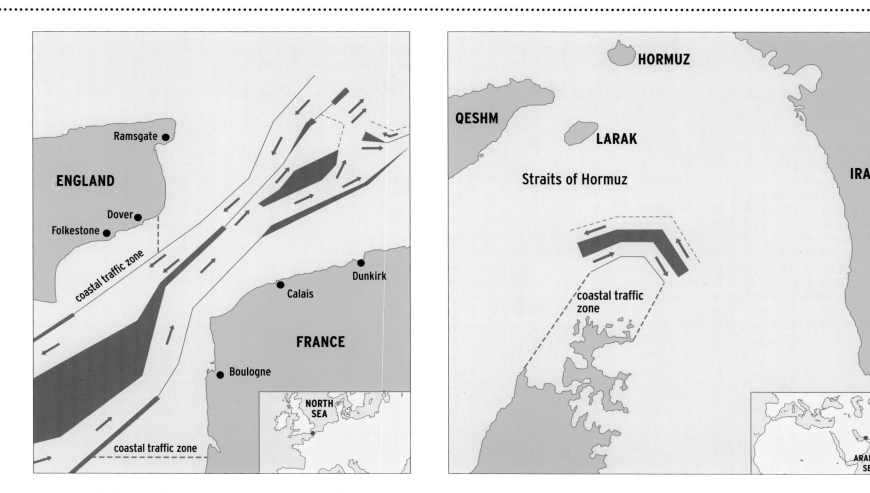

The English Channel links the North Sea and the Atlantic Ocean. Although shipping routes are fixed, ferries crossing from France to England are a constant source of danger.

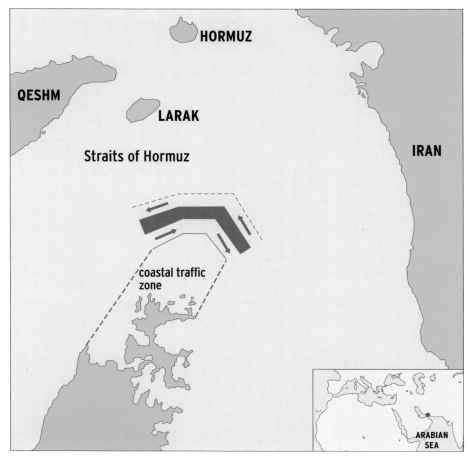

The transport routes for crude oil go from the Persian Gulf through the Straits of Hormuz into the Arabian Sea. The Straits of Hormuz can be used even by supertankers.

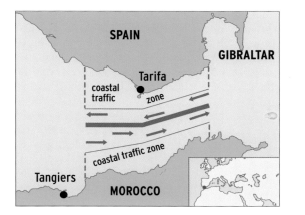

The Straits of Gibraltar link the Mediterranean Sea to the Atlantic Ocean. The main route between the Arabian oil ports and Europe is through these straits.

Should war break out over these islands it would mean a blockade of the Straits of Malacca. Freight charges would explode 500 percent, and the demand for transport capacities in Southeast Asia would increase. Ships from other parts of the world would be forced to go through the Indian Ocean, and the effects on world economy would be catastrophic.

The United States also keeps a particularly watchful eye on the Straits of Hormuz, which are the gateway to the Persian Gulf and lie in one of the most unsettled regions of the world. Because of the oil exports from Kuwait, Saudi Arabia, and other Arab states, the Straits play an important role in the world economy.

Supertankers leave the Persian Gulf daily through the Straits of Hormuz laden with a total of 15 million barrels of crude oil – approximately a fifth of the worldwide

requirements. Should these Straits ever be blocked in a military conflict, there would be an oil shortage throughout the entire world.

The most important bottleneck in Europe is the English Channel between France and England. Currently, at any given time, up to 300 large vessels are traveling daily through this passage from the Atlantic Ocean to the North Sea. In spite of modern maritime control technology, radar, and satellites, the Channel requires the utmost concentration. Ferries crossing between England and the Continent, frequent fog, drifting sandbanks, and high seas increase the risk of collisions.

A route under the sea

However, since the middle of the 1990s it has been possible to reach the British Isles "by land" – through the Channel Tunnel in an express train about 100 meters (330 ft.) under the surface of the sea. The modern high-speed trains only need three hours for the trip from London to Paris.

Because straits are strategically so important, the Great Powers began to negotiate contracts bound by international law regarding their use. The British and the Turks took the first step when, in 1809 Britain, the sea power of the time concluded the Dardanelles Agreement with the Osmanic Kingdom. This forbade all non-Turkish war ships from passing through the Dardanelles and the Bosporus to the Black Sea.

In the Treaty of Montreux, the Great Powers agreed with Turkey on a transit regulation for all nations. In 1982, similar contracts were concluded for all the important trading routes.

FACTS AND FIGURES

Electronics at sea

Today, even in the most congested straits, e.g., in the English Channel, modern vessels navigate in complete safety – that is, as long as the electronics on the bridge function correctly. The ship's position is determined nowadays by means of the Global Positioning System, or GPS, a satellite-supported navigational system. Every few seconds, the GPS calculates the exact position of the vessel down to just a few meters. In coastal waters, echo-sounding provides information on the water depth and, in critical positions, gives off a loud warning signal. High-resolution radar instruments penetrate even the thickest fogs, probing the coastline and surrounding ships – an important support for navigators, helping them to be aware of a collision course in good time and allowing them to pass in narrow shipping lanes, even in the very worst weather.

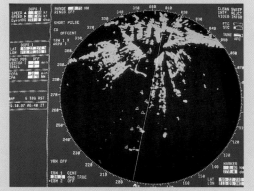

Radar and echo-sounding provide safety.

The lifelines of sea trade

The Panama, Suez, and Kiel canals – effective shortcuts for sea traffic.

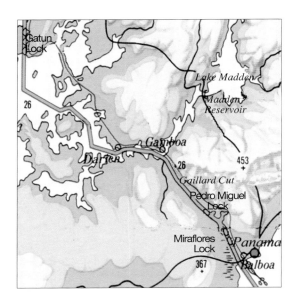

One trip through the Panama Canal can cost up to $150,000 US.

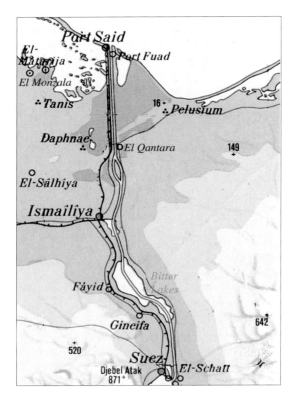

The Suez Canal shortens the sea route to Asia by 23 percent.

The Kiel Canal is the most heavily-used artificial waterways in the world.

●●● At the beginning of the 20th century, Punta Arenas at the southern tip of Chile was a thriving trading city. For ships from Europe destined for the ports on the west coast of the Americas, Punta Arenas (translated as the "sandy point") on the stormy Magellan Straits was always a strategic port of call, coaling station, and supply station rolled into one. But then, in 1914, the unavoidable demise of the Chilean city began.

The Panama Canal: a lucrative passageway

The cause was to be found about 8,500 kilometers (5,280 mi.) to the north. On 15 August of that year, the SS Anacona became the first vessel to pass through the Panama Canal, thereby opening up probably the most significant shortcut in the history of seafaring.

For its time, the construction of the Panama Canal was a magnificent feat of engineering. Even the Spaniards had planned to cut a channel through the isthmus a few years after Christopher Columbus discovered it in 1502. The French, too, made an attempt, but it was the USA which achieved the real breakthrough – in the truest sense of the word. Within just 10 years, hundreds of thousands of workers, mostly Chinese, dug the way from the town of Panama on the west coast to Colón on the east coast.

Since the opening of the 81-kilometer-long (50-mi.) canal, more than 800,000 vessels have passed through the narrowest point between the two Americas. By using the Panama Canal, modern ships save 18,000 kilometers (11,000 mi.) in distance and three weeks in time, so shipping companies do not think twice about paying up to $150,000 US in fees – per vessel, per trip. Today, more than 10 freighters a day take the shortcut. Per year all ship movements together amount to about 13,000, making the Panama Canal the most important economic factor for the small Central American country – especially since 1 January 2000, when the USA transferred the right to control the waterway to the Panamanians.

The Suez Canal: a shortened route to Asia

Ships coming from Europe and destined for Asia are also saved a detour, like the one in South America, by using the Suez Canal. They no longer need to take the route along the west coast of Africa around the tip of the continent past the Cape of Good Hope. Since 17 November 1869, the 195-kilometer-long (120-mi.) waterway between the Mediterranean Sea and the Red Sea has provided a 23 per cent shortcut in the shipping route from Rotterdam to Tokyo. Fourteen per cent of world trade passes along the almost 200-meter-wide (660-ft.) sea passage through the Egyptian desert. In contrast to the Panama Canal, even the largest ships of up to 500 meters (1,640 ft.) in length and 70 meters (230 ft.) in width pass the lock-free, 20-meter-deep (66-ft.) Suez.

It was the Pharaohs who created the first link by waterway between the two seas in the 6th century BC. However, the narrow channel filled with silt again and again until, by the 8th century AD, it fell completely out of use. It was not until the beginning of the 18th century that the idea of building a canal won the imaginations of new supporters. Napoleon Bonaparte investigated the feasibility of building a canal, but his engineers made erroneous calculations and advised him against the undertaking.

Finally, in 1854, the French engineer, Ferdinand de Lesseps, received the concession to build and operate a waterway. Construction began in 1859 and 1.5 million workers – forced labor – dug their way through the desert sand. During the 10 years until the opening of the Suez Canal, 125,000 of these laborers lost their lives and the budgeted building costs more than tripled. However, the opening ceremony of the Suez Canal was a giant show attended by 5,000 international guests. Guiseppe Verdi composed an opera especially for the occasion – "Aida" – which was performed for the first time two years after the opening of the Suez Canal in extravagant settings in Cairo.

The great powers of the day quickly recognized the strategic significance of the

The Panama Canal cuts off 18,000 km (11,000 mi.) from the route around South America.

The Suez Canal is 20 meters (66 ft.) deep and almost 200 meters (660 ft.) wide. It runs through 195 kilometers (120 mi.) of desert.

The Kiel Canal shortens the route between the two north European seas. It is a loss-making enterprise, however, as the time saved is almost negligible and, thus, no high charges can be made for the passage.

Suez Canal. Great Britain occupied the Canal Zone in 1882 until the Convention of Constantinople, which in 1888 declared the Suez open to ships of all nations in time of peace and war.

Shares in the operating company were divided. In 1956, the Egyptian President Gamal Abd el-Nasser claimed the Suez Canal for his country and nationalized the company. Israeli troops then advanced to Sinai, and the British and the French attacked Egypt.

The four-month conflict, which is remembered in the history books as the Suez Crisis, ended only upon diplomatic pressure from the USA and the Soviet Union. In the end, the Egyptians succeeded in their intentions, but guaranteed free passage through the Suez Canal. Today, the Suez is a major source of foreign currency for the North African country, in addition to tourism. The sea passage through the desert is used by 20,000 vessels a year, bringing in $2 billion US.

The Kiel Canal: shortcut to the Baltic

The Kiel Canal is more a subsidized enterprise than a source of income. The 95-kilometer-long (59-mi.) link between the North Sea and the Baltic Sea attracts 50,000 vessels a year, making it the most heavily-used artificial waterway in the world. But, unlike the Panama and Suez canals, the shortcut does not save enough time to justify any high charges.

Modern vessels save at most a day and half – not weeks – when they choose to travel from the North Sea to the Baltic via the Kiel Canal rather than rounding the Danish Peninsula. Ships using the Kiel are therefore not charged more than $4,000 US for the passage.

The waterway through Schleswig-Holstein was built more for military reasons than for economic ones. In the 19th century, Kaiser Wilhelm I wanted to transfer his fleet from the Baltic to the North Sea as quickly and as inconspicuously as possible. In 1887, the foundation stone for the Kaiser Wilhelm Canal was laid in Kiel. In 1895, 8,900 workers had a channel 67 meters (220 ft.) wide and 9 meters (29 ft.) deep as far as Brunsbüttel. It was widened to about 170 meters (560 ft.) in the following years and in 1948 was renamed the Kiel Canal.

Although more vessels pass through the Kiel Canal than the number through the Panama and the Suez put together, the proportion of freight in the latter two is 10 times higher.

In the meantime, the Panama Canal and the Kiel Canal have become too small for the really big container ships, the so-called post-Panamax and ultra post-Panamax class. And the limits of the Panama Canal's capacity are no more than 15,000 traffic movements per year. This could mean renewed opportunities for Punta Arenas which, in the meantime, has become the new center for the Chilean gas and oil industry.

The North Sea – Europe's turntable

The richest countries in the world are supplied with raw materials and industrial goods via the traffic lanes of the North Sea.

● ● ● The bows of the *Svendborg Maersk*, the largest container ship in the world, plough through the stormy Bay of Biscay at 22 knots bearing 30°. She is carrying 6,600 steel containers on board that are filled with electronic and consumer goods from Asia. The *Svendborg Maersk* is destined for Hamburg, the second largest container port in Europe, where freight can be discharged, i. e., unloaded, within 24 hours. However, before the floating giant reaches the Hanseatic city via the German Bight and the River Elbe, she must go through the English Channel – and that means pretty close quarters even for a high-tech freighter.

With more than 300 traffic movements per day, the 30-kilometer-wide (19-mi.) English Channel is one of the most heavily used waterways in the world. In addition to dense traffic, the weather is often inclement and the passage through the Channel demands the utmost concentration, even from the most experienced captain. And then, once the ship has passed safely through, the captain still does not dare to relax his or her concentration, as the English Channel is the gateway to the North Sea, where there is also some of the densest water traffic in the world.

The shallow continental shelf sea between Great Britain and the European continent is only 580,000 square kilometers (225,000 squ. mi.) in area and, on average, 70 meters (230 ft.) deep. The North Sea is bordered in the south by the English Channel and the Dutch and German coasts, in the east by Denmark, and in the north by a line from the Orkney Islands, past the Shetlands, up to Stadland in Norway.

Although the North Sea is not very large, it has always had great significance for trade. Today, it is a marine and transport link between the most important economic countries in the world. About 240 million people live in the bordering countries – all of them highly developed and industrialized.

A variety of vehicles grace the waterway

The great North Sea ports are therefore among the most important trading places worldwide. In Rotterdam, Antwerp, and Hamburg more than 510 million tons of goods are handled each year. Rotterdam benefits most from its position near the North Sea and its excellent connections to the inland waterways. With the movement of about 320 million tons of goods, the Dutch metropolis can claim to be the largest port in the world. Antwerp and Hamburg follow in the eighth and twentieth positions, respectively.

Be that as it may, the North Sea is not only important for freight traffic. It is also used by more than 35 ferry companies traveling, some of them daily, between the European continent and Great Britain, the Shetland Isles, Iceland and the Faeroes in the Atlantic. Modern ferries can handle up to 1,000 passengers, and there is also room for hundreds of cars and dozens of trucks in the

A bird's-eye view of the Europoort in Rotterdam: the Europoort is the largest port in the world, handling 320 million tons of goods.

loading decks. Traffic is densest on the English Channel – even after the Channel Tunnel was completed, a ferry sails at peak times every 45 minutes between Dover in England and Calais in France.

In addition to the ferries and freight ships, yachts and private motor boats make up more than 260,000 vessel movements per year in the Dutch part of the North Sea alone. Heavily frequented routes, such as the Le Havre–Antwerp–Hamburg range through the German Bight, have been split up into separate traffic zones. Ships going out to sea may not leave their allotted area, just as ships coming in may not leave theirs. The highest level of safety possible is provided by state-of-the-art traffic control technology and, in critical sections, a pilot will come on board.

Until late in the 20th century, the coastal inhabitants lived from fishing. To fish from sailing boats such as the Finkenwerder Ewer – a flat-bottomed, one- or two-mast craft which was in use until the middle of the 19th century – was a hard and dangerous job. Even on sea-

The fishing industry loses importance as catches decline.

worthy drifters equipped with powerful engines, fishing in the North Sea was certainly no picnic.

Today, modern factory ships fish the seas, heaving the catch of herring, mackerel, summer flounder, and pollock on board, where it is immediately processed. Although numerous small cutters still set out to fish, over-fishing, pollution, and prescribed catch quotas mean that it is hardly economical any more for the fisheries. German catches fell between 1984 and 1998 by about 50,000 tons to 90,000 tons of fish. Former fishermen have been forced to find new sources of income, such as those derived from tourism. After all, millions of people visit the dunes and the mudflat areas (unique in the world) for recreation and, today tourism provides more jobs than the fishing industry.

Underwater bounty

In the meantime, the resources under the North Sea – crude oil and natural gas – have become a much more significant economic factor. Norway is a clear example of a country which has changed its roles with the times – in the past 30 years, it has developed from a fishing nation to the second largest exporter of oil in the world.

This Scandinavian country owes its leading position to the deposits of crude oil lying under the shelf of the Norwegian North Sea. In 1970, production began in the Ekofisk Field, 440 kilometers (273 mi.) northwest of the German coast. The gigantic rigs, which can even stand up to hurricanes, pump more than 450,000 barrels of "black gold" everyday from deposits at depths of up to 5,600 meters (18,372 ft.). Although more than half of Europe's oil

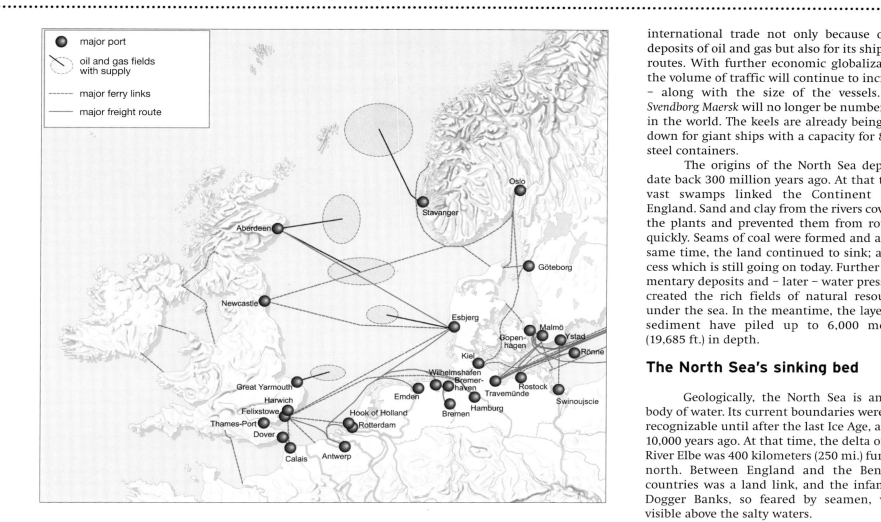

- ● major port
- ⬭ oil and gas fields with supply
- ----- major ferry links
- —— major freight route

Most of the traffic on the North Sea is destined for Rotterdam, Antwerp, or Hamburg. The lanes are crossed by ferries and freight ships going to England.

Deposits of crude oil and natural gas under the North Sea have made the marginal sea a gigantic industrial area. Norway, England, and Holland have the largest raw material resources.

resources lie off the Norwegian coast, the English also have richly productive fields.

The gas resources of the Norwegians are likewise very high-yielding. Approximately 3,400 billion cubic meters (119,000 bil. cu. ft.) are thought to be under the continental shelf – about three per cent of the world's resources. A system of underwater pipelines links the rigs in the middle of the North Sea to Germany, Belgium, and the Netherlands. So far, 13 billion cubic meters (455 bil. cu. ft.) of gas has been

supplied to Germany; from 2005 the sales volume is to increase to about 35 billion cubic meters (1,225 bil. cu. ft.). Around 1 billion cubic meters (35 bil. cu. ft.) from the Danish section of the North Sea and 24 billion cubic meter (840 bil. cu. ft.) from the Netherlands are piped to the Federal Republic of Germany.

Altogether, the crude gas deposits in the three countries are estimated at 5,520 billion cubic meters (193,200 bil. cu. ft.). The North Sea is thus gaining in importance in

international trade not only because of its deposits of oil and gas but also for its shipping routes. With further economic globalization, the volume of traffic will continue to increase – along with the size of the vessels. The *Svendborg Maersk* will no longer be number one in the world. The keels are already being laid down for giant ships with a capacity for 8,000 steel containers.

The origins of the North Sea deposits date back 300 million years ago. At that time, vast swamps linked the Continent with England. Sand and clay from the rivers covered the plants and prevented them from rotting quickly. Seams of coal were formed and at the same time, the land continued to sink; a process which is still going on today. Further sedimentary deposits and – later – water pressure, created the rich fields of natural resources under the sea. In the meantime, the layers of sediment have piled up to 6,000 meters (19,685 ft.) in depth.

The North Sea's sinking bed

Geologically, the North Sea is an old body of water. Its current boundaries were not recognizable until after the last Ice Age, about 10,000 years ago. At that time, the delta of the River Elbe was 400 kilometers (250 mi.) further north. Between England and the Benelux countries was a land link, and the infamous Dogger Banks, so feared by seamen, were visible above the salty waters.

Scientists speculate that in the geological near future, the Netherlands, Belgium, and parts of North Germany could all sink beneath the waves, as the bed of the North Sea is still sinking. The danger for the coasts has increased since the end of the 20th century due to the greenhouse effect.

FACTS AND FIGURES

Volume North Seaports 1998
(Grossweight metric tons transshipped)

Rotterdam	314,8
Antwerp	119,8
Hamburg	75,8
Le Havre	66,4
London	56,4
Bremen	34,4

Largest ports and their volume of goods.

Goods for Europe

Rotterdam is not only Europe's largest port, but is also the largest maritime terminal in the world. In addition, Rotterdam is the crude oil center on the Continent: 70 million tons of crude oil, chemicals, and crude oil products are moved yearly; 5 6 million containers are loaded and discharged.

Antwerp is the second largest port in Europe – based on the overall quantities moved. In the movement of containers, Hamburg is the second largest container terminal on the Continent. On the English coast are two ports whose significance to international shipping is expected to increase: Felixstowe and Thames Port at the mouth of the Thames.

A little sea with a great future

Tourism and growing trade among the bordering countries are bringing increased sea trade – a boom for the Baltic.

● ● ● Skagerrak, Kattegat, Belt, and the Sound – any weather forecast for the Baltic will most certainly begin with these shipping areas. The Skagerrak – the gateway to the North Sea – is known to seamen as a stormy area, and is the only way for large ocean-going vessels to travel from the North Sea to the Baltic as they cannot use the Kiel Canal. Traffic coming from the north through the Kattegat reach the west Baltic by means of the Belt and the Sound.

The Belts: gates into the Baltic

The "Lille Belt," or Little Belt, separates the east mainland coast of Denmark from the island of Fyn. In the north, vessels get into the shipping lanes at Frederica which brings them past numerous islands after about 70 kilometers (44 mi.) between the islands of Alsen and Aerø into the actual Baltic.

For floating giants the Little Belt is too narrow, and they choose to travel into the Baltic via the "Store Belt" – the Great Belt which separates the islands of Fyn and Langeland to the west from the island of Sjælland – the largest of the Danish islands – and Lolland. Since 1998, an impressive bridge has spanned the Great Belt between Nyborg and Korsør; it has a clearance height of 58 meters (190 ft.) and is thus navigable for even large, ocean-going vessels.

Thus the Great Belt remains an important lifeline for shipping in the Baltic. Denmark has to import about 70 per cent of all the raw materials processed in the country, most of them by sea. Even large oil tankers can pass through these waters, as an important center for Danish oil supply is on the tiny island of Omø at the edge of the Great Belt. Sea trade to and from the other Baltic countries also sets a course for the narrow strait, as do the ferry services from Kiel to Göteborg and Oslo.

The third waterway between the Kattegat and the Baltic is the Öresund Sound, a narrow passage between Sweden and the Danish main island of Sjælland. At the northern entrance to the Sound are Helsingør on the Danish side (with Hamlet's famous castle Kalundborg), and Helsingborg on the opposite, Swedish, side. The southern entrance to the Sound is guarded by the capital of Denmark, Copenhagen, and Malmö, the second largest city in Sweden. Malmö is an important port for the raw materials which have to be imported in order to manufacture industrial goods such as automobiles marked "Made in Sweden".

The Sound is very heavily frequented; the shipping lanes are narrow and are crossed

The Öresund link between Denmark and Sweden: The new bridge over the Sound between Copenhagen and Malmö brings Sweden closer to Central Europe.

The export of paper is one of Finland's major industries. Freighters deliver the goods on scheduled services.

in the north, between Helsingør and Helsingborg, and in the south, between Copenhagen and Malmö, by smaller ferry boats, jet-foils, and catamarans carrying tourists and numerous commuters between Denmark and Sweden. The new Sound Bridge, which was opened in 2000, has relieved this traffic. From Copenhagen a tunnel leads to an artificial island, and from there a 7,845 meter-long (25,740 ft.) bridge spans the Sound to Malmö.

Greatest depth only 460 meters

The Baltic Sea is comparatively shallow, with an average depth of only 55 meters (180 ft.); the deepest point, just north of Gotland, is no more than 460 meters (1,510 ft.). This makes the Baltic Sea especially sensitive

to ecological pollution – a particular danger for the fishing industry, which operates in the shallow coastal waters with small fishing boats and gill and drift netting. The larger fishing fleets that used to set out from Neksø on Bornholm, and from the Polish and German coasts, to hunt herring, cod, and salmon have seriously declined. Operating costs are too high and factory fishing on a large scale has caused prices to drop, making fishing in the Baltic simply unprofitable.

Ferry boat service continues to grow

In addition to the five main islands and Bornholm, Denmark is comprised of hundreds of small islands which are kept regularly supplied by busy shipping traffic. The countries bordering the Baltic can also be reached by numerous ferries providing services for passengers, their vehicles and, increasingly, by Roll-on, Roll-off vessels.

From the German harbors of Kiel, Lübeck-Travemünde, Rostock-Warnemünde, or Saßnitz on the island of Rügen, holiday-makers and, increasingly, trucks can reach Helsinki, Copenhagen, the Danish Gedser, Trelleborg in Sweden, Rønne in Bornholm, Klaipeda in Lithuania, the Latvian capital of Riga, Tallin in Estonia, and the Russian metropolis of St. Petersburg. Polish ferries set sail from Stettin to Ystad in South Sweden and Rønne, from Danzig to Tallin, St. Petersburg, and Stockholm; and the Swedish capital is linked to numerous Finnish harbors, to St. Petersburg and Tallin.

On 28 September 1994, between Tallin and Stockholm, the worst-ever ferry catastrophe in the Baltic occurred. Just 30 nautical miles south of the Finnish coast, the

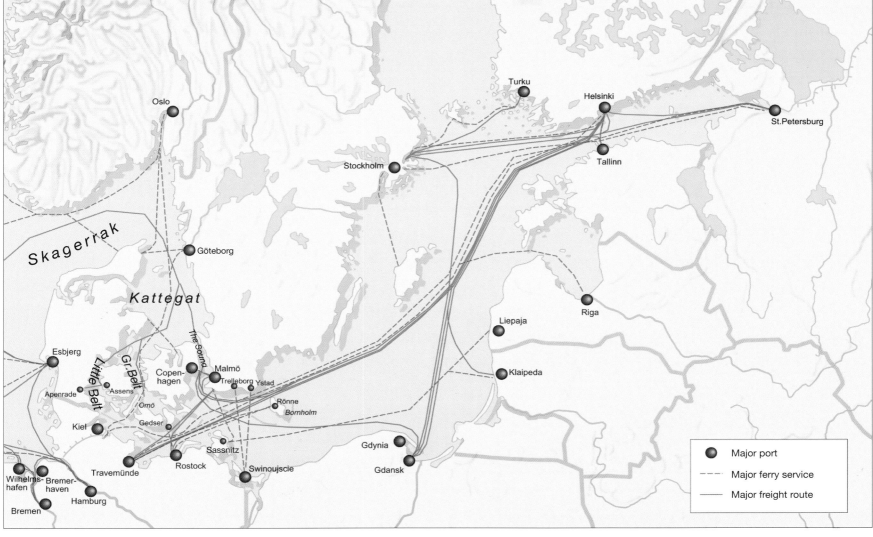

Shipping has reacted to increasing tourism and trade among the Baltic states with new ferry services and an intensification of existing routes.

Estonia sank in a heavy storm, with a loss of 852 passengers and crew.

The long traditions in the harbor towns along the Baltic bear witness that this sea has been heavily used since the time of the Vikings. Whoever controlled this comparatively small sea, also controlled trading. The rulers constructed strongholds and defenses at strategic bottlenecks, for example Hammerburg at the north tip of Bornholm. From there the Danes or the Swedes – depending on who happened to be in power on the island – had the Bornholmgat under their control.

Even today, the strait between the Swedish mainland and the idyllic island of Bornholm is the most used waterway in the Baltic. Sea vessels leaving Kiel on the Kiel Canal and setting course for the east coast of

Summer vacationers on the beach can watch the ferries go by at close hand .

Sweden, the Baltic countries, Finland, or Russia, pass through these straits along with the ferries and freighters coming from the Belts and the Sound with the same destinations.

Quick ferry services

About 50 million people live in the Baltic region, which is becoming more and more a market with European significance. And as international shipping grows in the Baltic, the ships get bigger and faster, and the shipping lanes increasingly overloaded. The fast ferry services attract more and more tourists – Scandinavians going south, and vacationers from Central Europe seeking recreation in Denmark, Sweden, Finland, or the new Baltic countries.

With the political changes in Europe and the ever-expanding European Union, the economic significance of the Baltic region and its waterways continues to increase. Poland's industrial goods and coal are exported mainly from the maritime centers of Danzig, Gdynia, and Swinemünde and raw materials are imported. On the coasts of the developing Baltic states, harbors are being improved in Lipaja in Latvia, and Klaipeda in Lithuania which – in contrast to St. Petersburg – remain free of ice the whole year round and so provide a bridgehead to the Baltic for Russian goods and services.

FACTS AND FIGURES

Skerries near Stockholm

Vacations in the Baltic
Every day, giant ferries transport tourists to Scandinavia. More and more vacationers are discovering the Baltic countries and the coast of Poland, where they find a unique landscape and coastal formations left after the last Ice Age 10,000 years ago – for example, the skerries not far from Stockholm, the center of Swedish Baltic traffic. Also a popular destination are the Finnish Åland Islands between Finland and Sweden, stretching along the southern edge of the Gulf of Bothnia. Of all the 6,554 islands and cliffs, only 80 are inhabited.

Transit traffic on the Mediterranean

Marseilles is the largest port, but Valencia, Genoa, Piraeus, Haifa, and Alexandria are all trading and transport centers.

●●● Water temperature in the Mediterranean rarely falls below the yearly average of 13° C (55° F) – the reason why the waters are sometimes referred to as the "bathtub of Europe." The water was let in 60 million years ago, when the African continent separated from Europe. A narrow crack gradually formed in the Atlantic which we refer to today as the Straits of Gibraltar. After

the Roman Empire all the coasts of the Mediterranean were under Roman rule.

After the fall of the Empire, the North African Moors began to advance into Europe via the Mediterranean and succeeded in reaching Europe via the Straits of Gibraltar and the Straits of Messina.

Today, the countries of the European Union have taken over the former role of the

Romans. From an economic point of view, the two Mediterranean basins are ruled by Spain, France, Italy, and Greece. Many freight ships take course for the large ports in these countries on their way to and from the Suez Canal.

Ports for citrus fruits and oil

Marseilles has the largest port, and the French town of 800,000 inhabitants is an important terminal for oil and a bridge to the Maghreb states. Almost 100 million tons of goods are moved in the French metropolis every year and a large proportion of trade between the former colony of Algeria and France – mostly oil and gas, but also citrus fruits and phosphate – is processed via Algiers and Marseilles.

Container ships increasingly take course for Valencia in Spain, which has one of the largest container terminals on the continent. The most important port in Italy is Genoa, which also plays a key role in oil imports – the raw material leaves Genoa by pipeline to Germany.

On the east side of the "boot" of Italy, from Bari and Otranto to the entrance of the Adriatic, numerous ferries make for Greece and Piraeus, the most important passenger port in the Mediterranean. The much-praised Piraeus is the starting point for many ferry services linking the Greek mainland to the islands of the Aegean and Turkey.

The major ports in the eastern Mediterranean are Haifa in Israel and Alexandria in Egypt. Mostly oil and citrus fruits are moved through these ports which, for their respective

The Mediterranean metropolis of Marseilles is the most important French port for the import of crude oil, and is the port of sail for numerous ferry services.

100 years, the 1,400-meters-deep (4,600-ft.) bathtub" was full.

As the Straits of Gibraltar are only 14 kilometers (9 mi.) wide, they have always been the "eye of the needle" for shipping. The opening of the Suez Canal increased their importance even more, as many of the heavily used shipping routes between Europe and Southeast Asia lead from the Straits of Gibraltar towards Port Said, and vice-versa. Seen in the light of world standards, the ports around the Mediterranean Sea are only of national importance.

Domination by EU countries

At one time the Mediterranean Sea was the world´s center of shipping. The Pharaohs used it for fishing and for trading with the Greeks, and later the Greeks colonized the coasts of Italy, the Black Sea, and France. The establishment of Marseilles and Naples can be traced back to the expansion campaigns of the Greeks.

After the Greeks came the Romans who were developing – albeit very slowly – into a seafaring nation. "Mare nostrum" – our sea – was how they named the Mediterranean following their victory over Carthage. The name was not altogether presumptuous, as at the zenith of

Spanish fishermen catching tuna: Once the fish have been driven into large nets, they are often brought on board in the traditional manner.

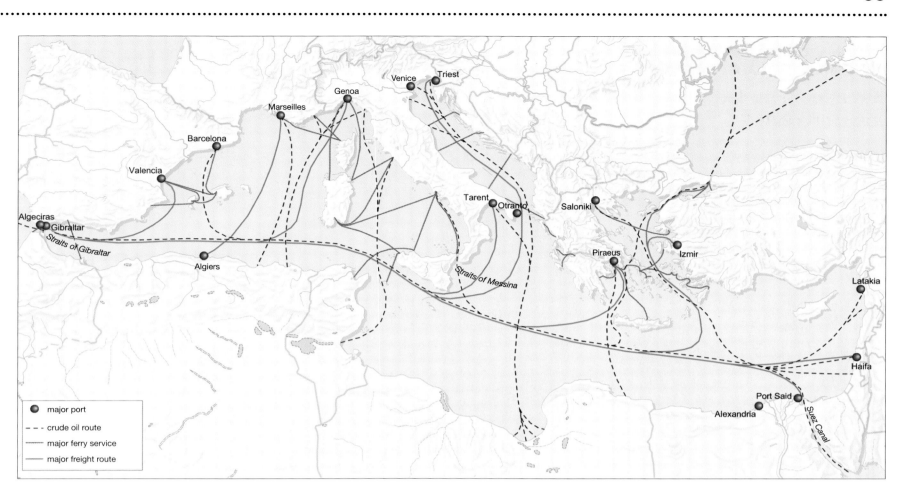

The exchange of goods between North Africa and Southern Europe is only of regional importance. However, many international shipping companies are destined for the large Spanish, French, and Italian ports.

After the Second World War, the Mediterranean beaches were systematically developed for tourism, bringing benefits to the inhabitants of the region, including the Greek islands.

country, are important centers of heavy industry, shipbuilding, and crude oil processing.

Fishing, which has been replaced by tourism as the most important economic factor, was for a long time the main source of livelihood for the coastal inhabitants of the Mediterranean. The main catch was tuna and it had the same significance for the people here as herring had in the North Sea. However, the fish population in the Mediterranean is now under threat from severely polluted water. Even today, 60 percent

of waste water is discharged into the sea untreated, as well as pollutants from the rivers. This has lead to outbreaks of troublesome algae, bringing death to many species of marine creatures and plants.

The European Union tries to combat these hazards with protective countermeasures. These measures are sorely needed since it is going to take the "bathtub" another 80 to 100 years to fill up with fresh water via its only inlet and outlet, the Straits of Gibraltar.

FACTS AND FIGURES

Genoa: Italian seaport

The Mediterranean ports

Based on the amount of goods moved, Marseilles and Genoa are the largest of the Mediterranean seaports. Marseilles in France moves just under 100 million tons a year, whereas Genoa in Italy deals with 45 million tons per annum. In a European comparison, these ports rank third and eighth, with the Italians leading when it comes to container business. In the Calabria container terminal of Gioia Tauro, 2.1 million steel containers are dealt with each year; in Algeciras in Spain, they number almost 1.8 million. Barcelona and Valencia follow with 1 million TEU. The most important passenger port in Greece is Piraeus.

The figures for the ports on the east and south shores of the Mediterranean are more modest. Alexandria in Egypt handles only about 23 million tons per year, and in Haifa in Israel about 17 million tons of goods are dealt with.

The Atlantic – bridge to the new world

The movement of most goods is concentrated in just a few mega-ports. Cape Town is still the most important port for Africa. International passenger services are no longer in demand.

● ● ● Most of the ships crossing the Atlantic from Rotterdam, Hamburg, or Le Havre are destined for New York – the city on the Hudson River. Besides Los Angeles, New York is not only the business center of the USA but is also the greatest seaport in the country, with 160 million tons of goods being moved on its piers each year, among them raw materials, vehicles, and machinery. Until the 1960s, New York was also a major passenger port, providing moorings in the docks of Manhattan for ocean giants owned by all the great shipping companies and destined for the city of 12 million inhabitants.

Millions of immigrants set foot on the American continent for the first time in New York – to be more exact, on Ellis Island, in the harbor.

Today, few passengers choose to take the sea voyage from Europe to the USA. Fast flights across the Atlantic – the "Great herring pond" as it is called – have diminished the importance of the scheduled trips made by the ocean steamers. All that remains is the British Cunard Line which regularly leaves Southampton and Le Havre, in France, bound for New York.

Halifax gains in importance

In the past few years, the Canadian port of Halifax has increased in importance with regard to routes across the Atlantic. Halifax lies on the east of the North American continent and has several decisive advantages for the modern shipping trade over New York. Ships bound from North America across the Atlantic through the Mediterranean and the Suez Canal to Southeast Asia gain one day of time.

In addition, Halifax lies on a unique natural harbor – the Bedford Basin on the coast of Nova Scotia. Its favorable position means the harbor basin and the shipping lanes are free of ice the whole year. Further-

Regional importance: The port of Lisbon is rich in tradition, but today is only frequented by cruisers.

more, the Bedford Basin is 18 meters (60 ft.) deep and has practically no tidal rise. So Halifax is the only port in North America which can accommodate fully loaded post-Panamax class container giants. From here, the goods can be distributed to American and Canadian business centers on the Great Lakes. The yearly movement is still quite modest – just about 14 million tons and 462,766 TEUs – but it can be assured of increasing growth rates.

In Europe, Le Havre is the biggest terminal in international sea trade next to Rotterdam – with movements of more than 66 million tons of goods a year Le Havre is the most important port for routes across the Atlantic. The town has 200,000 inhabitants

and is a major destination for oil tankers. A terminal has been constructed far out into the English Channel and can handle giants of up to 500,000 GRT.

At the port of Lisbon on the banks of the Tejus River, a monument to explorers and discoverers reminds us of seafarers who once left the Portuguese capital bound for expeditions into unknown territories. For a long time, the Lisbon port was not only the most important port on the Iberian Peninsula but was also the starting point for passages across the Atlantic to both North and South America.

Since then, Portugal's capital has retained only national importance for sea trade.Every year, 20 tons of freight are handled – 40 percent of Portuguese trade. The

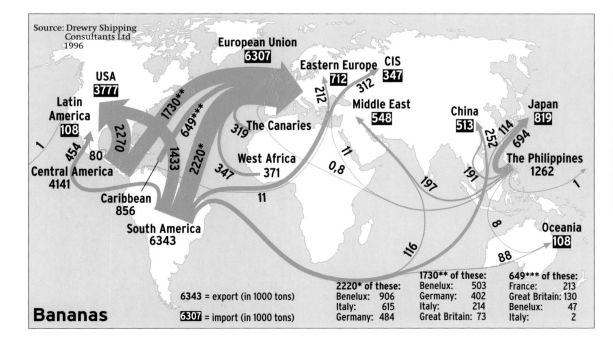

The cultivation of bananas is of major importance for the countries of Central and South America. The map shows the quantities which were exported to North America, European countries and the Pacific countries in 1996. The fruit is harvested while it is still unripe and is then transported in refrigerator ships.

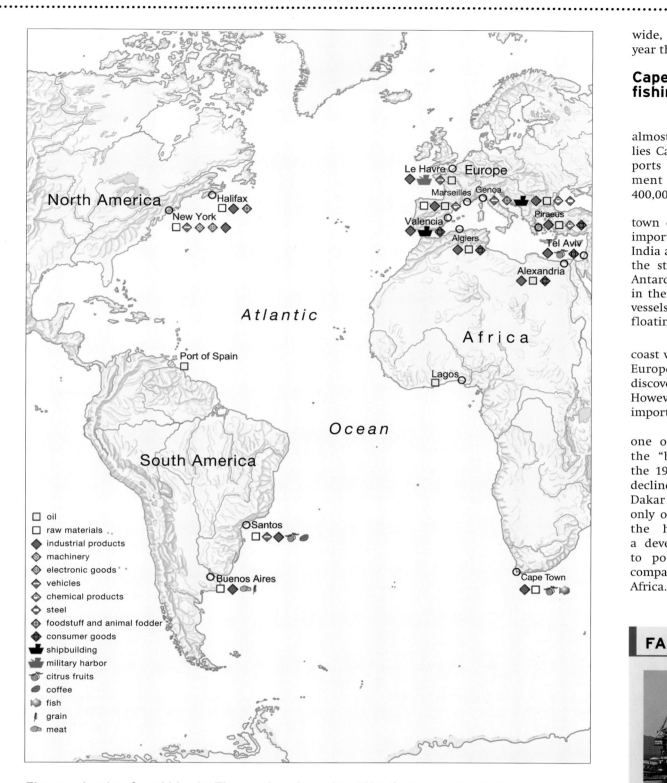

The race tracks of world trade: The great ports on the Atlantic are constantly increasing their share in the movement of goods across the seas.

Map legend:
- oil
- raw materials
- industrial products
- machinery
- electronic goods
- vehicles
- chemical products
- steel
- foodstuff and animal fodder
- consumer goods
- shipbuilding
- military harbor
- citrus fruits
- coffee
- fish
- grain
- meat

Map labels: North America, Halifax, New York, Atlantic, Port of Spain, South America, Santos, Buenos Aires, Ocean, Europe, Le Havre, Marseilles, Genoa, Valencia, Piraeus, Algiers, Tel Aviv, Alexandria, Africa, Lagos, Cape Town

natural harbor has, however, one advantage: it has the largest dry docks in the western world, which can even handle supertankers with 300,000 GRT.

Santos: gateway to Brazil

The most important port in the South Atlantic is Santos in Brazil. The town has 500,000 inhabitants and is the gateway to the business metropolis of São Paulo, a mega-city of at least 16 million inhabitants. From Sao Paulo comes about 77 percent of all Brazilian export goods, mostly shipped from Santos, which is 70 kilometers (44 mi.) away. Santos handles almost 30 million tons of freight a year, moving it on to ports of destination in the EU, the United States of America, and Argentina.

In Argentina, almost all of the international freighters – with few exceptions – are destined for the capital, Buenos Aires. With a population of 11 million, this metropolis on the Rio de la Plata is the most important Atlantic port next to Santos. Its founding father, Pedro de Mendoza, was brought here by the "buen ayre" – the good winds – in 1536 to the 45-kilometer-wide (28 mi.) delta of the "silver river," Rio de la Plata. At the end of the 19th century, the inhabitants at the port – the Portenos, as the people of Buenos Aires call themselves – became wealthy from the export of grain and cattle.

Like New York, Buenos Aires was also the first port of call for immigrants from Europe. Today, about 1.2 million containers are loaded and discharged in its five terminals. In spite of its location on the widest river in the world, Buenos Aires can only handle vessels with a draft of just around 10 meters (33 ft.).

But Buenos Aires does have one superlative to boast of. The Argentinian capital has the largest freshwater seaport world-wide, handling the more than 3,600 ships a year that sail into the Rio de la Plata.

Cape Town – the base of the fishing industry

On the other side of the Atlantic, on almost the same latitude as Buenos Aires, lies Cape Town – one of the most important ports of Africa, with a yearly goods movement of 6.2 million tons and just about 400,000 TEUs.

Until the opening of the Suez Canal this town on the southern tip of Africa was an important destination for ships bound for India and Southeast Asia. Today, Cape Town is the starting point for expeditions into the Antarctic and for international fishing fleets in the South Atlantic. A quarter of the 4,000 vessels sailing into Cape Town each year are floating fish factories.

Numerous ports on the west African coast were important bases for seafarers from Europe who were undertaking voyages of discovery around the Cape of Good Hope. However, most of them have declined in importance

The oil riches of Nigeria made Lagos one of the most important terminals for the "black gold", but after the boom in the 1970s its importance as an oil port has declined. Other ports such as Accra (Ghana), Dakar (Senegal), or Monrovia (Liberia) are only of regional importance or have become the home port for scrapped ships – a development which can be traced back to political unrest, corruption, and the comparatively negative economic situation of Africa.

FACTS AND FIGURES

Known to be a fast port: Santos

Trade routes in the Atlantic

The narrowest point of the Atlantic is between Brazil and Liberia measuring 2,848 kilometers (1,770 mi.); the widest point between the USA and North Africa is 4,830 kilometers (3,000 mi.). The northern boundary is an imaginary line from the southern tip of Greenland to Spitzbergen, in the south from the Drake Straits off the Antarctic. The following are considered the most important ports based on annual goods movements at the end of the 20th century:

New York	160 million tons
Halifax	14 million tons
Santos	30 million tons
Rio de Janeiro	18 million tons
Le Havre	66 million tons
Cape Town	6 million tons

New terminal centers in the Pacific

Japanese and Chinese seaports are competing with Singapore. In container traffic they lead the world.

● ● ● Up until the last 300 years, Valparaiso, Bombay, Djakarta, and San Francisco were all important ports of call in the Pacific sea trade. Since the 1970s, the great ports on the Japanese and Chinese coasts have replaced them in ranking.

In the top 10 container ports, there are two Japanese and two Chinese ports, with Rotterdam ranking only in fourth place. And even the Dutch are afraid of losing their title of the world's largest seaport. Singapore is hot on their heels with an annual transshipment of goods of more than 300 million tons.

Singapore is very favorably located, lying directly on the much frequented Straits of Malacca, within easy reach of 400 shipping companies that link the port to 130 countries around the world. Every year, 15.1 million TEUs (container units) are unloaded or loaded here.

The giant port of Hong Kong

In Hong Kong – "the harbor of fragrance" – only 200,000 containers fewer than that are handled. The former British crown colony is running neck-and-neck in the race for the top position in container traffic – sometimes Singapore wins, sometimes Hong Kong. In any case, the south Chinese metropolis has one of the most modern container terminals where even giant container ships can be handled within just 10 hours on the 6-kilometer-long (3.7-mi.) quay of Kwai Chung and Stonecutters.

Hong Kong has been the booming center of the financial world in Southeast Asia for many years, and since it was handed back to China it has increased in importance as a trading base for China's growing economic power. The goods reach the port from China via the Pearl River and are distributed to the

Container traffic has revolutionized transport. Kaohsiung port on Taiwan is the third largest container loading station in the world today.

whole world by 44,000 ships per year. In addition, countries like Vietnam and the Philippines make increasing use of the terminal – in this city of six million inhabitants – for transshipping their goods on to international lines.

The second largest port on the Chinese coast is Shanghai, which before Hong Kong was given back to China was the leading economic metropolis in this enormous country. The region around the millions-strong city is responsible for almost half of China's product needs; excluding Hong Kong, almost three million containers per year are

transshipped in Shanghai port. A large part is immediately reloaded on to ships and transported along the Yangtze River to the interior of the country. Although the Yangtze River brings wealth to the town, the masses of mud it transports into the Pacific prevent the giant post-Panamax containers from sailing into the port.

Three ports in the Bay of Tokyo

It is not the actual ports in Japan that present problems to deep-draft ships; more it is the danger from earthquakes and the lack of space which cause problems for the port managers in the Land of the Rising Sun.

One example is Kobe. In 1995, the port expansion project was interrupted by a massive earthquake. The port planners received another blow when a strong recession brought the growth of Japanese economy to a halt and the Asian crisis that followed had a negative influence on trade relationships in the Southeast Asian region.

Yokohama, the next largest port to Kobe, also had to cope with a serious upheaval; nevertheless, it can now boast of an impressive 118 million tons of goods handled per year. About 22.5 percent of Japanese export goods loaded in the Bay of Tokyo go to the United States of America and 20.7 percent to China. Each year, 45,000 vessels transport goods to and from Yokohama.

But in spite of the recession and the Asian crisis, Japan has five ports alone with annual transshipments of more than 100 million tons, and three of them are in the Bay of Tokyo – Yokohama, Osaka, and Kawasaki.

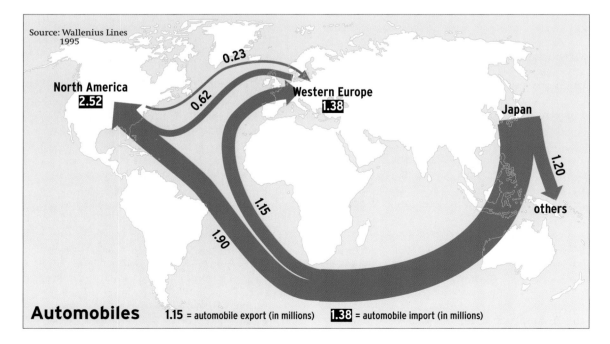

Automobiles 1.15 = automobile export (in millions) **1.38** = automobile import (in millions)

Japan leads the export market. The graphics show the number of vehicles manufactured in Japan that were shipped in 1995 to Europe and North America.

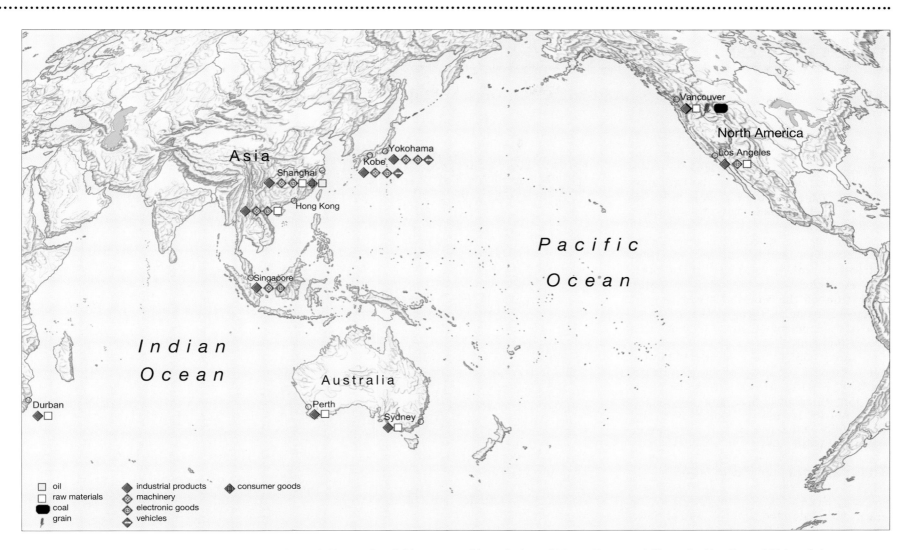

The economic boom in Southeast Asia has turned the ports of Singapore, Shanghai, and Hong Kong and those in the Bay of Tokyo into mega-ports, among the largest container terminals in the world.

Enormous cranes permit rapid loading and unloading of container ships.

The most important ports of destination for sea trade from Japan and the other Asian countries are Los Angeles on the American Pacific Coast and Vancouver in Canada.

Vancouver – important trading metropolis

Vancouver, with almost two million inhabitants, has developed into an important trading metropolis on the Canadian west coast, with its port being a major economic factor – employing almost 17,000 people. Every year, 72 million tons of freight and almost one million containers pass through the 20 terminals. Furthermore, 45 percent of Canadian grain and 75 percent of its coal are dealt with in the vast natural harbor.

San Pedro – port for high-tech

The second largest port on the west coast of America is 2,000 kilometers (1,245 mi.) further south – San Pedro, in Los Angeles. San Pedro comes after Hamburg among the eight largest ports in this category worldwide. It is the second largest port in the USA and handles an impressive 3.3 million containers per year.

A strong attraction for trading at the Los Angeles port is the proximity of the information and communication technology centers. The value of goods coming in and going out from San Pedro amounts to $80 billion US, with almost $50 billion US in products from Japan, China, and Taiwan – in that order – making up the main part.

Southeast Asia and eastern Asia are Australia's most important trading partners. Goods from these regions are mainly transshipped in Sydney – the most important port on the fifth continent. From there, and from other ports such as Perth on the west coast, Australia exports raw materials, for example, bauxite, into the large industrial countries.

When compared with other mega-terminals in the world, the Australian ports appear very modest – as do the ports of Valparaiso and Bombay. They are the most important ports in Chile and India respectively but, in comparison to others in the Indian-Pacific region, and with a yearly transshipment volume of 4.5 and 3 million tons a year, they have little significance.

FACTS AND FIGURES

A modern ship's propeller

The record-breaking ships

The modern container giants which today link up the ports of the Pacific with Europe and the USA are constantly setting new records. Some, like the "Susan Maersk" are up to 347 meters (1,140 ft.) long. The ship's engines could supply energy to a town of 50,000 people. The propellers, or screws, at 9 meters (30 ft.) across and 90 tons in weight, can drive the ship at 25 knots. A voyage from Kobe to Rotterdam around the Cape of Good Hope takes just under 20 days. The container ships are constantly at sea covering about 170,000 nautical miles a year – about seven and a half times around the Earth.

Sunken ships and treasure

Both treasure hunters and archaeologists scour the ocean bed looking for sunken relics of bygone shipping eras – ancient merchandise, coins and gold bars.

● ● ● On Tuesday, 8 September 1857, the vessel *Central America* set sail from Panama destined for New York. On board were about 581 people, including many who had made their fortunes in the California gold rush and were now returning with their riches to "better" addresses eastwards. But in addition to the passengers, the *Central America* was also carrying a secret cargo for the US government consisting of gold – a total of 21 tons of nuggets, coins, gold dust, and gold bars.

After a stopover in Havana, the steamer – which was powered by blade wheels on both sides – ran into a heavy storm in the Atlantic about 200 nautical miles off North Carolina. Soon the ship sprung leaks and water poured in everywhere. The boilers failed and the *Central America* drifted uncontrollably through heavy seas. The brig *Marine* and other sailboats crossing the route of the *Central America* were able to take on 153 survivors, but there was no saving the vessel. It sank with all its gold to 2,500 meters (8,200 ft.).

With the help of underwater cameras, she was discovered 130 years later. Never before had treasure hunters been face to face with so much gold – its value was estimated at about a billion dollars.

The oldest wreck in the world

Ever since human beings first went to sea, they have known what it is to be shipwrecked. Likewise, they have always attempted to reach sunken vessels, initially to save equipment, materials, or valuable cargo. In the 1950s, shipwrecks became a subject of interest to scientists; since then they have been scouring the historical trading routes with the help of modern technology to collect new insights and information.

In 1960, they discovered what is probably the oldest wreck in the world on the coast of Turkey just off Cape Gelidonya. Judging by the decayed remains and the salvaged hilts of weapons, tools and bronze artifacts it

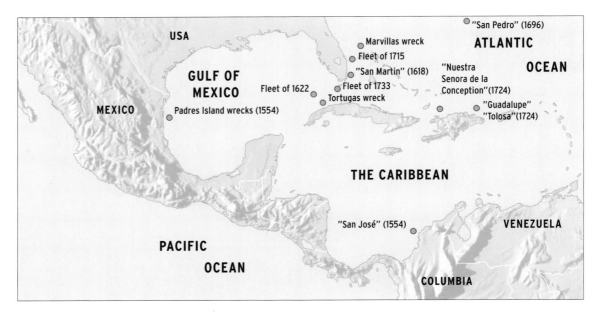

The Caribbean is a graveyard of sunken Spanish treasure ships. The map shows the locations of some of the most well-known wrecks.

was a Syrian ship from 13 BC, which was on its way from Syria to Greece.

Numerous wrecks found in the Mediterranean Sea allow us to draw conclusions regarding the busy trading routes and trade centers of the Ancient World. Off the French coast not far from Marseilles there is a mass of sunken ships from the time of the Roman Empire, and again on the west coast of Italy around the island of Elba, off Rome and Naples, in the Gulf of Tarent, and off the southern and eastern coast of Sicily.

Findings show that the smaller of the Roman traders could carry about 100 to 130 tons of cargo – for example fish, or up to 3,000 amphorae of wine – which in those days was a valuable trading commodity. The larger of the trading ships sailed with more than 1,200 tons of grain on board bringing it mainly from Egypt to the harbor in Rome.

Spanish galleons off Florida

Professional treasure hunters are not so much interested in the history of the ships but more in their valuable cargos. For them, the Caribbean is the preferred hunting ground because after Christopher Columbus first discovered the New World in 1492, numerous Spanish galleons cruised the Caribbean, heavily laden with rich cargo which the ruthless conquistadors had taken as booty during their raiding parties in Central and South America.

More than one of these heavy, bulky treasure ships never reached home port, as strong hurricanes and the treacherous

The Spanish fought their sea battles from their sturdy sailing ships. The oil painting by Reinier Nooms shows "Tromps flagship Amelia" prior to an encounter on October 21, 1639.

Salvaged from a Spanish galleon: coins in the hands of a treasure hunter.

depths of the Caribbean claimed many victims. The value of goods lost with Spanish ships up to 1690 is estimated at more than $28 billion US.

In the oldest wreck found to date in the Caribbean – a few miles north of the Cuban province of Pinar del Rio – vast quantities of gold and silver coins were found. The coins themselves, as well as the stamps on the gold and silver ingots that were salvaged from the same wreck, give rise to the assumption that the ship sank in 1554.

In September 1622, a fleet of Spanish galleons with their flagship *Nuestra Señora de Atocha* were caught in a hurricane. The 22 ships had been laden in Cartagena, Portobelo, and Havana with copper, silver, gold, precious stones, tobacco, and indigo and were bound for Spain. Eight of the ships did not survive the storm and sank south of Florida Keys, among them the *Nuestra Señora de Atocha*.

Most of the wrecks were found soon after they sank and were relieved of their treasures. The proud flagship, however, remained lost until 1985, when it was rediscovered by a contemporary maritime "gold-digger." After looking for 16 years, Mel Fisher finally found the *Nuestra Señora de Atocha* 35 nautical miles

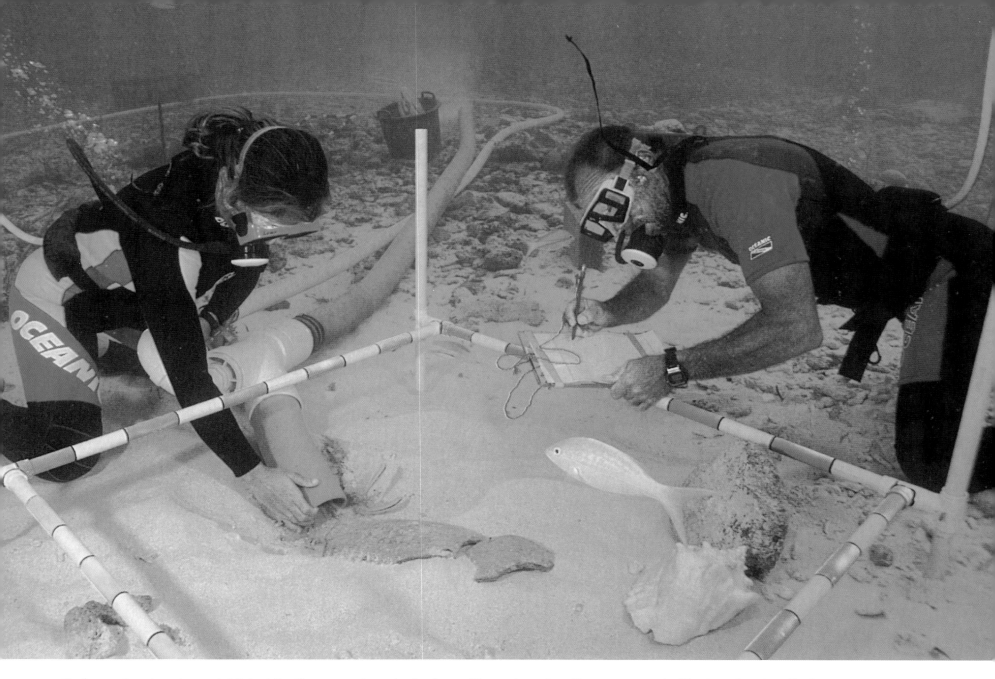

Marine archaeology has established itself as a new branch of science. The underwater sites are secured with utmost and meticulous care.

south of Key West, together with her treasure worth about $800 million US.

But it is not always modern deep-sea technology which leads to the finding of the sunken treasure – sometimes it is just pure luck. In 1987, four American hobby divers found the wreck of a treasure ship not far from the Bahamas. The *Maravilla* lay buried in only 4 meters (13 ft.) of sand; she had collided with another sailing ship in 1655 and sunk. In all, almost 300 Spanish galleons sank in the Straits of Florida laden with gold, silver, precious stones, and jewelry, and the *Maravilla* must have been the most valuable find of all as her cargo was worth almost $6 billion US.

No gold in European waters

In comparison, the wrecks found in European waters have more of a historical than commercial value, for example, the burned remains of a Celtic ship from 3 BC found near the British Channel Island of Guernsey, or a Viking sailing ship. In the Danish Roskilde Fjord, many wrecks of the Skudelev ships have been discovered – ships of the type Leif Eriksson must have used to sail to America.

Everywhere in the world where the discoverers and explorers of the great seafaring nations found noble metals, precious stones, spices, or other valuable commodities, there are numerous wrecks to bear

witness to their much frequented trading routes. The first in the Indian Ocean were the Portuguese; the Dutch founded the East India Company, which was the first worldwide trading organization. Spanish galleons cruised in the Pacific and, in this hemisphere, Great Britain set up the pillars of her Empire.

And finally, the fifth continent also claimed its tribute of seamen and ships, many of them breaking up on the reefs of the Australian east coast.

Underwater treasures: The Spaniards conquered large parts of Central America and the Caribbean Islands in the name of the Cross.

For whom the bell tolls ...

The great sea disasters of the 20th century – negligence, navigational errors, and technical troubles have been the causes of many spectacular wrecks.

● ● ● As soon as there is news that a ship is missing, the bell is tolled twice; just once means that a ship registered in Lloyd's Register of Shipping has sunk somewhere at sea. It is the bell that once belonged to the British frigate *Lutine*, which was stranded and sank in 1799 in a storm off the Friesian islands. The bell can be seen today in the entrance hall to Lloyd's of London, the famous insurance market which has been closely connected with shipping since its foundation in 1688.

Many a tolling of the bell has meant great expense for Lloyd's – all the ships which have sunk in the past 200 years are registered in the Loss Book, usually just referred to as "The Book." Among the entries is the *Titanic* – probably the best known of all sea disasters. The ocean giant, a floating symbol of its age, was said to be unsinkable. The luxury liner left Southampton on her maiden voyage on 10 April 1912, accompanied by pomp and ceremony, bound westward for New York with 1,316 passengers and a crew of 892 on board.

"S.O.S. Have hit an iceberg"

The tragedy occurred on 14 April. The *Titanic* was approaching Newfoundland, passing through the waters of the Labrador Current, known to be hazardous because of icebergs. But instead of reducing speed, Captain Edward J. Smith had given the command for full speed ahead through the clear, starry night. The lookout saw the iceberg too late, and below the waterline, the starboard hull of the *Titanic* was ripped open by the sharp-edged icy mass.

It was midnight when the radio operator John Phillips transmitted the historic distress signal, "S.O.S. Have hit an iceberg. Need assistance. Position 41° 54' N,

Twice for a missing ship, once for a ship lost at sea - the tolling of the historical bell at Lloyd's of London.

50° 24' W. Titanic." Two hours and forty minutes later, the *Titanic* sank, bow first. Ships hurrying to the scene were only able to rescue a few survivors. The Lloyd's list reports that 1,565 passengers and crew members lost their lives in the icy waters.

A few years later, an incident involving the *Lusitania* claimed the lives of many on 7 May 1915. This time the fault came down to negligence. The ocean steamer belonging to the English Cunard Line was returning from New York when it was hit by a torpedo – fired from a German submarine off the Irish coast. The U-20 attack on the *Lusitania* claimed 1,198 lives.

In comparison, a spectacular collision on the Atlantic was due to a fatal error. On 23 July 1956, the *Andrea Doria*, traveled at full speed across the Atlantic Ocean, bound for New York.

One day away from her destination, off the east coast of the USA, she met with dense fog. Captain Piero Calami gave the order to reduce speed and carefully observed the radar screen. At 10:45 PM, a ship appeared on the screen, just about starboard and coming towards them. At 11:03, the fog lifted briefly, and the *Stockholm*, an American-Swedish liner, came into full view.

At sea, in threatening situations like this one, there is a last minute maneuver – both ships steer hard starboard.

A critical error

But Captain Calami steered larboard, right into the wake of the *Stockholm*. There was no time to swerve, and the bows of the *Stockholm* bore into the side of the *Andrea Doria*. Fifty-one passengers and crew lost their lives in the collision. The *Andrea Doria* – the pride of Italy's fleet – sank one day later into the Atlantic.

But events such as these, which take their toll of human life and ships, are not restricted just to the high seas. One of the daily crossings of the English Channel was to be a fatal one for 197 passengers. On 6 March 1987, the *Herald of Free Enterprise* had only just left the Belgian harbor of Zeebrügge when the Roll-on, Roll-off ferry capsized. The loading doors had not been secured for sea.

Defective loading doors were probably the cause of the sinking of the *Estonia*. Another Roll-on, Roll-off ferry, the *Estonia*, sank on 28 September 1994,

When the Torrey Canyon ran aground in 1967 off the south coast of England, a vast oil slick polluted the coast of Brittany. Twenty years later, the ferry Herald of Free Enterprise capsized just outside of the harbor at Zeebrügge because the loading doors had not been secured and closed. The incident claimed 189 lives.

Lying 4,000 meters (13,100 ft.) down in the water since 15 April 1912, the wreck of the Titanic was found on 1 September 1985. The picture shows an artist's impression of the wreck at the bottom of the sea, using underwater photographs.

The Titanic sank on 15 April 1912 in the North Atlantic. Her position was 41° 54' N, 50° 24' W.

during its trip from Tallin to Stockholm – claiming the lives of 852 people.

On 20 December 1987, a collision with a small tanker proved to be calamitous for the *Doña Paz*. The ferry was drastically over-loaded with more than 4,000 passengers and was bound from Tacloban on the Philippine island of Leyte to the capital, Manila, 600 kilometers (373 mi.) away. Around 10:00 PM, the *Doña Paz* collided with a tanker whose cargo caught fire. The *Doña Paz* was not able to call for assistance, as it was not carrying a radio. The authorities later estimated the number of casualties who either died in the flames or in the Sibuyan Sea at 4,317.

The forces of nature or human error (negligence, too much trust in technology, navigational errors) – in some cases, it is often difficult to say exactly what are the causes for disasters and damage at sea. In the case of the *Torrey Canyon* it was "a chain of unfortunate

circumstances" as the experts later found out. The supertanker was at sea in March 1967 carrying 122,000 tons of crude oil from the Persian Gulf to its destination in Milford Haven, Wales. The Loran system, a radio-controlled navigational aid, had been defective for hours as the *Torrey Canyon* approached the Scilly Isles at about 16 knots. However, when the first officer noticed the islands on the radar screen, they were not straight ahead on the starboard side – as had been calculated – but larboard. The current and the wind had shifted the course of the vessel eastwards.

No reaction from the rudder

The first officer changed course to the east in order to round the Scilly Isles at a safe distance. Captain Pastrengo Rugiati deemed this to be an unnecessary detour and brought the *Torrey Canyon* back on her northerly course.

Between the Scilly Isles and Lands End, the most southwesterly tip of England, are two shipping lanes separated from the dangerous Seven Stones Rocks. Rugiati decided on the narrower and more westerly lane and switched the automatic pilot on without reducing speed. A few minutes later, the men on the bridge saw the first rocks straight ahead. If appropriate actions had been taken, there would still have been time to steer clear of the shallows.

As the helmsman proceeded to carry out the captain's command to steer larboard, he found to his dismay, that there was no response from the rudder. The automatic

pilot blocked the steering system, the *Torrey Canyon* ran aground on the rocks, and the oil from the supertanker polluted the beaches of Cornwall, Brittany, and the Channel Islands.

The authorities and the experts usually find the cause and an explanation for most disasters at sea but, in many cases, they will forever remain a secret.

FACTS AND FIGURES

New life-saving regulations

After the Titanic tragedy, new life-saving regulations were set up for ship-ping. Among them was the regulation that there should be a sufficient number of life boats. After an incident, the ship-ping company must be able to prove that there was enough life boat space to accommodate each and every person on board. Furthermore, an operator must be present in the radio room around the clock. The SOS signal from the Titanic did not reach the freighter California, which was only 20 nautical miles away, because the radio officer was in bed at the time of the collision. Furthermore, powerful searchlights and binoculars must be on board. The Titanic had neither. Had they been available, the disaster might never have happened.

Food from the sea

The methods of catching fish practiced by modern fishing fleets are a threat to the fish population worldwide.

● ● ● Sea fishing concentrates on just a very few species. Of the approximately 200 species that are of economic interest, no more than six make up a quarter of the total catch: anchovy, Alaska pollock, Chilean horse mackerel, Atlantic herring, tuna mackerel, and capelin. Large species such as the Atlantic cod, ocean perch, haddock, sardine, anchovy, swordfish, and many types of tuna have all become scarce.

Fishing contributes only about 10 to 15 percent of the total protein supply needed by humans, but this creates demands on the oceans' ecological system that are leading to its ruin. Forty-four percent of the fish population is being exploited to the very edge of its existence, and 16 percent are over-fished. Six percent have already disappeared. Off the coasts of Canada, thousands of fishers have become unemployed and many harbors are now ghost towns.

The fishing grounds of the Northwest, Southeast, and East Atlantic have suffered particularly under intensive exploitation, which actually climaxed decades ago. The limits of economic utilization of the Northeast, Southwest and East Central Atlantic fishing grounds have now been reached, and the same applies to the East Central and Northeast Pacific. Fishing in the Mediterranean and the Black seas are likewise no longer profitable.

It is only in the Indian Ocean and in the western parts of the Central and North Pacific that catches have increased slightly. The latter is the main fishing region in the world. In 1996, just under 25 million tons of fish were caught in the North Pacific.

In the golden years between 1950 and 1980, sea fish production rose each year by six percent; in the 1980s it was only a 1.5 percent increase per year. The year 1996 was a record year, with a catch of 87.1 million tons. A year later, this figure dropped by 1 million tons.

Fishing right on the doorstep

Experts from the Fishing and Agricultural Organization of the United Nations forecast for 2010 very noticeable bottlenecks in the supply of fish that is suitable for consumption. This would be a disaster for the people living in poorer countries, as fish and

Salmon farming in the high north: the Norwegians are world leaders in pisciculture.

sea products represent an important source of animal protein for billions of people in Asia, for example. In Third World countries, 60 percent of the population get at least 40 percent of their animal protein from the sea.

The fishing grounds all lie directly along the coasts where 90 percent of all sea fish are caught. These regions are so productive, in biological terms, because it is only there that sufficient nutrients reach the surface waters where ample sunshine activates the light-dependent growth of plankton algae. These microscopically small plants are the indispensable basis of the marine food network; for example, it is food for krill, which in turn are also food for plankton-eating fish such as the herring.

In the shallow shelf regions, storms churn up the sea bed but only the nutrients brought up in spring and early summer are put to good use. After the storms in the fall, it is too cold in the winter, and at high latitudes the plankton do not get sufficient light for growth. On the continental shelves, sea currents running parallel to the coast cause water laden with nutrient salts to be brought up from the cold deep waters. The west coasts of the continents, where the Humboldt, Benguela, Alaska, or Canary currents flow, are particularly productive.

Fish as animal fodder

Nutrients also come up to the surface in regions where cold and warm ocean water converge, such as off Newfoundland, where the cold Labrador Current and the warm waters of the Gulf Stream meet, or where the Norwegian Current and the East Greenland Current flow past one another.

The major fishing countries in the world are China, Peru, Chile, Japan, the USA, Russia, and Indonesia – accounting for half of the fish caught. Fish exports represent 75 percent of the total proceeds from foreign trade for Iceland, the Faeroes, Greenland, the Maldives, and the Seychelles.

Differences in productivity between privileged and underprivileged countries are dramatic. In Iceland, 5,600 fishers land 280 tons a year of fish, while 6 million Indian

Off the coasts of Third World countries people still fish using traditional methods. Foreign fishing fleets that harvest shoals of fish on the high seas are depriving the natives of their main source of food.

Modern fishing fleets are highly equipped technically and can locate shoals of fish precisely. When one fishing ground has been depleted, the factory ships move on and plunder the next. The only protection is a 200-mile prohibited zone off the coasts.

fishers catch about 5 million tons – not even 1 ton per fisher.

But not everything the fishers catch is meant for human consumption. A good quarter of the catch is processed as fish meal and fish oil – particularly anchovies, sand eels, capelin, smelts, but also herring and sprats. Almost 40 percent of North Sea fish ends up in the mill as fish meal, and is used to feed valuable aqua-culture fish, as well as pigs and chickens. Fish oil is used as an ingredient in baked goods and cosmetics.

The end of unwanted catches

The so-called "discarded catch fishery" also effects the population of fish caught for our tables. For example, small fry are important for cod and haddock but fishers deny them this source of food.

Another problem is the "throwaway" mentality, with more than a quarter of the catch being thrown overboard as waste – every year about 27 million tons of (mostly) dead fish – simply because the nets catch more types of fish than the fishers are interested in. This is particularly the case where drag nets are used. They are plowing up all the shelves and continental shelves with 90 percent of the fish caught in the nets unwanted.

The fishers also throw away the catch when the assumed market prices are too low or the boat is too small. They then partake in so-called "high-grading." Inferior fish, most of which have already been gutted, are thrown back into the sea and only those that will fetch a high price on the market are kept in the storage.

Quotas, originally planned to protect fish populations, simply encourage the fishers to throw back unwanted fish. If fishers find out by radio that the price for their catch has fallen, the fish are simply dumped overboard. Officially on paper, the fishers have not fulfilled their quota, which they then keep for better days and better prices.

An increased demand for shrimps is not just a fad. There are simply too few fish, so more and more "fish feed" is finding its way to the table, i. e., sea creatures that normally serve as food for other fish are now appearing on menus, praised as delicacies.

Today lobster and king prawns are increasingly bred in aqua-farms.

Source: FAO 1999

FACTS AND FIGURES

Fishing in the Bay of Tokyo

The largest fishing nations
Half of the sea fish caught worldwide lands in the nets of seven large fishing nations. The El Niño phenomena of 1997/98, when the seas off the coast of South America increased in temperature, meant reduced yields for Chile and Peru by 10 percent to 20 percent. The fish swam out into cooler waters where they were more difficult to catch (quantities given in 1,000 tons):

China (VR)	14,222	Indonesia	3,729
Peru	9,515	India	3,491
Chile	6,692	Thailand	3,138
Japan	5,964	Norway	2,638
USA	5,000	South Korea	2,413
Russia	4,675	Iceland	2,060

International fishing

As a result of giant fishing fleets depleting fish stocks, the fishing nations of the world protect their own grounds with a 200-mile zone.

●●● Actually, all the big fishing fleets in the world ought to register as bankrupt. While the market value of their catches are given as well over $224 billion US, about $400 billion US are invested in the building of boats, purchasing of fishing equipment and tackle, wages, costs for borrowed funds, and operating costs. State subsidies of $176 billion US per year balance out the deficit in order to keep the fishing industry alive.

A modern factory trawler costs about $120 million US and daily operating costs are far above $40,000 US. The ships are equipped with 10,000-PS machines, dragging nets costing $300,000 US at high speed behind them.

With the help of GPS, the global positioning system, the ships can navigate in the ocean within an accuracy of 5 meters (16 ft.). Gigantic nets are cast using strong winches. For example, purse seines, up to 1,6 kilometers (1 mi.) long and reaching down to 140 meters (460 ft.), more or less wrap the fish shoal up and haul it in. Drift nets 20 kilometers (12.5 mi.) long can be cast out and hauled in within just a few hours.

Long-line fishing boats can spool off 60 kilometers (37 mi.) of line a day, with 40,000 machine-baited hooks hung per line. The opening of a modern drag net is 140 meters (460 ft.) wide and up to 110 meters (360 ft.) high. Each haul can bring in 20 to 30 tons of fish.

Helicopter guides in the fishing grounds

Satellites help ocean fishers to find their catches. Their data comprises exact information on water temperature, currents, water eddies, and the color of the sea, all helping the captain to recognize a potentially rich fishing ground. The helicopter then guides the fleet directly to the shoal. For what the pilot's eye cannot see, special cameras are used that can measure the exact size of a herring shoal.

When the trawler comes within reach of the targeted area, the sound waves of a sonar device probes the surrounding sea 3 kilometers (1.9 mi.) around, Reflection data appear on the monitor in color, and an experienced captain can tell by the shades of color not only the size of the shoal and the direction it is swimming in but also the type and size of the fish.

The fishing tackle can be controlled from the bridge of the ship. Under water, a probe signals the position and quantity of fish in the net. One movement of the joystick and the net can be lowered or raised. The maneuverable ships can follow even the slightest changes in the movements of the shoal.

There will never be "the last fish caught," as only relatively few fish are necessary to create a new population. However, the enormous over-capacity of international fishing fleets hardly gives the fish time for sustainable reproduction. The crisis is obscured by the fact that more and more young fish are

The herring is an important source of income for the coastal fishers on the Baltic.

being caught, the industrial nations are importing large quantities of fish from developing countries, and the amount of fish-farming is growing.

Although the cutbacks in the fishing industry are subsidized in many countries in order to reduce the fishing capacities, money is also being spent on its modernization. Ships which are sold far below their value because of state grants often end up in the harbors of poorer countries.

From a global point of view, the fishing capacities have not been reduced by doing this, but the ships have simply changed their location. Ships sold off cheaply can still fish for a profit even if the fish population has been exploited and only a few fish land up in the net. So the pressure builds and the remaining fish population has even less chance of recovering. This frequently leads to local conflicts between the large foreign factory ships and the small indigenous coastal fishers for whom little remains.

But there is also a merciless war waging among the major fishing nations regarding distribution. Since the end of the 1950s, the Cod War that has been waged off the Icelandic coast among Iceland, England, Norway, and Germany has flared up time and time again. In some cases, war ships have had to

intervene. In the 1990s, Spain led several battles against France and Italy over tuna; in the North Pacific, there was a dispute over shrimps; in the Sea of Okhotsk, a skirmish took place over haddock; and off the Horn of Africa, Somalia and EU fishers argued about the lobster population.

Skirmishes on many coasts

In 1975, when Iceland became the first country to extend its fishing zone to 200 sea miles it was treated as a scandal. Since then, the 200-mile economic zone has become recognized around the world.

Canada's efforts to limit cod fishing off its coast had little success because foreign trawlers would wait on the edge of the 200-mile zone for a shoal of cod to cross the line. In 1992, Canada stopped cod fishing altogether, causing 50,000 people to lose their livelihood.

After the cod population had recovered, the quota off Canada was limited to 27,000 tons in accordance with the North West Atlantic Fisheries Organization. Of this, Canada claimed 60 percent and the European Union were allotted 3,400 tons. Under pressure from Spanish and Portuguese fishers, the EU arbitrarily approved 16,300 tons for itself. The Canadians looked upon this act as robbery and grounded a Spanish trawler which, on top of everything, had been fishing with prohibited small-meshed nets.

As all the efforts to reduce fishing capacities

Coastal fishing boat

Fish trap

Lobster pot

Fishing as it is practiced today: with gigantic nets, the highly equipped factory ships can pull a whole shoal of fish from the sea, while in Third World countries, many people still earn their living by conventional fishing methods.

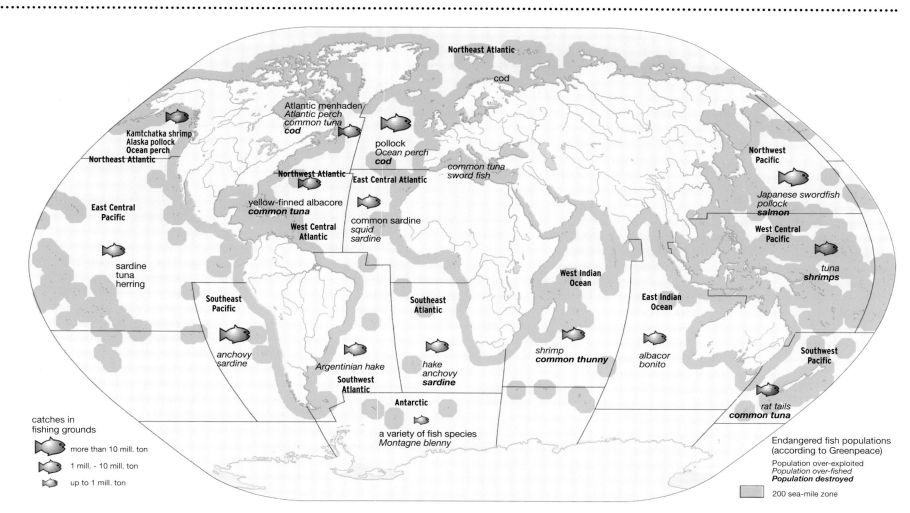

Northeast Atlantic
cod

Kamtchatka shrimp
Alaska pollock
Ocean perch
Northeast Atlantic

Atlantic menhaden
Atlantic perch
common tuna
cod

pollock
Ocean perch
cod

Northwest Pacific

Northwest Atlantic

East Central Atlantic

common tuna
sword fish

Japanese swordfish
pollock
salmon

**East Central
Pacific**

yellow-finned albacore
common tuna

common sardine
squid
sardine

**West Central
Atlantic**

**West Central
Pacific**

sardine
tuna
herring

**West Indian
Ocean**

tuna
shrimps

**Southeast
Pacific**

**Southeast
Atlantic**

**East Indian
Ocean**

anchovy
sardine

Argentinian hake
**Southwest
Atlantic**

hake
anchovy
sardine

shrimp
common thunny

albacor
bonito

**Southwest
Pacific**

Antarctic

a variety of fish species
Montagne blenny

rat tails
common tuna

catches in
fishing grounds

more than 10 mill. ton

1 mill. - 10 mill. ton

up to 1 mill. ton

Endangered fish populations
(according to Greenpeace)

Population over-exploited
Population over-fished
Population destroyed

200 sea-mile zone

The map shows the parts of the oceans where factory fishing has strongly decimated, or even ruined, the fish population. As a result, in many parts of the world, fishermen in their own countries have been robbed of their living.

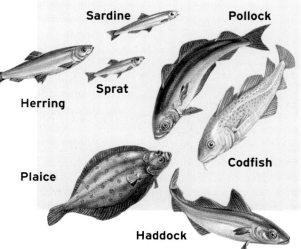

Factory ship

Trawler

Purse seine

Whale-catcher

Fyke nets

have had little success, rich countries are seeking new fishing grounds for their fishers and subsidy licenses for the fish population of poorer countries. The EU pays $304 million US to Morocco so that the Spanish can fish off the North African coast.

In order to make better use of their resources, many countries and groups of states determine quotas for individual types of fish. Most of them are, however, too high and encourage overexploitation rather than prevent it.

The quotas are set according to information from scientists who base their figures on research results and recommend maximum quantities which can be caught without endangering the fish population. In the course of subsequent political discussions, many countries insist on higher quotas, against their better judgment, as a concession to the lobbyists in their own national fisheries organizations.

Whether these quotas are then adhered to by the fishers is not sufficiently monitored – especially not on the coasts of very poor countries. Therefore,the fishers have ample opportunities to exceed the legal limits by means of manipulation. For example, the catch is entered into the logbook simply for another region, or fish which have already been gutted are thrown overboard because the expected price for them on land is too low.

However, there have been some success, such as the well-managed salmon, cod, herring, and sprat population in the Baltic. In addition, there are agreements regarding the population of hake between Argentine and Uruguay, the North Sea herring among the Faeroes, Iceland and Norway, Pacific salmon between Canada and the USA, the pilchard between Angola and Namibia, and sardines among the Ebony Coast, Ghana and Togo. These fish have long provided good, steady yields for the fishers.

FACTS AND FIGURES

Catches of sea fish

The figures for fishing since 1995 show there has been a shift in the proportion of certain types of fish. In 1995/96 the figures for capelin, Spanish mackerel, and Japanese anchovies increased, while those for South American sardines and Peruvian anchovies decreased. In 1996, six of the most frequently caught fish species made up 25 percent of the overall catch (catch in 1,000 tons):

Peruvian anchovy	8,863
Alaskan pollock	4,533
Chilean horse mackerel	4,378
Atlantic herring	2,330
Spanish mackerel	2,167
Capelin	1,527
South American sardine	1,493
Striped tuna	1,479
Atlantic cod	1,329
Cutlass fish	1,275
Janese anchovy	1,254

Sardine **Pollock**

Sprat

Herring

Codfish

Plaice

Haddock

Source: FAO 1999

Giant pumps on the high seas

Offshore oil production in deep, rough seas makes the highest demands on technology. The oil platforms must be able to withstand heavy storms and high waves.

●●● It was 27 March 1980. An angry west wind raged across the North Sea with gale force, creating waves almost 15 meters (50 ft.) high, too strong and too high for the accommodation platform, or "flotel" of the *Alexander Kielland*. This was home to 212 men working on the production platform on the oil field Ekofisk, about 260 kilometers (160 mi.) west of the Norwegian coast. One of the pontoon piers broke and the man-made steel island capsized. In a dramatic rescue operation, only 89 of the team were saved from the raging seas; the remainder were dragged down with the *Alexander Kielland*.

Despite all the modern technology available, oil production at sea is still a dangerous business. But offshore platforms not only take their toll on human lives; they are also a constant threat to the environment. Any accidental discharge of oil can have disastrous effects on marine organisms.

Floating platforms

The oil-producing companies therefore demand the highest safety standards. Modern offshore platforms bear no resemblance to the steel rigs which were simply put into the sea bed in shallow, coastal waters in the early years of oil exploitation in the oceans. The first oil rigs, built in the 1960s for the North Sea, weighed up to 35,000 tons. They were mounted on three to five steel or reinforced concrete barges which were simply "floated" into the sea bed at a depth of about 90 meters (295 ft.). Since then, they have become more modern and lighter and are now standardized worldwide in the production of oil at sea – in the Persian Gulf, the Gulf of Mexico, and in the offshore fields of Southeast Asia.

An alternative to stationary installations, and more suitable for deeper waters,

are the so-called "semi-submersibles" – free-floating platforms, secured by a wide cast anchor. These semi-submersibles are secured to the sea bed only by means of the drilling lines.

British vs. Norwegian construction

The platforms have gradually developed into giants to cope with greater depths and higher production output. However, the British and the Norwegians use different construction methods.

The Norwegians specialize in structures made of reinforced concrete, and build gigantic support towers in the deep fjords near Stavanger, dragging them individually or in "three-packs" that float upwards to their locations, then are sunk into the sea bed.

British oil fields, however, are dominated by constructions made of steel tubular scaffolding, up to a length of 170 meters (560 ft.), built in special, purpose-built dry docks and then towed out to sea lying on barges. On reaching their location, the barges are flooded in a complicated process so that the constructions are brought into an upright position and then carefully lowered to the sea bed and anchored with "nails" several feet in length.

It is possible to reach depths of up to 350 meters (1150 ft.) with similar steel towers which are then additionally anchored by means of hawsers. In even deeper waters and in smaller oil fields this function is taken over by so-called SWOPS – Single Well Offshore Production Systems – which resemble giant oil tankers. They have their own conveyor system and are connected to the well head with a drilling line that pumps the crude oil out of the sea bed and serves as an interim storage facility.

A steel colossus: The production platform is mounted on a steel construction that is firmly anchored in the sea bed. It is equipped with numerous drilling lines through which the oil field is developed up to an area of about 15 square kilometers (3.6 sq. mi.). The oil produced is transported via pipeline direct to a storage facility on the mainland or into an underwater or floating interim storage container. The platform is equipped with a helicopter landing area, the production derrick, and supply cranes. Technical installations and material are on the lower decks. At the end of the long beam, the gas, which has been separated from the oil, is "flared off". The crew is accommodated in containers on the upper deck during their two-week shift.

Oil rigs in the North Sea. The modern steel structures are designed to withstand rough waters, strong currents, and giant waves.

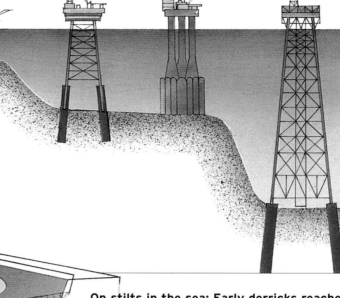

On stilts in the sea: Early derricks reached down to depths of about 90 meters (295 ft.). Today, modern platforms are anchored as deep down as the Empire State building is high.

The hard stuff: Rotating chisel bits (see picture) are used for drilling in layers of earth and soft rock. Bore heads tipped with diamond teeth are used in harder layers.

FACTS AND FIGURES

Energy from the sea

Fossil fuels are not inexhaustible. Scientists forecast that the Earth's resources of crude oil will last about another 40 years, and natural gas about 70 years. The days of "cheap oil" will soon be a thing of the past as the oil companies begin to exploit deposits which today are seen as non-profitable – such as those offshore productions beyond the comparatively shallow continental shelves.

In this regard, the oceans have an enormous energy potential, combined with the advantage of being more environmentally friendly than burning fossil fuel. Up to now, there have only been isolated uses of these opportunities, such as the tidal power station in Saint-Malo on the French coast of the English Channel. A further variation on the tidal power station is the wave power station which could make use of the power from constant sea currents to generate electricity – a sort of underwater "windmill".

Crude oil – the gold of the seas

There is no lack of new site developments for offshore production. The Persian Gulf and new fields in Southeast Asia are the main centers in the Indian and Pacific oceans.

● ● ● When the American Edwin Drake sank the first wells in a gigantic oil field in Titusville, Pennsylvania, USA in 1859, he triggered a worldwide rush for the "black gold." Demands for oil and oil products increased rapidly and, likewise, there was a dynamic increase in the number of oil companies searching for new sources.

The treasure hunters also assumed that there were huge deposits in the sea. As it turned out, they were right, and in 1896 they found what they were looking for off the coast of California. The oil field discovered there was developed with conventional methods by means of piers built out into the sea. The first real offshore oil deposit was tapped in 1947 in the Gulf of Mexico.

A consequence of the oil crisis

Since then, the proportion of crude oil produced offshore has risen rapidly. Intensification of exploration at sea was expensive, and as long as the oil wells on the mainland continued to gush, offshore production remained a side business for the multinational oil companies.

This situation changed overnight in 1973 when the cartel of oil producing countries, OPEC, pushed up the price for the black gold.

Within a short space of time, a barrel of oil (42 US gallons) shot from $3 US to just under $30 US. In view of this development, the production of offshore oil began to make economic sense. Furthermore, oil from the sea gave the industrial countries more independence from the crisis-prone Gulf region, which was still the number one oil supplier.

In the great oil terminals such as this one in Singapore, crude oil is stored in tanks and then processed in local refineries. The harbor waters must be deep enough for the jumbo tankers.

Close to the Arabian deserts, geological surveys also revealed rich deposits of oil under the sea – in the Persian Gulf. Oil pumped from the tank farms into the bowels of supertankers or via pipelines to harbors at the Red Sea and the Mediterranean is offshore oil – from storage tanks off the coasts of Bahrain, Qatar, and Kuwait.

However, these deposits are not so high-yielding and cannot compete with the enormous Ghawar Field in the desert of Saudi Arabia, which has been producing oil for many years.

Rich deposits on land explain why offshore exploitation began relatively late. Not only are the oil fields in the Persian Gulf very substantial, but also the sea between the Arabian Peninsula and Iran is ideal for offshore production. The waters are shallow and protected from the open sea and the area is only very seldom plagued by heavy storms, such as those experienced in the North Sea.

Just off the United Arab Emirates, on the tanker route through the Straits of Hormuz, are numerous small oil fields, like a patchwork quilt in the Persian Gulf. The largest of them, Kahfij, extends close to Saudi Arabia. Next to Abu Dhabi and Qatar, the kingdom is the largest offshore producer on the Persian Gulf. Qatar has an even more lucrative source of income in the Persian Gulf – just off the coast is the Northwest Dome, a gigantic deposit of natural gas.

Black gold in Southeast Asia

Other regions where oil companies produce significant quantities of black gold from the sea are in Southeast Asian waters. Compared with fields in the Persian Gulf, they are small; but for the Kingdom of Brunei on the east coast of Borneo they are the source of the country's fabulous wealth.

As in the Persian Gulf, the offshore activities are offshoots of production on land, especially in Indonesia and Malaysia. Malaysia produces oil from the South China Sea off the coast of the Malayan Peninsula and the east coast of Borneo.

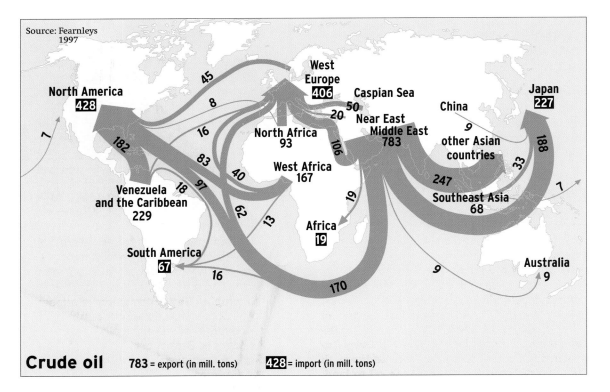

Crude oil   783 = export (in mill. tons)   428 = import (in mill. tons)

The industrial countries meet their requirements for crude oil mainly from Arabian and Caribbean sources. This map indicates what quantities of crude oil are exported to which countries.

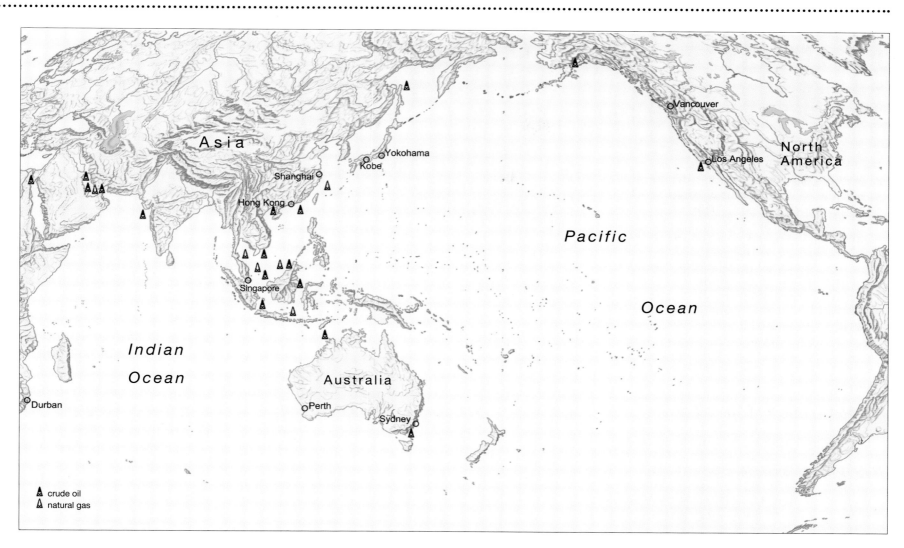

The greatest oil deposits are to be found in Arabia and the Persian Gulf. Increasing prices mean that even smaller sources are profitable, which accounts for the development of oil fields on the coasts of Southeast Asia. The map gives an overview of new production areas.

The Indonesians discovered oil sites in the Java Sea north of Java and east of Sumatra, as well as in the Straits of Makassar between Borneo and Sulawesi. On the other hand, Thailand can only meet its energy requirements from significant deposits of natural gas in the Gulf of Thailand, which are linked to the mainland by means of one of the longest underwater pipelines in the world.

Other western Pacific deposits

In the 1990s, the attention of the oil companies turned to the coast of Vietnam where there were thought to be rich deposits. After decades of war and subsequent isolation, production is still modest and international companies have long since staked their claims on the east and south coast.

Recently, there has been a marked improvement in anchoring methods and technology on oil rigs.

Further to the north, off the coast of China, and even further to the Yellow Sea, numerous small fields are producing oil. However, they can in no way meet the requirements of China, even if the flat shelves reaching far out into the South China Sea do provide excellent prerequisites for offshore production. As well, there is a snag – the rigs and their anchorage are regularly lashed by tropical storms.

All around Australia are numerous oil fields – small, but producing enough to be profitably exploited. They lie at the east exit of the Bass Strait between Victoria and Tasmania and off the northwest coast in the Indian Ocean, where small gas fields have also been discovered. And last, but not least, small deposits of crude oil and natural gas are to be found under the shallow waters of the Timor Sea.

Difficult production from the sea

Crude oil production from the sea bed remains both a technical and an environmental problem. The more shallow and more calm the waters, the easier it is to erect the rigs on steel barges on the sea bed.

The required technology becomes more costly at depths of more than 50 meters (165 ft.) and particularly at the edge of the continental shelf. The floating platforms must be anchored firmly enough to withstand storms and waves. In addition, it is often difficult to transport the oil to land. All these reasons are why the rich deposits under the sea have not been fully exploited – at least, not yet.

FACTS AND FIGURES

The gas-guzzling automobile.

Crude oil from the sea
The annual world production of crude oil is about 3.4 billion tons. Deposits from the Near East account for about 28 percent, with 1 billion tons; approximately 15 percent of world production comes from North America, and West Europe contributes about 10 percent, with 330 million tons.
The proportion of offshore-produced oil is presently at 20 percent. Even countries in the Near East are now pumping increasing amounts of black gold from the Arabian Gulf – Abu Dhabi is already up to 55 percent. Elsewhere, the quota of offshore oil is even higher: In the Kingdom of Brunei the figure is 60 percent, in Australia 85 percent. And there are numerous other countries, for example Malaysia, who extract the sought-after commodity only from the sea.

Atlantic and Alaskan oil deposits

New oil fields are being developed continuously in continental shelf regions. The North Sea production triggered an "oil rush" in the surrounding countries.

●●● The experts from the oil companies remained skeptical. How could we pump oil out of the sea without a fixed link to the land? One small company from Oklahoma took up the challenge. The managers of the company saw no opportunity to compete with the mighty worldwide production companies of the day and claim rich deposits on land, so they turned their attention to where competition was not so fierce: to the sea; to be more exact, to the Gulf of Mexico, where the oil explorers struck it lucky.

On a clear Sunday morning in October 1947, they discovered a high-yield deposit 15 kilometers (9 mi.) off the coast of Louisiana.

The oil finds in the Gulf of Mexico were at that time, as they still are today, of great importance for the USA. Soon, row upon row of oil rigs could be seen in the Gulf.

A dense network of pipelines

The oil companies no longer restrict their activities to the comparatively flat shelf of the Gulf of Mexico, but are drilling at depths of more than 1,500 meters (5,000 ft.) into the sea bed. The numerous fields are linked to the refineries and harbors on land by a dense network of pipelines. In the Gulf and off the coast of Mexico, the oil fields are strung like pearls on a chain, producing oil south of the port town of Tampico and the

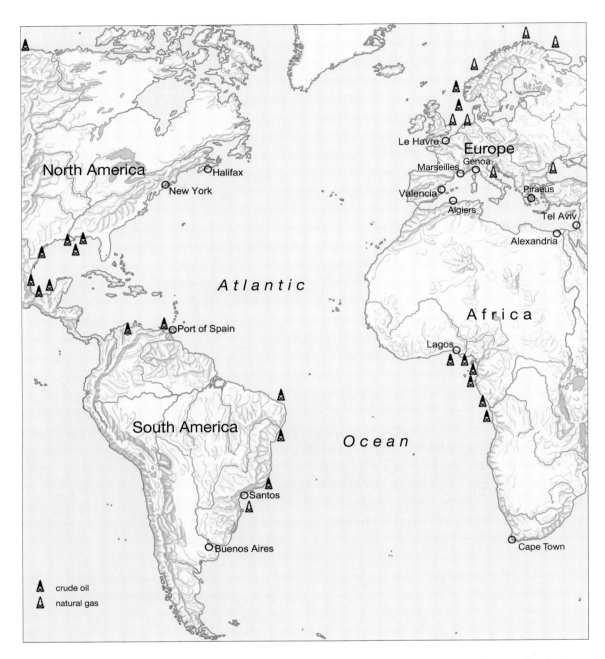

On the double American continents, the most important oil fields are to be found off Alaska and in the Caribbean. For Northern Europe, the North Sea is the major site.

An oil rig is towed out to sea and positioned off the coast of Norway.

oil center Coatzacoacos, in the Bay of Campeche.

Oil still comes from where offshore exploration had its early successes – off the coast of California. The deposits are modest in comparison to the fields in the Gulf of Mexico region, but the exploitation of resources on the continental shelf of the Pacific between Santa Maria and south of Los Angeles is still worthwhile.

The Americans also exploit the significant oil fields off the north coast of Alaska in Prudhoe Bay. However, extreme weather in these arctic latitudes make production dif-

ficult, particularly since transport of the oil by sea is not possible. The oil is pumped by pipeline straight across country to Valdez on the south coast of Alaska.

The town on the Prince William Sound was made sadly famous in 1989 when the supertanker *Exxon Valdez* ran aground on the rocky Bligh Reef a few kilometers off the coast on 24 March. It lost 240,000 barrels of oil – resulting in a disastrous oil slick that devastated the natural habitats in Alaska.

Search parties looking for offshore deposits struck lucky in the 1920s in the Maracaibo Sea of Venezuela. Most experts at the time were certain that every dollar invested in looking for oil in the tropics was a wasted dollar. But the facts were to prove the opposite. In 1922 the Borrosso deposit in the La Rosa Field broke out with such force that suddenly all the oil companies became interested in Venezuela. Besides these rich

deposits, a large number of other deposits – albeit small – were discovered in the coastal waters to the north of the country. Venezuela owes its position as a leading oil-producing country mainly to the deposits in the Maracaibo Sea and on land.

Not far from the mainland, off the delta of the Rio Grande and south of Trinidad, the oil seekers later discovered numerous minor deposits on the continental shelf.

Along the South American coast, larger offshore fields have only been developed on the continental shelf that lies off Brazil – about 200 kilometers (125 mi.) into the Atlantic and linked by pipelines to the port town of Campos.

Oil rush in the North Sea

The greatest challenges in offshore business for oil companies can be met in the North Sea. The rough and stormy sea

An environmental disaster amid picturesque scenery: the British tanker "Braer" ran aground on 5 January 1993 just off the Shetland Isles. In total 84,413 tons of light crude and 1,700 tons of heavy crude were spilled, polluting large areas of natural beauty along the coastline.

makes the highest demands on technology and much patience is needed to search for oil on its bed.

After finding only a series of "dry holes," the US company Phillips Petroleum were ready to break off their explorations in the North Sea, which had begun in the 1960s. But because the oil rig *Ocean Viking* was on charter, they undertook one last attempt – in extremely adverse weather. The rig threatened to capsize and an emergency evacuation of the men had already been arranged, but the rig and the men held out.

In November 1969, the *Ocean Viking* found oil in the Ekofisk Field at 3,000 meters (10,000 ft.) – and it was oil of an astonishingly good quality.

This triggered an oil rush in the North Sea, which was later intensified in the 1970s by the oil crisis. The neighboring North Sea countries – Britain, Norway, Denmark, the Netherlands, and Germany – had agreed on their claims prior to this, and now these "newcomers" started to erect one rig after the other, scoring one bull's eye after the other.

In 1971, the British came across the gigantic Brent Field about 200 kilometers (124 mi.) east of the Shetlands. Names like Stafjord, Piper, Columba, and Balder were given to the new sites.

Well-paid but gruelling work: oil workers on an oil rig in the North Sea

The giant oil rigs erected today in the North Sea are frequently exposed to gale force winds and heavy seas as high as 17 meters (58 ft.). However, they are designed to withstand "the wave of the century" of twice that height if need be. Still, oil production in the North Sea remains an adventure. When "Blanke Hans" (the name given by German seamen to the North Sea, when it is really rough) is in a bad mood, it can be decidedly harsh – a hard job for the crews on the rig, for the nippy supply boats, the pipe-laying barges, and the helicopter crews that sometimes have to land on the platforms by performing neck-breaking maneuvers.

FACTS AND FIGURES

Commuters to the platform

The loading area of a drilling platform is limited. Everything needed for drilling and transporting the oil has to be brought from land including fuel, water, technical equipment, machines, drilling rods, and pipes. Special supply boats are used. These are particularly seaworthy and maneuvrable, and are usually designed as stern loaders with open loading areas, so that they can be quickly unloaded by cranes on the platform.

Urgently-required materials or spares are transported by helicopter from the supply base to the platforms. The same is true for the staff, i.e., the drilling teams, when there is a shift change, and specialists who are only on the platform for a short time to carry out special work, for example, divers who control and check the underwater parts of the platform, the pipelines, and safety precautions at regular intervals.

Mineral resources under the sea

In the search for new sources of raw materials, exploration of the sea's mineral resources has produced some interesting findings.

● ● ● Oil and gas exploration at sea has shown that modern technology allows exploration at greater depths. And it is in these depths that the sea keeps treasures other than black gold. However, it is still extremely awkward and uneconomical to develop these sources. But as the resources on land slowly decline, marine geologists are certain that the exploitation of offshore mineral resources will gain in importance in the coming years.

The first offshore mines

Today, quartz and carbon-rich sand, pebbles, shells, and clay from coastal waters are being extracted worldwide, in particular by the USA, Japan, the Netherlands, Great Britain, and Denmark. Specially-designed ships pump the material into large transport vessels, using bucket excavators or suction dredgers, or it is washed directly ashore through pipelines.

These materials are used in the building industry, in civil engineering for above-ground and underground workings, in road building, and last but not least, to repair what the sea has eroded. Sand and pebbles are used to fill in beaches that have been washed away and to secure whole lengths of coastline.

Much more sought after than sand, pebbles, and shells are "strategic" raw materials deposited in the sea – metals such as gold, platinum, copper, titanium, manganese, and tin, as well as phosphates and other minerals such as salts and barytes.

The extraction of metals from the sea is still not common, although titanium is extracted from the shelf waters off western Australia and tin off the coast of Indonesia. Every year in the waters northeast of Sumatra, particularly around the islands of Bangka and Belitung, a fleet of more than 30 ships equip-

"Hot springs" found on the edges of the Earth's plates and on volcanic subsoils spew out mineral substances from the interior of the Earth. Objects referred to as "black smokers" - tubes that are many meters in length - develop from these deposits. Some of these tubes have been brought up to the surface. Bacteria that are the basis of existence for life in the deep seas surround the hot springs.

ped with bucket excavators extract up to 40 million cubic meters (1,400 mill. cu. ft.) of sediment containing tin from 50 meters (160 ft.) down.

Enormous fields of manganese nodules

For decades, marine geologists have explored the oceans looking for deposits that would one day be economically worthwhile to extract.

At great depths, they have discovered enormous fields of manganese nodules. Made of brittle sedimentary rock in a variety of shapes and sizes, these contain not only manganese but also copper, iron, nickel, and cobalt. The richest deposits with the highest metal concentration are in the Clarion and Clipperton Fracture Zones between Hawaii and the North American continent, where they are already being "fished" out of the sea on large scale by specially designed dredgers.

More of these nodule fields are to be found in the South Pacific between New Zealand and South America, as well as in the North Pacific. Deposits discovered in the Indian Ocean and Atlantic Ocean are smaller, however, and the mineral concentration in the nodules is lower.

In addition, sediments containing metals and sulfides are thought to occur where the tectonic plates of the oceans and continents meet and slide against one another, for example on the East Pacific Ridge and between the Galapagos Islands and the coast of Ecuador.

The bed of the Red Sea also has a layer containing metals at a depth of 100 meters (328 ft.). These fields have a high concentration of minerals, particularly iron, but also manganese, tin, and copper.

Ownership issues

Exploitation of the resources under the sea encounters not only technical limits, but also numerous political and economical discussions on the question of who is allowed to exploit the international waters. Therefore, it is a matter that takes on both economic and ecological issues. As yet, there are no worldwide, binding regulations to prevent international consortiums and mining companies from claiming concessions to exploit resources in the sea, especially in the Pacific between Hawaii and the USA.

For the Americans in Alaska it is easier. Directly off the coast, west and east of the town of Nome, are considerable gold deposits. These sites have been known since the 19th century. In those days, the precious metal was washed out of the sand from the beaches for as long as the hard arctic winter allowed. Later, piers were built in the shallow waters. Deposits in deeper waters are reached today by drilling holes through the ice – which covers the sea for almost the

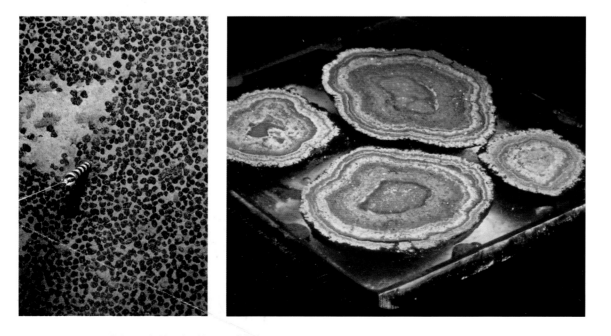

Manganese nodules at the bottom of the deep sea contain copper, iron, nickel, and cobalt. When cut open, they reveal their development over millions of years.

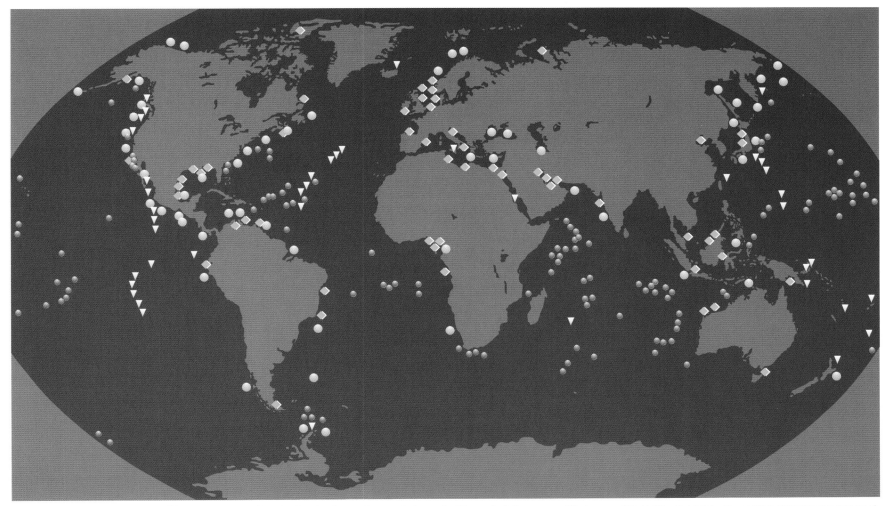

manganese　▼ massive sulfide 🖤 methane hydrate ◇ crude oil, natural gas　　Sources: Spektrum der Wissenschaft, Resources and Environment/World Atlas, Part I, Peter Herzig, TU Bergakademie Freiberg et al.

Manganese nodules, sulfides, methane, and crude oil are the most important raw materials, which are interesting for mining. This map shows the oceanic regions where particularly large reserves are deposited.

whole year – into the sea bed, bringing the gold-bearing sand to the surface.

Since the 1960s, there has been exploration of the sea bed off the southwest coast of Africa for the hardest material on Earth – diamonds. Several companies, including the diamond magnate De Beers, excavate from ships or from supported platforms in the sea off Namibia and South Africa at depths of 180 meters (590 ft.).

On site, the rough diamonds are washed out of the extracted sediments. In the future, excavator ships will be replaced by remote-controlled underwater bulldozers which, with their suction nozzles, will pump sand and stones through a pipeline into a waiting vessel.

The need for energy

Not all these marine explorations are concerned with sought-after metals or precious stones. Energy is often the main issue. It is hoped that, in the future, a large part of the increasing worldwide demand for energy can be met with fuels from the oceans.

Geologists speculate that there are gigantic reserves of coal under the continental shelves, stretching from the mainland seams far out into the sea. In the North Sea, drilling in already-developed gas fields has produced high-grade coal from a depth of approximately 7,000 meters (23,000 ft.).

Such depths are too great for present-day extraction methods, but engineers are already developing processes that would make coal extraction from the seas an economically viable project.

Furthermore, the oceans also conceal a far greater energy potential. In the sea bed of deeper waters there is a layer of sediment several hundred meters thick containing vast amounts of methane in the form of frozen, ice-like gas hydrates. Scientists estimate that the amount of methane bound up in the sea is twice as large as all the known resources of fossil fuel on Earth. That leads them to hope that in the not too distant future, methane could become an increasing component in our energy mix and could gradually replace conventional fossil fuels. However, a profitable method of extracting the gas from the sea must be developed.

The treasures of the sea: suction dredgers haul up sand and pebbles to be used for coastal reconstruction work.

FACTS AND FIGURES

Energy on ice

The deposits of underwater methane gas could be the answer to the world's energy problems. But so far, there is no technological process to extract it economically, as methane requires extreme physical conditions. In the sea it occurs on the continental slopes, and then only at a depth of 500 meters (1,640 ft.) or more. It is difficult to gather as it is stored in sediment several hundred meters thick at near-freezing water temperatures. It occurs in an icy form due to the pressure of the deep sea. As soon as methane hydrate leaves these temperatures and pressure conditions, at the surface, it decomposes and the flammable gas escapes.

Those industrial countries who speculate that there are extensive methane deposits on their coasts are investing in methane gas technology with the goal of being able to harvest the energy-rich gas fields. However, so far no-one has come up with a cost-efficient method, so it will probably take decades before these deposits can be extracted in economically viable volumes.

The Arctic Ocean and its perpetual ice

Mineral resources from the north polar region require safe transport routes through the icy seas – hence the use of the Northwest and Northeast Passages.

●●● The Arctic is the smallest ocean on Earth, with an area of 12.2 million square kilometres (4.7 mill. sq. mi.). It is up to 4,000 meters (13,000 ft.) deep. In the winter, 95 percent of it is covered in a thick layer of ice, and in the short Arctic summer, about half of it remains covered.

Most of the ports in the north polar regions are only open for shipping during a few weeks of the year. Icy conditions, heavy storms, low temperatures, and frequent fog severely limit shipping, unless, of course, the ships "take a dive", as the American *Nautilus* did in 1958 when it proved that there is a passageway under the ice. The nuclear-powered submarine submerged off the north coast of Alaska and, after crossing under the North Pole, resurfaced off Spitsbergen.

Vega's journey

The underwater journey of the *Nautilus* beneath the Arctic ice cap was nothing more than a demonstration of military strength in the days of the Cold War. It fueled the imaginations, however, of those who dreamed of underwater freighters or underwater tow trains, but these dreams all came to no avail.

Of greater interest, and more economical, was a safe passageway during the Arctic summer, when the ice masses have melted to a minimum. In the 16th century, the English tried without success to find a way along the Norwegian coast. But it was a Swedish baron

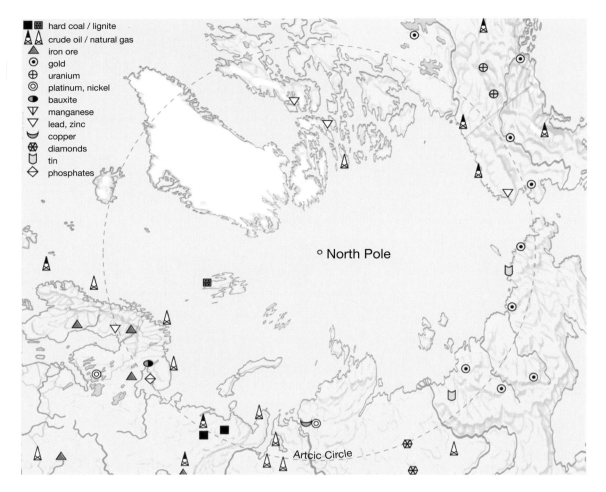

hard coal / lignite
crude oil / natural gas
iron ore
gold
uranium
platinum, nickel
bauxite
manganese
lead, zinc
copper
diamonds
tin
phosphates

° North Pole

Artcic Circle

Mineral resources in the Arctic catchment area: sea routes on the Russian and North American sides are not navigable throughout the year, as shipping is hindered by polar ice.

The port of Murmansk is of major importance for Siberian mineral resources as it remains more or less free of ice, thus allowing the shipment of goods.

named Adolf Erik Nordenskjöld who, on his ship the *Vega*, in 1879, succeeded in crossing from the Norwegian Tromsö, through the Barents Sea and south of Novaya Zemlya into the scarcely 85-kilometer (53-mile) wide Bering Strait that separates Alaska from Russia and leads into the North Pacific.

Today the Northeast Passage is used by specially-equipped freighters and tankers, although only for a short time during the year. Giant icebreakers, some of them nuclear-powered, keep the sea routes along the northern Siberian coast free of ice in the months from June to October.

A shortcut was also sought by English seafarers, who hoped to find a shorter route to India and China from the west side of the Atlantic – through a northwest passage from the northeast coast of the American continent through the Baffin Sea, along the west coast of Greenland and through the Canadian Arctic Archipelago. The first to succeed was the Norwegian polar explorer Roald Amundsen, who took the 4,820-kilometer (3,600-mi.) route between 1903 and 1906.

Passageways for shipping natural resources

Neither the Northwest Passage nor the Northeast Passage has declined in importance for shipping since its discovery, because in the following years rich mineral resources were found around the Arctic. The gold-seekers in Alaska were followed at the beginning of the last century by the mining companies who successfully explored for coal, ore, and minerals.

Later they were joined by the powerful multinational oil companies who discovered rich deposits in the Canadian Arctic and Alaska. The Americans gave a spectacular demonstration on how to transport the "black gold" from polar regions into the industrial centers of the world in 1969: They piloted the icebreaking supertanker *Manhattan* through the Northwest Passage 4,800 kilometers (3,000 mi.) from the North Atlantic to Prudhoe Bay in

The cruiser "Hanseatic" makes regular tourist trips through the ice off Spitsbergen. For $20,000 US, adventure-seeking travelers can even book the journey through the entire Northeast Passage.

Alaska and back. In the end, however, it turned out that it is more cost-efficient to build pipelines through which the oil can be pumped to ice-free ports on the North Pacific coast of Alaska.

Other mineral resources also find their way south by road or rail, in so far that it is worth extracting them in the inhospitable north. The Northwest Passage, therefore, does not truly meet the initial and daring expectations made of it by shipping.

In comparison, the Northeast Passage is much busier, especially the western part. Siberia is held to be one of the richest regions in the world with regard to mineral resources. For years, rivers have been used in attempts to transport wood, coal, ore, and minerals north over almost impassable distances. The rich oil and gas deposits are taken via pipelines from the west Siberian lowlands to the large ports of the Northeast Passage – to Murmansk and Archangel, to Salechard or Nowy Port on the Ob delta to Dudinka or Ust-Port on the Yenisey delta. Practically all of the sea freight from there – more than 5 million tons a year – goes to the West.

For some years now, the polar routes have become a standard part of the tourist economy. Cruisers call at Spitsbergen or travel to the edge of the pack ice and, for just under $20,000 US, the complete Northeast Passage can be booked.

FACTS AND FIGURES

Arctic sea routes

In the vast expanses of the Arctic lie rich deposits of mineral resources which can only be extracted under extremely difficult conditions. Siberia's permafrost ground is practically impenetrable, thawing out a little for just a short time in summer. In addition, the rivers along which the mineral resources could be shipped to the seaports in the north are frozen solid from October to May. Siberia contains almost all the mineral resources that are significant for a national economy today: coal, nickel, copper, platinum, cobalt, gold, silver, and diamonds, as well as crude oil and natural gas, produced from the impassable swamplands of the Siberian lowlands and the provinces of northern Siberia, and then pumped directly to western Europe via pipelines.

Resources are not so high-yielding in the Arctic around the Northwest Passage. In the last century, hundreds of thousands of people joined the gold rush in Alaska. Today this valuable metal is still extracted in many places in the American state, and so are silver, lead, and tin. Small deposits of these minerals are also found in the Arctic islands of Canada. In spite of crude oil and natural gas deposits in the Arctic, the only significant fields to be explored are in the Canadian Mackenzie Bay, and on Melville and Bathurst Islands.

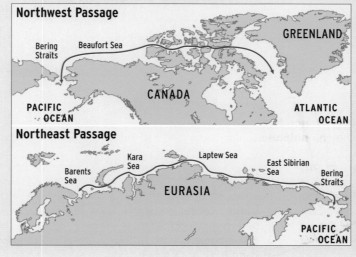

Northwest Passage

Bering Straits Beaufort Sea GREENLAND CANADA PACIFIC OCEAN ATLANTIC OCEAN

Northeast Passage

Barents Sea Kara Sea Laptew Sea East Sibirian Sea Bering Straits EURASIA PACIFIC OCEAN

Antarctica – the white continent

The Antarctic, with an area of 13.7 million square kilometers (5.3 mill. sq. mi.), is the fourth largest continent on Earth. It is rich in fish, but poor in mineral resources.

●●● The Antarctic is the highest, driest, coldest, windiest, and most desolate place on the planet. The Russian research station Vostok measured temperatures of −89.2° C (−128° F) and winds up to 320 kilometers an hour (199 mph) raging across the icy wastes.

The Antarctic measures 13.7 million square kilometers (5.3 mill. sq. mi.) including all the islands and the shelf ice; the landmass alone is 11.9 million square kilometers (4.6 mill. sq. mi.) – around 2.5 million square kilometers (965,000 mill. sq. mi.) more than the area of the USA. However, the continent is 99 percent hidden by a thick sheet of ice. The thickest point measured by researchers was in Adélie Land, at 4,476 meters (15,700 ft.).

This inhospitable continent is separated from Australia by over 3,600 kilometers (2,237 mi.), and the nearest point in South America is still about 1,400 kilometers (870 mi.) away from the Antarctic Peninsula. The Antarctic was discovered comparatively late – not until 1820. The first expedition was led by the Norwegian-born Carsten Borchgrevink, who went on land at Cape Adare after spending the winter under extreme conditions of cold.

On 14 December 1911, a Norwegian team led by the polar explorer Roald Amundsen was the first to reach the South Pole. Only 21 days later, the British explorer Robert Scott, along with two of his companions, froze to death on the return journey. His countryman Ernest Henry Shackleton became a popular hero as a result of his polar expedition. After his ship, the *Endurance*, had become enclosed and crushed in the pack ice in November 1915, the explorer and his crew set out on a long foot march and then took an open boat over 800 miles by sea from Elephant Island to a manned whaling station at South Georgia.

No-man's land

The world's great powers were always keen to legally claim land in the Antarctic, especially as they hoped to find valuable resources in the south polar regions. Geologists speculated that the rock under the ice would contain coal, ore, rare metals, and precious stones.

Scientists have discovered that the geological formation of Antarctica is similar to that of Australia. About 250 million years ago, Africa, Australia, South America, India, and the Antarctic were one landmass – the supercontinent of Gondwana. Then the Earth's crust began to move again and the landmasses began to drift apart. About 30 million years ago, Antarctica finally separated from Australia and moved gradually to its present location.

The dreams of the Great Powers to claim land in the Antarctic came to nothing. Today, an international treaty, signed by 42 nations, stipulates that the south polar region is a no-man's land. The whole area

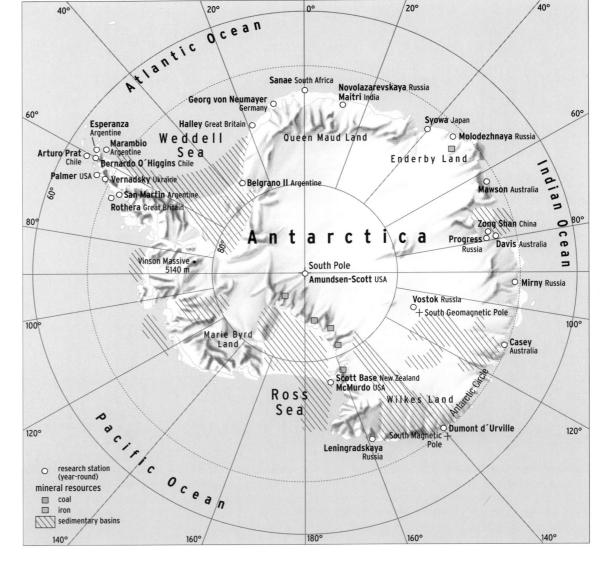

There are no permanent settlements in the inhospitable Antarctic; only numerous research stations have been established there. Under international law, the Antarctic is no-man's land.

On 11 December 1911, Roald Amundsen became the first man to reach the South Pole.

south of 60° latitude is to be used solely for peaceful scientific investigation. The extraction of mineral resources was excluded definitively by an additional clause to the Antarctic Treaty.

Besides, exploitation of any possible deposits would hardly be profitable. In order to reach the sites, the great sheet of ice would have to be penetrated, and the construction and maintenance of any infrastructure to transport resources to ice-free waters and then to load them onto ships would be much too costly.

Fresh water as a commodity

However, one raw material that could become an extremely rare commodity in the coming years can be found in vast amounts in the Antarctic: fresh water. In fact, Antarctica holds about 70 percent of the world's total fresh water reserves in the form of ice. These almost inexhaustible resources could one day become a popular Antarctic export. "Little" icebergs comprising 10 million cubic meters (350 million cubic feet) of water could be towed by powerful

The great ice shelf seas spread out from the Antarctic continent. The picture shows the German research vessel "Polar Star" lying at the edge of the Filchner Ice Shelf hoisting the dismantled buildings of a research station on board.

ships to the coasts of countries suffering water shortages.

Even if 20 percent were to melt on the way, the remaining water reservoir could supply a whole country for months on end. To make a comparison: A city like Hamburg, with its 1.7 million inhabitants, uses 120 million cubic meters (4,200 mill. cu. ft.) of water annually.

An enormous biomass

The southern regions of the Atlantic, the Pacific, and the Indian oceans that surround the Antarctic are decidedly rich in fish and are home to, in particular, the Atlantic krill. There are an estimated 500 million tons of these minute crustaceans representing the greatest biomass on Earth. They feed on plankton and are themselves food for whales, penguins, and seals – they could also become an important part of the human food chain. The Ukraine, Poland, and Japan already fish around the Antarctic for these protein-rich sea creatures.

The extreme climatic conditions in the south polar regions have made the Antarctic an international scientific investigation project. Numerous countries "share" the territory for their scientific research, among them France, Norway, Great Britain, Argentina, New Zealand, the USA, Germany, and Russia.

They maintain research stations there and investigate global warming, the expansion of the hole in the ozone layer, and possible changes in climate. Geologists collect information regarding the formation of the Antarctic landmass, oceanologists observe changes in the surrounding seas, experts in ice and snow measure glaciers, and astronomers observe the stars as seen from the Antarctic. All the countries have undertaken to make the results of their research work accessible to all.

As before, life in the now 42 stations, which are also maintained over winter, is hard even though they are equipped with modern conveniences. The big camps are regularly supplied by air, weather permitting, and in favorable weather conditions the research vessels and supply ships set off for support bases near the coasts.

In the meantime, there are numerous worldwide enterprises that have specialized in maintaining links to the Antarctic. Some of them offer trips to the Antarctic as a tourist attraction – why not take a trip to the endless south polar ice fields, in the tracks of Amundsen and Scott?

A Garden of Eden in the sea

Coral reefs only grow in the warm, clear waters of the Tropics. They serve as a habitat for a great number of marine organisms.

● ● ● Without the coral reefs our planet Earth would have a very different appearance. The great mountain ranges, such as the Dolomites or the Dachstein Massif, owe their existence to the corals. They, too, were fossil reefs pushed upwards when the Alps were formed.

The Great Barrier Reef – the largest construction on Earth

Uncountable islands were formed (and are still being formed) by corals. The island world of Oceania consists only of reefs. Coral reefs also shape the appearance of the planet indirectly. Since they live exclusively in shallow, sunlight-intensive waters mostly near coasts, they act as breakwaters, protecting the land and its inhabitants from the destructive power of the waves.

The architectural skills of coral are unsurpassed by any other living creature. The largest construction on Earth is not man-made, but coral-made – it is the Great Barrier Reef off the northeast coast of Australia. It is an awe-inspiring natural wonder that is 2,000 kilometers (1,242 mi.) long and up to 250 kilometers (155 mi.) wide, covering an area of more than 200,000 square kilometers (77,200 sq. mi.).

Compared with their construction feats, corals are minute, barely an inch in size. All corals belong to a group of organisms that scientists call coelenterates, from the Greek word *koilos*, meaning "cave," and *enteron*, meaning "intestine."

Indeed, the coral is a small polyp consisting of a short, hollow cylindrical structure that functions like an intestine, digesting food. At the upper end is a mouth-like opening surrounded by tentacles with which the polyp catches the tiniest marine animals, paralyzing its prey with poison.

Other types of coral, however, have another, much more important source of energy. They have a symbiotic relationship with minute algae that is beneficial to both species.

Clear water is essential

The algae live in the cells of the coral polyp, which supplies them with carbon dioxide, nitrates, and phosphates. The metabolism of the polyp results in waste products which the algae then in turn convert into hydrocarbons and oxygen. However, in order for this conversion to happen, the algae need sunlight – and that is why coral can only survive in clear, sun-filled, light-intensive, waters and are not found at greater depths.

Using the carbon of the hydrocarbons and the calcium of the sea, the coral polyp produces a tiny skeleton of calcium carbonate (limestone). Numerous other polyps do the same – and so, little by little, a coral reef is formed.

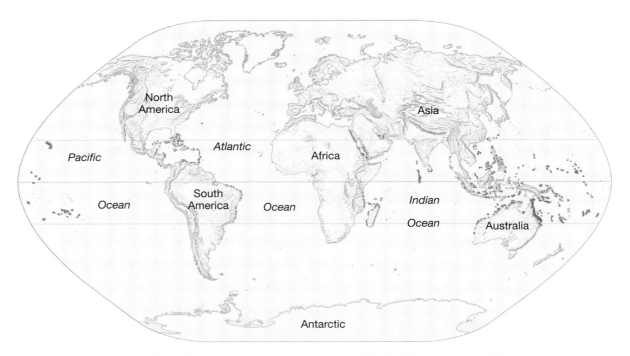

North America

Asia

Atlantic

Pacific

Africa

Ocean

South America

Ocean

Indian Ocean

Australia

Antarctic

Coral reefs (marked in red) are limited to the Equatorial Belt. They can only thrive in clean water and are considered to indicate the ecological balance of the seas.

The colorful splendor of healthy corals.

Scorpion fish off the coast of the Maldives.

Coral banks are paradise for fish.

Corals reproduce by a simple dividing process called budding. The parent coral divides itself to produce a "daughter" polyp that remains attached to the parent. Continuous division gradually results in a colony where the surface consists of living creatures and the center is formed from the dead skeletons of former polyp generations.

Asexual and sexual reproduction

Corals can also reproduce sexually and often all of them spawn in one single night. On the Great Barrier Reef this event always takes place in the week in which there is a full moon in March, around the time of the spring equinox – such synchronized behavior of more than 130 species and several million individual creatures is unique in the animal kingdom.

Millions upon millions of eggs and sperm swim about in the water, fertilize one another, and develop into larvae. These drift around for several days or even several weeks on the surface of the water, then settle down on to a hard surface, which could be a piece of dead coral, a rock, or a shipwreck. The larvae then turn into polyps, begin to excrete calcium carbonate, and found new colonies by budding.

No colony resembles another. The confusing variety of shapes and sizes does not depend on the type of coral polyp but on the location where they are created. Where waves are strong, the polyps grow together as a stable flat patch; if the environment is more protected, however, the form is often graceful and extensively branched.

Coral reefs will only grow in warm, shallow waters, away from river deltas. Most of them can be found between the two

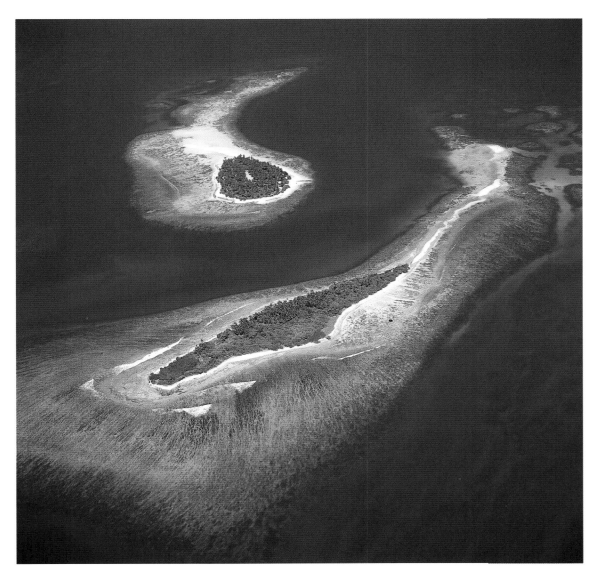

Coral banks act like breakwaters, protecting the islands in the open sea. In the Pacific Ocean, Indonesia owes part of its attraction to the ecological system of the coral reefs.

Tropics, mainly in the Caribbean, surrounding the islands in the Indian Ocean and the South Pacific, in the Red Sea, and in the Persian Gulf. However, coral will also settle where the warm ocean currents flow, for example, off the coasts of Florida, or the Bermudas which are washed by the warm Gulf Stream.

A coral reef is not a uniform formation but consists of different zones. The reef top is sometimes dry and can be colonized by particularly robust species. The slope falling into the lagoon (the so-called reef terrace where the currents are weaker) is especially rich in corals. Thanks to its structure, the coral reef is a habitat for a great variety of organisms and is always teeming with life.

A paradise for predatory fish

Each morning, as soon as it is light, the active predators, such as sharks or barracudas, are off hunting their prey; bright yellow butterfly fish swim along the reef to nibble coral polyps with their long, drawn out mouths; colorful parrot fish bite off branches of coral with their beak-like mouths; enormous shoals of fusilier fish meander through the reef looking for minute marine organisms; and puffers blow themselves up to an impressive size to frighten away their enemies. Then, when evening comes, they all disappear to their hiding places in the reef.

Soon the nocturnal hunters are out and about. Groupers hang around beneath overhangs; cardinal and hussar fish go off looking for food. It is also at night that the coral polyps unfold their tentacles to catch their prey, since their helpers, the algae, cannot supply them with food in the dark.

Since the beginning of humanity, the riches of the coral reef have supplied humans not only with food, but also with building materials, medications, and jewelry. Coral reefs form natural harbors, and in coastal areas they are a major form of protection against the breakers. If they were to disappear, a great deal of money would have to be spent on measures to compensate for their loss.

And yet, the world's reefs are very much threatened by human activities. Reefs are subjected to waste waters and toxic chemicals. They suffocate under the eroded earth and mud from coastal building sites. They are smashed by the anchors from tourist boats and luxury cruisers, and are destroyed by ignorant and inconsiderate divers.

There are often hundreds of different types of coral living together in a coral reef. The upper part of a polyp's body is edged by tentacles, with which it catches its prey. Many coral types can form gigantic colonies.

FACTS AND FIGURES

Types of reefs

A FRINGING REEF grows near the coast and is the most common form worldwide. It begins to form directly on the shore and grows outwards into sea. In an advanced stage of its growth, a lagoon is formed between the coast and the reef. Reefs in the Red Sea are almost exclusively fringing reefs.

A BARRIER REEF forms on the edges of continental shelves and from the beginning is separated from the land by a lagoon. The best-known example is the Great Barrier Reef off the north coast of Australia, which consists of a conglomerate of individual reefs and accounts for 3 percent of all the world's reefs.

AN ATOLL is a fringing reef round a volcanic island in the open sea. If the  island submerges, the fringing reef becomes a circular barrier reef with a 30-80 meter (98 to 262-ft.) deep lagoon in the middle. The Maldives in the Indian Ocean are atolls.

A PLATFORM REEF is formed in the middle of the sea in shallow regions on the sea bed. Unlike fringing reefs and barrier reefs, it grow out to all sides and is mostly oval in shape. An example is the Cardagos reef of the northern Mascarene Plateau in the Indian Ocean.

Sun, sea, and white beaches

The coasts of the Mediterranean and the Caribbean, Southeast Asia and Hawaii, which have become centers of the booming tourist industry, are under threat.

● ● ● In the late 1950s, sun-seeking vacationers from northern and central Europe discovered the south and the Mediterranean Sea. Hundreds and thousands of Germans, Britons, Dutch, and Scandinavians made their way across the Alpine passes into Italy. The beaches on the Adriatic and the Riviera attracted the tourists, and Italy's boom as a vacation destination began.

A few years later, hordes of vacationers invaded Spain – and Greece soon followed. Enormous holiday centers were built along the Costa Brava, on the Balearic Islands, the Canary Islands, and the islands of Greece.

The Mediterranean is still one of the major vacation areas in the world. About 120 million people spend their annual vacation in the surrounding countries, making up about 20 percent of all the tourists who are traveling around the globe. The nickname "bathtub of Europe" is aptly applied to the Mediterranean.

Vacation destination

Spain remains the tourist magnet, with 50 million visitors per year – 20 percent of them coming from Germany. The top destination is Majorca on the Balearic Islands.

But the boom has left its traces on the island. Although the people of Majorca earn good money from pale-faced northerners, the ecological and sociological consequences are, in some cases, disastrous. Drinking water is becoming scarce, village life is disappearing, and conventional economies such as agriculture are being crowded out completely – many a "campesino" has had to make room for a golf course.

Similar developments can be observed in other vacation regions of the Mediter-

Overseas tourism is becoming more and more synonymous with active vacations: sailing, scuba diving, and surfing are some of the attractions aimed at enticing tourists to visit the more remote parts of the globe.

ranean. The coasts of the Aegean islands, the Turkish Riviera, the Adriatic, or the Côte d'Azur hold an enormous attraction for vacationers from all parts of the world. And, naturally, the guests have to be provided with every possible facility – so competition is fierce! As a result, huge hotel complexes, restaurants, and sports and leisure centers have built up near the beaches of the Mediterranean.

The Mediterranean countries can be reached quickly, and immigration formalities are simple. Prices are on an international average; for example, a last-minute booking for a week under the Majorcan sunshine can be had for about $250 US – normally it would cost twice that much.

Be that as it may, the Europeans have already discovered a new cheap holiday island. Since the beginning of the 1990s, charter jets have been on course for the Dominican Republic, the second largest island in the Antilles. There is nowhere else where the vacationer can enjoy a Caribbean holiday for such a reasonable price. Traditionally, the dream beaches of the Bahamas were reserved for the wealthy, Jamaica was somewhere for dropouts, and Cuba was the destination of revolutio-

nists, but the "Dom Rep," as it is referred to, is within the reach of almost anyone's budget. Each year, 2.6 million tourists visit this Caribbean island; of these, half a million come from Germany. The tourist industry has long since become the major economic factor in this bitterly poor country. In the meantime, Cuba has also gone into business with its beautiful beaches and has opened up for tourists and foreign currencies.

One traditional vacation destination lies just 150 kilometers (90 mi.) from Cuba – the state of Florida. This peninsula on the southeast tip of the USA is not only a sunny retirement locale for US pensioners, but also a unique vacation experience for many Europeans. South Americans from Argentina or Chile enjoy the Spanish flair; literature fans from all over the world are drawn to Hemingway's house in the picturesque Florida Keys; bikers would not want to miss the annual bikers' rally at Daytona; and surfers seek to measure their strength against the waves on Cocoa Beach.

The fine, sandy beaches on the Atlantic side and along the Gulf of Mexico have long since become an alternative for former Mediterranean fans, and a flight across the Atlantic today can be had for around $350 US.

Other exotic locations

Many Europeans can book a two-week beach vacation in Thailand or Bali for little more than $750 US. Phuket, Bali, and Borneo

The South Sea islands are dream vacation spots for many tourists. The Beachcomber Hotel on Tahiti caters to the visitor's every wish.

are the most popular vacation regions in Southeast Asia, with the guests ranging from the ordinary tourist to the well-heeled undersea diving enthusiast.

The Maldives, Sri Lanka, and the Seychelles are also high on the list of sun-seekers. The beach at Goa on the Indian west coast is a venue for backpackers, dropouts from civilization, and hippies from all parts of the globe. Scuba divers explore the waters of the Indian Ocean, the Caribbean, the South Seas, and the Red Sea, with Egypt and Israel leading as destinations.

Only a few holiday-seekers get to see the real paradises – the small atoll states in the South Seas. No more than 200,000 people make the trip to French Polynesia. However, the reason for the relatively small number of visitors is not due to a lack of interest, but more to poor flight connections and high hotel prices.

The north also has its share of traditional bathing resorts stretching along the Baltic coast. Many resorts, with well-known names such as Heringsdorf, Binz, and Ahlbeck, have experienced a renaissance. Vacation destinations in Poland, Russia, and the Baltics are slowly recovering from the consequences of a planned economy. The climate with its hot summers is certainly one reason for a vacation at a Baltic beach resort.

In comparison, the North Sea is noticeably cooler and rougher – nothing for the sun worshippers. In spite of that, millions of people still visit the windy coasts each year, in Germany, the Netherlands, and the North Sea islands. The Danes have also focused on the tourists by building holiday homes, some of them directly on the dunes, for those who enjoy the wind and the weather on the North Sea at any time of the year.

In recent years, other coastal areas far away from traditional destinations have experienced an upswing. Bulgaria and Senegal are no longer a well-kept secret, and the Ukraine is planning to make Crimea more attractive to visitors.

The most famous beach in the world – the Copacabana in Rio de Janeiro – cannot complain about a lack of tourists. The French and the Portuguese fell to the charms of this beautiful bay on the South American Atlantic coast when they settled here in the 16th century at Sugarloaf. Today, Copacabana and the neighboring beach Ipanema have become the sandy catwalks for the vain, and in spite of the crime rate, economic crises, and low-quality water, the beaches have lost none of their attraction.

FACTS AND FIGURES

Surfing - not without its dangers

The Perfect Wave

Raging storms in the Bering Sea means just one thing for Hawaii – that fun is on the way. Far out in the ocean the heavy seas produce waves that wander southwards. Where the Hawaii islands jut out of the water, the long rolling waves are stopped and become higher and steeper. Off the north shore of Oahu they become enormous breakers, making the Pacific dream island, between Kahuku Point and Kaneohe Bay, a mecca for surfers. The origins of artistic riding of the waves are to be found in Polynesian culture. The sport boomed in the 1960s and, since then, has become an Olympic discipline.

Endangered marine life

The tropical shores of East India and the West Pacific, as well as the coasts of Asia, Africa, and the Caribbean, offer habitats to a rich variety of marine creatures. Today, however, these zones are in grave danger.

● ● ● Measured in terms of the Earth's history, the world's oceans remained physically and chemically stable for a long time. About four billion years ago, they were the cradle of all life. At the same time they were varied enough to promote the development of species able to cope with rapid change – which are found, for example, at the delta of a large river – or species happy to live under extreme conditions like brackish waters or next to hot springs on the sea bed.

Every now and then species became extinct – on average 90 per 100 years. Humans have accelerated this figure by a factor of 240,000. According to estimates, we are currently witnessing the death of 50 to 100 species every day.

Of all the known species of plants and animals, about 250,000 are believed to live in the sea. This observation is based on the fact that species living on land or in freshwater have been better researched than those in the sea. In any case, those in the sea belong to more families – groups with basically differing biological blueprints. Only one of the 33 animal families on Earth cannot be found in the sea, but there are 15 which can be found only there.

The ocean regions with the greatest variety of creatures lie in the Tropics off the coasts of Asia, eastern Africa, northern Australia, and the Pacific Islands. The various biological development forms spread from these regions, including the Caribbean, to other oceans.

There are few investigations concerning the real extent of the variety in the sea and whether or not it is changing. Nevertheless, it can be seen that dramatic changes are taking place in all marine habitats, even if only a few species are threatened with extinction.

If the population of one species declines or, in some regions, completely disappears, the genetic variety of this species also disappears and, with it, the ability to withstand and cope with new conditions.

The decline of a species may also have unforeseeable consequences for other organisms. For example, the sea otter in the Aleutians plays a major role in maintaining enormous kelp forests, as they feed on the sea urchins that live on these large algae. After the sea otters had been decimated on some of the islands, the kelp forests died together with all the organisms living there – eaten up by the sea urchins.

Only in 50 years' time, we will know how serious the situation is regarding the variety of animal and plant life. That is the agreed-upon time period that must pass after the last sighting of an organism in order to declare it extinct. Other species which live for a very long time, such as the sea turtle, can be observed for many more years, even if their population is much too low to keep it alive.

A third of all the biomass in the sea grows around the coastal zones, which are

Most of the sea turtle populations are under threat. Humans are slowly destroying the spawning grounds to which they always return after their birth.

small compared with the vastness of the oceans. Ecosystems such as the deltas of rivers, and including mangrove forests, are some of the most productive on Earth. At the same time, they serve as breeding grounds and nurseries for creatures that normally live in the open sea. Three-quarters of all economically valuable fish live near the coast at some stage of their development.

Coastal zones vs. settlement zones

But most of the people in the world live at the coast, too. About 70 percent live and work not more than 80 kilometers (50 mi.) from the sea. Half of the cities in the world with a population of a million or more are on the coast, particularly at the

mouths of rivers. The sea provides them with food, building materials, building ground, new agricultural areas, and recreation. In return, humans use the sea to dispose of wastewater, garbage, and toxic chemicals, tipping 6.7 million tons of waste into coastal waters each year.

Those who do not live by the sea usually live near a river. Pollution and inconsiderate agricultural methods, damming and irrigation installations in the land's interior all contribute to changing the physical and chemical state of the coasts downstream.

The mangrove forests are particularly affected. They border one-quarter of all coasts, but more than 50 percent of them have been destroyed. In the Philippines, 70 percent were felled for firewood and building materials, or

A look at what coastal waters are subjected to: agricultural pesticides, municipal waste water, toxic substances from the chemical industry, and ships illegally discharging oil residues.

else to provide new ground for shrimp farming and other types of ponds for aqua-culture.

In many places, the damming of rivers in the interior led to an increased salt content in the water and all the trees died.

Bleached coral reefs

The oceanic ecological systems that contain the greatest variety of organisms are the coral reefs. Already 5 to 10 percent have been destroyed. Soil that has washed into the sea from the land has buried the corals beneath it. The limestone, which has built up over thousands of years, is being dynamited and used for building purposes. Prussic acid is being used to paralyze fish for the aquarium market, and at the same time, it kills numerous other organisms.

A completely new form of disaster has affected the corals in the last 20 years – in many places, they are bleached. Corals live in a close symbiosis with minute algae, called zooxanthellae, which give the corals their color. If the corals are stressed, the algae move away and leave behind the white skeletons – which then die off.

The cause of the bleaching is not yet fully understood, but one reason for the stress is increasing water temperatures. Corals live in warm water with a temperature of 20° C to 28° C (68° F to 82° F), which is often just about the limit of their tolerance. An increase of just one degree can cause the zooxanthellae to disappear, and the tropical seas have increased

Polluted beaches in the Baltics: During some years, algae affect the ecological balance.

in the last hundred years by exactly one degree. This temperature increase is expected to continue.

The sea is also endangered by "stowaways." Up until a hundred years ago, only those organisms that could attach themselves to the bows of wooden vessels or could bore into the wood were transported across the oceans. Today, giant freighters and tankers carry about 3,000 species around the world in the bilges, waste water, and ballast tanks. Most of these exotic organisms do not survive very long in their new environment, but if they do happen to find a new habitat, they often have no enemies there and can spread uncontrollably.

Even if the creature is not so exotic, it can still interfere with the genetics of the existing population or introduce diseases. For example, Baltic salmon were introduced into the Norwegian Sea to increase the salmon

population there. But they brought parasites that were unknown on that side of Scandinavia and are now a danger to the natural Norwegian salmon population.

Our knowledge concerning the condition of the seas is very shaky. Only about seven percent of the oceans have been explored, and less is known about the sea bed than about the moon. So, it is really not surprising that scientists in recent years have come back from their diving expeditions with news of hitherto unknown species, particularly those that live around the hydrothermal vents, the "black smokers." And even these have the potential to be endangered if humans, one day, begin to exploit the resources in and on the sea bed.

FACTS AND FIGURES

Toxic waste in the North Sea and Baltic Sea

Like all coastal areas, shelves, and marginal seas are subjected to great volumes of pollutants. The hazardous substances reach the sea via rivers or the air, often from deep in the land's interior:

yearly quantities in tons	North Sea	Baltic Sea
Cadmium	340	170
Mercury	75	90
Lead	11,000	3,800
Arsenic	950	930
Copper	4,500	3,500
Zinc	28,400	14,000
Chromium	5,000	-
Nickel	2,150	2,900
Oil	170,000	-
Chem. warfare ag.	-	12,035
Nitrogen	1,300,000	1,009,000
Phosphorus	78,000	37,700

Sources: Warnsignale aus der Nordsee, Warnsignale aus der Ostsee, HELCOM, BSH; source: FAO 1999

Countries with little awareness of the environment use the sea as a garbage dump.

How the oceans are polluted

More than half of oceanic pollutants are transported along rivers and into the seas; the rest are carried there by wind and rain.

● ● ● It is a drama which goes unnoticed. Every year, millions of tons of nitrogen, hundreds of thousands of tons of phosphorous, and ten thousands of tons of zinc, lead, chromium, arsenic, and cadmium dissolve in the sea. And, even worse, the marine ecosystem has to cope with several tons a year of chlorohydrocarbons – substances that do not occur in nature.

The seas contain 1.3 billion cubic kilometers (0,3 bil. cu. mi.) of water. Once diluted in such an enormous quantity of water, is it possible that these substances will have any effect at all? Yes, if you keep in mind that the human body consists of billions of cells, and if changes occur in just one of them, it can trigger a fatal disease.

About half of the pollutants that are discharged directly into the sea are carried there by rivers or simply dumped from ships. The other half comes from automobile exhaust and industrial gases. These fumes are carried by the wind; 30 percent are blown directly out to sea while the remaining 70 percent bind with dust particles and are carried by rain clouds across the sea to fall in the most remote places. They infiltrate the ground water and the rivers, thus adding to the pollutants from municipal and industrial waste water.

However, not all pollutants reach the sea. Some of the rivers clean the water and deposit the pollutants in the river bed. It is estimated that only 50 percent of the cadmium and one percent of the lead dissolved in river water actually reaches the sea.

The impact of fertilizer

The agricultural industry uses vast amounts of fertilizers and pesticides, half of which are washed out, unused, by the next rainfall. These substances then infiltrate the rivers and eventually reach the coasts.

Nitrogen and phosphorous stimulate algae growth. Algae often multiply more quickly than the zooplankton organisms can cope with and die off after a few days, sinking to the sea bed where they are further decomposed by bacteria. In doing so, the microbes use up all the oxygen which is dissolved in the water and so-called "oxygen holes" occur on the sea bed. If there is no current to wash in fresh water, there is a spread of bacteria types which can live without oxygen. Instead they give off a gas – hydrogen sulfide – which is toxic to the sedentary inhabitants of the sea bottom. Fish can avoid such zones by swimming around them and moving off to other areas.

Excessive quantities of fertilizer also promote the growth of particularly small unicellular algae species, including many that emit toxic substances into the water and, in a few cases, even into the air. They poison all of the water column and can even be hazardous to people.

Most of the poisonous organic compounds are made by humans. However, no one

The female polar bear can lose her ability to reproduce when PCB residues absorbed from the food she eats, are deposited in her fatty tissues.

really knows their number and many have not even been identified.

Pesticides belong to this category of compounds. They are not easily degraded in nature – a prime example being the infamous DDT. At one time, people had high expectations of this poison, but its use has now been prohibited in most countries. Ninety-five percent of this sprayed poison reached the sea by air. It became concentrated in the fatty tissues of many higher animal species, such as sea birds, through the food chain. It can still be found today in marine mammals, even in those in remote polar regions.

PCBs and DDT in the fatty tissue of animals

The many varieties of polychlorinated biphenyls, better known as PCBs, are also hazardous. They are used in plastics, as well as insulating materials in electrical installations. Like DDT, these chlorinated organic substances also become concentrated in the fatty tissue of animals, including seals and polar bears, through the food chain. They are suspected of weakening the immune system of sea mammals, making them more prone to disease. In sea turtles, they are even said to cause tumors. Scientists also suspect that the mutated formation of male genitals in female polar bears that hunt near the Svalbard Islands can be traced to high concentrations of PCBs in the fat.

Destructive heavy metals

Cadmium, lead, and other heavy metals reach the seas mainly via the atmosphere. They are released during the combustion of oil and coal. And approximately 80 percent of the lead still comes from automobile exhaust, as unleaded gas is only available in a few countries in the world.

The toxic metals combine with dust particles and, once in the sea, are eaten first

Dumping oil residues: As here in the North Sea, too many ship captains think nothing of it.

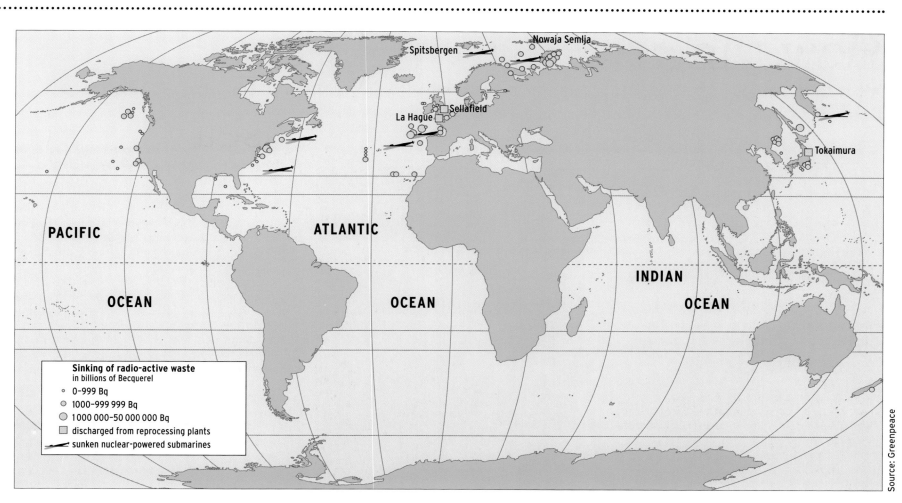

Source: Greenpeace

Sinking of radio-active waste
in billions of Becquerel
- 0-999 Bq
- 1000-999 999 Bq
- 1 000 000-50 000 000 Bq
- ▢ discharged from reprocessing plants
- ▬ sunken nuclear-powered submarines

A particular form of environmental pollution by the industrial nations: The Americans, Russians, British, French, Japanese, and Chinese have all dumped a portion of their nuclear wastes into the sea. A number of nuclear-powered submarines have also been sunk deliberately at sea.

The issue of environmental protection: Even in industrialized countries, untreated waste water is still discharged into the sea.

by plankton. Bacteria then attack the excretions of organisms or dead plankton and decompose them, whereby some of the heavy metals such as cadmium are again released into the water where, in the course of time, they enrich, especially in enclosed sea basins.

Others, such as lead, are not released to the same extent during decomposition but sink down to the bed with the dead organism. If the sea is not too deep, they endanger those organisms that live on the sea bed, which are especially numerous in those places where the most pollutants come into the sea – in the shelf areas off the coasts. These creatures live on what trickles down from the water's surface. What they have digested is again dissolved in the water and once more becomes part of the food chain.

Oil pollution caused by tanker incidents are disasters, but are limited to a particular location, where the damage is usually

redressed within 5 to 10 years. In contrast, incidents in polar and subpolar regions leave behind traces in the ecological system which can be seen even decades later.

As oil is a natural product, however, there fortunately are bacteria which specialize in degrading oil. After all, about 250,000 tons of oil trickle from natural sources on the sea bed every year. Just how quickly the microbes can deal with the task of decomposing depends on how warm the water is and whether there are enough supplementary nutrients and oxygen available.

Slow and treacherous oil pollution

Far worse for the ecological system is the gradual pollution by oil. Each year, an estimated 3.2 million tons of oil finds its way into the sea – 400,000 tons of which is leaked through tanker accidents. More than 1 million tons are from bilge and machine oil used on ships that are simply dumped overboard.

Municipal and industrial waste water carry another 1.2 million tons into the sea, and exhaust from automobiles and the oil industry make up another 300,000 tons that contribute to the pollution. In comparison, the offshore rigs are cleaner, as a "mere" 50,000 tons flow into the seas through leaks or during loading operations.

This low-scale but nevertheless permanent pollution can affect the sense of smell of many marine animals and can lead them astray when they migrate or are seeking a mate. Even the tiniest amounts of oil affect plankton populations, as the more resistant of the species gain the upper hand, which throws the perfectly attuned natural balance of the food chain into disorder.

FACTS AND FIGURES

The warning signals

The United Nations believes the oceans of the world are threatened by the following causes (shown in the sequence of weighting).

OVER-UTILIZATION OF MARINE SPECIES: Since the Second World War, the expansion of global fishing and the increased sophistication of fishing methods for hauling vast volumes of wild living organisms on board have threatened practically every species of marine creature.

POLLUTION FROM THE MAINLAND: Pollutants in the air, industrial waste, municipal sewage, agricultural pesticides and fertilizers, and erosion caused by deforestation and agriculture have an enormous impact.

EXPLOITATION OF THE SEAS: Normal shipping operations and accidents are responsible for oil entering the seas. Offshore drilling, exploitation for building materials, and the sinking of industrial waste are destroying the marine environment.

CLIMATIC CHANGE: Man-made climatic changes are causing major upheavals in coastal regions. The polar ice caps are melting, leading to a rise in the sea level.

TOURIST INDUSTRY: The sea has always been a tourist attraction. The tourist industry, however, exerts immense pressure on coastal zones, especially sandy coasts and the coral reefs.

Surveying the seas

An armada of research vessels is collecting data on the characteristics of the world's oceans. The first General Bathymetric Chart of the Oceans (GEBCO) appeared in 1904.

A view of the bridge of a modern ferry ship. Since the introduction of depth sonars, measuring water depths has become increasingly more precise.

● ● ● Seafarers through the ages have always asked for "a hand's breadth of water under the keel," because to run aground often meant the loss of a ship and the crew. The plumb line, or sounding line, was invented a long time ago and used to find hidden shallows.

Pictures from Egypt from 3,500 years ago depict seamen at the bow of a ship sounding the depths with a long pole. In the 5th century BC, the Greek historian Herodotus described how depths were measured using a sounding line weighted with a piece of lead. The depths measured in shallow waters with a hand plumb have been entered into navigational charts since the 16th century. Later, much-frequented coastal regions were measured systematically and the depths – or rather, the shallow areas – were surveyed. The depth lines, called isobaths, were entered into the sea charts for coastal regions in the same way as contour lines on a land map.

For thousands of years the depths were sounded purely for reasons of safety. Some, for certain, would like to have known how deep the sea was at greater distances from the coast, but the plumb lines were not long enough for that, and so it was left to guesswork.

"Fishermen, fishing for corals at depths of 275 and 360 meters (900 and 1,180 ft.) and whose lines are not long enough to reach greater depths, speak fearlessly of the bottomless sea," wrote the Italian Count Luigi Marsigli in his book *Histoire Physique de la Mer* in 1725. "They claim it is impossible to reach the bottom. This opinion is shared by experienced seafarers and appears to me to be absurd as it is based simply on the fact that no one so far has ever taken the trouble or has had the necessary means to carry out such a sounding."

The first successful sounding in deeper waters was made by the British captain Constantine Phipps in 1733 in the North Atlantic, between Iceland and Norway, on returning from an expedition in the Arctic. "On 4 September, at two in the afternoon," reported Phipps, "sounded with all our lines totaling 800 fathoms (1,464 meters/4,800 ft.). Shortly before all the lines had completely run off, we noticed that they were not running as quickly as before. When we hauled the lines in the first roll, the following 20 fathoms ran easily. But from then on, we had trouble to move the lines. The point at which we felt the weight was marked and the line was measured. We established a depth of 683 fathoms (1,250 meters/4,100 ft.). The plumb weighed more than 330 kilograms (727 lbs.) and we could see from the line that it had sunk almost 3 meters (10 ft.) into the ground which was of very fine, blue soft clay."

Record-breaking sounding in 1840

In 1840, the British admiral and polar explorer James Clark Ross sounded a depth of 4,463 meters (14,642 ft.) during a voyage through Antarctic waters. He had had the sounding line, which was 6,500 meters (21,300 ft.) long spooled onto a large drum that revolved from the weight of the plumb. Otherwise, sounding in deep waters remained an exception and in 1845, the Prussian scholar Alexander von Humboldt deplored the fact that no one was interested in the oceans. No one knew how deep they were. In fact, practically nothing was known about them. But changes were already in sight.

Two Americans were to ring them in: marine officer Matthew Maury and the financier Cyrus Field. Maury had become unfit for active naval service after an accident with a stagecoach and now was the head of the Depot of Charts and Instruments of the

Marine research under full sail. The painting shows the research vessel "Challenger" close to icebergs in stormy seas. The naval sailing boat was converted to use steam power and undertook the first research expedition through all the oceans between 1873 and 1876.

A cable-laying vessel in operation: Following the invention of telegraphic transmission, permanently-installed cable connections became essential. In the 19th century, cable-laying vessels installed inter-continental lines across the oceans of the world.

US Marines in Washington. His job was to evaluate the specially-prepared logbooks he had distributed among the sea captains and to compile charts and sailing instructions based on observations regarding maritime winds and currents collected from all over the world. Maury was fascinated by the idea of a systematic exploration of the oceans. In 1853, he organized the first oceanographic congress in Brussels and in 1855 published the first textbook on oceanography.

A cable across the Atlantic

Following a successful career in the paper business, Cyrus Field became extremely interested in what was then an adventurous plan to lay a transatlantic telegraph cable. After the American artist and inventor Samuel Morse had created the written telegraph in 1837 and decisive improvements had been made by 1844, cables were being put down everywhere – and water was to be no obstacle. Rivers were soon crossed, and from 1850 to 1851, so were the Straits of Dover, followed by the Irish Sea and the North Sea – all relatively shallow and comparatively well-known waters.

However, in order to lay a cable under the Atlantic Ocean it would be necessary to have at least a rough idea of the depths that could be expected.

Field turned to Maury, who had soundings made. In 1854, Maury's first bathymetric chart of the Atlantic – based on fewer than 200 soundings of more than 1,800 meters (5,900 ft.) between 10° S and 52° N – was published. Many measurements had been obtained with knotted lines and were therefore inexact. Nevertheless, the cable layers made progress. After three unsuccessful attempts to bring Europe and America closer together by cable, the first link was made between Ireland and Newfoundland in 1866. At the time, shorter lengths of cable had been successfully installed 51 times.

Due to the interest in laying cable in the sea depths, the method for sounding was gradually improved. Thanks to a new type of construction, the heavy plumb weight was released from the line as soon as it touched the bottom and no longer had to be heaved laboriously back on board. Piano wire, which offered the water less resistance and did not drift so easily in deeper currents, was spooled from the drums instead of the old hemp lines. Steam-driven machines replaced the conventional manual operation.

Nevertheless, deep-sea sounding remained a difficult business. The ship had to remain exactly in position, sometimes for hours, and since ships were unable to cast anchor in deeper waters – at least, not until 1920 – it was an almost impossible task. In

any case, in order to take any soundings, the sea had to be calm and so the number of soundings were limited. The scientists on board the British research vessel *Challenger*, which from 1873 to 1876 made the first major inventory of the oceans, brought 492 deep-sea soundings home with them and are thus deservedly mentioned in literature on the subject.

Depth sounding was not a routinely performed task until it became possible to measure the depths without wires and weights, and independent of wind and waves, i.e., with sonic pulses. Rather than light and radio waves, water is an excellent conductor of sonic waves. A sonic pulse is sent from the surface of the water and is reflected, or "echoed," by the sea bed back to the ship, whereby the depth is determined by the time taken for the sound to return.

The invention of the echo sounder

In 1838, an American named Bonnycastle had already attempted to implement this easy-to-understand principle of echo sounding. Using an ear-trumpet, he tried to catch the echo of a detonation on the sea bed on the surface of the water, but without success. Further attempts were not made for a considerable time as it was assumed that the sea bed absorbed the sound so much that an

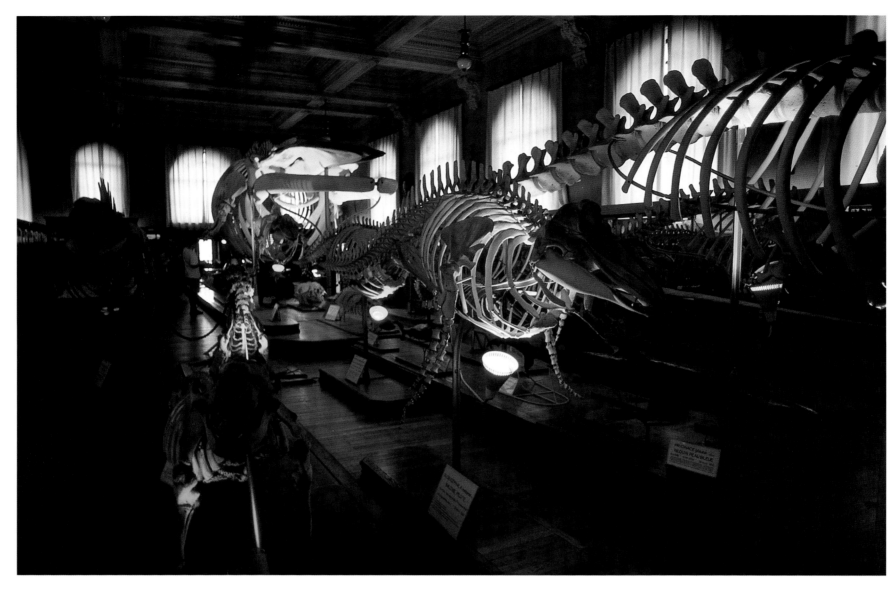

In the exhibition rooms of the Oceanographic Museum in Monaco, the skeletons of whales and numerous rare fish are on view.

echo would not be generated. And, actually, a rocky sea bed does absorb 40 to 70 percent of the sound, while mud absorbs up to 90 percent.

The first echo sounders were meant for completely different tasks at sea. After the 1912 collision of the *Titanic* with an iceberg, the German physicist Alexander Behm and the American wireless pioneer Reginald Fessenden began work on such a device, independently of one another. Sonic pulses were to be emitted straight ahead underwater from the ship's bow, and the reflected echo from an iceberg would then give the captain time to change course.

The marvelous efforts of Meteor

When the First World War broke out in 1914, it was no longer just a question of locating icebergs but of enemy submarines. Military technical development work was put to good use for depth measuring for civilian purposes. In 1919, Behm presented the first reliable, operational echo sounder. The American destroyer *Stewart* was the first to take an echo sounder on board in 1922. Oceanographers were now able to make series of depth measurements instead of laborious single soundings.

German scientists used the technology on board the *Meteor* research vessel, which measured and surveyed the oceans more intensively than ever before between 1925 and 1927. The *Meteor* crossed the Atlantic

13 times from east to west, during which time the scientists made continuous soundings. After 67,000 depth soundings had been carried out, the first modern bathymetric chart of an extensive part of the sea was created. On it, the Mid-Atlantic Ridge could be clearly discerned running like a backbone from north to south.

Knowledge of the depths increased rapidly. Depth sounding had become easier but also presented the scientists with problems that were only solved with increased experience and improved instruments. "The exactitude of depth sounding depends on time measurement, knowledge of the mean speed of sound, the grouping (of sonic waves), the movement of the ship, and the type of sea bed" could be read in a classical textbook *General Oceanography*, written by Günter Dietrich, Kurt Kalle, Wolfgang Krauss, and Gerold Siedler.

The speed at which sound waves travel through water is 1,485 meters (4.872 ft.) per second – so even a tiny fraction of a second counts when measuring the time. This speed applies when the temperature is 20° C (68° F). In order to be able to make exact measurements, the temperature layers in the ocean must be known and taken into account when evaluating the measured traveling times, in the same way as fluctuations in measured values from the rising and falling of the ship.

To ensure that the sound waves do not spread, attempts are made to "bundle" them.

If the waves were not bundled sufficiently and the sea bed was strongly contoured, the measuring didn't show the depth under the ship, but the distance to an elevated region sideways. On the other hand, if the waves were bundled sharply and the sea was rough, causing the ship to move heavily, the sonic pulse may not be emitted to the sea bed in a perpendicular line or may miss its target when returning.

Problems with precision

It was finally decided on a large bundling. In the 1930s, low-frequency sound was replaced by ultrasonic sound, which achieves a better and sharper directivity. Exact targeting is provided by a gyroscopic system control that keeps the "swinger," or oscillator – which transmits and receives the sonic pulses – always in a horizontal position. Another decisive innovation was the echograph, which records the measurements of the sonic pulse on paper tape. The individual signals combine to produce a line representing the contours of the sea bed in profile.

Not only were there problems with precision in sounding the depths but also in determining the respective location. The classical astronomical determination of geographical longitude and latitude at sea, with the help of sextant, chronometer, and nautical tables, was inexact to an extent of 1.8 kilometers (approximately 1 mi.). This corresponds to a circle with an area of

10 square kilometers (3.9 sq mi.) – meaning there could be depth differences of up to 2,000 meters (6,600 ft.). No wonder there had been repeatedly different values of measurements assumed to be made at the same position. Not until the 1970s was it possible to record exact positioning with the help of satellites.

A vote for Mercator projection

In view of the increasing number of soundings made towards the end of the 19th century, it was decided in 1899, at the VII International Geographical Conference in Berlin, to create a comprehensive bathymetric chart of the oceans. A commission, with Prince Albert I of Monaco (an enthusiastic and renowned marine explorer) taking a prominent role, established the guidelines for the chart sections and layout of the planned General Bathymetric Chart of the Oceans (GEBCO). The first issue of the chart is shown on page 120 in this atlas.

To show the surface of the spherical Earth on a plane chart is only possible by making compromises. Geographical details can only be "correct" according to one of three criteria. They can be displayed with their proportions true to either length, area,

Prince Albert I of Monaco played a prominent role in the development of oceanography.

or angle. In the tradition of sea charts, the true angle is decisive, therefore the GEBCO Commission decided on the Mercator projection, on which the Earth is shown as if it has been projected on a cylinder around the Earth.

As this method of projection leads to extensive distortions in higher latitudes, the "gnomic" projection was used to show the Poles, whereby the curved surface of the Earth is projected on a plane which just touches the Earth's surface (the tangential plane).

On a scale of 1:10,000,000 at the Equator – 1 centimeter (0.39 in.) on the map stands for 100 kilometers (62 mi.) – the Commission divided the Earth's surface between 72° N and 72° S into 16 charts. In

The Oceanographic Museum for documenting the development of oceanography was founded by Prince Albert I of Monaco. To this day, it has remained the center for oceanography.

addition, eight charts exist for the Poles on a scale of 1:3,100,000 (based on 72°). Albert I of Monaco took over the costs for the preparation and production of the GEBCO. In 1904, he presented the first edition containing 18,400 soundings. A second edition with 29,000 soundings was begun in Monaco in 1910 and was published between 1912 and 1927.

Cooperation in the grand style

The death of the patron Prince Albert in 1922 was not the only reason why the updating of the charts took so long. After the invention of the echo sounder, the number of soundings made increased rapidly, and much effort and many means were required to collect, look at, and judge the quality of all of them. In 1955, the International Hydrographic Office in Monaco published 18 charts of the third edition after 23 years of preparatory work, while charts of the Poles remained unchanged. The preparatory work consisted of entering the 370,000 soundings known at that time into 1,001 work charts on a scale of 1:1,000,000. Fifty-four thousand of these were included in the 18 new GEBCO charts.

In a fourth edition, only two charts were published 1958 and 1961. For the fifth edition, 16 Mercator charts and two charts on a scale of 1:6,000,000 for the polar regions were published between 1975 and 1982 after enormous international efforts commissioned by the Intergovernmental Oceanographic Commission of UNESCO and the International Hydrographic Organization of the Canadian Hydrographic Service. The Federal Republic of Germany, represented by the German Hydrographic Institute (today the Federal Office for Shipping and Hydrographics), carried out the preparatory work for the North Atlantic.

Thanks to the GEBCO editions, oceanographers were able to make increasingly exact pictures of what the world looks like under the vast ocean areas. These illustrate the character of our planet and how the shelf regions and continental slopes, the deep-sea trenches and plains, the Mid-Oceanic Ridge and numerous seamounts, and extinct volcanoes rising up from the sea bed are distributed.

Knowledge of the topography of the ocean floor is essential for finding the answers to many questions regarding the physics, chemistry, and biology of the oceans. Also the marine geology, currents and tides, the expansion of earthquakes or underwater landslides, the triggering of tsunamis, the upsurge of nutrient-rich water, the mixing of varying water masses, and other marine processes with their manifold effects on the animate and inanimate environment which are strongly influenced by conditions on the sea bed.

The charts have become an essential working tool for representatives from a variety of oceanographic disciplines, from sedimentologists to fishing scientists. And without the global overview provided by the charts, it would be difficult to understand the dynamics of our planet or to decipher the mystery of the drifting tectonic plates. (See page 70.)

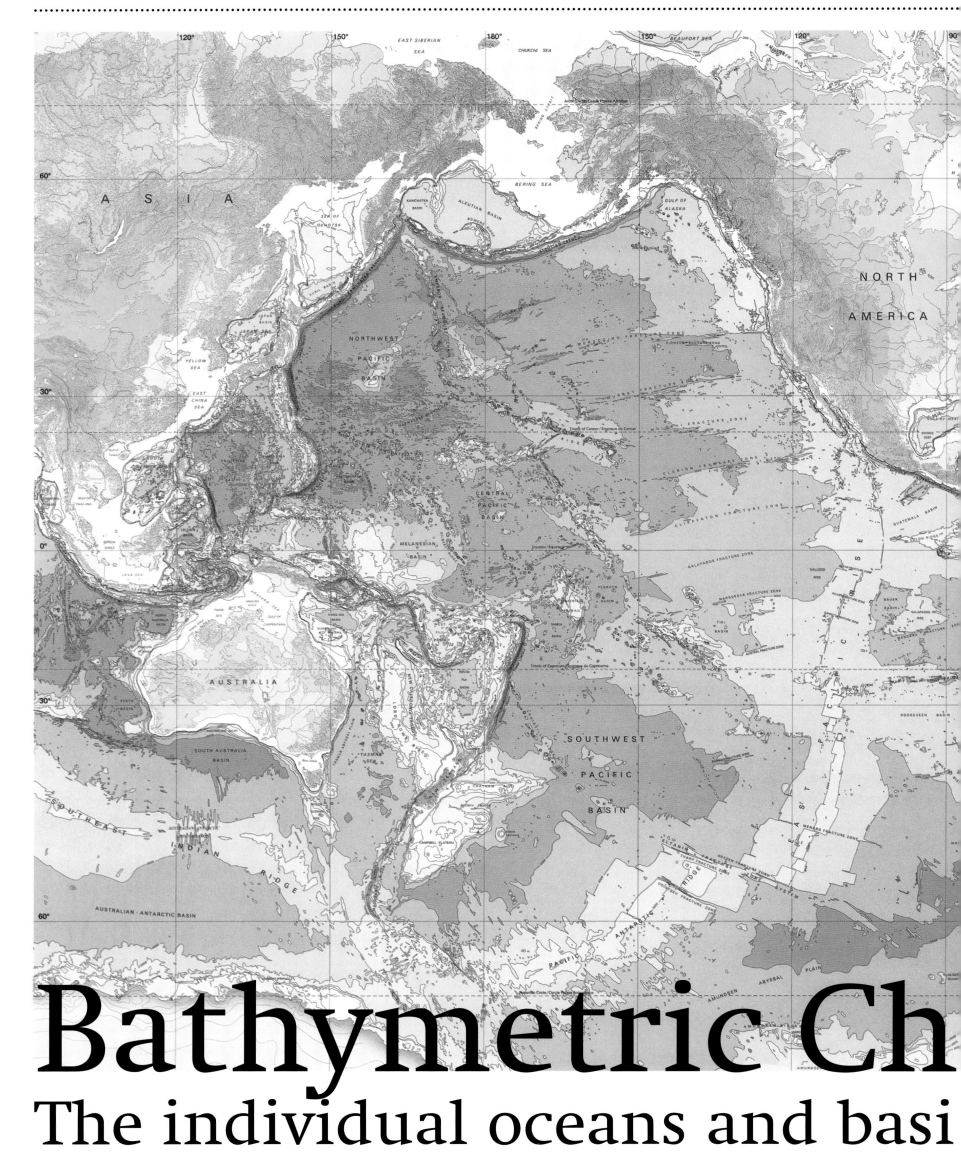

Bathymetric Ch

The individual oceans and basi

arts

ns

The Northwest Passage

●●● The Davis Strait is part of the Atlantic Ocean, located between Baffin Island and southwestern Greenland, connecting the deep Baffin Sea in the north with the Labrador Sea in the south.

At 650 kilometers (400 mi.) long and 320 kilometers to 650 kilometers (200 to 400 mi.) wide, it is part of the Northwest Passage leading to the west, through the Canadian Arctic to the Bering Strait on the Pacific Coast.

British navigator John Davis made one of the first attempts to find a passage between the Atlantic and the Pacific oceans via the Canadian Arctic Archipelago. Between 1585 and 1587, he undertook three voyages through the Labrador Sea. During the first, he explored the sea strait that was later named after him, and used it as a passageway two years later on his last voyage into the Baffin Sea, touching at Disko Island (recently renamed Qeqertarsuaq) on his journey back.

Davis succeeded in establishing and maintaining an amicable long-term relationship with the Inuit. To this end, he hired minstrels for his journeys to play music for his sailors to dance to in order to get the natives to join in their celebrations.

At 130 kilometers (80 mi.) long and 32 kilometers to 120 kilometers (20 mi. to 75 mi.) wide, Qeqertarsuaq was explored as early as 985 by Erik the Red and his men. Having been expelled from Iceland for manslaughter in 982, Erik sailed the Greenland Currents in search of a new place – somewhere in Greenland – to settle with his men. As the settlers found no signs of life at the first site they explored in the south of Greenland, they traveled further north along the west coast, where they discovered the island.

Immediately off Greenland's coast, the West Greenland Current carries relatively warm water to the north. It is supplied by the East Greenland Current flowing from the island's eastern part, around Cape Farvel, the island's southernmost point, and into the Labrador Sea.

In the opposite direction, the cold Baffin Current drifts from the coast off Baffin Island to the south and further towards the Labrador Current. It is a mixture of the water brought into the Baffin Sea by the West Greenland Current and the cold Arctic water crossing the channels of the Canadian Arctic Archipelago. It carries huge amounts of drift ice and a large number of icebergs that continually break off the inland ice on Greenland's coast.

These icebergs usually have a life-span of between three months and two years. On their way south, the ice melts at an ever-faster rate, and once they reach the area around the Grand Banks off Newfoundland, it takes them only few days to melt away completely.

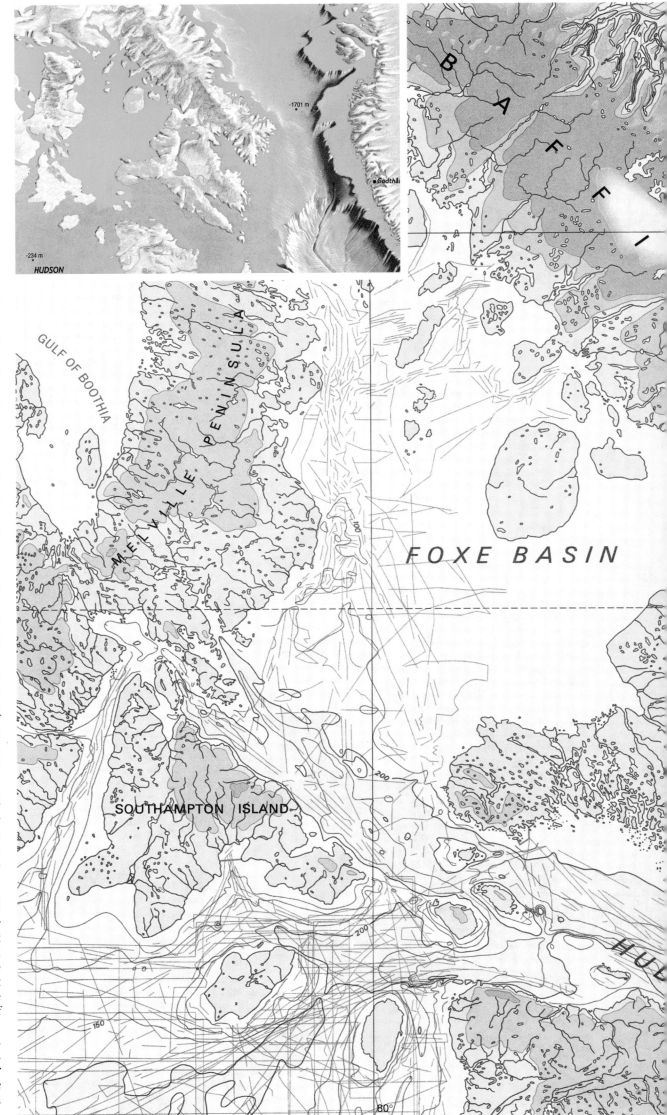

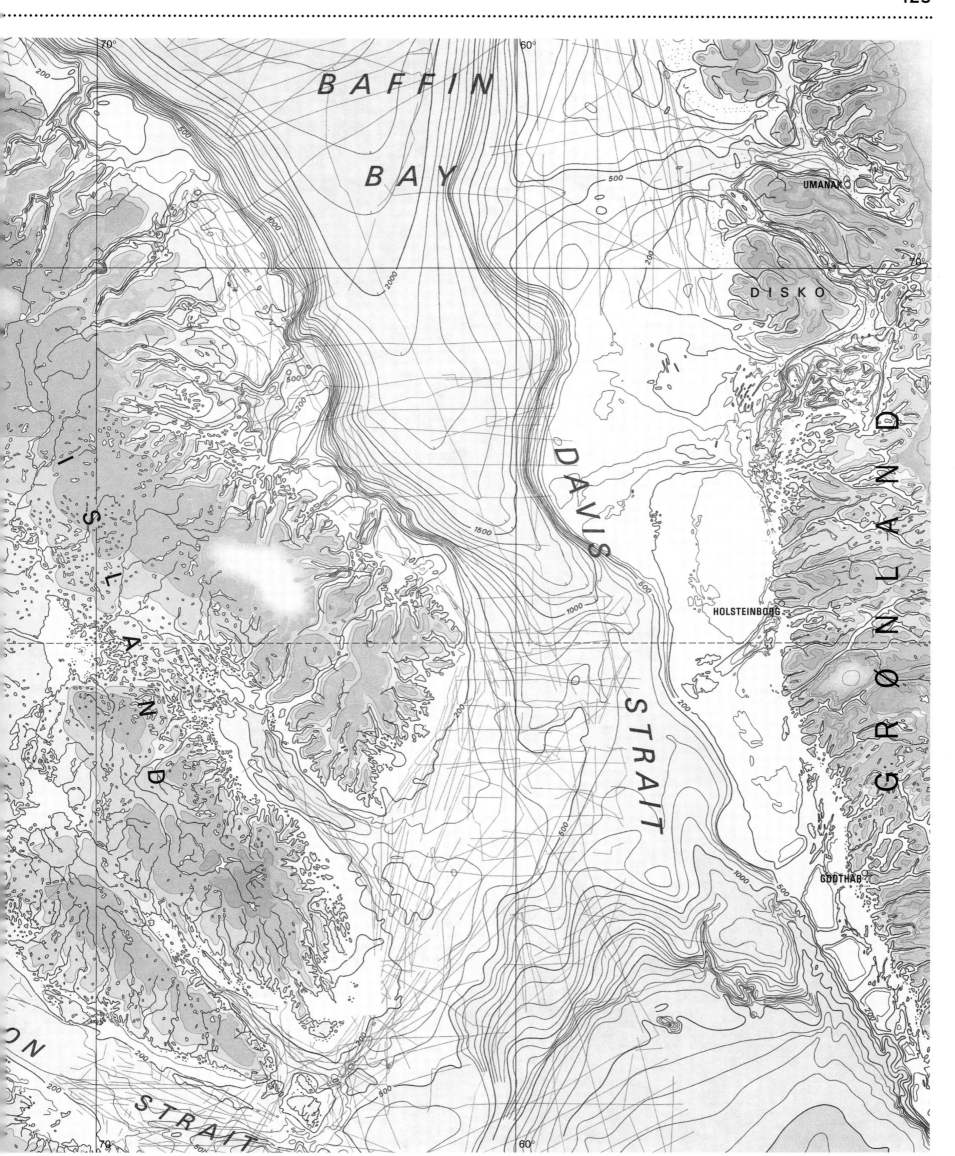

The peak of the Atlantic

●●● Viking settlers reached Iceland more than a thousand years ago. From there, Norwegian sailors and adventurers undertook voyages to Greenland and even North America, which they called Vinland.

The island constitutes the part of the Mid-Atlantic Ridge visible above water level. The lava emerging from the center of the ridge creates a new sea bed on both sides of it. The island's approximately 200 active volcanoes reach deep into the Earth's restless core. The region, one of the most active volcanic areas on our planet, has been particularly agitated over the last 30 years. An estimated one-third of the Earth's total lava has emerged from these volcanoes since the year 1500.

Iceland is separated from Greenland by the 290-kilometer (180-mi.) long Denmark Strait. On its surface, the cold East Greenland Current flows southwards, carrying drift ice and icebergs originating from the Arctic and Greenland's ice cap – one of which was supposed to have caused the *Titanic* disaster. Off Cape Farvel, Greenland's southernmost tip, the current changes direction, flowing north into the Labrador Sea and, as the West Greenland Current, into the Davis Strait.

In the opposite direction, near Iceland's coast, the warm Irminger Current drifts northwards. This branch of the North Atlantic Current reaches the island from the southeast and divides into two currents west of it. One branch flows north through the Denmark Strait and surrounds Iceland in the east, while the other flows southwestward to merge with the East Greenland Current.

The Irminger Current is rich in salt. Its mixture of relatively warm North Atlantic water and cold Arctic water provides the basis for the rich fishing grounds around the Icelandic coasts.

Between the east coast of Iceland and the Faeroe Islands runs a sub-marine ridge which blocks off the Norwegian Basin from the open Atlantic and extends further to Scotland. To its north, cold, saline Arctic water is pooled in the Norwegian Sea, often spilling over into the Atlantic, where it sinks quickly to the bottom of the Iceland Basin. Scientists refer to this phenomenon as "overflow."

At irregular intervals, this overflow renews the Atlantic deep-sea water. As these water masses move downward from the surface of the Arctic Sea, they are particularly rich in oxygen and therefore are able to ventilate the bottom of the sea, although the oxygen is slowly used up while the bottom water flows southward.

The oceans' lungs

●●● Svalbard, the "cold coast" with its main island of Spitsbergen, was created by the continental drift separating Greenland and the Eurasian Plate.

When the Eurasian basin, i.e., the eastern part of the Arctic Sea, opened up some 60 million years ago, Svalbard began drifting southeastwards. Since then, the group of islands has traveled some 400 kilometers (248 mi.). Towards the end of the drift, the Fram Strait formed between Greenland and Svalbard, the only deep-sea connection between the Polar Sea and the oceans of the world.

Cold Polar water emerges from there and moves southward along the coast of Greenland forming the East Greenland Current, whereas off the Norwegian coast, the relatively warm waters of the Norway Current pass Svalbard on their way towards the Polar Sea. The Norway Current is the continuation of the North Atlantic Drift, which is formed by whirling water masses branching off from the Gulf Stream. It is so warm that ships can sometimes call in Spitsbergen even in winter.

Both currents converge at the passage between the Greenland Sea and the Norwegian Sea, and this mixture of waters provides the foundation for the rich fishing grounds in the north. On occasion, ice floes traveling southward with the Greenland Current are captured by the Norway Current and driven back to where they came from.

The northern tip of the Atlantic Ocean acts as the "lung" of the oceans because most of the ocean's bottom water is produced there. When cooling down, oxygen-rich surface water becomes heavier and descends. At the sea floor, it spreads slowly to all the other oceans after crossing the Iceland-Faeroe barrier. To replace the descending water, new surface water must flow in from the south – a continual process referred to as "thermohaline circulation."

However, the currents and winds from the south also bring toxic industrial pollution to the seemingly pristine wilderness of the north. They accumulate in the tissues of the animals at the top of the food chain. The PCB concentrations in the tissues of polar bears roaming the Svalbard region are, for instance, 20 times higher than in the bears in Alaska. As of 1996, female polar bears have often been found with male and female genitalia – believed to be the result of hormonal malfunction caused by pollution.

Sometimes, however, the toxins do not even have to travel very far. On Jan Mayen, a foggy island situated halfway between Norway and Greenland, the Norwegian army dumped wastes with high PCB contents so near the coast that the poison is leached out by the waves.

BARENTS

SEA

SPITSBERGEN

BOREAS
ABYSSAL PLAIN

BJORNØYA
BANK

Bjornøya

GREENLAND

ABYSSAL PLAIN

North Cape

VARDØ

FUGLØY
BANK

MOHNS RIDGE

TROMSØ

NORWEGIAN SEA

NORGE

DUMSHAF

ABYSSAL PLAIN

NARVIK

BASIN

Vestfjorden

RØST
BANK

VØRING PLATEAU

SVERIGE

TRAENA
BANK

On the icy inland sea

●●● Hudson Bay is a shallow inland sea that is connected with the Atlantic in the northeast via the Hudson Strait, and with the Arctic Ocean in the north via the Foxe Channel.

Although only 100 meters (330 ft.) deep on average, in some parts the inland sea reaches a depth of 270 meters (886 ft.). In winter, it is completely frozen. In August, the deep-sea water temperature reaches a mere −2° C (28.4° F), although it may rise to 9° C (48.2° F) in September.

Currents flowing in from the Foxe Basin in the north wash in cold polar water sometimes charged with pack ice, while the numerous rivers flowing into the basin deliver huge amounts of fresh water. The Hudson Strait drains the inland sea into the Labrador Sea, especially in July, when snow and ice have melted.

In the summer, the light fresh water brought in by the rivers along with the melted ice result in a relatively low salt content of 20 parts per thousand (ppt) in the uppermost 2 meters (6.6 ft.) of the water. Below 25 meters (82 ft.), the salt content rises to 31 ppt, which corresponds roughly with the saline concentration of the oceans. Like most of the shallow polar waters, the water of Hudson Bay is rich in nutrients. When the sun reappears in spring, unicellular algae growth explodes, providing rich food for the many animals on the sea bed and fish which, in turn, feed the numerous ringed seals, as well as the walruses, dolphins, and killer whales that reside further north.

In the winter, polar bears from the north wander out onto the frozen sea to hunt for seals that hide in crevices and holes within the ice. It is, however, becoming more and more difficult for the bears to survive. In contrast to Spitsbergen, for instance, where they are threatened by environmental toxins, the problem here is due to the warming of the global climate, which makes the ice thaw earlier from year to year.

Over the last 20 years, the ice season on western Hudson Bay has shortened by three weeks. Polar bears must leave their rich hunting grounds earlier and return onshore where they find less food. They are thus in danger of starving, and, what is more, the females give birth to fewer cubs because they can no longer find enough food. And, unfortunately, those last weeks before the ice breaks up are of vital importance, because it is the time when polar bears develop the layers of fat needed during gestation. If the ice sheet thaws just one week earlier, the females return onshore with some 10 kilograms (22 lb.) less weight than they should. Since, on all accounts, they lose about 24 kilograms (53 lb.) of body mass during the barren summer, they can easily become roughly 34 kilograms (75 lb.) underweight.

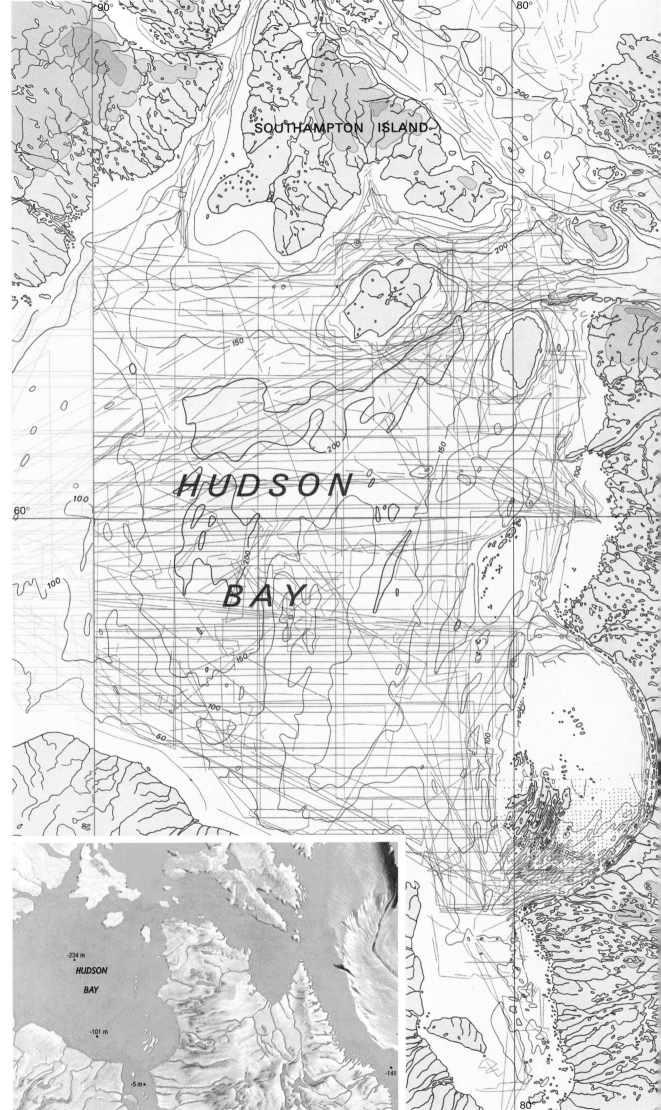

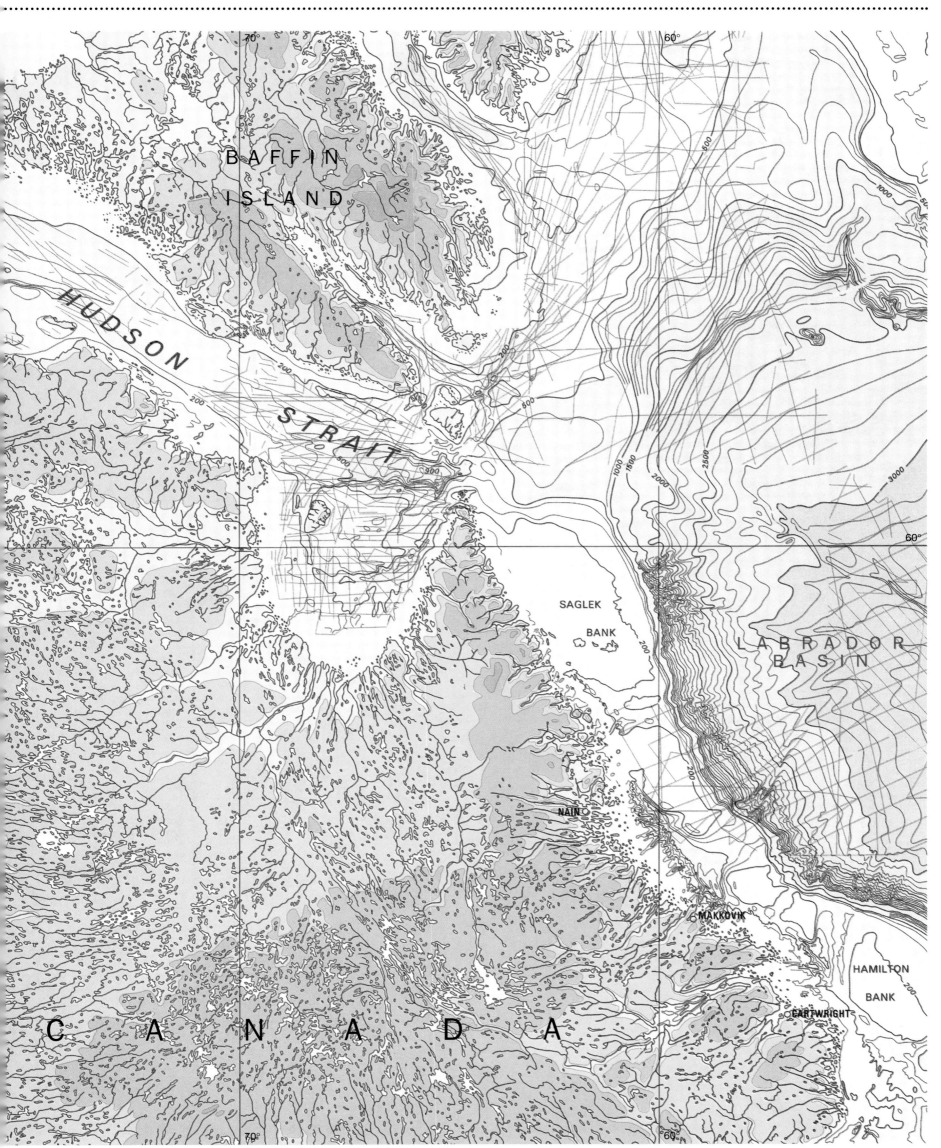

The Grand Banks' currents

● ● ● With its surface area of some 155,000 square kilometers (60,000 sq. mi.), the Gulf of Saint Lawrence bears more resemblance to a sea than the mouth of the Saint Lawrence River draining North America's Great Lakes. Its subsoil consists of submerged parts of the northern Appalachian mountain range, which extends to Newfoundland, and the southeastern rim of the vast Canadian Shield. Atlantic and Arctic deep-sea waters flow in through the Cabot Strait separating Newfoundland from the peninsula of Nova Scotia and into the gulf, where they converge with the waters of the Saint Lawrence River, rise jointly to the surface, and flow back out.

A counterclockwise current circulates within the gulf, moving around the northeastern sub-marine mountains and sometimes even up the river itself as far as 100 kilometers (62 mi.) north of Quebec. In the opposite direction, it flows southward as the Gaspé Current towards the island of Anticosti until it merges with the Cabot Strait and flows into the Atlantic.

The Laurentian Trough below the Cabot Strait was carved out by ice. It is 80 kilometers (50 mi.) wide, almost 520 meters (1,700 ft.) deep and extends eastward through the gulf from the mouth of the Saint Lawrence River to the edge of the continental shelf.

On the shelf, southeast off Newfoundland, lie the Grand Banks of Newfoundland extending 560 kilometers (348 mi.) in a north-south direction and 675 kilometers (420 mi.) in an east-west direction. Here, the average water depth is merely some 55 meters (180 ft.), although in some places, the sea bed descends to more than 180 meters (590 ft.).

Near the Grand Banks, the cold Labrador Current from the north encounters the warm Gulf Stream from the southwest. The air currents blowing over these contrasting water masses often produce dense fogs that jeopardize the work of the fishers just as much as icebergs and heavy storms. Nevertheless, the Grand Banks of Newfoundland are popular international fishing grounds because the mixture of cold and warm waters creates a favorable nutritional resource for sea organisms.

Unfortunately, since the mid-20th century, irresponsible over-fishing has depleted the formerly rich fish populations. Although the fishing nations agreed to increase the mesh size for fishing nets to safeguard reproduction by letting young fish escape, restrictions on fishing quotas could be imposed only after Canada extended its fishing zone to 200 sea miles in 1977.

Nevertheless, there are still conflicts with foreign (mainly European) fishers that wait outside national borders for shoals of fish, using the prohibited close-meshed nets.

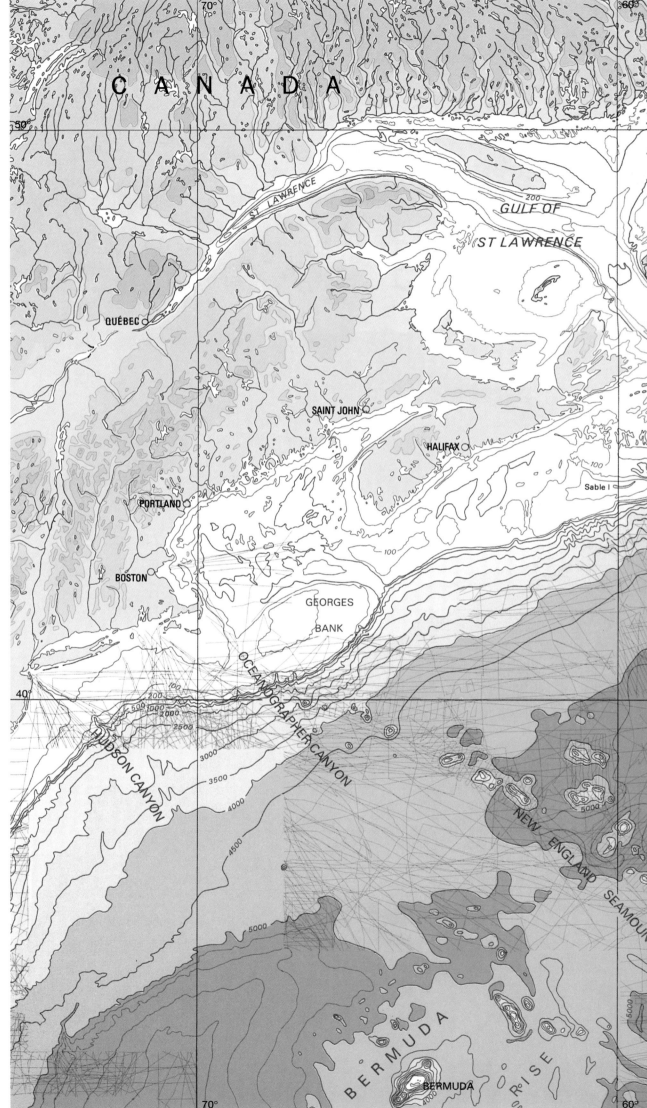

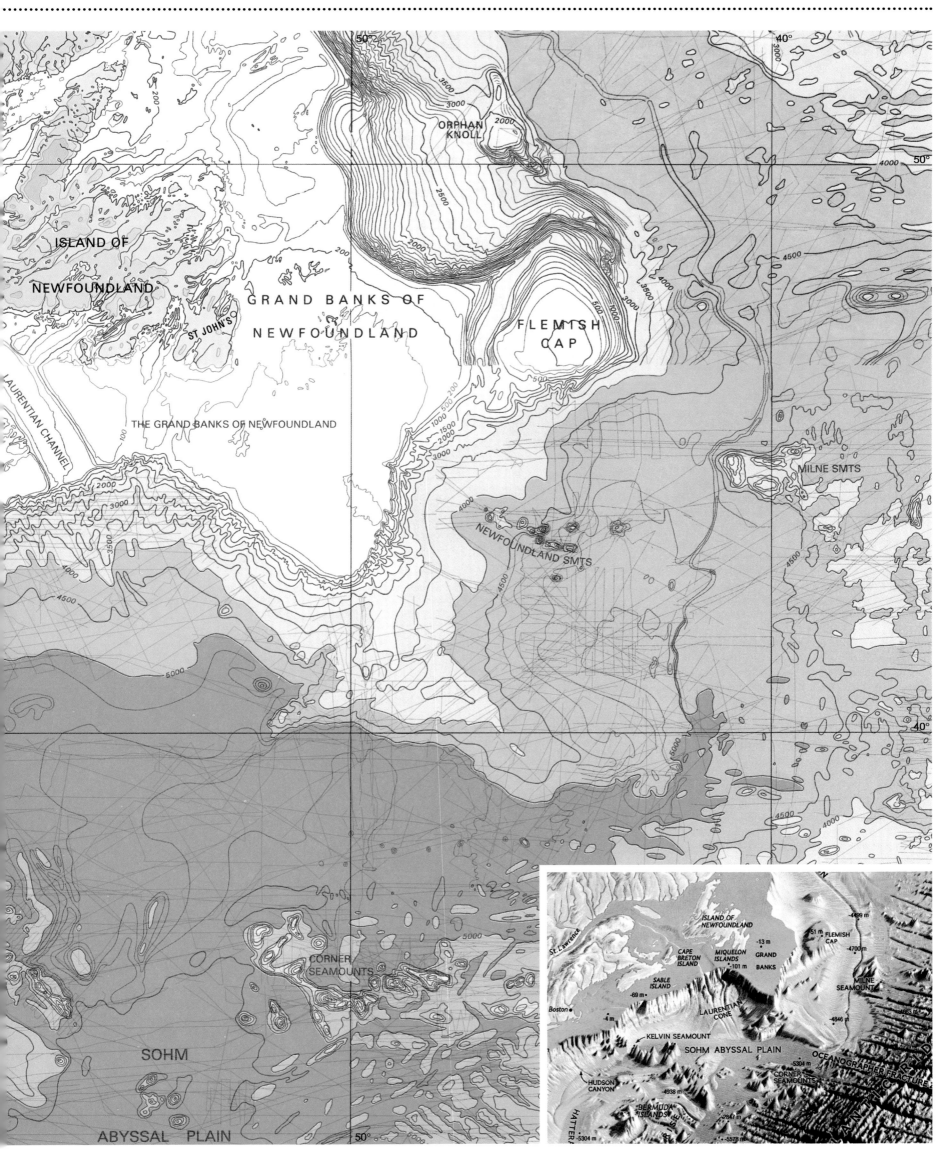

ISLAND OF
NEWFOUNDLAND

LAURENTIAN CHANNEL

ST JOHN'S

GRAND BANKS OF
NEWFOUNDLAND

THE GRAND BANKS OF NEWFOUNDLAND

ORPHAN
KNOLL

FLEMISH
CAP

MILNE SMTS

NEWFOUNDLAND SMTS

CORNER
SEAMOUNTS

SOHM

ABYSSAL PLAIN

St. Lawrence
ISLAND OF
NEWFOUNDLAND
CAPE
BRETON
ISLAND
MIQUELON
ISLANDS
-101 m
-13 m
GRAND
BANKS
51 m
FLEMISH
CAP
-4499 m
-4700 m
SABLE
ISLAND
-69 m
Boston
-4 m
LAURENTIAN
CONE
MILNE
SEAMOUNT
-4846 m
KELVIN SEAMOUNT
SOHM ABYSSAL PLAIN
OCEANOGRAPHER FRACTURE
HUDSON
CANYON
-4938 m
-5304 m
CORNER
SEAMOUNTS
BERMUDA
ISLANDS
-2847 m
HATTERA
-5304 m
-5578 m

The warm north of the Atlantic

●●● Ireland and southern England owe their particularly mild climate to the North Atlantic Current, Europe's "central heating." The large and small whirls of the Gulf Stream, which dissolves off Labrador, are driven across the Atlantic Ocean by the wind and the Earth's rotation, transporting its warmth up to northern Norway.

The shelf regions off western Europe gradually incline to a depth of some 200 meters (660 ft.) below the coastline, then its edge drops sharply to the sea floor. Numerous deep valleys are carved into this slope, extending over roughly 20 kilometers (12.5 mi.) before reaching the sea bed at a depth of some 2,500 meters (8,200 ft.).

It was the debris, sand, and mud that slid down the incline or broke off the slope and gathered at its base, that gradually built up the continental shelf that sits on the bottom of the sea 4,000 meters (13,120 ft.) deep.

Many of the slopes contain huge deposits of methane hydrate – frozen compounds of gaseous methane and water. This methane-water ice remains stable only under a particular pressure or beneath a certain temperature. As soon as the surroundings become warmer or the sea level decreases, the methane gas is released and may cause the slope to slip. About 8,400 years ago, one of the largest slides set off a 3- to 5-meter (10-ft. to 16-ft.) high tsunami, traces of which geologists are able to pinpoint to this day on the coasts of Scotland, Iceland, and Norway.

Methane is not only a source of energy, but is also a potent greenhouse gas. With increasing warmth, the oceans would release more methane gas, thus boosting the greenhouse effect. But the ensuing rise in sea level would increase the pressure so that additional methane could be absorbed.

At 470 kilometers (292 mi.) to the west of the Hebrides, a 27-meter (89-ft.) wide rock rises 23 meters (75 ft.) above the Atlantic sea level. Ever since soldier Brian Peel took possession of Rockall on behalf of Great Britain on 18 September 1955, Denmark and Iceland have been arguing with Britain over who should be the true owner, since owning the rock means imposing an economic area 200 sea miles around. When crude oil was found beneath the Rockall bank in 1969, the argument escalated. In 1975, the British set down two guards complete with guardhouse to symbolically represent the Crown for just three hours to demonstrate its title to the rock.

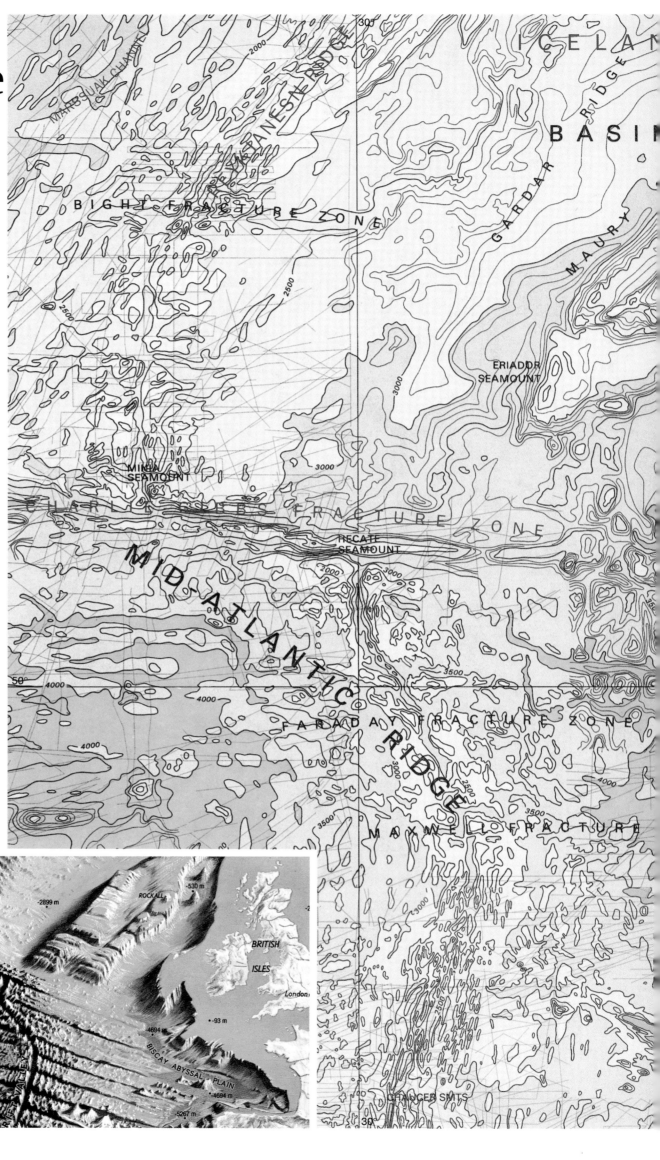

20°

10°

ROSEMARY
BANK

GEORGE
BLIGH
BANK

ROCKALL

HEBRIDEAN SHELF

1000

ROCKALL
ISLAND

ANTON DOHRN
SEAMOUNT

HATTON-ROCKALL BASIN

PLATEAU

500

HEBRIDES
TERRACE
SEAMOUNT

GLASGOW

ROCKALL BANK

1500

ORAS
K

UNITED

LOREN
BANK

FENI RIDGE

1000

500

BELFAST

ROCKALL TROUGH

LIVERPOOL

KINGDOM

AST
HULEAN
ISE

4000

4000

PORCUPINE BANK

DUBLIN

IRELAND

2000

CELTIC

50°

PORCUPINE ABYSSAL PLAIN

4500

GOBAN
SPUR

3000

SHELF

CHANNEL

PLYMOUTH

ENGLISH

N E

4500

4000

4500

4000

BREST

BISCAY

BAY OF

AZORES-BISC

3500

CHARCOT SEAMOUNTS

3500

ABYSSAL

4500

BISCAY

BORDEAUX

F
R
A
N
C
E

4000

THE GAP

3500

PLAIN

CAP
BRETON CANYON

ROUGH

3000

GALICIA
BANK

LA CORUÑA

GIJÓN

BILBAO

20°

10°

ESPAÑA

The source of the Gulf Stream

●●● The Central American Sea, comprising the Gulf of Mexico and the Caribbean Sea, developed from repeated shifting of the North American Plate and the South American Plate.

More than 245 million years ago, continental drift caused the Caribbean to detach from the Mediterranean Sea as the Atlantic Ocean emerged. Up to 67 million years ago, it was also connected to the Pacific Ocean, but this connection was closed by the formation of the Central American land bridge.

The passages between the southern Antilles allow surface water to flow into the Caribbean Sea where the trade winds drive it further into the Gulf of Mexico through the 1,600-meter (5,280-ft.) deep, narrow Strait of Yucatan between Cuba and the Yucatan Peninsula. The water accumulates in the Yucatan Basin and in the Gulf of Mexico, thus generating hydrostatic overpressure, which is believed to be the main source of energy for the Gulf Stream. Water is pushed through the Straits of Florida into the Atlantic Ocean.

The Gulf of Mexico is surrounded by a shelf area that reaches a width of more than 300 kilometers (186 mi.) off Florida and the Yucatan Peninsula. Hidden at various depths of the shelves as they descend to the deep but unusually flat seafloor, lie salt domes which are often connected with oil and gas deposits. In the period from June to November, the northern Caribbean and the Gulf of Mexico are plagued by hurricanes, most of which race over the sea at speeds of at least 120 kilometers per hour (75 mph), although as much as 500 kilometers per hour (310 mph) has been recorded.

Most of the hurricanes originate on the other side of the Atlantic, in the region of the Cape Verde Islands, and follow the route of the trade winds towards Central America. The surface water must reach at least 27° C (80.6° F) for them to pick up sufficient energy. Over the last several years, such tropical cyclones have occurred more frequently, presumably because climatic changes have heated up the Earth to such an extent that the ocean temperatures exceed this minimum more often.

Northeast of the Central American Sea, the Sargasso Sea extends to the Bermuda Islands. It is located in the calm, windless center of the great circular current of the North Atlantic; on its western rim, the Gulf Stream rolls slowly north along the North American coast. The surface is often covered with masses of sargassum weed (also known as gulf weed), a seaweed kept afloat by its characteristic bladders. Eels from European rivers come here to spawn before they die; it takes their larvae three years to cross the Atlantic and return to Europe.

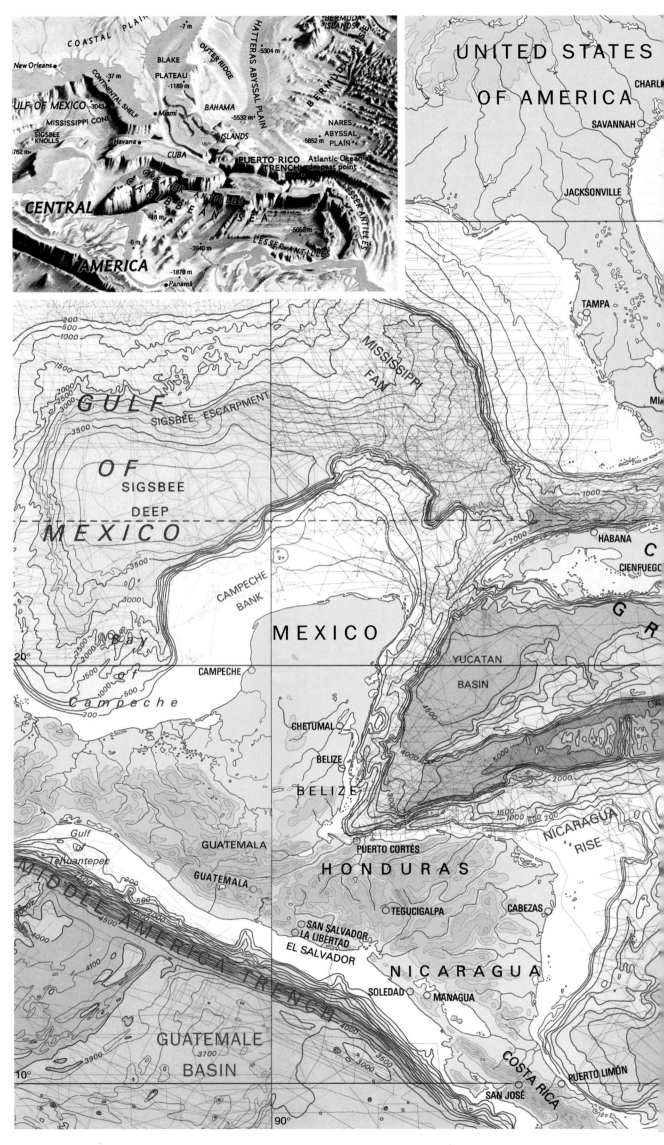

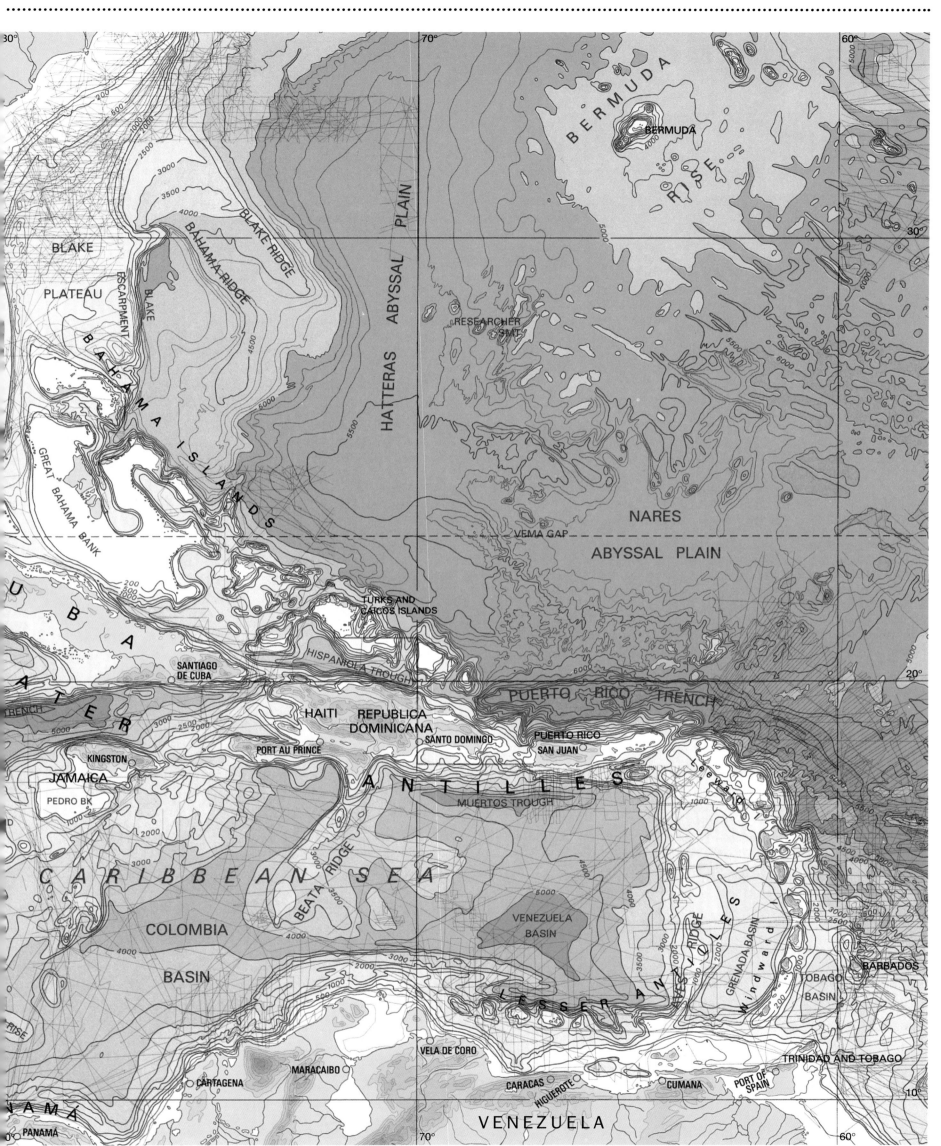

BERMUDA

BERMUDA

BERMUDA RISE

5000

BLAKE

PLATEAU

200

600

2000

2500

3000

3500

4000

BAHAMA RIDGE

BLAKE RIDGE

BLAKE ESCARPMENT

BLAKE

HATTERAS ABYSSAL PLAIN

RESEARCHER SMT.

5000

5500

6000

B A H A M A   I S L A N D S

GREAT BAHAMA BANK

4500

5000

5500

NARES

VEMA GAP

ABYSSAL PLAIN

200
800

TURKS AND CAICOS ISLANDS

HISPANIOLA TROUGH

U   B   A

SANTIAGO DE CUBA

TRENCH

5000

3000

2500 2000

HAITI

PORT AU PRINCE

REPUBLICA DOMINICANA

SANTO DOMINGO

PUERTO RICO

SAN JUAN

PUERTO   RICO   TRENCH

6000

Leeward I.

20°

KINGSTON

JAMAICA

PEDRO BK

1000

2000

3000

A   N   T   I   L   L   E   S

MUERTOS TROUGH

1000

4500

3000

4000

C A R I B B E A N   S E A

BEATA RIDGE

4000

3500

VENEZUELA BASIN

5000

4000

3500

Aves Ridge

Windward I.

GRENADA BASIN

2000

2500

3000

3500

4500

4000

3000

BARBADOS

COLOMBIA

BASIN

4000

3000

2000

1000

500

L   E   S   S   E   R   A   N   T   I   L   L   E   S

1000

2000

TOBAGO

BASIN

RISE

VELA DE CORO

CARTAGENA

MARACAIBO

CARACAS

HIGUEROTE

CUMANA

PORT OF SPAIN

TRINIDAD AND TOBAGO

10°

PANAMÁ

PANAMA

VENEZUELA

70°

60°

Oases in watery wastes

●●● Some 1,600 kilometers (990 mi.) away from their mother country of Portugal, the Azores are located on the rim of the Mid-Atlantic Ridge. Frequent earthquakes and volcanic eruptions serve to remind the inhabitants that new sea floor is continually being formed in their immediate surroundings. Situated some 1,200 kilometers (750 mi.) further to the southeast, the archipelago of Madeira, another inhabited and two uninhabited islands, also owes its existence to volcanoes which sit directly on the sea bed. They became extinct millions of years ago.

Perhaps one of the most exotic "islands", however, lies below sea level, 1,300 kilometers (800 mi.) west of the Canary Islands: Great Meteor Seamount. Such tablemounts, or submarine mountains, are abundant in all the oceans, and new ones are discovered regularly. Estimates suggest that there are 20,000 in the oceans of the world. Many once protruded above sea level as islands, and most of them are flat-topped with a limestone cap – the remains of former coral reefs. These seamounts are named "guyots" after a 19th century American geologist.

One of the most imposing guyots is Great Meteor Seamount, which was discovered as one of the first deep-sea tablemounts in 1938 during an expedition undertaken by the German research vessel *Meteor*. Although the 1,500-square-kilometer (580-sq.-mi.) plateau lies a mere 300 meters (984 ft.) below sea level, it rises steeply to more than 4,000 meters (13,100 ft.) above the sea floor. The mountain constitutes an oasis amidst the endless desert of deep blue, crystal clear water. There is hardly enough plankton present to cloud the waters of these windless horse latitudes, as they lack the turbulence to whirl up nutrient-rich deep-sea water to the surface.

Around the Great Meteor Seamount, however, wildlife is abundant, as the water is rich in plankton. Squid and moray eels hide between sponges and corals, while myriad of fish crowd the waters above the plateau, always in danger of being hunted by the otherwise rare, yet abundant here, seven-gilled sharks.

This guyot presents a natural obstacle for the passing sea current, which is forced upwards – thereby washing nutrients to the surface – where it is deflected by the Earth's rotation, resulting in a continual whirlpool circulating above the plateau. Countless microscopic crustaceans living in deeper water layers during the day rise to the surface at night, pooled by the eddy circulating above the plateau. The suction in the center of the whirlpool balances their buoyancy, and when they start to descend in the morning they land on the plateau, thus providing rich food resources for the wildlife on the Great Meteor Seamount.

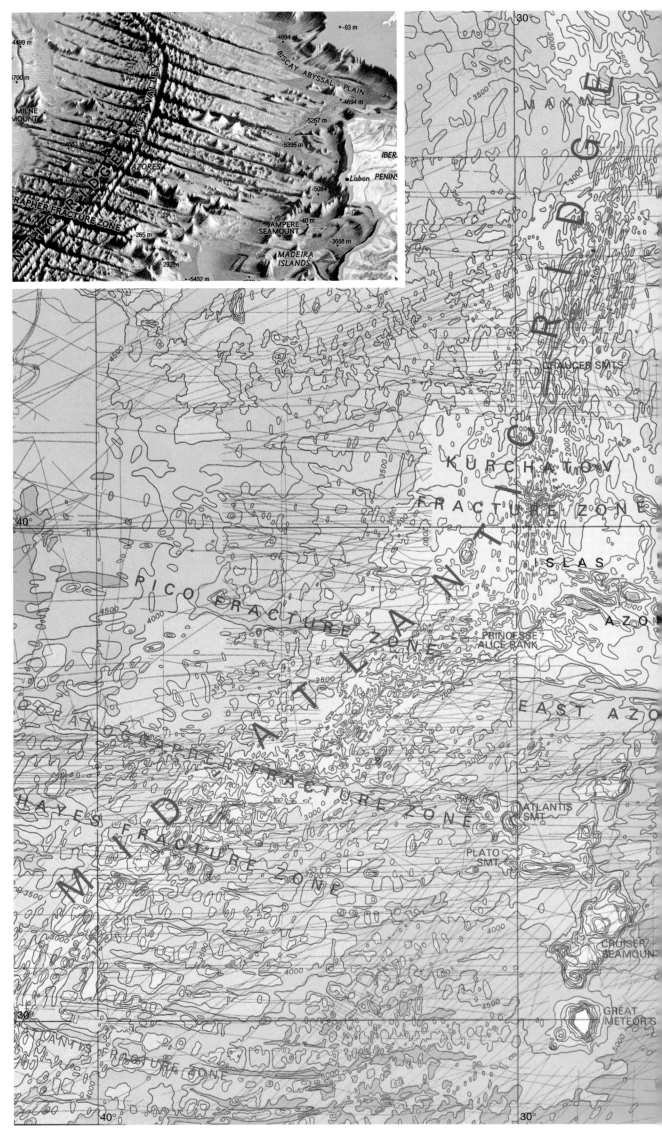

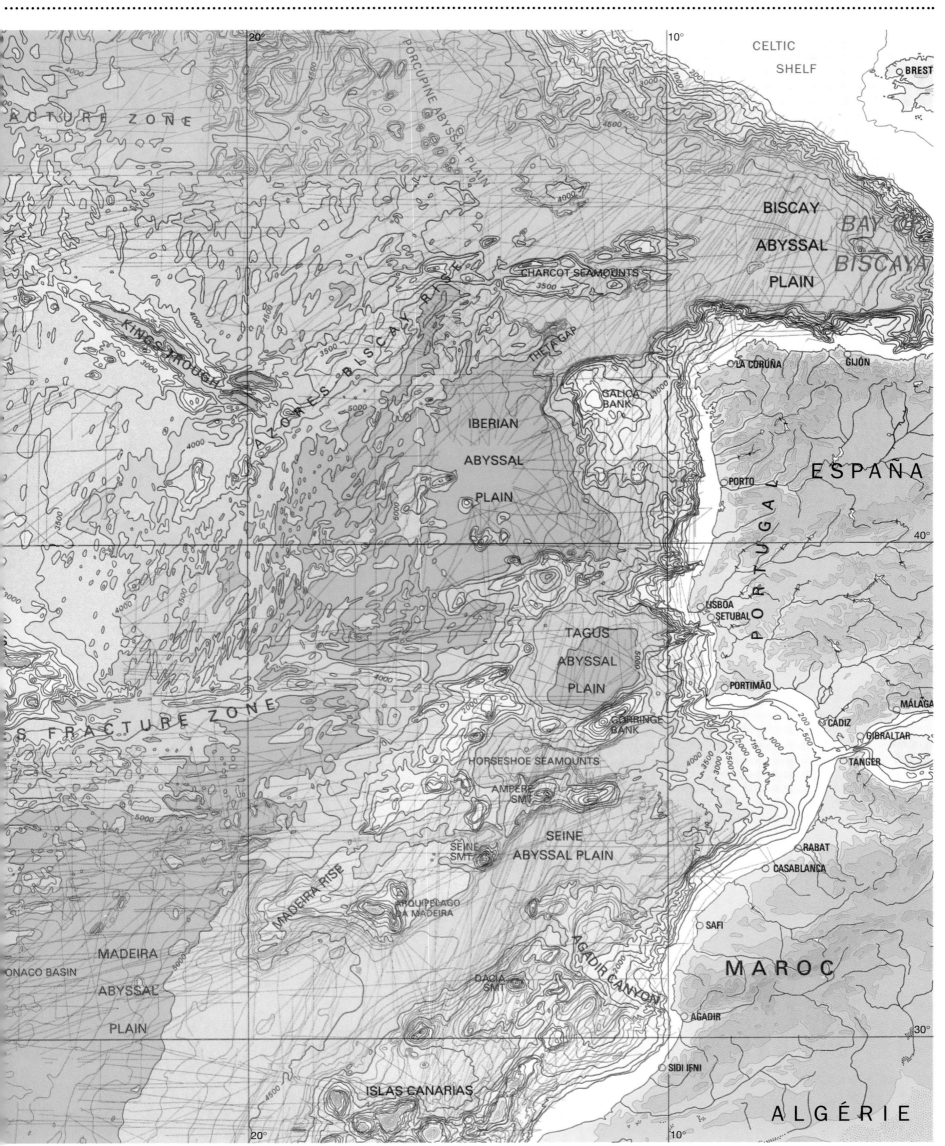

ICTURE ZONE

4000

PORCUPINE ABYSSAL PLAIN

CELTIC SHELF

BREST

20°

10°

BISCAY

ABYSSAL

PLAIN

BAY OF

BISCAYA

CHARCOT SEAMOUNTS

3500

3500

3000

4000

4500

KING'S TROUGH

AZORES BISCAY RISE

THETA GAP

GALICIA BANK

LA CORUÑA

GIJÓN

IBERIAN

ABYSSAL

PLAIN

ESPAÑA

PORTO

PORTUGAL

40°

TAGUS

ABYSSAL

PLAIN

LISBOA
SETUBAL

ES FRACTURE ZONE

4000

GORRINGE BANK

PORTIMÃO

MÁLAGA

CÁDIZ

GIBRALTAR

TANGER

HORSESHOE SEAMOUNTS

AMPERE SMT

5000

SEINE SMT

SEINE

ABYSSAL PLAIN

RABAT

CASABLANCA

MADEIRA RISE

ARQUIPÉLAGO DA MADEIRA

SAFI

MADEIRA

ONACO BASIN

ABYSSAL

PLAIN

DACIA SMT

AGADIR CANYON

MAROC

AGADIR

30°

SIDI IFNI

4500

ISLAS CANARIAS

ALGÉRIE

20°

10°

America approaches Africa

●●● The 11,300-kilometer (7,000-mi.) long mountain range of the Mid-Atlantic Ridge divides the Atlantic Ocean into a western and an eastern basin. The ridge is up to 1,600 kilometers (990 mi.) wide and represents one-third of the Atlantic ocean floor. Peaks rise 2,500 meters to 3,500 meters (8,200 ft to 11,500 ft.) above the sea bed, on average 2,500 meters (8,200 ft.) below the surface. Some of the peaks protrude as islands like São Paulo or Ascension.

Running along the crest of the mountain ridge is the central rift from which new sea floor continuously wells up, spreading the continents apart at a rate of 1 centimeter to 10 centimeters (0.4 in. to 4 in.) per year.

The Mid-Atlantic Ridge is interrupted at right angles by numerous rifts and crevices. The valleys are up to 500 kilometers (310 mi.) long, 25 kilometers (16 mi.) wide, and 3 kilometers (2 mi.) deep. Along these rifts, individual sections of the ridge shift against each other in an east-west direction.

At its narrowest point, between Cape São Roque in Brazil and Cape Palmas in Liberia, the width of the Atlantic amounts to a mere 2,850 kilometers (1,770 mi.). Here, just below the equator, the 7,758-meter (25,454-ft.) deep Romanche Gap divides the Mid-Atlantic Ridge into a northern and a southern section. Along the edges of the 300-kilometer (190-mi.) long, 19-kilometer (12-mi.) wide deep-sea gap, the southern part of the ridge arches some 640 kilometers (400 mi.) towards Africa.

The gap is one of the few deep-sea trenches neither situated along continental rims nor created by the collision of continental plates. Instead, the ridge sank into a so-called "cold spot" – as opposed to a "hot spot" – an opening in the ocean floor devoid of volcanic activity through which parts of the Earth's crust slide deep into the planet's core. The deep cut in the middle of the Atlantic Ridge allows bottom water from the Antarctic to flow into the eastern basin of the Atlantic, given that, normally, the eastern Atlantic is sealed off against the direct inflow of Antarctic Bottom Water by the Walvis Ridge, located at a right angle off the coast of southwest Africa.

Together with the overlying deep-sea water layers of the lower North Atlantic, Antarctic Bottom Water discharges through the Romanche Gap from the Brazil Basin into the Guinea Basin off the West African coast. From here, it spreads southward as well as northward at the bottom of the eastern Atlantic. On crossing the trench, however, the bottom water mixes with the slightly warmer deep-sea water flowing in from the north. This means that while it measures only 0.7° C (33.3° F) at the western entrance to the Romanche Gap, it is 0.6° C (1.1° F) warmer just 300 kilometers (190 mi.) further east – an important difference at this depth.

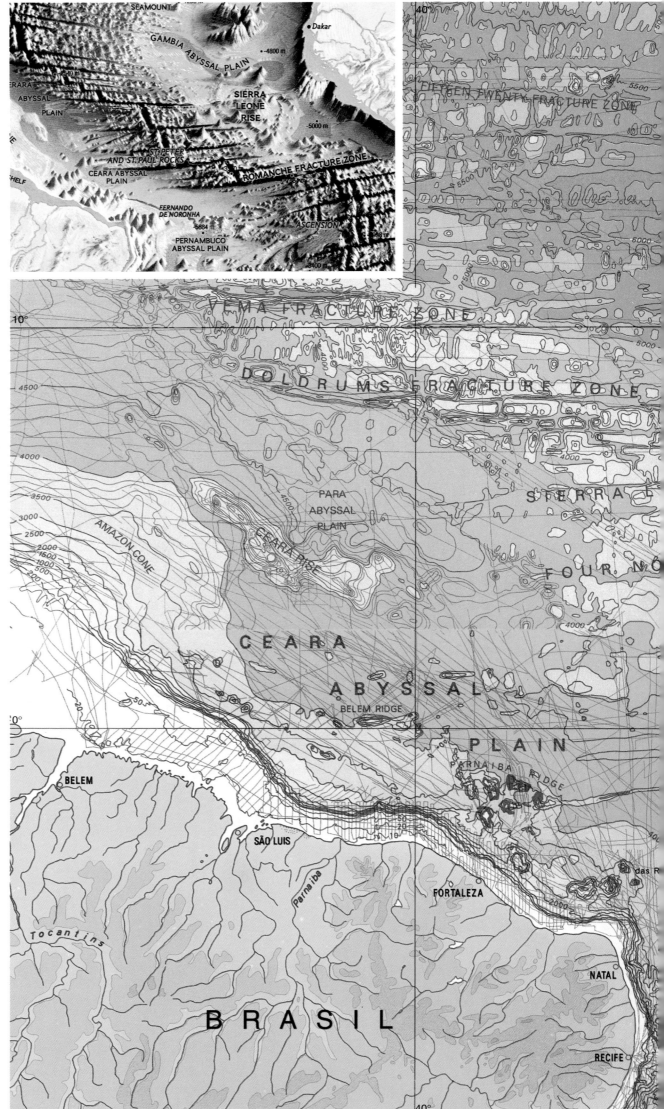

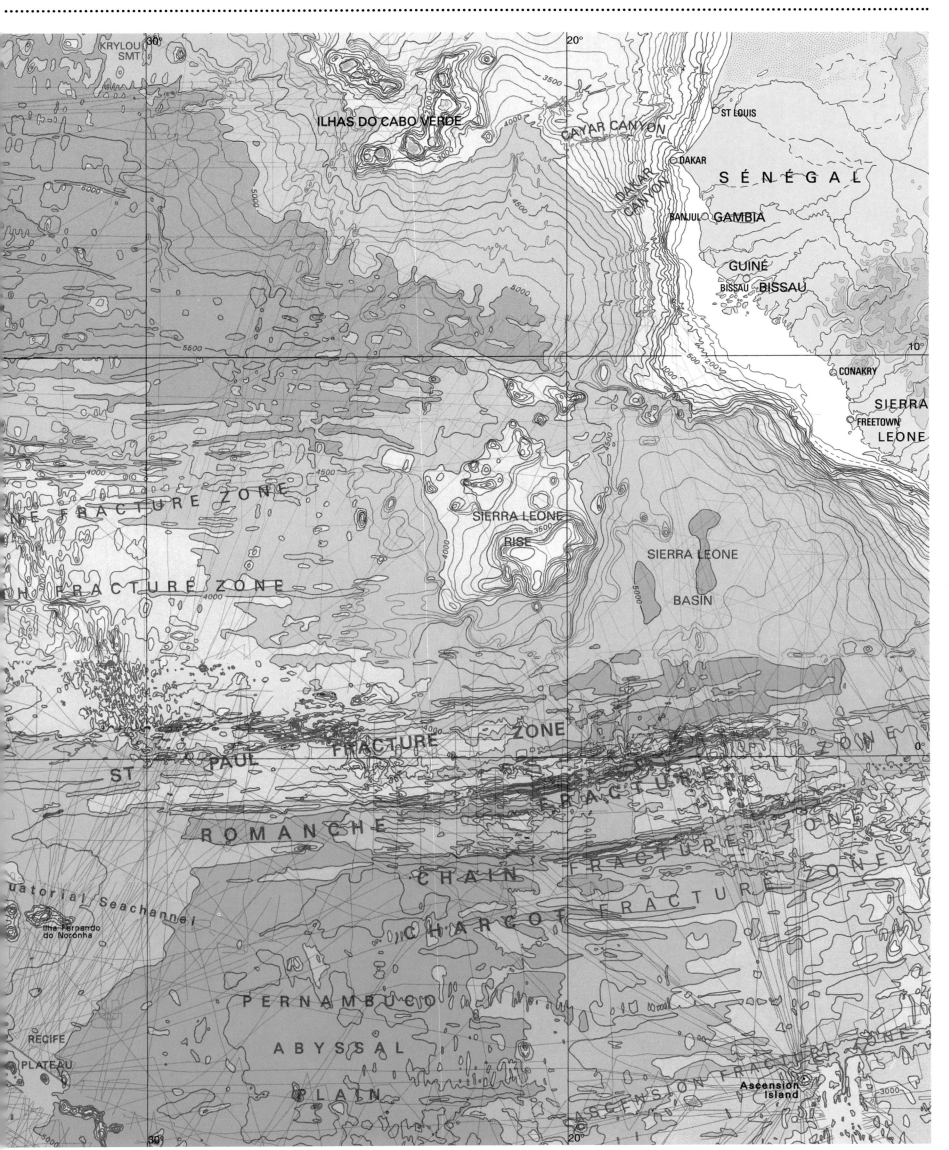

Sahara sands in the deep seas

●●● The Cape Verde Basin is a deep-sea plain located between the Mid-Atlantic Ridge and the West African coast.

While the bottom of most ocean basins is covered with mud consisting of the remains of dead organisms, this area is coated by red clay made from extremely fine-grain particles blown out to sea by Saharan winds. As the clay contains 15 percent to 20 percent aluminum, this deep-sea clay could one day become an attractive source of raw material.

The Canary and Cape Verde island groups are located between the Cape Verde deep-sea plain and Africa. The Canary Islands developed from volcanoes several million years ago.

At a distance of merely 108 kilometers (67 mi.) from Africa, the island of Fuerteventura is closest to the continental coast. The western islands of Tenerife, Gran Canaria, La Palma, Gomera, and Ferro are all mountain peaks rising directly from the sea bed, whereas the islands closer to the shoreline are located on the same sub-marine plateau, the Canary Ridge, rising 1,400 meters (4,590 ft.) above the ocean floor.

The Cape Verde Islands are also of volcanic origin, with Mount Cano on Fogo Island still an active volcano. The ruggedly jagged mountains were sculpted by sands driven there by high winds from the Sahara.

Near the Cape Verde Islands, Jacques Piccard tested the first model of his bathyscape, the deep-sea submersible vessel *Trieste*. Although the vessel was damaged during its first test dive in 1948, Piccard eventually managed to dive to a depth of 4,000 meters (13,100 ft.) off Dakar in 1954. In 1960, he reached the bottom of the 11,000-meter (36,100-ft.) deep Mariana Trench with this vessel.

Along and around the Canary Islands, the Canary Current flows southward along the African coast. It is part of an enormous clockwise eddy system – a gyre – in the North Atlantic Ocean. The Canary Current branches off from the northern part of the circular current, the North Atlantic Current, and then follows the African coast, finally turning westward, south of the Cape Verde Islands, to converge with the North Atlantic Equatorial Current, the southern branch of the gyre.

The Canary Current is cold because the offshore winds drive the surface water away from the coast and into the open sea. This results in cold waters rising from the depths, loaded with nutrients for plankton algae which, in turn, provide the basis for the rich fishing grounds of the region. The cool current is also responsible for the comfortable temperatures prevailing on the Canary Islands, as it fends off the Saharan heat.

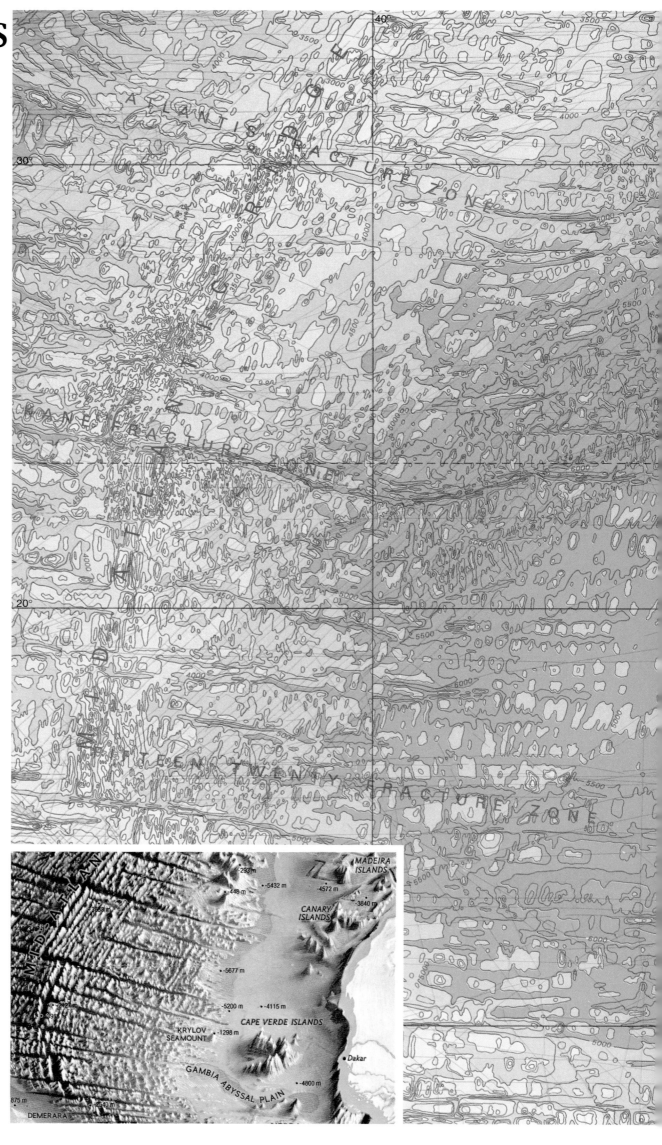

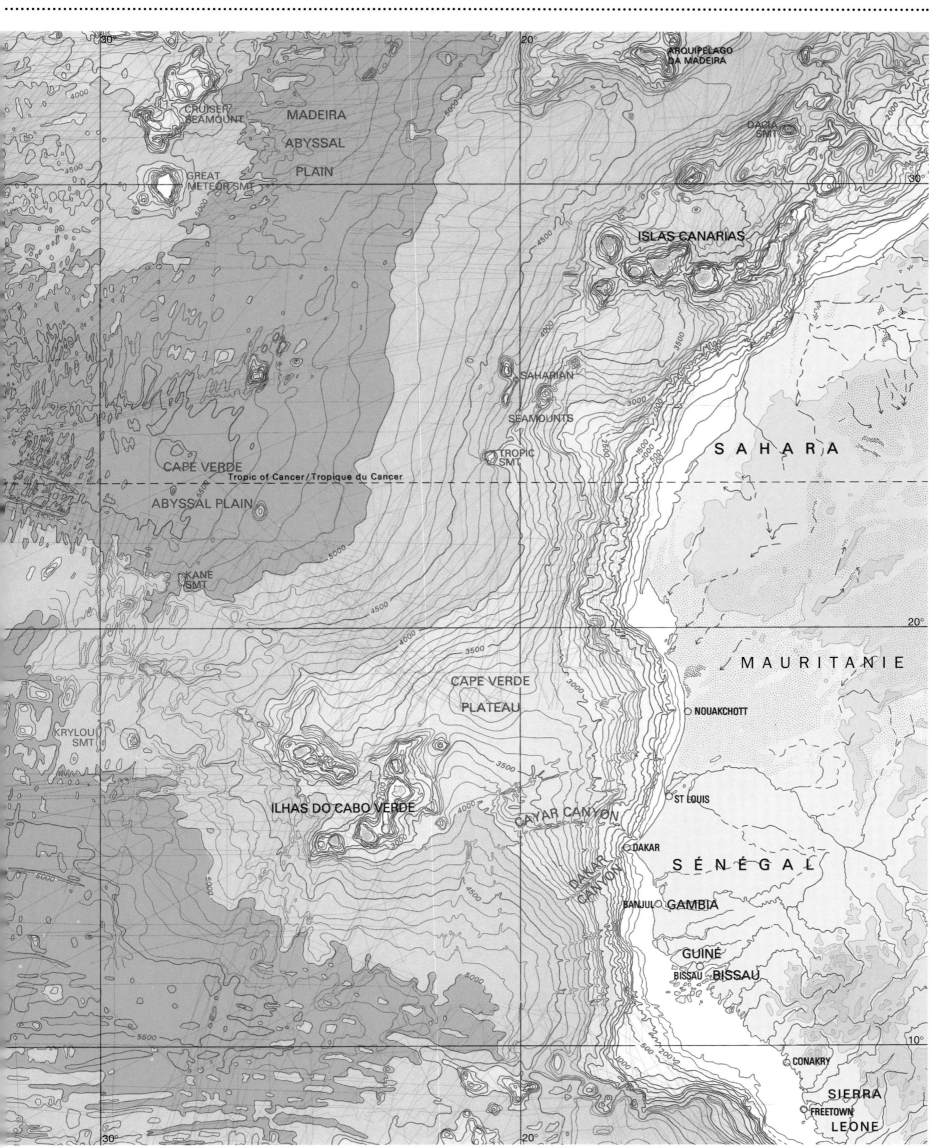

ARQUIPELAGO
DA MADEIRA

CRUISER
SEAMOUNT

MADEIRA

ABYSSAL

PLAIN

GREAT
METEOR SMT

DACIA
SMT

ISLAS CANARIAS

SAHARIAN

SEAMOUNTS

TROPIC
SMT

SAHARA

CAPE VERDE

Tropic of Cancer / Tropique du Cancer

ABYSSAL PLAIN

KANE
SMT

CAPE VERDE

PLATEAU

MAURITANIE

NOUAKCHOTT

KRYLOU
SMT

ILHAS DO CABO VERDE

ST LOUIS

CAYAR CANYON

DAKAR

SÉNÉGAL

DAKAR
CANYON

BANJUL GAMBIA

GUINÉ

BISSAU BISSAU

CONAKRY

SIERRA

FREETOWN

LEONE

A passage for Antarctic waters

●●● In the southwestern part of the Atlantic, the Rio Grande Rise separates the Brazil Basin in the north from the Argentine Basin in the south.

Just like the Walvis Ridge on the eastern side of the Mid-Atlantic Ridge, the Rio Grande Rise formed over a so-called "hot spot" – a point of volcanic activity within the Earth's mantle. This particular hot spot, which gave rise to both these aseismic ridges more than 80 million years ago, is located near the Tristan da Cunha island group. After both ridges had drifted away from the middle of the ocean, the Rio Grande Rise underwent no further transformation.

Like the Walvis Ridge, the Rio Grande Rise is a natural barrier preventing Antarctic deep-sea water from spreading into the subtropical South Atlantic. Unlike the Walvis Ridge, however, the Rio Grande Rise presents two passages: the Vema and the Hunter seachannels.

While it was formerly believed that deep-sea water could flow north off the South American coast only by crossing the deep Vema Seachannel, researchers have recently discovered that huge amounts of Antarctic waters can, also at intervals, reach the Brazil Basin via the shallower Hunter Seachannel.

On the surface, the Brazil Current flows south in the opposite direction. It is part of the subtropical gyre, a counterclockwise circular current in the South Atlantic. The Brazil Current is weak, however, in comparison to similar coastal currents of other ocean basins. Off South America's eastern tip, it branches off from the South Equatorial Current, which comes from Africa and splits into several branches at this point. Most of the water is shifted towards the Caribbean so that little is left for the Brazil Current.

The Tristan da Cunha island group, where the Rio Grande Rise once developed, consists of six small islands that were discovered in 1506 but remained uninhabited for a long time. When a British garrison on the main island closed down in 1817 after just one year of service, three of the soldiers decided to stay.

Over the years, they were joined by shipwrecked sailors, European settlers, and women from Saint Helena. By 1886, the population had increased to 97 inhabitants living in a settlement called Edinburgh. When the place was threatened by volcanic eruptions in 1961, the islanders were evacuated to England. After the danger was over, however, 198 of them returned to their homes in 1963.

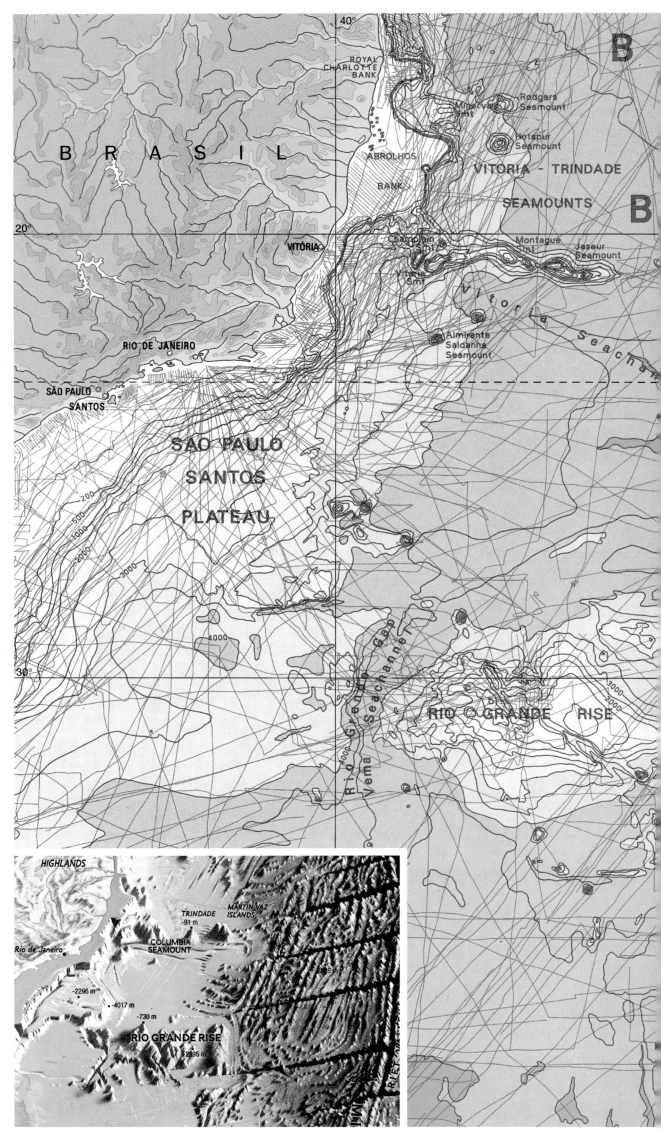

The edges of Africa

●●● West Africa's coastline shows a remarkable correspondence to the continental rim of South America on the other side of the Atlantic. This similarity, not only in shape but also in geological features, is a visible confirmation of the concept of continental drift.

The West African coastal shelf is mostly very narrow, broadening to 160 kilometers (100 mi.) only in the Bay of Biafra where the mud carried by the River Niger created a huge delta over the course of 10,000 years. To the southeast, more than 700 kilometers (440 mi.) into the open sea, lies the region's only volcanic island chain, including Bioko, Principe, São Tomé, and Annobón (Pagalu), although these volcanoes have long been dormant. The mainland continuation of the chain comprises Mount Cameroon, rising 4,095 meters (13,435 ft.) above the coast.

On a stretch of some 400 kilometers (250 mi.) in width, along the entire northern flank of the Gulf of Guinea, the Guinea Current heads for the Nigerian coast. Coming from the south, the cold Benguela Current reaches the Gulf of Guinea, then branches off westward to merge with the South Equatorial Current flowing along the equator in the opposite direction to the Guinea Current. At the latitude of the mouth of the River Congo, the Benguela Current is separated by a sharp ridge from the tropical waters of the Gulf and the Bay of Biafra.

The highly saline Guinea Current is a continuation of the north Equatorial Counter Current approaching from the west, and supplemented by parts of the Canary Current off North Africa. Here, the variety of oceanic organisms is surprisingly low compared with the numerous life forms found on the other side of the Atlantic, or in Indonesia. Scientists suppose that the cooling down of the climate some 5 to 24 million years ago led to the extinction of many more organisms in the Atlantic than in the Indo-Pacific region.

Yet there is another reason for this biological poverty. The Guinea Current is very turbulent, and its calmer areas are relatively low in salt because the fresh water brought in by the Rivers Niger and Congo dilutes its surface water. These conditions impede the development of the ecological system associated with coral reefs, which is dependent on calm waters and normal oceanic salt concentration.

Fish, however, are abundant due to the upwelling of nutrient-rich bottom water off the coasts of Senegal and Congo, which stimulates the growth of plankton algae. Furthermore, the offshore wind coming from Cote d'Ivoire and Ghana drives the surface water out into the open sea in July and August, thus making space for deep-sea waters. However, the fish populations in these West African waters are threatened by unchecked over-fishing.

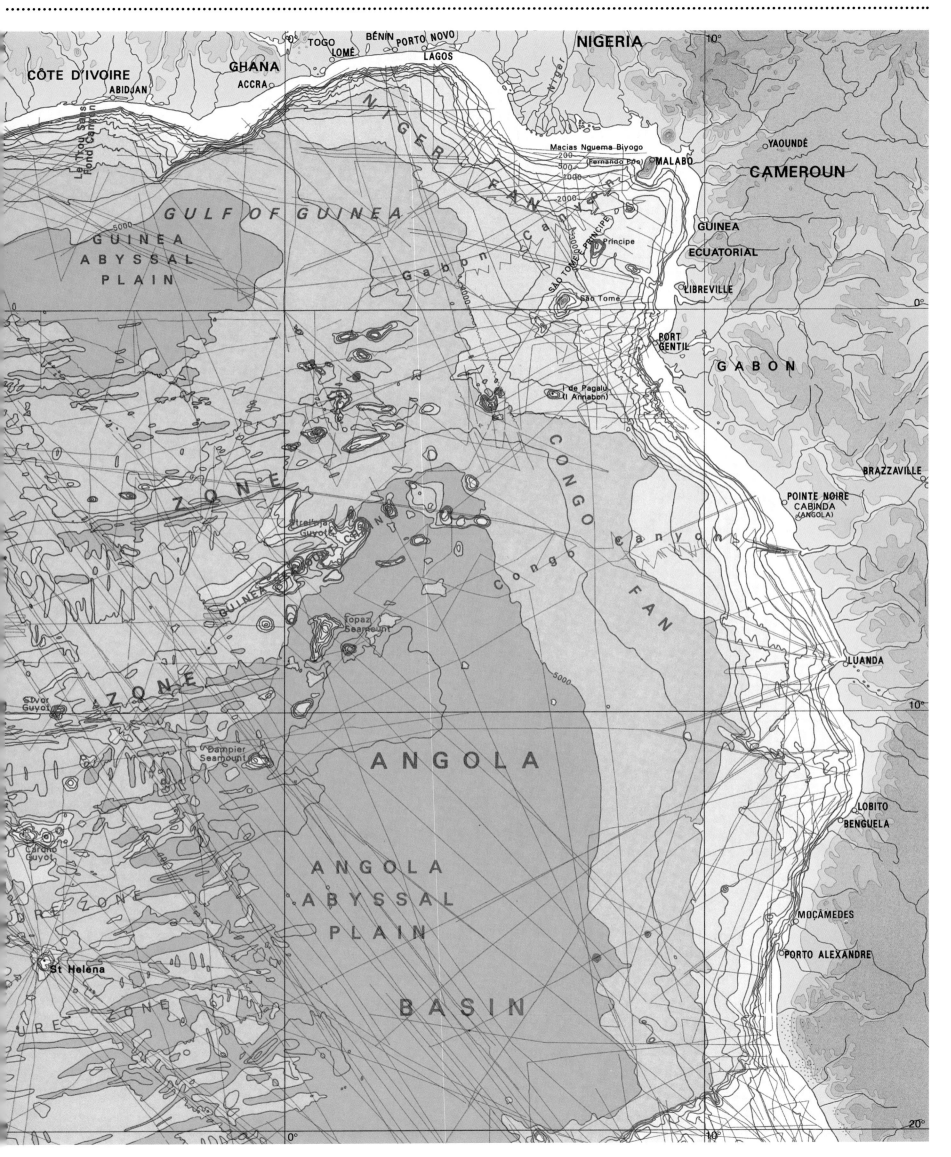

Icebergs off South America

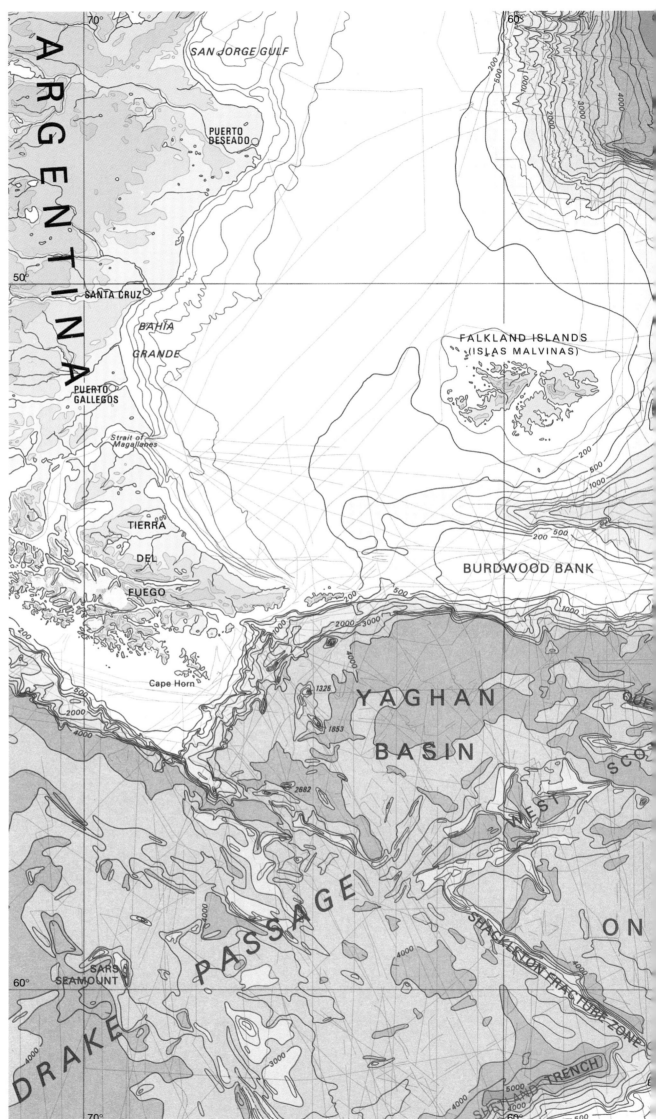

● ● ● The 1,000-kilometer (620-mi.) wide Drake Passage is the narrowest passage encountered by the Antarctic Circumpolar Current, as it circulates around the Antarctic continent. Trapped between the tip of South America and the Antarctic Peninsula, the current crosses the passage at high speed. Immediately off the shore of Tierra del Fuego, it is referred to as the Cape Horn Current.

East of Tierra del Fuego, the Falkland Current branches off from the Antarctic Circumpolar Current and flows up the South American coast to the latitude of the mouth of the Rio de la Plata near Buenos Aires and Montevideo. This cold current carries a considerable number of icebergs into this area. Strong westerly winds, the ill-famed "furious fifties," rage around South America's southern tip, especially near the mainland. The southern part of the Drake Passage is often plagued by cyclones developing in the South Pacific.

Roughly along 60° latitude, in the southern third of the Drake Passage, the water temperature suddenly changes. This line constitutes the Antarctic Convergence, a transition zone separating cold, low-saline polar water from subantarctic surface water. In this area, the sea is some 3,400 meters (11,160 ft.) deep, in some places reaching up to 4,800 meters (15,750 ft.) deep. At a depth between 500 meters and 3,000 meters (1,640 ft. and 10,000 ft.) a layer of relatively warm, high-saline deep-sea water hovers over the bottom water.

The Falkland Islands, also known as Malvinas Islands, lie almost 500 kilometers (310 mi.) northeast of South America's southern tip, at almost the same distance from the Strait of Magellan on a branch of the continental shelf where roughly 200 islands rise above sea level. The 80-kilometer (50-mi.) long and 2-kilometer to 32-kilometer (1.2-mi. to 20-mi.) wide Falkland Sound, with its many tiny islands, separates the two main islands of East Falkland and West Falkland.

Owing to their location in the middle of the ocean, the Falkland Islands have no major seasonal variation. All year long, air temperatures range between 3° C and 9° C (37.4° F and 48.2° F). From the west, however, a strong wind continually blows over the island at some 31 kilometers per hour (19.3 mph) – the same wind that also propels the ocean currents.

The first British settlers came to the Falkland Islands in 1765, but only for nine years. In 1820, Argentina proclaimed sovereignty over the abandoned archipelago. In 1831, however, a US warship destroyed the Argentinean settlement after seal-catching ships had been captured. Thus, Great Britain was able to retake possession of its old colony. In 1982, Argentinea made an attempt to reconquer the islands with force, but was defeated by Britain.

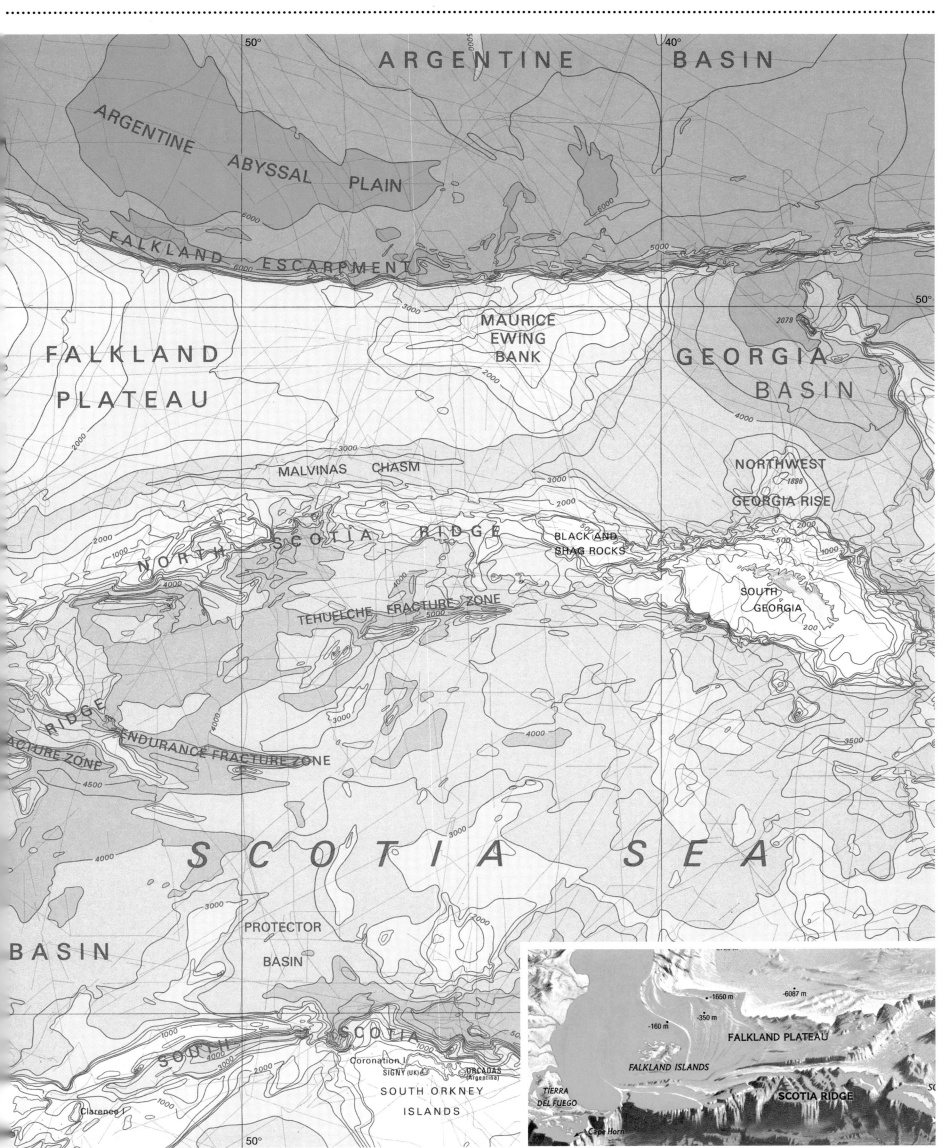

ARGENTINE BASIN

ARGENTINE ABYSSAL PLAIN

FALKLAND ESCARPMENT

FALKLAND PLATEAU

MAURICE EWING BANK

GEORGIA BASIN

MALVINAS CHASM

NORTH SCOTIA RIDGE

BLACK AND SHAG ROCKS

NORTHWEST GEORGIA RISE

TEHUELCHE FRACTURE ZONE

ENDURANCE FRACTURE ZONE

RIDGE

ACTURE ZONE

SOUTH GEORGIA

SCOTIA SEA

PROTECTOR BASIN

BASIN

SCOTIA

Coronation I.
SIGNY (UK)
ORCADAS (Argentina)

SOUTH ORKNEY ISLANDS

Clarence I.

TIERRA DEL FUEGO

FALKLAND ISLANDS

FALKLAND PLATEAU

SCOTIA RIDGE

Cape Horn

-1650 m
-6087 m
-160 m
-350 m

The "sulfur pearls" of Namibia

● ● ● Walvis Ridge is a sub-marine mountain range in the northwestern part of the Cape Basin off South West Africa – formerly an island rising 2,000 meters (6,600 ft.) above sea level. Its counterpart is the Rio Grande Rise located on the other side of the Mid-Atlantic Ridge. Both emerged over the same so-called "hot spot" – an active volcanic site in the Earth's mantle that draws hot magma up from the depths. The ocean crust moves slowly over this hot spot and its emerging magma, leaving a trail of volcanic outpourings on the sea floor which later disappear. The hot spot over which these mountains developed more than 80 million years ago is located between the two ridges of the Tristan da Cunha island group.

Although the South West African coast is bordered by hot deserts, the surface water off the coast is cold. The Benguela Current, a branch of the West Wind Drift of the Southern Hemisphere, flows along the coast almost to the equator, where it converges with the Atlantic South Equatorial Current drifting westward. On its way north, the Benguela Current draws up cold deep-sea water which surfaces directly at the shoreline.

This upwelling carries nutrients to the surface, thus providing the rich fishing grounds off South West Africa. In the nutrient-rich waters, microscopically small plankton algae thrive so quickly that not all of them can be eaten by plankton animals which in turn provide food for fish. The algae die off and sink to the sea floor where they rot, eventually forming a greenish, slimy layer. As their decomposition uses up oxygen, it produces sulfide (a sulfur compound).

In this slimy layer, a young German scientist recently discovered the world's largest bacterium, which she designated as the "Sulfur Pearl of Namibia." It is just recognizable with the naked eye and thus many times larger than any other known microbe.

In addition, the "sulfur pearl" is highly specialized. It subsists on sulfide which is found in particularly high concentrations on the sea floor off Namibia. To process this compound, however, the microorganism needs nitrogen which is not available there. When one of the rare storms stirs the water down to the sea floor, these bacteria are whirled into high-nitrate surface layers where they take up as much nitrogen as they can store in a bubble representing up to 95 percent of their cell volume. When they sink back to the bottom, this stock lasts them for a long time, so they are able to take up and process their primary food – sulfide.

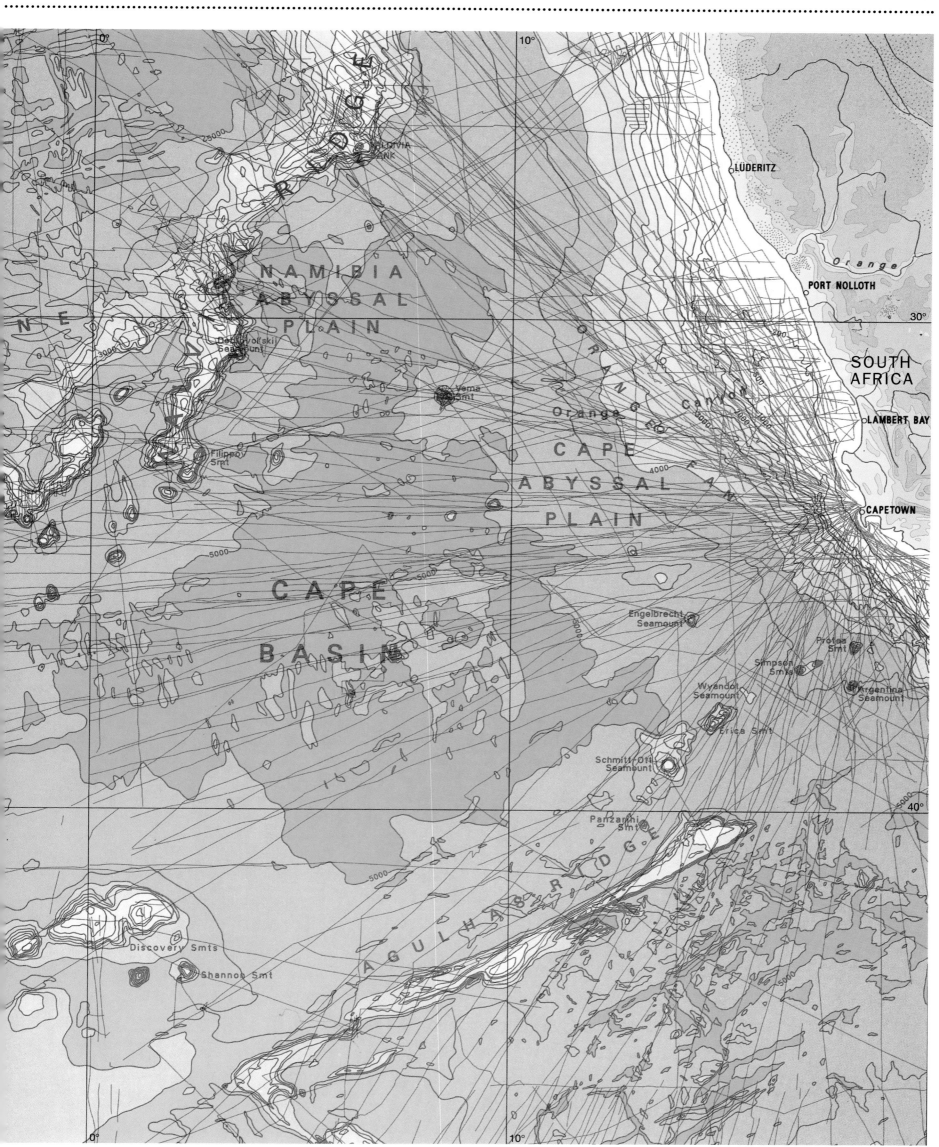

The south polar hydro-logic circle

●●● The Scotia Arc, comprising the sea of the same name, consists of the submarine Scotia Ridge with the mountainous South Atlantic islands and the Antarctic Peninsula – including its outermost tip, the Trinity Peninsula. From there, the Scotia Arc turns eastward and performs a hairpin turn to merge with Tierra del Fuego and the South American Andes.

Unlike the Pacific, where such island arcs are quite common, there is only one comparable structure in the Atlantic: the Antilles Arc in the Caribbean. Because of this northern counterpart, the Scotia Arc was, therefore, also called the South Antilles Ridge. The entire bow is 4,350 kilometers (2,700 mi.) long and declines sharply in the east into the more than 7,900-meter (25,920-ft.) deep South Sandwich Trench.

As of the 17th century, the region had been explored in greater detail than most other oceanic areas. During the 18th and 19th centuries, the reason for such intense exploration was mainly the relentless search for more abundant, new hunting grounds for whales and seals. Many of these marine mammal species were hunted almost to the point of extinction by the 1960s.

A weak barrier connects South Georgia Island with the South Orkney Islands, dividing the Scotia Sea into two smaller basins. Water from the Antarctic Circumpolar Current pushes through the 1,000-kilometer (620-mi.) long Drake Passage into the Scotia Sea. More or less unhindered by mainland branches, the Antarctic Circumpolar Current circulates clockwise around the southern continent, driven by the "furious fifties" and "screaming sixties," – the strong westerly winds of the 50° and 60° latitudes.

Occasionally in winter and spring, melting icebergs from the Weddell Sea float into the Scotia Sea. In the center of the Antarctic Circumpolar Current lies the Antarctic Convergence, a water barrier where warmer subantarctic water from the north converges with cold, high-nutrient water from the Antarctic. Plankton is found in abundance where the current picks up speed, and this was once a major feeding ground for numerous baleen whales. Today, this water stretch offers a rich supply of food to almost 100 different fish species and a large number of birds.

The northern and southern branch of the Scotia Ridge belong to different climatic zones. While South Georgia Island is located in the subantarctic region, the South Orkney Islands are already part of the Antarctic proper. The latter are covered almost completely by glaciers, and the vegetation there is mostly limited to lichen, moss, and algae. Dogs, cats, mice, and rats, which were mostly unintentionally introduced to some of the Scotia islands, today threaten important seabird rookeries.

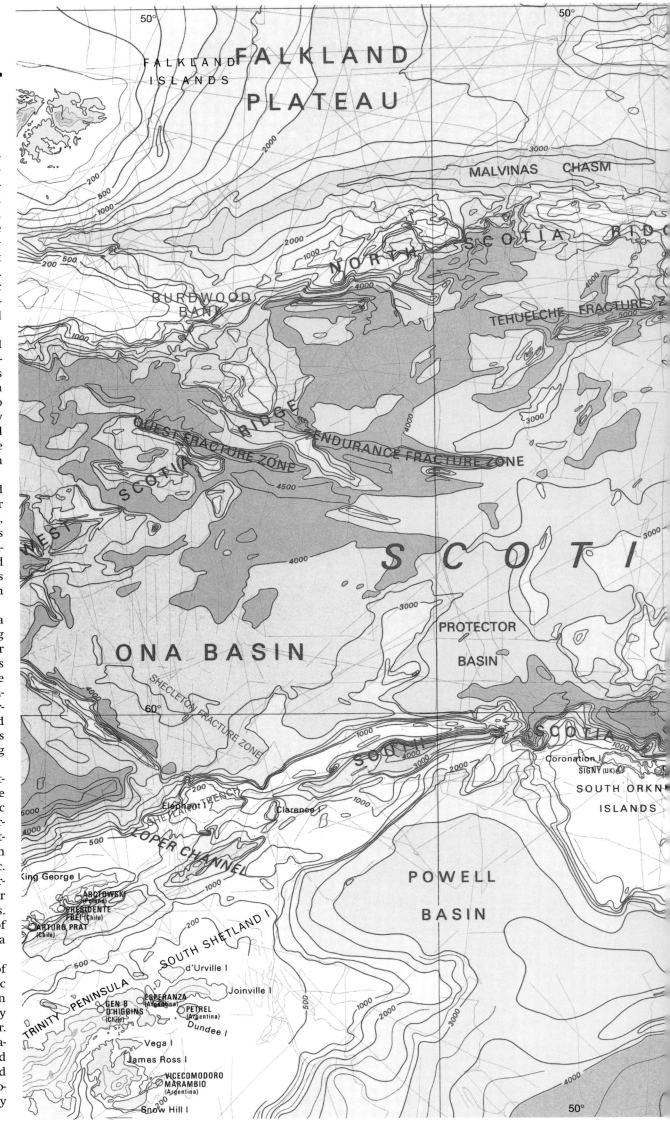

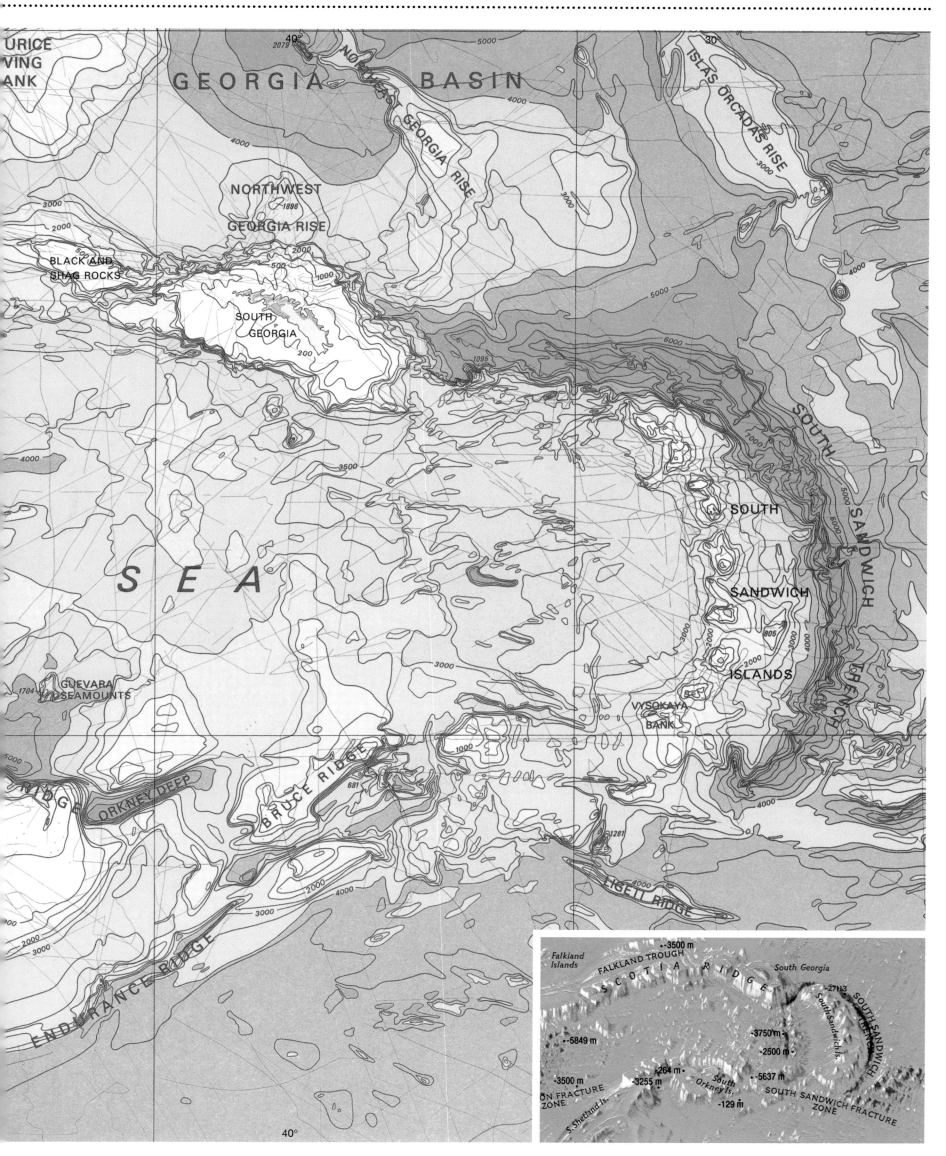

URICE
VING
ANK

G E O R G I A   B A S I N

5000

40°
2079

NORTHWEST GEORGIA RISE

4000

4000

30°

ISLAS ORCADAS RISE

3000

NORTHWEST

1896

3000

GEORGIA RISE

2000

2000

3000

4000

3000

BLACK AND
SHAG ROCKS

500

500

1000

2000

SOUTH
GEORGIA

200

5000

1095

6000

5849 m

4000

3500

6000

SOUTH

S E A

3000

SANDWICH

805

SANDWICH

7000

SOUTH

5000

TRENCH

2000

ISLANDS

GUEVARA
SEAMOUNTS

1704

3000

2000

VYSOKAYA
BANK

3000

4000

2000

1000

RIDGE

ORKNEY DEEP

BRUCE RIDGE

681

4000

1281

4000

3000

2000

EGETT RIDGE

ENDURANCE RIDGE

200

2000

3000

Falkland
Islands

-3500 m

FALKLAND TROUGH

S C O T I A   R I D G E

South Georgia

-27113

-5849 m

-3750 m

SOUTH SANDWICH TRENCH

-2500 m

South Sandwich Is.

-264 m

-5637 m

-3500 m

-3255 m

South
Orkney Is.

SOUTH SANDWICH FRACTURE
ZONE

-129 m

ON FRACTURE
ZONE

S. Shetland Is.

Where tectonic plates meet

●●● In the far south of the Atlantic Ocean, far from anywhere, lies Bouvet Island. It belongs to Norway and is probably the most remote of all islands on Earth, at a distance of 2,400 kilometers (1,490 mi.) from the Cape of Good Hope and some 1,600 kilometers (1,000 mi.) from the Antarctic mainland. The steep, rocky island is completely buried under ice, making landing on its shores extremely difficult.

After the French navigator Jean-Baptiste-Charles Bouvet de Lozier had discovered the island in 1739, it fell into oblivion until a German expedition rediscovered it in 1898. The Norwegian flag was first hoisted in 1927, although the island was annexed to Norway only in February 1930. Since 1971, the island has been a nature preserve.

Bouvet Island is the result of volcanic activity. It is situated at the beginning of the Atlantic-Indian Ridge, i.e., the southernmost part of the Southwest Indian Ridge. The ridge extends in a more or less straight line eastward, where it separates the Antarctic Plate from the African Plate before its main part turns north. A third element, the South American Plate, meets the other two plates at this point.

This meeting of the three oceanic ridges situated on the seams of their respective continental plates is known as the Bouvet Triple Junction. Its current structure is no more than two million years old, making it relatively young.

The three plates are drifting apart as new sea floor continually emerges from their spreading centers – the ridges – at varying speeds. The border between the South American and African Plates, the Mid-Atlantic Ridge, is the most active of the three sub-marine mountain ranges, and some 35 millimeters (1.4 in.) of new rock are formed each year.

The Southwest Indian Ridge is the calmest of all oceanic ridges, driving the oceanic plates apart at a rate of merely 13 millimeters to 18 millimeters (0.52 in. to 0.72 in.) per year. Nevertheless, it possesses the thinnest "skin" of all, since over much of its length, its crust is not as thick as would be expected. Up until now, it has hardly been explored, so nothing is known to date about the presence of hot springs or the ecosystems associated with them. To date, most research activities have focused on the faster expanding Mid-Atlantic Ridge and the very active East Pacific Rise.

Unlike other oceanic triple junctions, the Bouvet Triple Junction is very static and hardly moves. It is connected with a hot spot in the oceanic crust where molten magma emerges from the depth of the Earth's core and volcanoes rise.

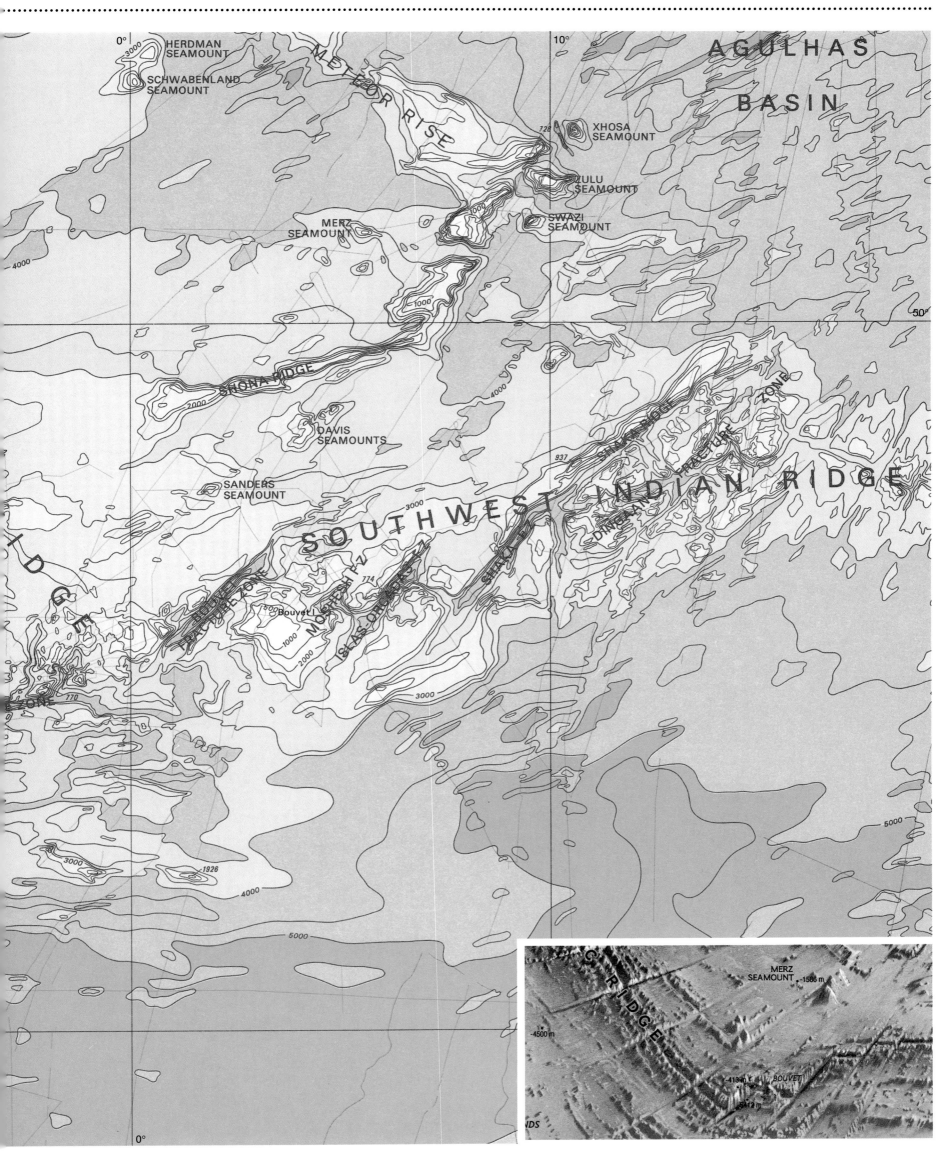

0°

HERDMAN SEAMOUNT

3000

SCHWABENLAND SEAMOUNT

METEOR RISE

10°

AGULHAS

BASIN

XHOSA SEAMOUNT

128

ZULU SEAMOUNT

MERZ SEAMOUNT

SWAZI SEAMOUNT

4000

2000

1000

50°

SHONA RIDGE

2000

4000

DAVIS SEAMOUNTS

937

SHAKA RIDGE

SANDERS SEAMOUNT

S O U T H W E S T   I N D I A N   R I D G E

FRACTURE ZONE

DINGAAN

3000

RIDGE

FRACTURE ZONE

SHAKA F.Z.

ISLAS ORCADAS

774

MOSHESH F.Z.

500 Bouvet I.

1000

2000

ZONE 770

3000

3000

4000

1926

4000

5000

5000

MERZ SEAMOUNT -1586 m

RIDGE

-4500 m

-418 m BOUVET

-3412 m

NDS

0°

Sea strait and land bridge

●●● The Bering Strait connects the Pacific Ocean with the Arctic Ocean. To its south, the Bering Sea basin extends as the northernmost part of the Pacific while, to its north, the Chukchi Sea is part of the Arctic Ocean.

The Bering Strait separates Asia from North America. At its narrowest point, the distance between the two continents is a mere 85 kilometers (53 mi.). The average depth of the strait ranges between 30 meters (98 ft.) and 50 meters (164 ft.).

Only small quantities of water flow from the Bering Sea in the south through the strait to the Arctic Ocean. Although parts of the deep water of the Bering Sea rise to the surface from the 4,000-meter (13,120-ft.) deep basin, they are driven back into the Pacific as surface water. Nevertheless, a small amount of deep water does reach the Arctic Ocean via the Bering Strait, the main reason for this being a slight difference in sea levels between the North Pacific and the Arctic Ocean.

In addition, the water exchange seems to be influenced by irregular movements of the Alaska Current as well as the large-scale atmospheric eddies over the North Pacific.

The tidal rise in the Bering Strait is only some 30 centimeters (11.8 in.). In winter, heavy storms rage over the strait, and at air temperatures between −35° C and −45° C (−31° F and −49° F), the sea is covered with pack ice, more than 1-meter (3.3-ft.) thick, south to the Aleutian Island arc. Ice floats are seen in the Bering Strait even in the warmest summer months.

Almost halfway between Cape Dezhnyov on the Russian shore and Cape Prince of Wales in Alaska lie the two Diomede Islands. The International Date Line runs between them, while to the south, the St. Lawrence Island is situated diagonally across the entrance to the strait.

The Bering Strait was discovered in 1648 by the Russian navigator Semyon Ivanov Dezhnyov and was explored in detail – on orders of the Russian czar Peter the Great – by the Danish seafarer Vitus Jonassen Bering in 1728. During the last glacial period lasting up to some 10,000 years ago, the sea level was about 100 meters (328 ft.) lower than it is today. Instead of the sea strait, a land bridge (Beringia or Beringland) connected Asia and America for a period of 100 million years, allowing numerous plant and animal species to cross from one continent to the other.

Even early humans migrated from Asia to America some 10,000 years ago, although most recent findings raise questions with respect to the conventional research concept – recent linguistic investigations indicating, for instance, that the first migration wave must have taken place as far back as 40,000 years ago.

UKCHI SEA

170°

Icy Cape

160°

Colville

BROOKS RANGE

Pt Hope

50

KOTZEBUE SOUND

C. Dezhneva

PENINSULA

BERING STRAIT

C. Prince of Wales

SEWARD PENINSULA

ALASKA

50

NOME

KIVAK

NORTON SOUND

St Lawrence I

Yukon

50

ALASKA RANGE

St. Matthew I

Nunivak I

QUINHAGAK

COOK INLET

Asia's coldest sea

●●● To the north and northwest, the Sea of Okhotsk has a relatively narrow continental shelf. The other two-thirds of the sea, which is on average 1,500 meters (4,920 ft.) deep, declines from north to south towards the Kuril Basin to a depth of 3,500 meters (11,480 ft.).

Of the great Siberian rivers, only the Amur empties into the Sea of Okhotsk, pushing huge amounts of sediments through the Tatar Strait between Sakhalin Island and the mainland and into the ocean. A lot of fresh water is, however, also washed into the waters off the western and northern shores by the many smaller rivers. Between the Kuril Islands, Pacific water enters the Sea of Okhotsk from the south. Under the influence of this warm ocean water, a powerful current moves along the eastern side to the north, with the result that the eastern part of the sea is warmer than the western part. Supported by Siberian fresh water, a similar strong current flows south off the mainland and Sakhalin Island.

The continental climate on the Asian mainland is not much different from that over the Arctic Ocean. This determines the weather and ice conditions within the Sea of Okhotsk, making it Asia's coldest sea. During winter, from October to April, the northeastern, northern, and western regions of the Sea of Okhotsk lie under a dense cover of ice, while due to the Pacific influence, the southern and southeastern parts remain more or less ice-free.

The fresh water washed into the sea by the rivers, as well as the thorough blending of waters by currents and winds, allow nutrient-rich deep-sea water to well up. In biological terms, the Sea of Okhotsk is therefore known to be one of the most productive seas of the world. During the few warm months of the year, there is an explosion of life. While the abundant fish stocks are used by commercial fishing fleets, they are also essential for the survival of the large populations of local marine mammals including seals and sea lions. Even gray whales, which pass the winter near the equator, undertake long migrations to these rich feeding grounds.

On the northern shelf, deposits of crude oil and natural gas have been discovered, and also what is supposedly the largest barite deposit on Earth. This mineral is used mainly in the nuclear industry to seal off radioactive radiation.

Scientists have recently discovered sites where large amounts of gaseous methane escape from the sea floor. Their findings point to the Sea of Okhotsk being one of the most important source regions for this greenhouse gas, implying that this sea exerts massive influence on the development of the global climate.

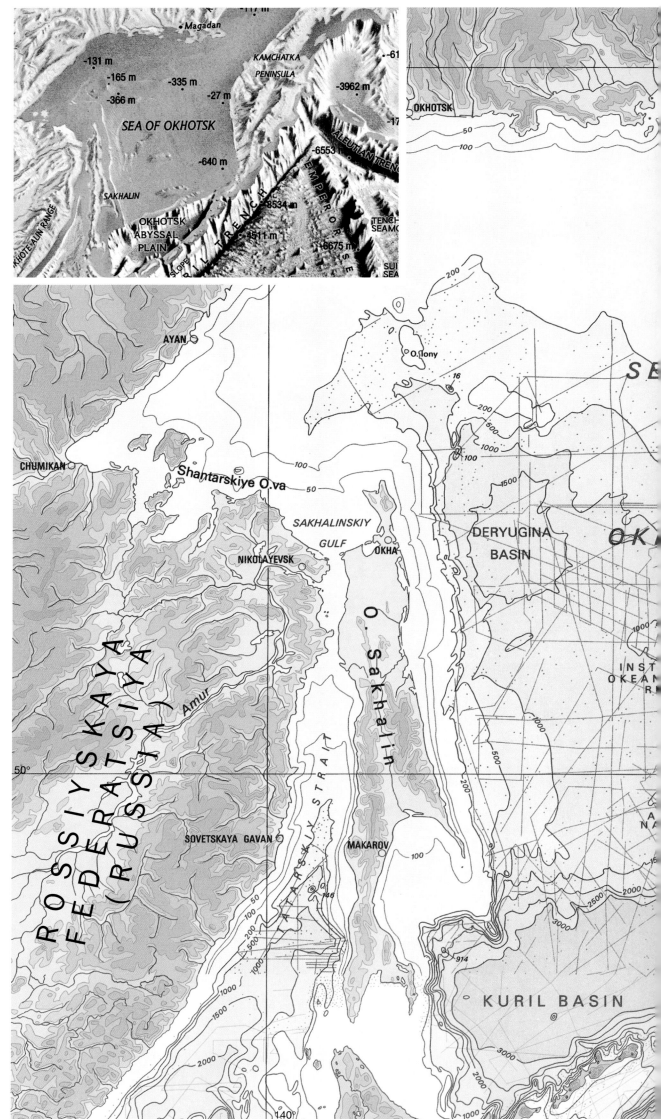

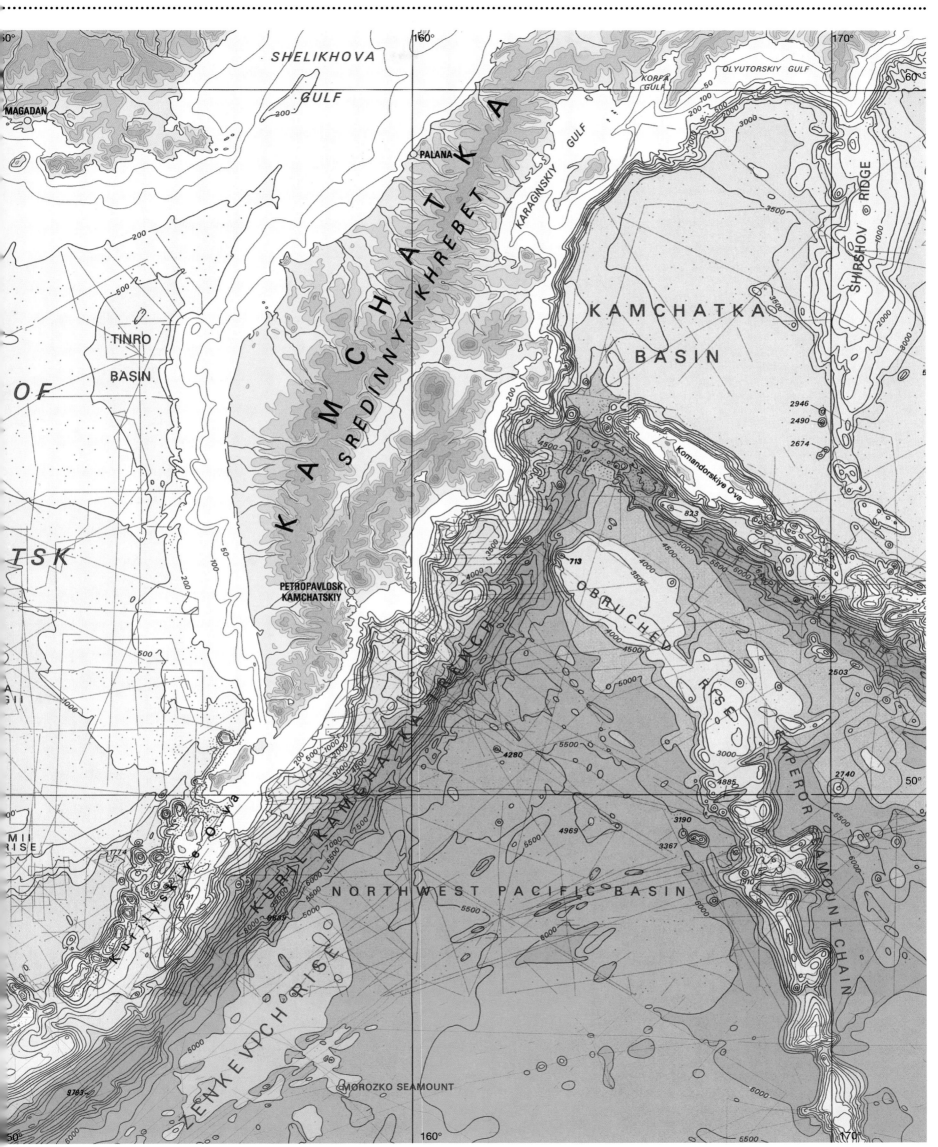

SHELIKHOVA
GULF

MAGADAN

OLYUTORSKIY GULF

KORPA GULF

PALANA

KARAGNSKIY GULF

SHIRSHOV RIDGE

K A M C H A T K A

KAMCHATKA BASIN

TINRO BASIN

OF

SREDINNYY KHREBET

Komandorskiye Ova

2946
2490
2674

823

713

TSK

OBRUCHED

PETROPAVLOSK
KAMCHATSKIY

2503

4280

4885

2740

KURIL KAMCHATKA TRENCH

4969

3190

3367

1910

MII
RISE

1774

Kurilskiye Ova

NORTHWEST PACIFIC BASIN

EMPEROR SEAMOUNT CHAIN

9585

ZENKEVICH RISE

9783

MOROZKO SEAMOUNT

The "Arctic" of the Pacific

●●● The Bering Sea, the northern-most part of the Pacific, is a more or less triangular basin between Siberia in the west, Alaska in the east, and the merely 85-kilometer (53-mi.) wide Bering Strait in the north. To the south, the 1,600-kilometer (1,000-mi.) long Aleutian Island arc separates the Bering Sea from the Pacific Ocean.

The Bering Sea is made up of two basins of roughly the same size – on the one hand the relatively shallow continental shelf in the north and east, which is merely 150 meters (490 ft.) deep, and, on the other hand, the much deeper region in the southwest.

Sub-marine ridges divide this part into three basins all between 3,700 meters and 3,900 meters (12,100 ft. and 12,800 ft.) deep. The huge Aleutian Basin extends from north to south. To the west, off the Kamchatka Peninsula, the Shirshov Ridge separates the Kamchatka Basin from the Aleutian Basin. In the south of the Bering Sea, directly at the Aleutian arc, the Bowers Ridge seals off the basin known by the same name.

Virtually the whole of the water of the Bering Sea originates in the Pacific. The Alaska Current, flowing towards Asia on the Pacific side of the Aleutian Islands, pushes it mainly through the Blizhny Strait opposite the Shirshov Ridge, and to a lesser extent also past the islands.

After entering the Bering Sea, the water masses change direction and follow the island chain eastward, thus creating a gyre, i.e., a counterclockwise circular current. Off Alaska, the gyre divides into two branches, one of which constitutes the Lawrence Current flowing north towards he Bering Strait, whereas the other converges with the Anadyr Current and drives the very powerful Kamchatka Current southward along the Asian coast and out of the Bering Sea.

Because of the warm current flowing north off the Alaskan coast, the ice conditions on the east coast are less extreme than those on the west coast. Yet this pattern of currents is rather unstable because tides, storms, and the varying sea level of the Pacific bring about continual changes.

At the continental shelf, the deep-sea water of the Bering Sea rises and returns to the Pacific as surface water. It is rich in nutrients and, therefore, forms the basis for the high biological productivity observed in the Bering Sea. Roughly 25 species of fish are caught on a commercial scale, among them salmon, herring, cod, flounder, halibut, and haddock. During the summer, some whale species including gray whales, migrate into the Bering Sea to feed, although the marine mammal populations have already declined due to intensive fishing in the area.

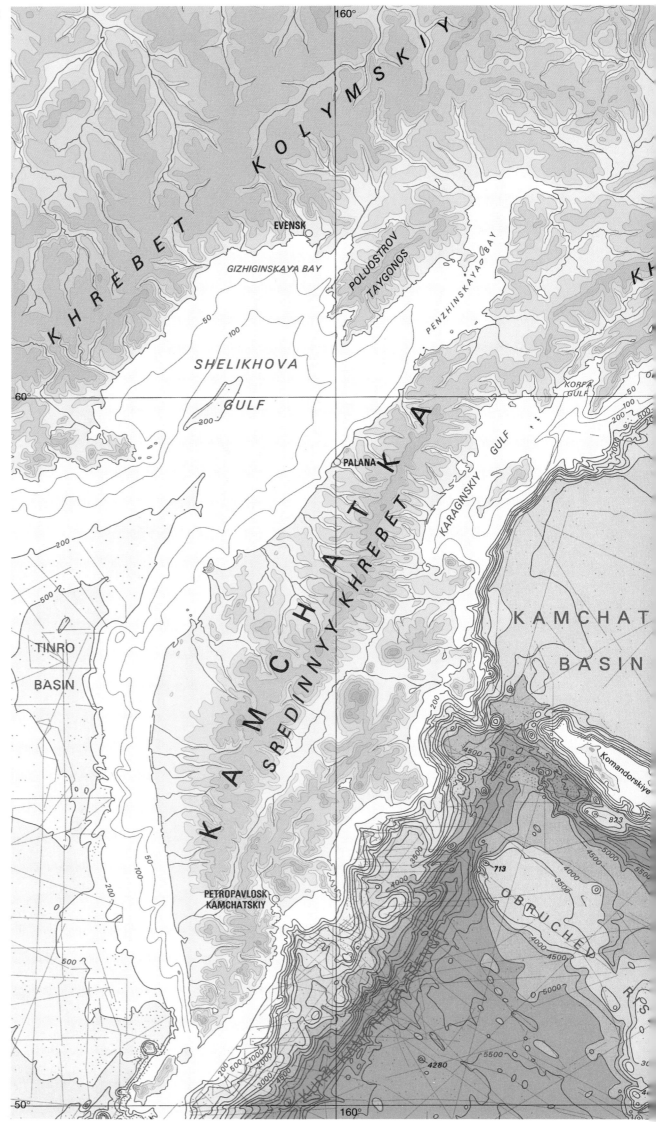

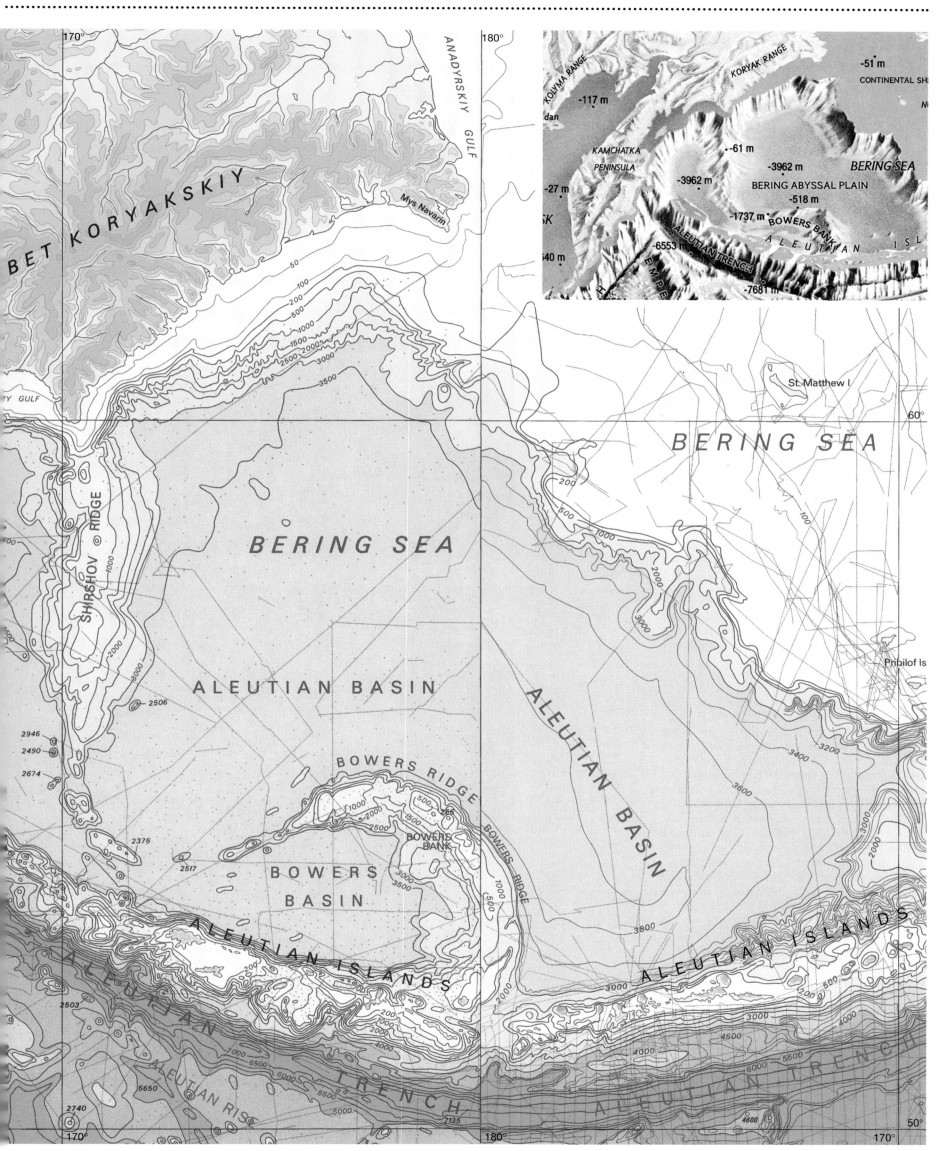

BET KORYAKSKIY

ANADYRSKIY GULF

Mys Navarin

GULF

50

100

200

500

1000

1500

2000

2500

3000

3500

170°

180°

60°

BERING SEA

St. Matthew I

200

500

1000

2000

3000

100

SHIRSHOV RIDGE

1000

2000

3000

ALEUTIAN BASIN

2506

2946

2490

2674

2376

2517

3400

3200

3600

3800

3000

2000

Pribilof Is

ALEUTIAN BASIN

BOWERS RIDGE

500

1000

2000

2500

1500

BOWERS BANK

BOWERS RIDGE

1000

500

BOWERS

BASIN

3000

3500

2503

2740

5650

5500

5000

6500

6000

5500

5000

4000

3000

2000

200

1000

2000

ALEUTIAN ISLANDS

ALEUTIAN RISE

ALEUTIAN TRENCH

7135

2000

3000

4000

4500

4600

3000

4000

5000

5500

6000

ALEUTIAN ISLANDS

ALEUTIAN TRENCH

170°

180°

170°

50°

KOLYMA RANGE

KORYAK RANGE

-51 m

CONTINENTAL SH

-117 m

dan

KAMCHATKA PENINSULA

-61 m

-27 m

-3962 m

-3962 m

BERING ABYSSAL PLAIN

-518 m

BERING SEA

-1737 m

BOWERS BANK

ALEUTIAN

ISL

ALEUTIAN TRENCH

-6553 m

40 m

EMPE

-7681 m

Alaska's unique climate

● ● ● Off the shores of the Gulf of Alaska, the Alaska Current flows north and converges with the Aleutian Current near the Aleutian Island arc. It represents the northeastern part of the North Pacific subpolar gyre, a counterclockwise circular current extending over the whole North Pacific, carrying warm water to the North American coast. For this reason, the Alaskan coast up to Prince William Sound remains ice-free even in winter. Tankers can enter the Sound all year round and call at Valdez to load the crude oil that is brought in via the trans-Alaskan pipeline from the oil fields along the margins of the polar sea.

While the salmon populations off Alaska are today considered rather depleted, catches still reached historic record numbers of one million tons per year in the 1990s, even though similar record quantities were recorded in the 1930s.

Fishers attempt to increase their yields by raising salmon spawn and releasing the fry at a stage when their chances of survival are most favorable. Nevertheless, their efforts do not seem to be successful, for the survival of the salmon is much more dependent on climatic conditions than was once believed.

The Pacific Decadal Oscillation (PDO) is a climatic phenomenon altering the wind pressure system, and thus the sea currents, around Alaska over several decades. If the winter low-pressure areas are strong, west coast salmon are abundant in the Gulf of Alaska, while weak winter cyclones provide good conditions for the Alaskan salmon in the Bristol Bay north of the Alaska Peninsula.

Since 1977, a "positive" PDO has influenced the salmon-fishing grounds. The Alaska Current carries warmer water to the north, bringing Alaska warm, dry winters with little snow. During fall and spring, the sea has been plagued more often by cyclones than before. Although they have whirled up more nutrients from the sea floor, the warmer conditions were too unfavorable for west coast salmon in the Gulf of Alaska. In addition, the declining populations were almost completely destroyed by irresponsible over-fishing. Simultaneously, however, the same oscillation provided the backdrop for record catches in the Bristol Bay in the eastern Bering Sea. The oscillation is expected to reverse in approximately ten years, which will again provide more favorable conditions for Pacific salmon, albeit at the disadvantage of the salmon species in the Bering Sea.

Obviously, though, the situation relies not only on the climate, the fishing industry, and the breeding of millions of young salmon. Despite positive forecasts, the populations in the Bristol Bay suffered a surprisingly sharp decline in 1998 and 1999.

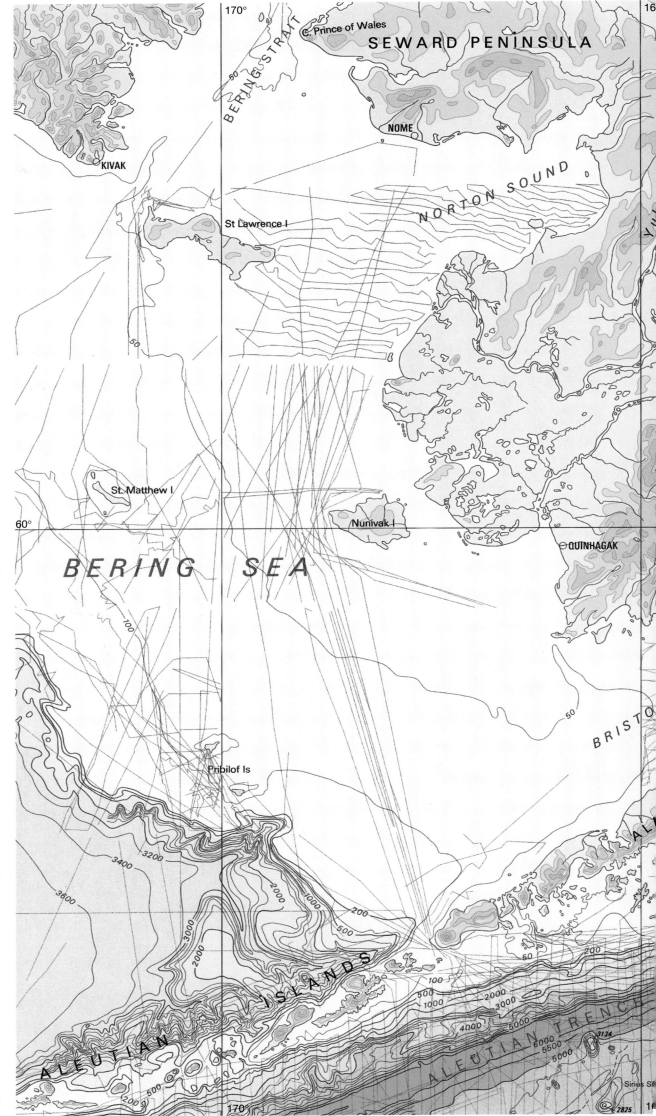

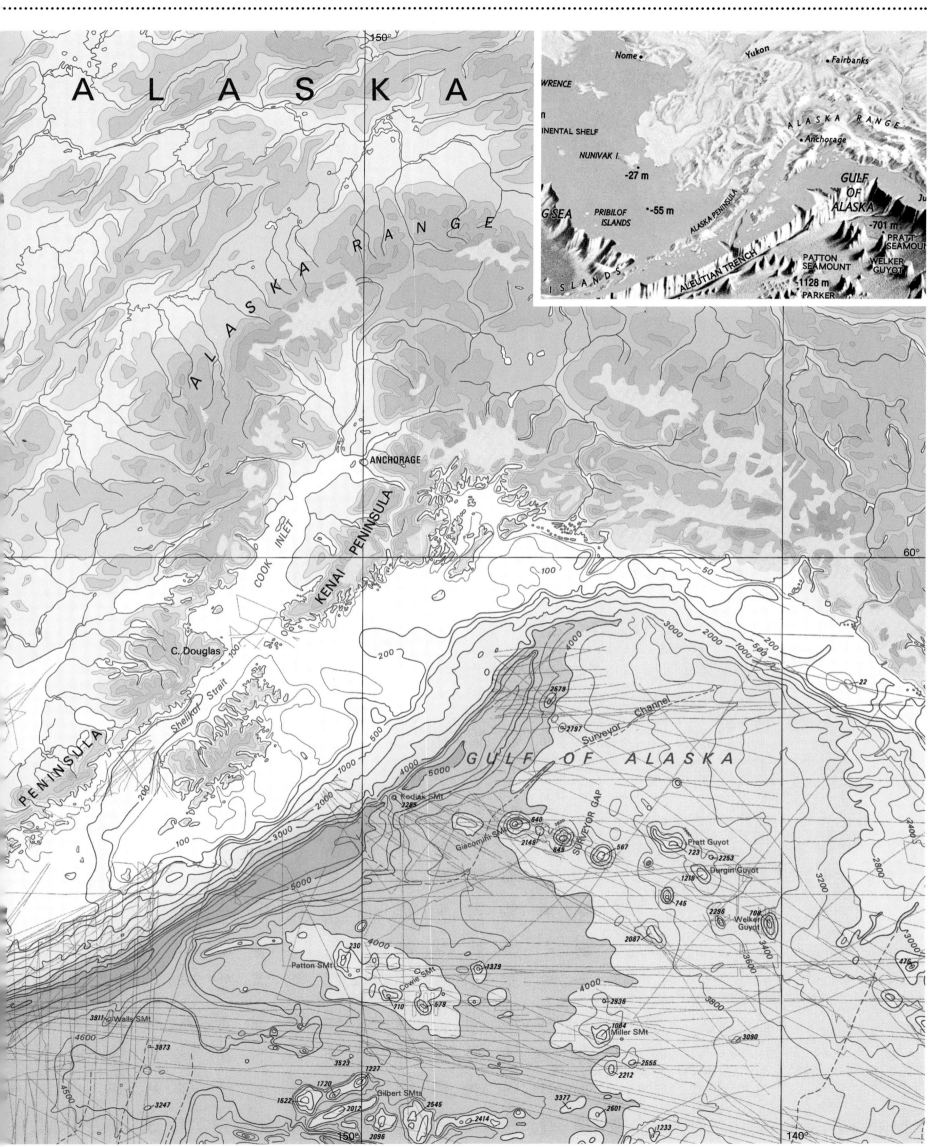

A L A S K A

ALASKA RANGE

ANCHORAGE

KENAI PENINSULA

COOK INLET

C. Douglas

PENINSULA

Shelikof Strait

GULF OF ALASKA

Surveyor Channel

SURVEYOR GAP

Kodiak SMt
2205

Giacomini SMt

Pratt Guyot

Durgin Guyot

Welker Guyot

Patton SMt

Cowie SMt

Walls SMt

Miller SMt

Gilbert SMts

150°

60°

140°

Inset map:

G SEA

WRENCE

Nome

Yukon

Fairbanks

INENTAL SHELF

ALASKA RANGE

Anchorage

NUNIVAK I.

-27 m

GULF
OF
ALASKA

PRIBILOF
ISLANDS

-55 m

ALASKA PENINSULA

-701 m

PRATT
SEAMOUNT

ISLANDS

ALEUTIAN TRENCH

PATTON
SEAMOUNT

WELKER
GUYOT

-1128 m
PARKER

Ju

The land below the sea

●●● It is hardly conceivable that two marginal seas so close to each other could differ so much. The Yellow Sea between China and Korea is only 60 meters to 80 meters (197 ft. to 262 ft.) deep and is basically just a stretch of land that was flooded during the last ice age 10,000 to 15,000 years ago. In contrast, the Japan Sea is an elliptical basin declining steeply from the Asian continent to a depth of 3,743 meters (12,281 ft.) before becoming shallower again towards the Japanese coastline.

Both these seas belong to the group of areas that are most abundant in fish. Whereas the shallow Yellow Sea provides mainly catches of marine animals living near the sea floor, Russian, Korean, and Japanese trawler fleets used to bring in large shoals of herring, sardines, and tuna prevailing from the open waters of the Sea of Japan. However, all these species are severely threatened by over-fishing and can scarcely be found anywhere today.

In the Yellow Sea, the future of the fish and seafood industry does not only depend on the industry itself. Climatic changes and new agricultural methods adopted deep in the north of China threaten to starve the entire ecosystem because the great rivers carry less of the fertile yellow clay mud into the sea.

As recently as 1980, the Huang Ho, or Yellow River, alone pushed more than a billion tons of mud into the sea with each 25,000 cubic kilometers (6,000 cu. mi.) of water. By 1997, the water quantity had already decreased dramatically, while the amount of mud had dropped to less than one percent of what it was. One reason is that the farmers now protect their fields more effectively against erosion, but hydraulic engineering projects implemented to ensure the navigability of the Yellow River play an important role as well. Chinese shrimp fishers are already aware of these changes, as their catches have noticeably decreased.

The people living on the coast have always suffered from the adverse effects of climate and weather. When the northwestern monsoon drives cold polar air over the relatively warm Japan Sea, it picks up the foggy humidity hovering over the water during winter and releases it as snow over the Japanese mountains. The rough seas common during winter cause serious damage to the Japanese coastlines and further erosion.

The winter monsoon also rages over the Yellow Sea, often building up to dangerous blizzards in the innermost bay of Po Hai where water and mud are whirled up by the storms. In the summer, typhoons agitate the shallow sea and threaten ships and seamen, for unlike the Japan Sea, the Yellow Sea is used extensively by shipping traffic between the adjoining regions.

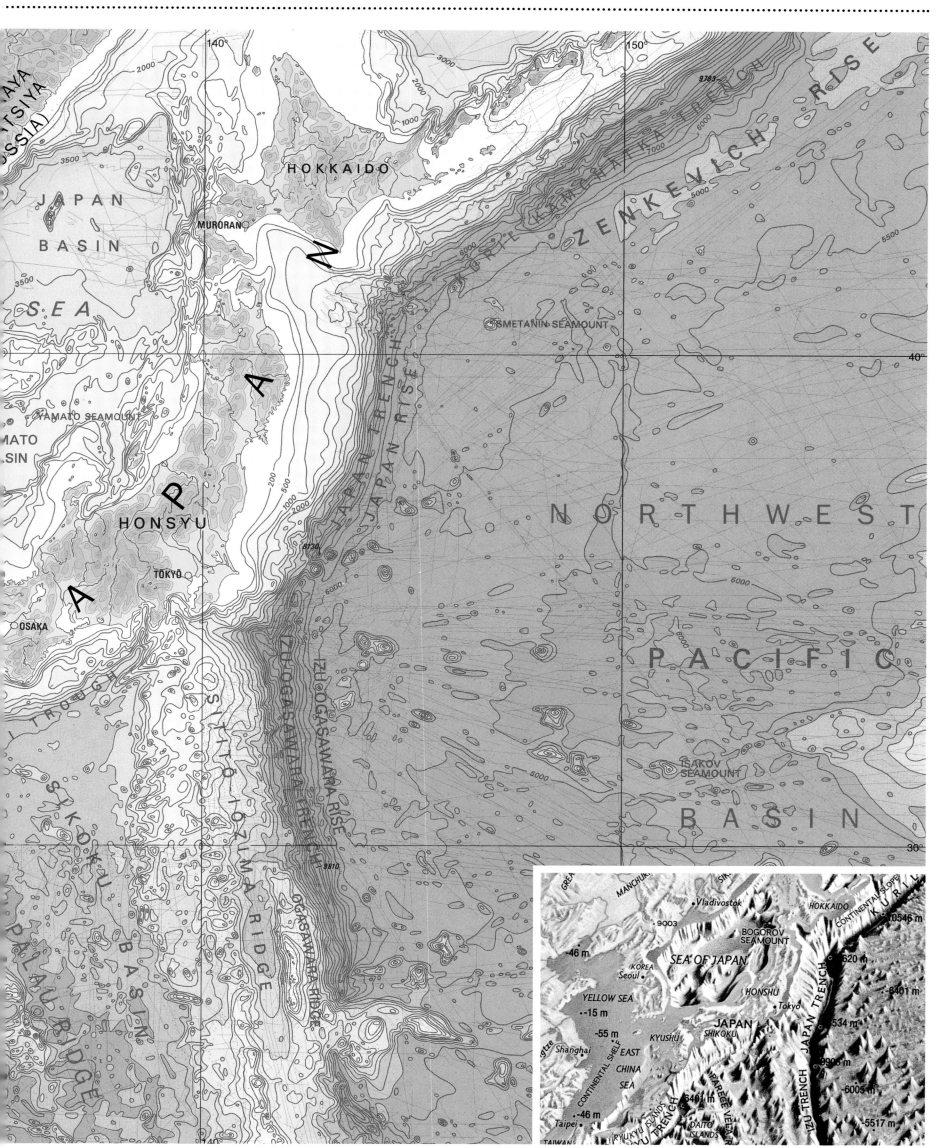

140°

150°

9763

2000

3000

3000

2000

1000

HOKKAIDO

JAPAN

BASIN

MURORAN

3500

SEA

3500

YAMATO SEAMOUNT

MATO

SIN

HONSYU

TŌKYŌ

OSAKA

SMETANIN SEAMOUNT

40°

NORTHWEST

6000

7000

6000

5000

5000

5500

6000

6000

PACIFIC

200

500

1000

1500

2000

6000

6000

ISAKOV
SEAMOUNT

BASIN

30°

JAPAN TRENCH

JAPAN RISE

IZU-OGASAWARA TRENCH

IZU-OGASAWARA RISE

SI-TÔ-IÔZIMA RIDGE

OGASAWARA RIDGE

SIKOKU BASIN

PALAU RIDGE

TROUGH

8730

9810

KURIL-KAMCHATKA TRENCH

ZENKEVICH RISE

EAST PACIFIC RISE

"Black smokers" in the Alaska current

●●● North of San Francisco, between the Queen Charlotte Islands and Cape Mendocino, the Alaska Current reaches the North American continent. Part of the gyre – a huge circular current – it circulates counterclockwise off Canada and Alaska, fed by the relatively warm North Pacific Current – driven from Japan over the Pacific Ocean by constant westerly winds. Storms are common and violent, mainly in winter, and they thoroughly mix the sea waters, whirling up plankton nutrients from the sea floor near the coastline. These provide the base for the abundant fishing grounds off the Canadian coast.

North of San Francisco, the Mendocino Fracture Zone extends 400 kilometers (248 mi.) into the Pacific Ocean. Although it looks like a stair step, it is in fact an uneven sub-marine ridge. Whereas its northern flank is very flat, the southern flank declines rather sharply. At this point, two oceanic plates rub against each other – both part of the big oceanic plate which subducts beneath the American continent along the coastline.

The area of the Juan de Fuca Ridge at the rim of the Cascadia Basin, off Vancouver Island, holds many sites where sulfuric, boiling-hot water and lava escape from the sea floor. For more than 20 years, the ridge, which is more than 2,000 meters (6,560 ft.) underwater, has been explored on numerous scientific diving excursions. In these surroundings, which seemingly defying any kind of life, scientists discovered completely new ecosystems with more than 350 unknown species, almost all of them endemic.

Most of these thriving deep-sea oases are located around so-called "black smokers" – several-meter-high vents that eject hot water with a temperature of 350° C (662° F) and which are loaded with dark mineral particles whirled up from the Earth's core. When sea water seeps through clefts and crevices in the ocean floor, often several kilometers deep, it is heated up by the Earth's warmth, reacts with the rock, and is loaded with minerals and gases. As with a coffee percolator, the heat drives the water back upwards. As soon as it makes contact with the cold sea water, minute particles precipitate from the ejected hot water, turning into vents or rising to the surface as "black smoke."

This hot broth, containing sulfur and heavy metals, is the natural habitat of bacteria that are able to reproduce at a 115° C (239° F) water temperature. They are fed on by exotic, often giant annelids, shells, and crustaceans obviously unperturbed by the heat, the mixture of sulfur and heavy metals, and the darkness.

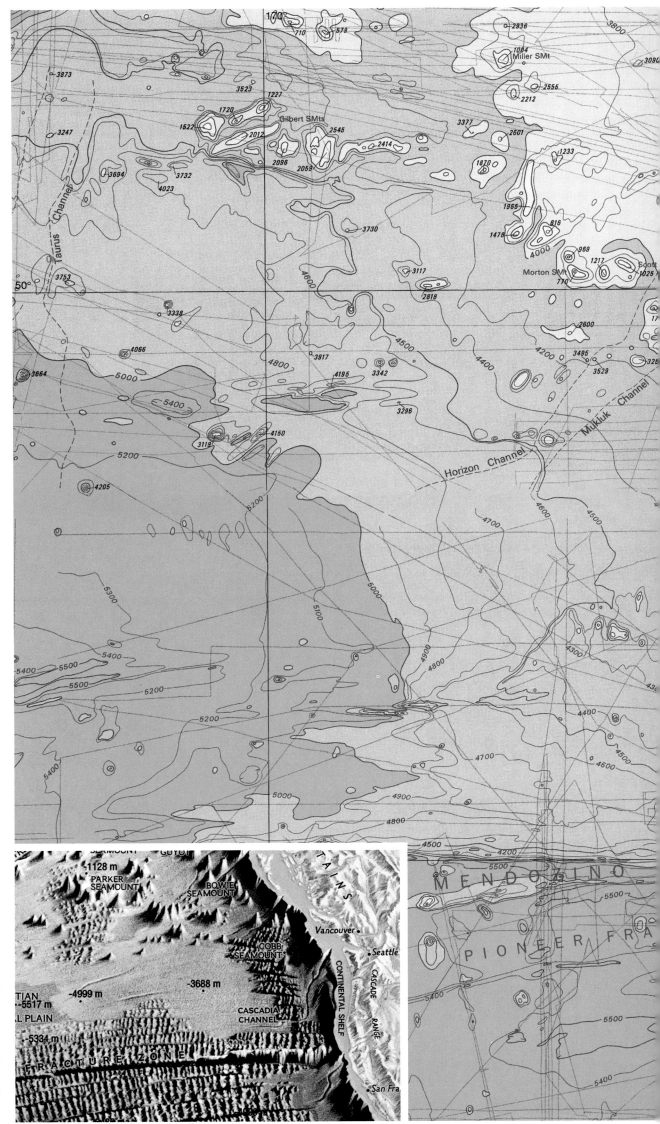

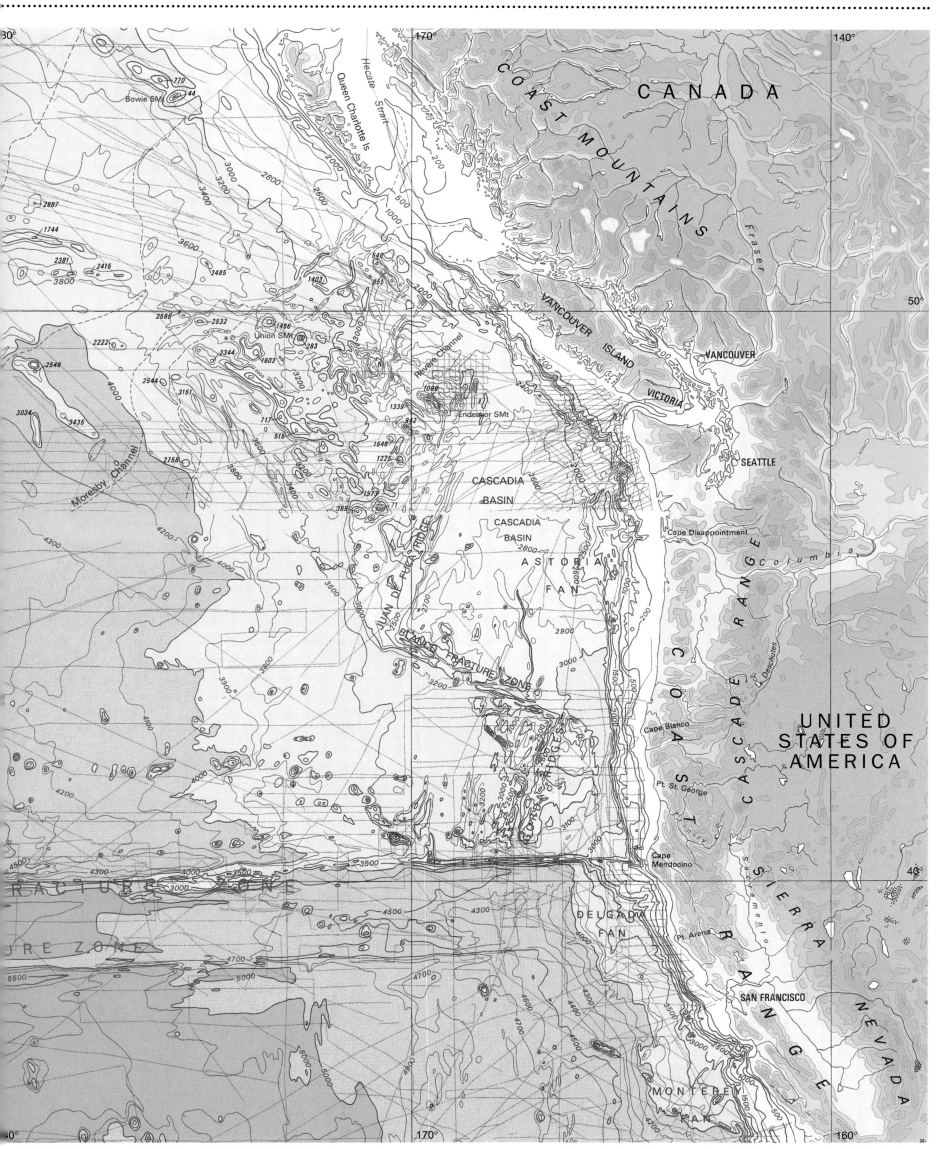

Where the sea is at its deepest

●●● In the northern part of the Pacific, the enormous sea-bottom plate of the Pacific is subducted under the Asian continent and forms a deep trench. This process is accompanied by immense pressure, provoking volcanic eruptions and seaquakes. While islands emerge and grow on the continental plate, the Pacific Plate merges with the mantle deep inside in the Earth.

The Mariana Trench is the deepest part of the Earth's oceans. The gap is 2,550 kilometers (1,600 mi.) long, but on average only 80 kilometers (47 mi.) wide. Its continuation lies further north in the deep-sea trenches off the Japan, the Kuril, and the Aleutian Trenches. Together, they form a "ring of fire" around the Pacific Ocean, given that of the approximately 800 active volcanoes on Earth, some 75 percent are located on the rims of the deep-sea trenches. For more than 50 years, scientists have searched the Mariana Trench for the lowest point on the Earth. Whether or not they have actually found it yet is still uncertain because the available figures are as numerous as the measurements.

In 1949, Russian scientists measured down 11,022 meters (36,163 ft.) at one point and named the spot Vityaz Deep after their research ship. To illustrate the enormity of that depth, consider that a steel ball weighing 1 kilogram (2.2 lb.) thrown into the water there from a ship would need about one hour to reach the bottom. In 1951, English researchers measured 10,915 meters (35,812 ft.) at a point west of the Vityaz Deep. This so-called Challenger Deep (named after their research vessel) was sounded by Japanese hydrographs as actually being 9 meters (30 ft.) deeper, i.e., 10,924 meters (35,842 ft.) deep.

Although it was known at the time that the bottom of the trench held a lot of mud and scarcely any animals, many researchers were keen on seeing it with their own eyes. In 1960, Jacques Piccard and Don Walsh reached the bottom of the Challenger Deep at 10,916 meters (35,815 ft.) with their bathyscape *Trieste*. However, their bathymeter was set to fresh water so that an accurate value of depth could only be calculated by applying complicated corrections for salt concentration, pressure, temperature, and acceleration. In fact, there was nothing much to see, for this desert of light-cinnamon-colored mud contained merely one 2.5-centimeter (1-in.) long shrimp and what they designated as a "flat fish" – in all probability a sea cucumber.

For researching the deepest deep-sea areas, the future is likely to favor unmanned submersible robots since their video recordings and photographs can reveal much more than human beings will ever be able to see at these depths.

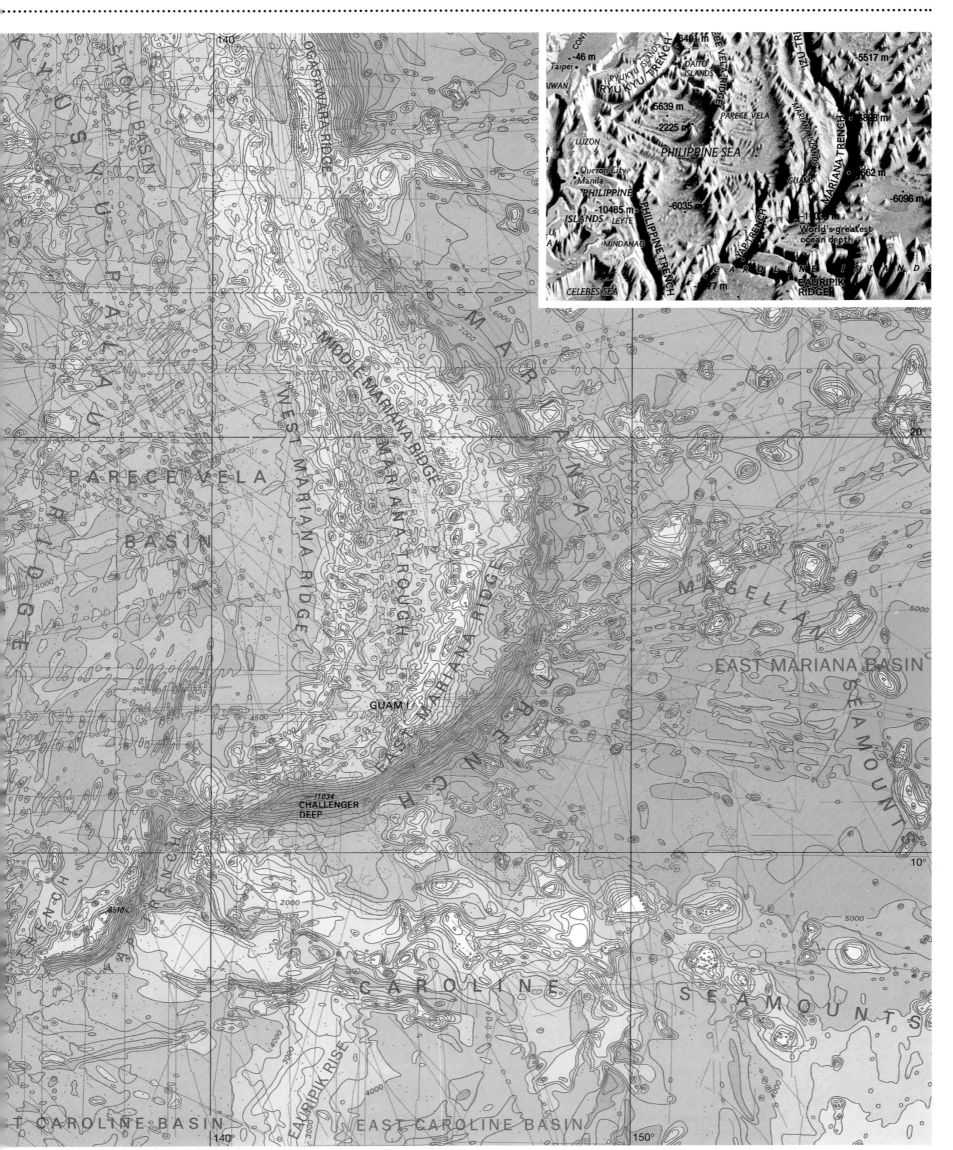

KYUSYU

KYUSYU BASIN

OGASAWARA RIDGE

140

MIDDLE MARIANA RIDGE

WEST MARIANA RIDGE

MARIANA TROUGH

M A R I A N A

6000

7000

PARECE VELA

BASIN

RIDGE

5000

20°

EAST MARIANA RIDGE

GUAM I.

M A R I A N A   T R E N C H

4500

3000

—11034
CHALLENGER
DEEP

MAGELLAN

EAST MARIANA BASIN

SEAMOUNT

5000

10°

TRENCH

—8510

2000

5000

C A R O L I N E   S E A M O U N T S

EAURIPIK RISE

4000

4000

3000

3000

T CAROLINE BASIN   EAST CAROLINE BASIN

140°   150°

CONT

-46 m
Taipei

RYUKYU ISLANDS

RYUKYU TRENCH

-6401 m

DAITO
ISLANDS

GE VELA RIDGE

IZU-TRE

-5517 m

IWAN

5639 m

-2225 m

PARECE VELA

MARIANA

MARIANA TRENCH

-5893 m

LUZON

PHILIPPINE SEA

GUAM

-662 m

Quezon City
Manila

PHILIPPINE

-6096 m

-10485 m

PHILIPPINE TRENCH

-6035 m

YAP TRENCH

-1 03 m

ISLANDS   LEYTE

World's greatest
ocean depth

MINDANAO

C A R O L I N E   I S L A N D S

EAURIPIK
RIDGE

CELEBES SEA

77 m

The formation of Hawaii

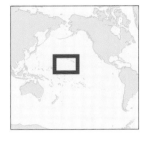

●●● Geologically, Hawaii is considered a "hot spot." Below this group of islands, the Earth's mantle arches upwards like an enormous bubble. Geologists call this phenomenon "plume", and it is especially pronounced below this group of islands. Hot rock rises from the mantle to the surface, passing through crust and ocean floor on its way.

Something similar also occurs at the oceanic ridge, where magma emerges from the mantle and rises to the surface. For Hawaii, however, the situation is different since the magma here has a chemical composition which is unlike the liquid lava that wells up from the oceanic ridge.

The mantle is a 3,000-kilometer (1,860-mi.) thick rock layer between the crust and the metallic core of the Earth. Recent findings suggest that the mantle consists of two layers. While the upper 2,000 kilometers (1,250 mi.) are constantly shifting, pulling the continental and oceanic plates on the Earth's surface, the 1,000-kilometer (620-mi.) thick lower layer is immobile and contains a different magma composition than the floating upper layer.

For plates descending under continental plates – for instance, along the deep-sea trenches – this lower layer presents a barrier that stops the plates at a depth of 2,000 kilometers (1,250 mi.). Unable to merge with it, they can only dissolve in the upper, floating layer. This is why the chemical properties of the two mantle layers show so many differences.

Only at few points in the mantle's "cellar" – the exact hot spots – is the magma able to bubble up under the floating layer and rise directly to the surface of the Earth. Tremendous eruptions accompany the emergence of seamounts. These are often even more impressive than their continental counterparts.

The Pacific Plate bottom, which is continuously reborn at the oceanic ridge and drifts along with the floating upper mantle, slides over the Hawaiian Islands. The hot spot below the islands, therefore, continues to open new spots emitting lava, thus creating the row of volcanoes of the 130 Hawaiian Islands. These are arranged in a straight line like a string of pearls 2,400 kilometers (1,490 mi.) long.

Hawaii is the most active hot spot on Earth. The sub-marine mountain range – the peaks of which form today's islands – emerged some 80 million years ago. With the volcano Mauna Loa rising 9,100 meters (29,857 ft.) above the otherwise flat sea floor, it is even higher than the mountains of the Himalayas.

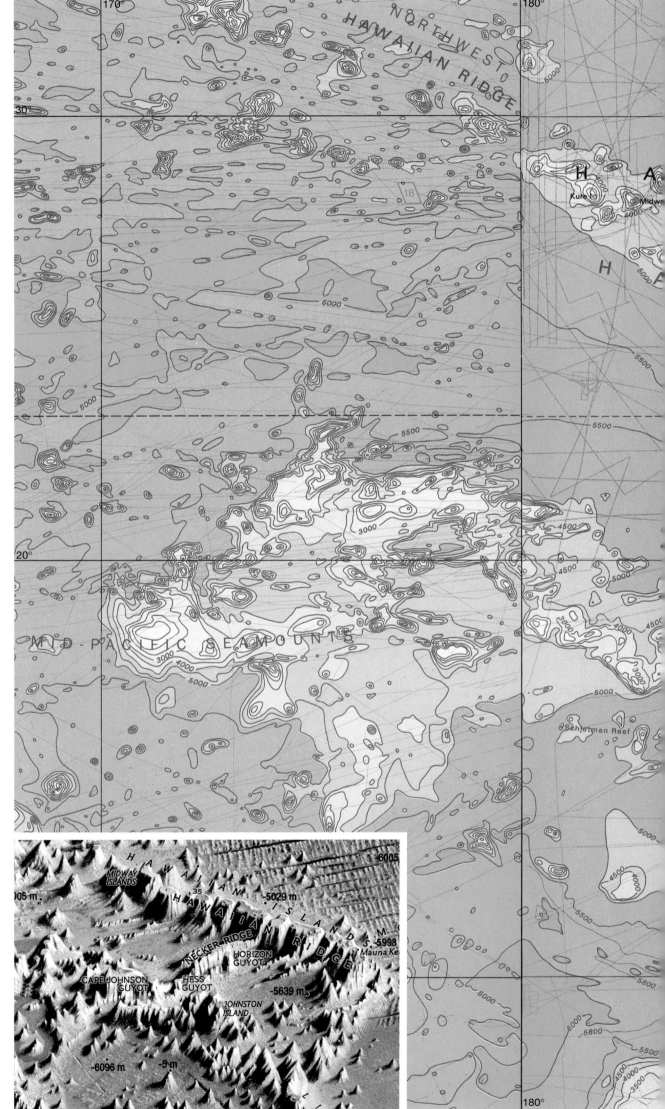

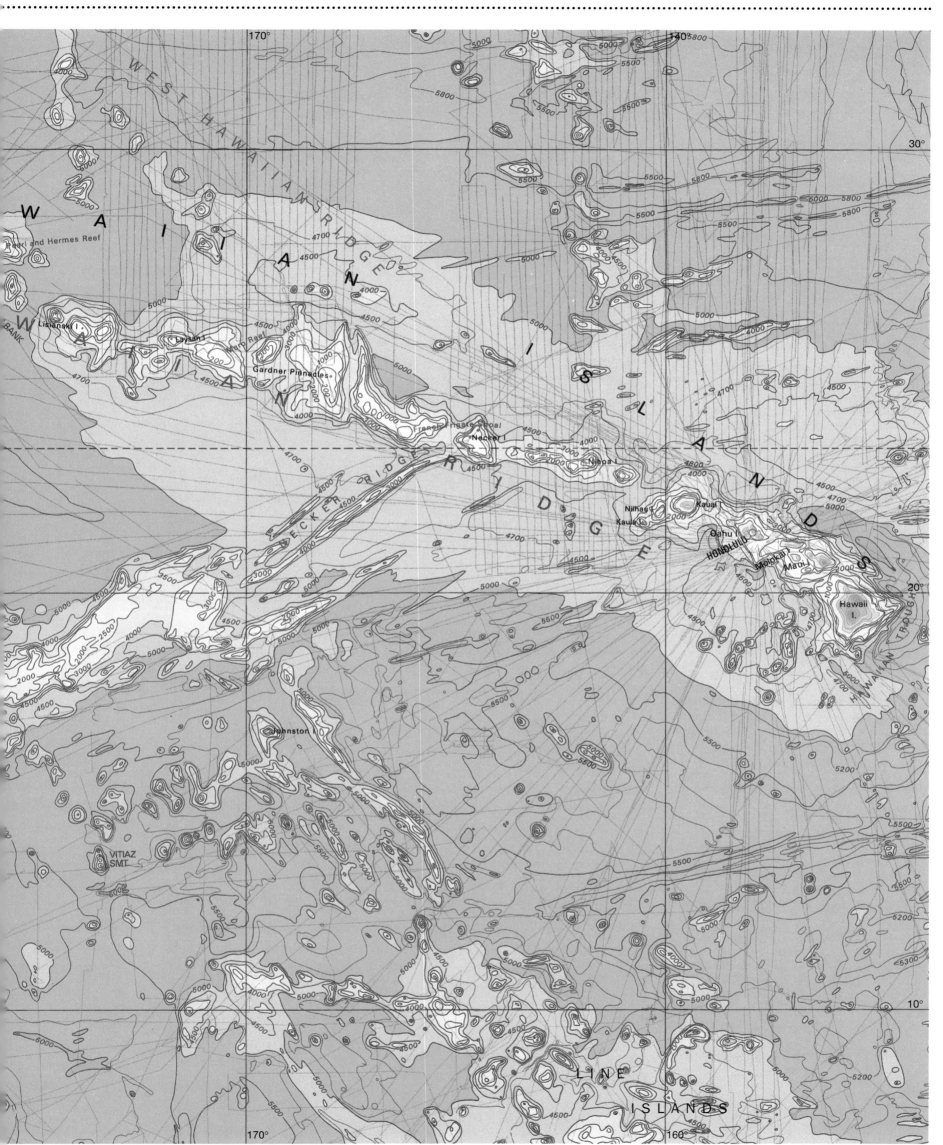

WEST HAWAIIAN RIDGE

W A I I A N

W A I I A N

Pearl and Hermes Reef

Lisianski I

BANK

Laysan I

Maro Reef

Gardner Pinnacles

French Frigate Shoal

Necker I

Nihoa I

I S L A N D

R I D G E

Niihau I

Kauai I

Kauai I

Kaula I

DECKER RIDGE

Oahu I

HONOLULU

Molokai

Maui

Hawaii I.

HAWAIIAN TROUGH

Johnston I

VITIAZ SMT

L I N E

I S L A N D S

The whales of Baja California

●●● South of the Baja California peninsula, the rim of the great Pacific Plate, curving in from the south, meets the smaller Cocos Plate off Central America. The mountainous stretch of land may have emerged from the sea when the East Pacific Rise, part of the Pacific Plate, collided at this point with the North American Plate.

Another possibility is that the peninsula broke off from the Mexican mainland and drifted away from the continent by sliding north along the San Andreas Fault, which is frequently subject to earthquakes. The exact course of events is still disputed among geologists. However, it seems certain that Baja California, with its 3,300-kilometer (2,050-mi.) long coastline, has migrated over the last 100 million years, probably by some 480 kilometers (300 mi.), thereby opening up the narrow Gulf of California.

The Gulf of California (also known as the Sea of Cortés) is 1,200 kilometers (750 mi.) long and some 150 kilometers (93 mi.) wide. In the south, its deepest point reaches 3,000 meters (10,000 ft.). The strong tidal current, which caused so much trouble for the Spanish conquerors on their sailing ships, continually stirs up the nutrient-rich sea floor, thus stimulating a plankton growth so abundant that the Gulf of California represents one of Mexico's most important commercial fishing grounds.

Off the Pacific flank of the spit, some 250 gray whales arrive each year in late fall. For thousands of years, these baleen whales have came here from the cold Alaskan Bering Sea some 8,000 kilometers (5,000 mi.) away. The shallow lagoons in the center of Baja California are some of the most important mating and breeding grounds for the 12-meter to 14-meter (39-ft. to 46-ft.) long giants, weighing 45 tons. In these shallow waters they are protected from their most dangerous enemies, the killer whales.

In the 1950s, gray whales were the first of their species to rouse the interest of whale watchers, as the whales were at the point of extinction at the time. Their name refers to the characteristic gray mottling on their skin, which is due to the pronounced growth of barnacles on it. Like a giant aspirator, these whales strain their food – crustaceans and small fish – through their baleen while they are browsing through the shallow bottom waters, whirling up mud clouds that are often visible from the surface.

The Pacific off Baja California is also frequently visited by humpback whales – like the grays, a type of baleen whale – although most of them prefer the open sea near the islands. The harmonious noises issued by the male humpbacks are considered to be the longest and most complicated songs in the animal kingdom.

Sahul: the submerged land

●●● The sunken land of Sahul, today a continental shelf reaching into the Indian Ocean, extends from the western part of Australia's north coast to New Guinea. Some 40,000 years ago, this stretch of land was still inhabited. At its bottom, the shapes of old river beds are still visible. When Sahul sank, its rims bent downwards while coral atolls – their base reaching down to a depth of 600 meters (1,969 ft.) – grew upwards at the same pace.

What remains today is the second largest island on Earth: New Guinea. It is 2,400 kilometers (1,500 mi.) long and, at its largest point, 650 kilometers (400 mi.) wide. The remains of the old land bridge with Australia are still visible in the shape of three island groups within the 130-kilometer (80-mi.) wide Torres Strait. The numerous coral reefs and shoals have given this strait the reputation of being dangerous. The same applies to the Arafura Sea, which is 50 meters to 80 meters (160 ft. to 260 ft.) deep; it presents countless shallows that reach almost to the water surface and are not registered by sea maps. The Aru Islands in the northern part of the 3,660-meter (12,008-ft.) deep Aru Trough were created by a local buildup of the Earth's crust.

Also part of the Arafura Sea is the Gulf of Carpentaria which is nowhere deeper than 70 meters (230 ft.). From the western plains of Queensland, the country slopes so gently towards the north and northwest that the coast is bordered by a broad rim of salt plains which are flooded by sea water during the monsoon season from November to April.

In the 20th century, manganese and bauxite were discovered in the Gulf of Carpentaria. A principal source of aluminum, bauxite is found here in layers up to 10 meters (33 ft.) thick. Since the end of the 1960s, shrimp fishing has become another important economic factor.

To the west, the Arafura Sea converges with the Timor Sea. This shelf sea is some 200 meters (656 ft.) deep and belongs to the most important oil-producing areas of Australia. The area is governed by the West Australian Current, which flows in from the southeast at a constant speed of 1.6 kilometers per hour (1 mph).

The Bismarck Archipelago to the east of New Guinea is not part of Sahul. This chain of volcanic island arcs stretches from Japan to New Zealand. Consisting of volcanic rock and surfaced coral limestone, the archipelago emerged when the Indo-Australian Plate submerged under the Pacific Plate from the Solomon Sea.

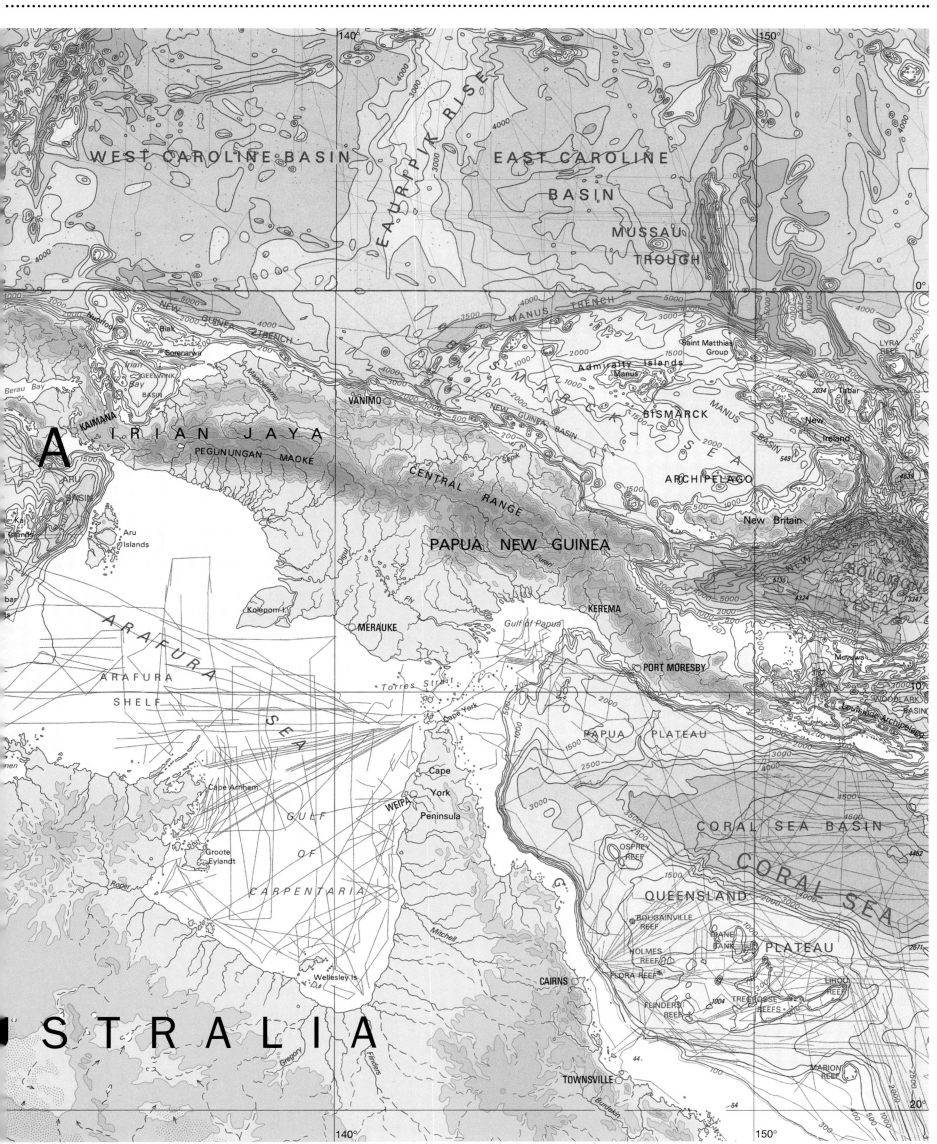

WEST CAROLINE BASIN

EAST CAROLINE

BASIN

MUSSAU

TROUGH

FAURIPIK RISE

NEW GUINEA TRENCH

MANUS TRENCH

Nubflod

Biak

Sorenarwa

Irian

GEELVINK

BASIN

Berau Bay

KAIMANA

IRIAN JAYA

PEGUNUNGAN MAOKE

Aru

ARU

BASIN

Kai

Islands

Aru

Islands

Kolepom I.

Digul

Fly

Purari

Sepik

Mamberamo

VANIMO

CENTRAL RANGE

NEW GUINEA BASIN

Admiralty Islands

Manus

Saint Matthias

Group

BISMARCK

ARCHIPELAGO

BISMARCK

SEA

MANUS

BASIN

New

Ireland

New Britain

LYRA

REEF

Tabar

SOLOMON SEA

PAPUA NEW GUINEA

MERAUKE

KEREMA

Gulf of Papua

PORT MORESBY

Misima

ARAFURA

ARAFURA

SHELF

ARAFURA SEA

Torres Strait

Cape York

PAPUA PLATEAU

WOODLARK

BASIN

Louisiade Archipelago

Cape

York

Peninsula

Cape Arnhem

WEIPA

GULF

OF

CARPENTARIA

Groote

Eylandt

Roper

Mitchell

Wellesley Is

CAIRNS

Gregory

Flinders

Burdekin

TOWNSVILLE

CORAL SEA BASIN

QUEENSLAND

PLATEAU

CORAL SEA

OSPREY

REEF

BOUGAINVILLE

REEF

DIANE

BANK

HOLMES

REEF

FLORA REEF

FLINDERS

REEF

TREGROSSE

REEFS

LIHOU

REEF

MARION

REEF

STRALIA

A STRALIA

Island arcs on deep-sea slopes

●●● The island arcs of Melanesia form an almost closed chain stretching from the north over the Solomon Islands, Vanuatu (formerly the New Hebrides), and the Fiji islands to Tonga. They are accompanied by deep-sea trenches such as the 7,000-meter (23,000-ft.) deep South Solomon Trench, the 9,165-meter (30,070-ft.) deep New Hebrides Trench, and the almost 11,000-meter (36,100-ft.) deep Tonga Trench.

The arcs were formed by the collision of two oceanic plates. From the west, coming from the Coral Sea, the Indo-Australian Plate submerges under Melanesia; while in the southeast, the Southwest Pacific Basin, moving in from the south, descends below Fiji and the Lau Basin.

The islands emerged at the rim of the upper plate, with two main arcs directly adjoining each other. While the islands of the outer arc merely drifted upward, the inner islands were formed by volcanoes. The third, innermost arc frequently shows signs of submarine ridges which, just like the outer arc, display no volcanic activity.

Islands and deep-sea trenches are frequently shaken by seismic activity. Unlike the collision points of continental plates, this center is located deep within the Earth, in most cases 600 meters (2,000 ft.) or more below the island bases.

To the west of this system of deep-sea trenches and island chains, the Coral Sea extends from here to Australia. The sea has a subtropical climate and is often churned up by typhoons, mainly in the period between January and April.

The Vityaz Trench in the northwest of the Fiji Basin constitutes a peculiarity among the deep-sea trenches because it registers no seismic activity whatsoever, and its rims are completely immobile. Just how this trench came into being still puzzles marine geologists.

The seas trapped between these arcs are typically extremely flat regions like, for instance, the western Fiji Basin. Fiji, the easternmost of the Melanesian island groups, comprises some 300 larger and 540 tiny islands distributed over 3,000,000 square kilometers (1,158,000 sq. mi.). No more than 100 of the larger islands are inhabited.

The geological history of the island group is complicated. It is located on an old, submerged plain and owes its existence to volcanoes as much as to the accumulation of sediments and the growth of coral reefs. Countless tiny islands and shoals impede navigation in the central Koro Sea.

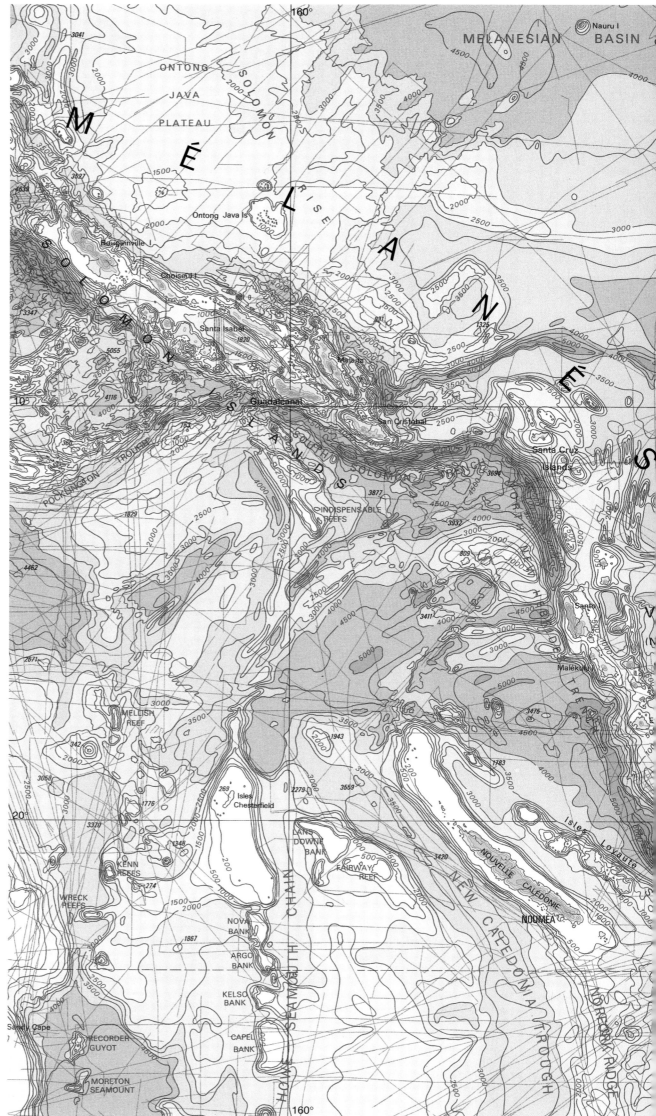

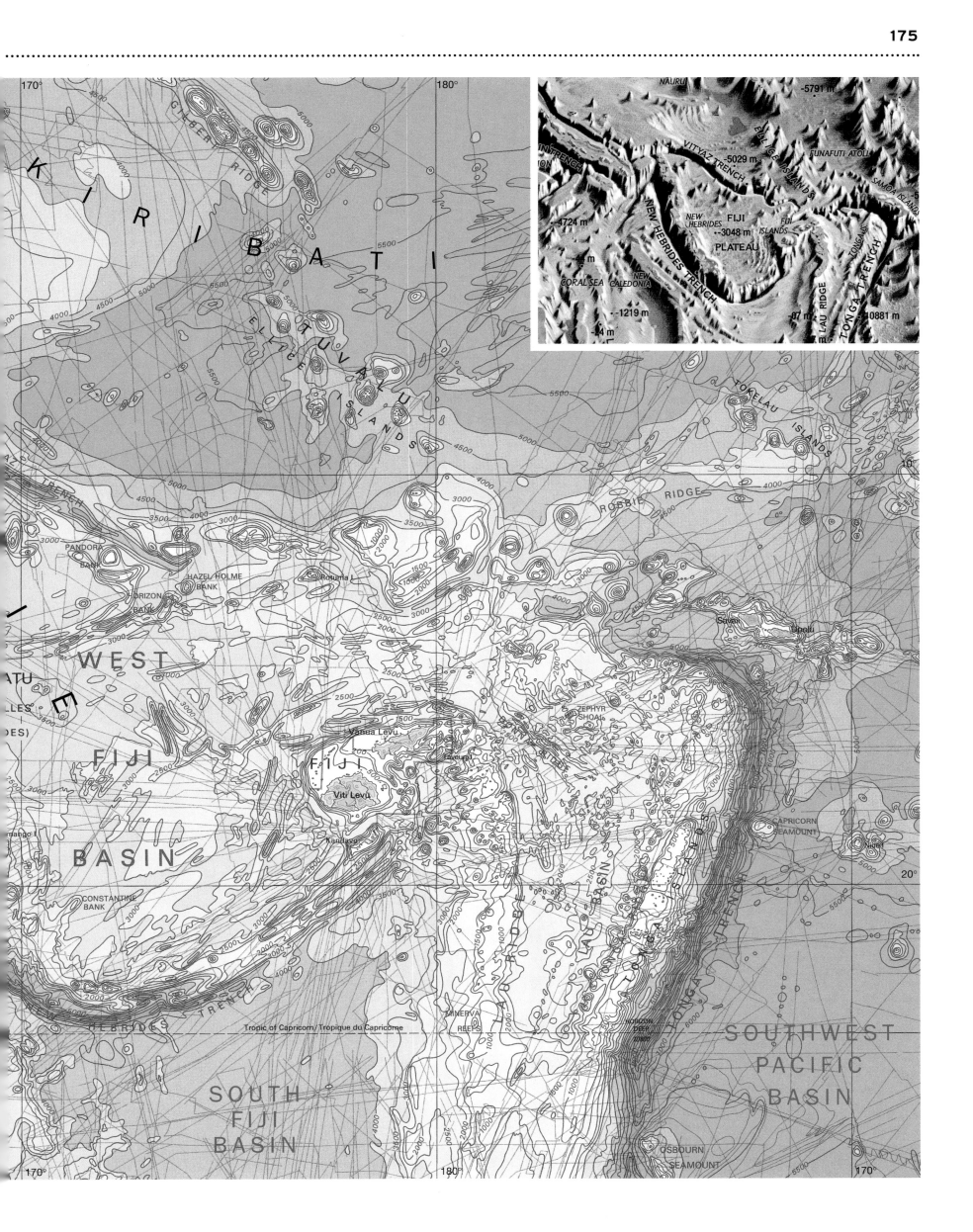

K I R I B A T I

GILBERT RIDGE

TUVALU

ELLICE ISLANDS

5500

5000

4500

4000

TOKELAU ISLANDS

ROBBIE RIDGE

PANDORA BANK

HAZEL HOLME BANK

HORIZON BANK

Rotuma I.

ZEPHYR SHOAL

(Savai'i)

Upolu

W E S T

F I J I

Vanua Levu

F I J I

Taveuni

Viti Levu

B A S I N

Kandavu

CONSTANTINE BANK

CAPRICORN SEAMOUNT

Niue I.

20°

LAU RIDGE

SOUTH FIJI BASIN

MINERVA REEFS

HORIZON DEEP 10800

TONGA TRENCH

S O U T H W E S T
P A C I F I C
B A S I N

Tropic of Capricorn / Tropique du Capricorne

HEBRIDES TRENCH

SOUTH
FIJI
BASIN

OSBOURN SEAMOUNT

170°   180°   170°

NAURU

VITYAZ TRENCH   -5029 m

ELLICE ISLANDS

FUNAFUTI ATOLL

SAMOA ISLANDS

NEW HEBRIDES   FIJI
-3048 m

FIJI ISLANDS

TONGAS

PLATEAU

NEW HEBRIDES TRENCH

-4724 m

-5791 m

CORAL SEA   NEW CALEDONIA

-1219 m

LAU RIDGE   TONGA TRENCH

-87 m   -10881 m

-14 m

The Galapagos Archipelago

●●● The Galapagos Islands are located in the Pacific Ocean, some 1,000 kilometers (600 mi.) off the coast of Ecuador. As of 1890, the group of islands has been officially known as the "Archipiélago de Colón." Despite its location directly on the equator, the climate is dry and relatively cool. This is due to the cold Humboldt Current. Its waters originate in the Antarctic and flow northward off the South American coast. Near the Galapagos Islands, the current turns west and spreads into the Pacific, forming the South Equatorial Current.

Although the 13 islands are extremely barren – some of them consisting merely of bare black lava rocks – they have formed the backdrop for the development of a unique world of animals and plants. The fact that the islands are merely 14 million years old, while the endemic marine and land iguanas developed 20 million years ago, means that the iguanas originally lived on similarly isolated islands which have long since disappeared.

Like Hawaii, the Galapagos Islands owe their existence to a "hot spot," a point in the Earth's crust where hot mantle material continually breaks through the surface. While the crustal plates slide over it, the hot spot continues to generate volcanic islands that migrate with the plate until they disappear into the sea again.

Here, at a depth of 2,500 meters (8,200 ft.), two researchers made one of the most important discoveries in marine biology. In 1977, they dived into the Galapagos Fracture Zone with their 7-meter (23-ft.) long submersible *Alvin* to verify whether or not this fracture zone contained geysers and hydrothermal vents similar to those in the Yellowstone National Park. During their dive, however, they not only found the hydrothermal vents they had hoped for, but also living organisms – a complete ecosystem swarming in the immediate surroundings of the hot geysers, which emit 350° C (662° F) hot water. They found annelids up to 3 meters (9.8 ft.) long and thick as an arm, but devoid of mouth, stomach, or intestines, as well as giant yellow shells. Among these, they found pale crustaceans, eyeless shrimp, and even fish.

Since then, similar strange oases have been found at the bottom of all oceans at depths of more than 2,500 meters (8,200 ft.). The key organisms of these ecosystems are specialized bacteria able to utilize the large amounts of high-energy sulfur escaping from the hot springs as a source of energy to subsist on. They, in turn, serve as food for all other animals living around the springs.

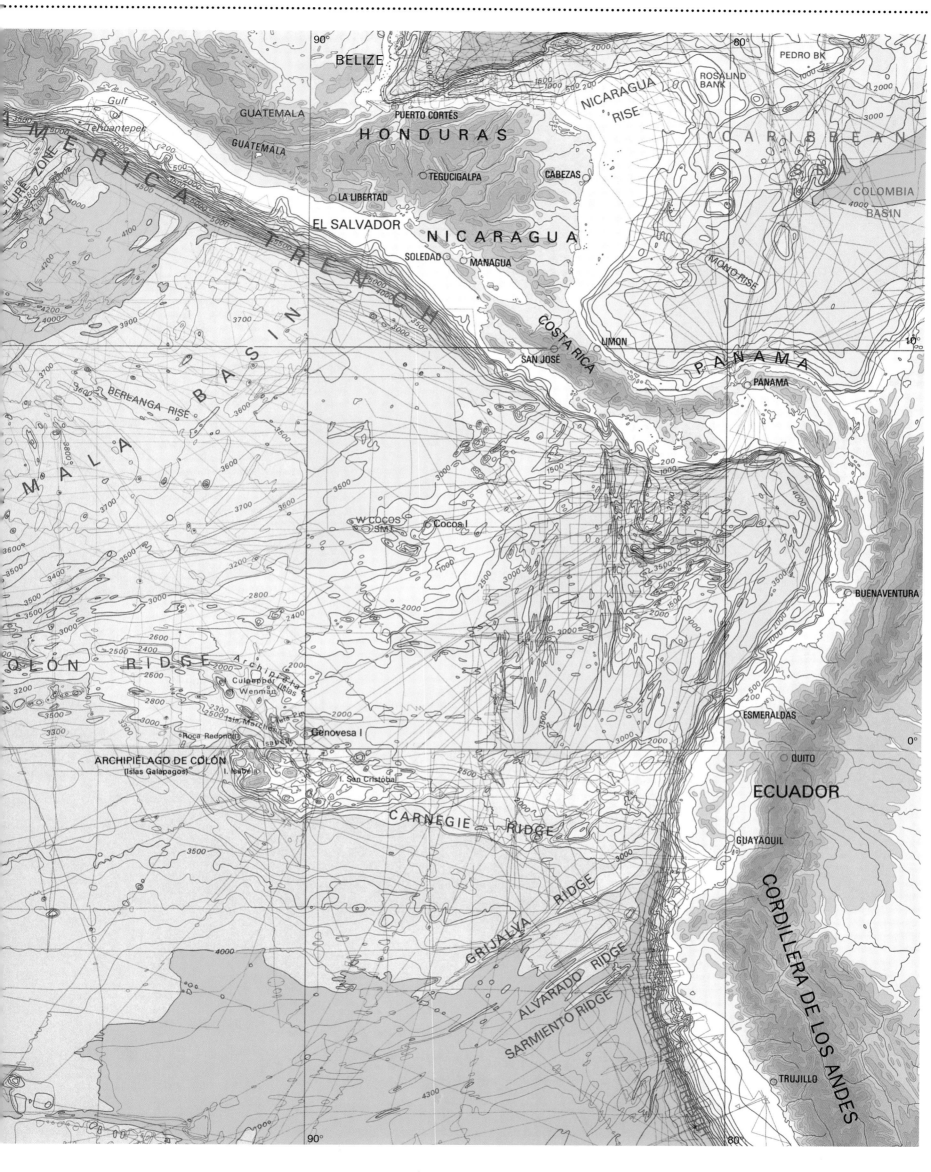

BELIZE

GUATEMALA

Gulf
of
Tehuantepec

GUATEMALA

HONDURAS

PUERTO CORTÉS

TEGUCIGALPA

CABEZAS

NICARAGUA
RISE

ROSALIND
BANK

PEDRO BK

CARIBBEAN

COLOMBIA
BASIN

LA LIBERTAD

EL SALVADOR

NICARAGUA

SOLEDAD

MANAGUA

MONO RISE

FRACTURE ZONE

AMERICA TRENCH

AMERICA BASIN

BERLANGA RISE

MALA

COSTA RICA

SAN JOSÉ

LIMON

PANAMA

PANAMA

W COCOS
SMT

Cocos I

BUENAVENTURA

COLÓN RIDGE

Archipiélago

Culpepper Islas
Wenman

Isla Marchena

Roca Redonda

Genovesa I

ESMERALDAS

ARCHIPIÉLAGO DE COLÓN
(Islas Galápagos)

I. Isabela

I. San Cristóbal

QUITO

ECUADOR

CARNEGIE RIDGE

GUAYAQUIL

GRIJALVA RIDGE

ALVARADO RIDGE

SARMIENTO RIDGE

CORDILLERA DE LOS ANDES

TRUJILLO

In the land of the giant squid

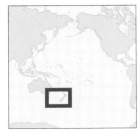

●●● Owing to the Lord Howe Rise, New Zealand separated from Australia 60 to 80 million years ago, opening the Tasman Sea in the process.

The East Australian Current approaches from the south, driven by the South Equatorial Current and trade winds. Nevertheless, it remains weak and has hardly any impact, particularly during winter in the Southern Hemisphere. Consequently, cold water from the south can at times reach the Lord Howe Island with its coral circle. South of this island, however, there are no more coral reefs. Navigators dread the frequent violent storms that rage over the Tasman Sea which is located in the zone of the "roaring forties" – the frequent, often extremely strong westerly winds prevailing between the 40° and 50° latitude.

Besides the coral species surrounding the southern sea islands, there is another group forming thickets in cooler water which later extend to banks rather than reefs. In winter, they tolerate water temperatures between 4° C and 15° C (39.2° F and 59° F) and live in depths between 60 meters and 200 meters (197 ft. and 656 ft.) – for instance, in shallow areas of the Chatham Rise that extends eastward at the latitude of New Zealand's South Island.

This sub-marine plateau is about the size of Denmark; the area surrounding it is supposedly inhabited by large numbers of giant squid, the creature of legends. Scientists have been trying to track down this species for more than 130 years. They have been sighted time and time again in the Kaikoura Canyon between the South Island of New Zealand and the Chatham Rise, obviously a favorite habitat for the enormous mollusks weighing up to one ton.

Two of their 10 tentacles attain a length of 14 meters (46 ft.). With a diameter of 40 centimeters (15.4 in.), their eyes reach the size of volleyballs. Their chitin jaws are shaped like a parrot's beak and are hard as rock. Their bodies can be twice the size of a human being. So far, however, nobody has ever seen a giant squid alive, although some 200 dead animals have been found to date.

The 800-meter (2,625-ft.) deep Chatham Rise is a "land of milk and honey" for these giant squid, their favorite food being Hoki fish of which enormous shoals roam depths below 300 meters (984 ft.).

In the giant squid's hunting grounds, however, sperm whales – their major enemies – are never far away. Giant squid beaks have been found in the stomachs of many dead whales. Yet even 40-ton sperm whales do not escape unscathed from fights with giant squids, for their bodies are often marked with large round scars inflicted by the squid's suckers.

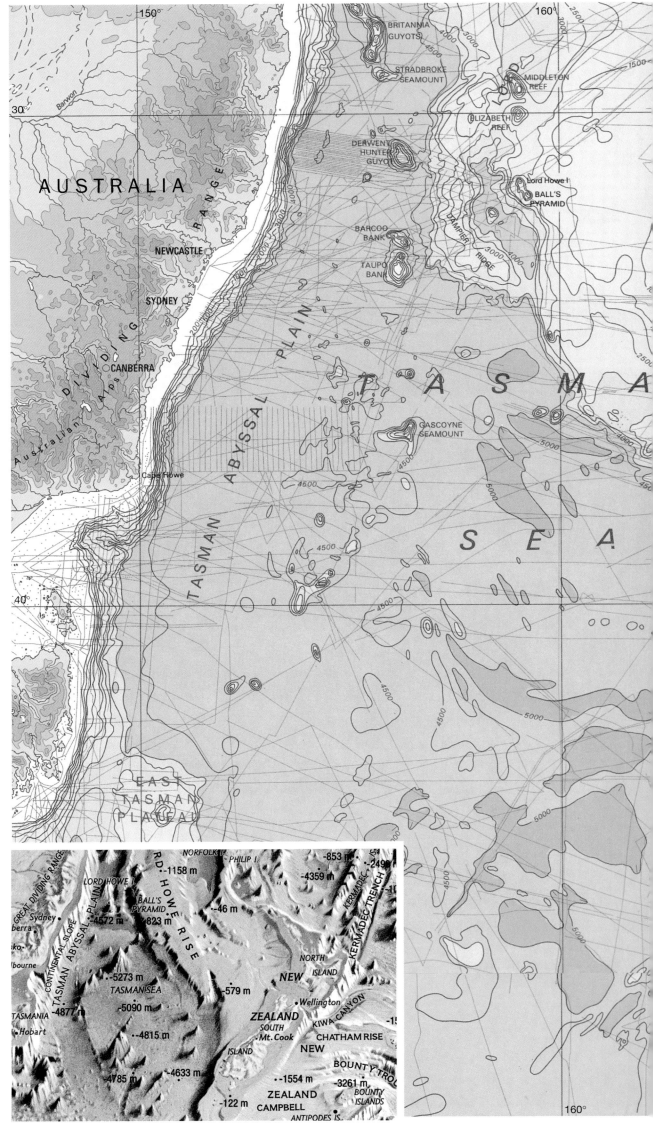

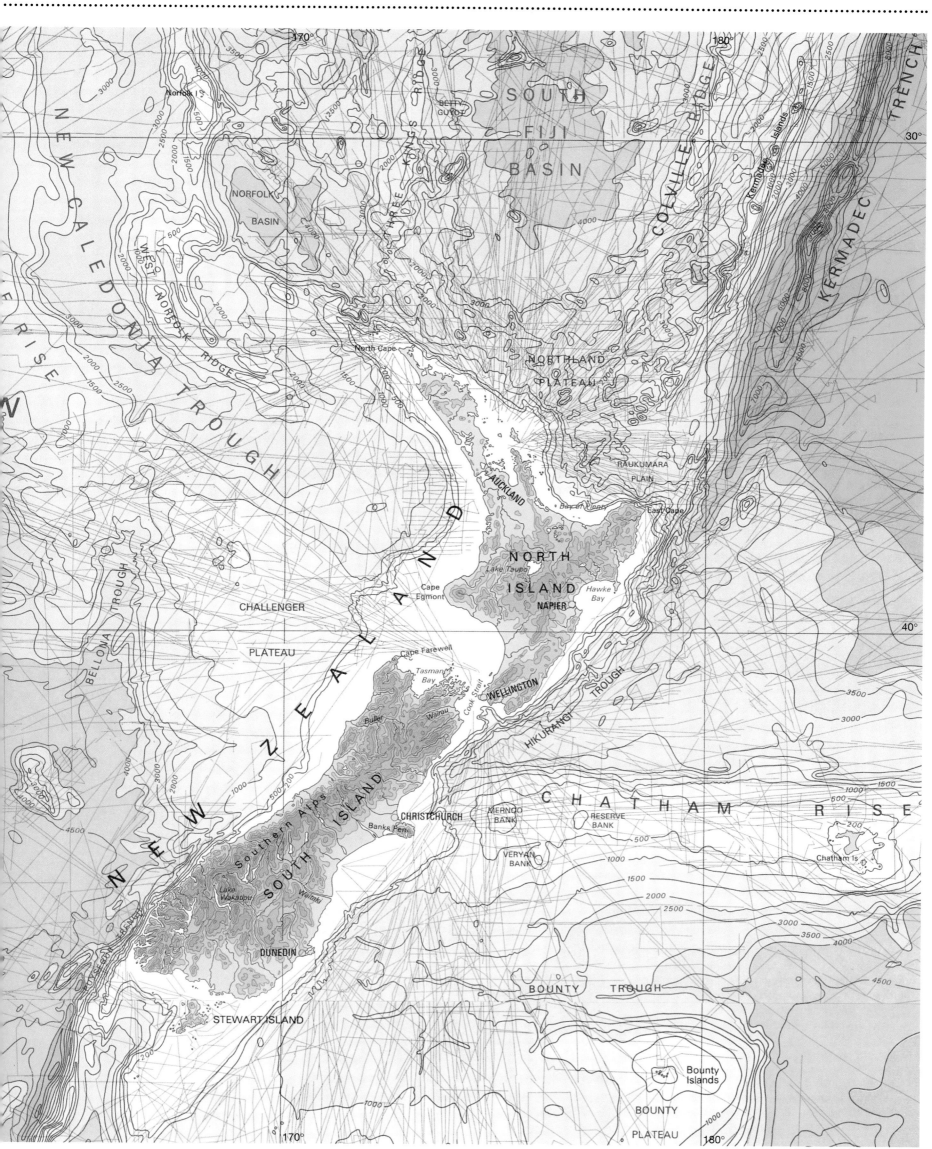

A sea of sinking volcanoes

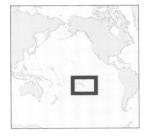

●●● French Polynesia comprises only some of the many islands located in the triangle between Hawaii, New Zealand, and Easter Island – known as Polynesia. The French overseas territory consists of some 130 islands belonging to the groups of Tuamotu, Gambier, Marquesas, Tubuai (also called Austral Islands), and the Society Islands, all situated on the ledges of parallel sub-marine ridges.

Tahiti is the largest of the "Windward Islands," as the southernmost group of Society Islands is called. The two eroded volcanic cones, the 2,237-meter (7,340-ft.) high Orohena and the 1,323-meter (4,341-ft.) high Roniu are surrounded by a protective ring of coral reefs.

Volcanoes that erupted from the sea floor in primeval times now sit heavily on the sea bed and are slowly sinking down, while corals readily grow in the shallow, 23° C to 25° C (73.4° F to 77° F) warm Pacific waters surrounding them. They develop into fringing reefs protecting the basaltic mountain against the surf. If the corals grow at the same speed as the volcano sinks, lagoons emerge between mountain and reef, slowly filling up with volcanic debris.

Long after a volcanic cone has disappeared in the sea bed, a coral ring surrounds the shallow lagoon. Such atolls can remain in place up to 40 million years. If, however, the corals lose the competition, the volcanic stumps submerge and become guyots, flat submarine mountains covered by caps of coral limestone.

Corals are firmly installed polyps with bodies similar to a bag, with the upper end – the mouth – being surrounded by tentacles that are used to draw food into their digestive tract. Indigestible remains are also eliminated through the mouth.

Over 6,000 species of these colorful and varied animals are known today. The reefs are built up by stony corals which grow a limestone foot in the lower part of their body and surround themselves with an outer limestone skeleton.

Although these animals could, in principle, grow independently from light, they thrive only in depths of up to 11 meters (36 ft.) and are hardly viable below 40 meters (131 ft.). This is due to the zooxanthellae, microscopic algae that live symbiotically with the coral in their tissue. Like all plants, the zooxanthellae need light to perform photosynthesis. From the polyp's metabolism, they take up nitrogen and phosphor, thus altering the chemistry of the water around the reef in a way that allows their hosts to develop limestone skeletons more readily. If the algae die, for example, because the sea water becomes too warm, the coral become pale and also die.

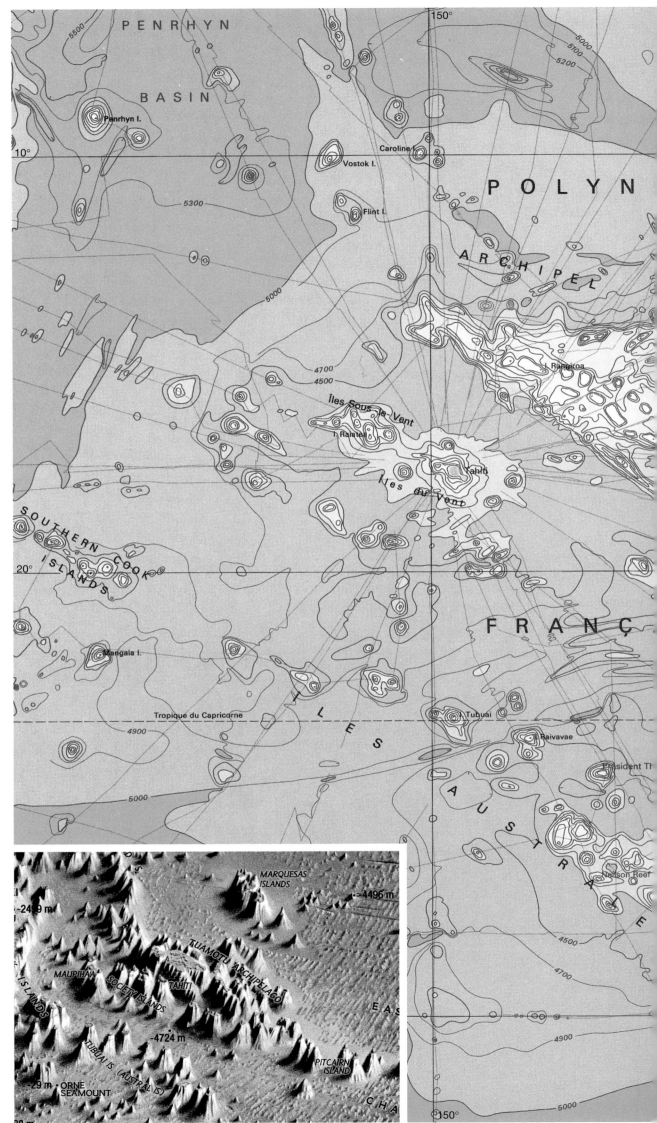

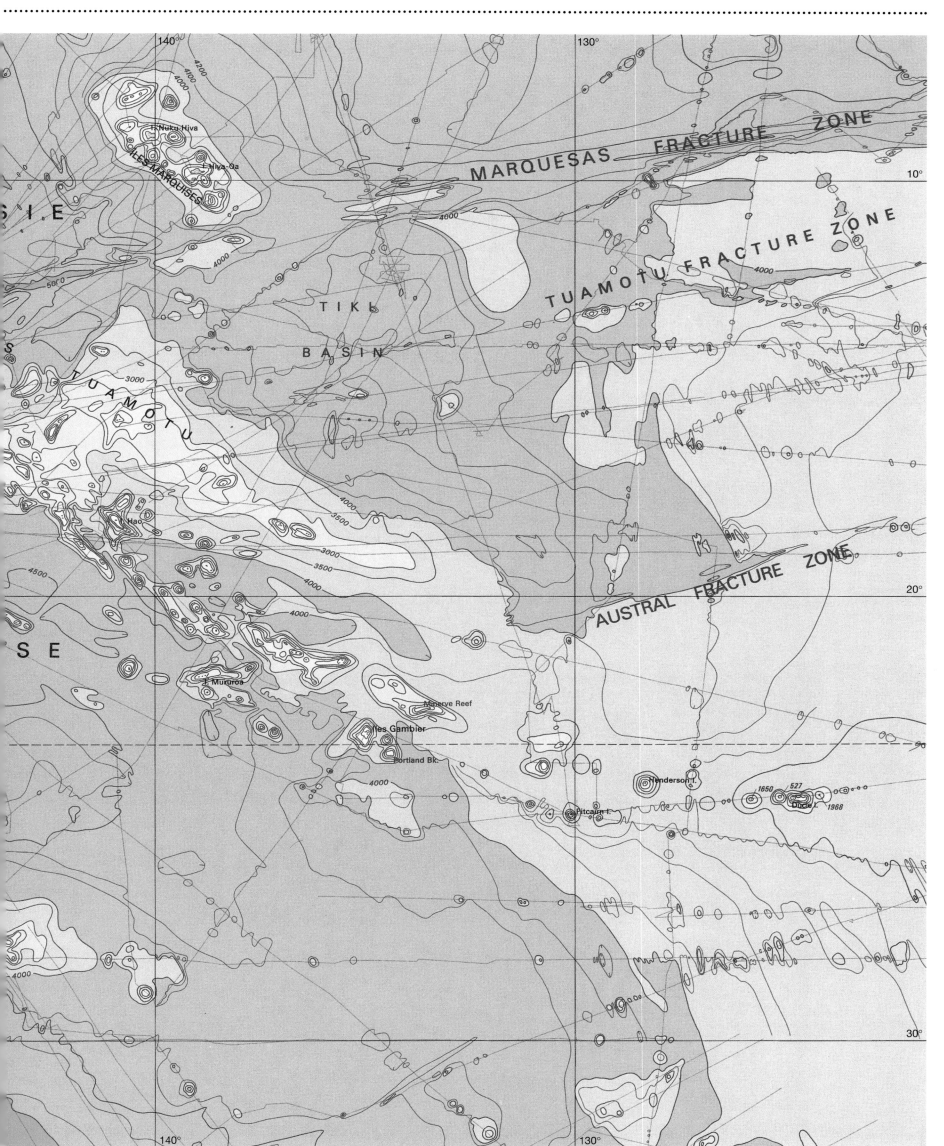

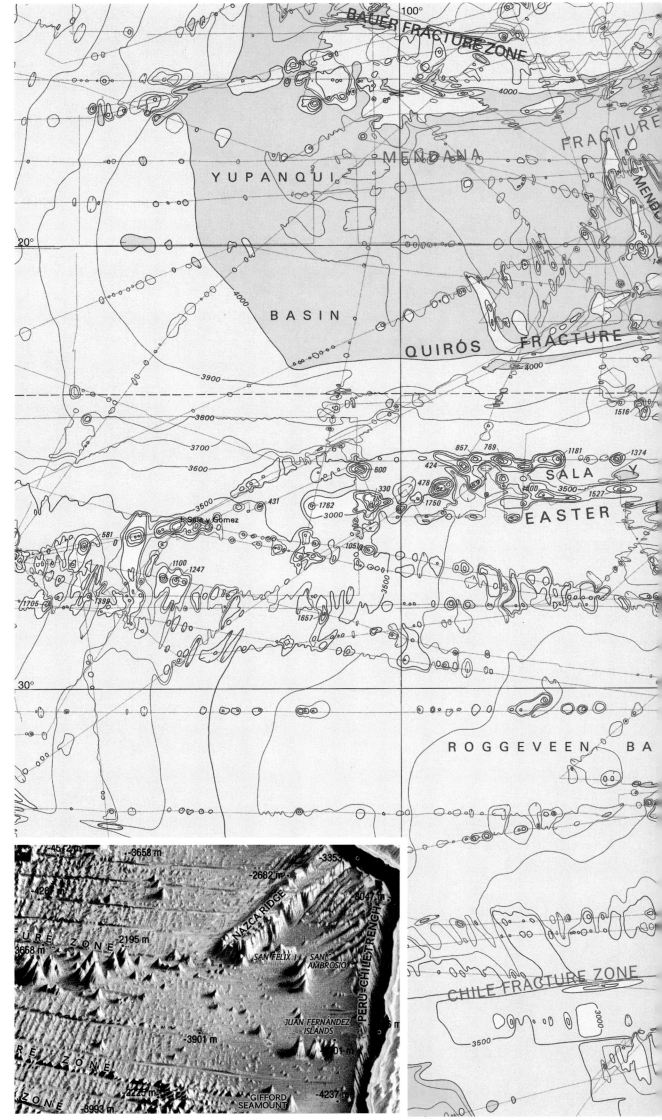

El Niño begins off Peru's coast

●●● About 160 kilometers (99 mi.) off the South American Pacific shore, the Peru-Chile Trench, also known as the Atacama Trench, digs itself into the sea floor. It is up to 8,000 meters (26,200 ft.) deep, almost 4,000 kilometers (2,500 mi.) long and 60 kilometers (37 mi.) wide. For the last 170 million years, the Nazca Plate has descended under the South American Plate on the bottom of the southeastern Pacific, pushing up the Andes Mountains in the process.

Off the coast, the cold and shallow Peru Current, also known as the Humboldt Current, moves slowly northwards at a width of 900 kilometers (559 mi.), fed by the cold circular current surrounding the Antarctic. Near the equator, it turns to the west and converges with the Pacific South Equatorial Current. This current accounts for the dense fogs frequently shrouding the coastline and for the fact that the slope of the Andes is one of the most arid regions of the world.

Together with the Earth's rotation, the southwestern wind continually blowing from the sea to the mainland draws water from the depths, carrying a wealth of nutrients to the surface. This provides for an abundance of plankton which, in turn, caters to the food requirements of the huge sardine and tuna shoals populating the offshore waters. The fish serve as food also for the sea birds which then leave behind guano, a valuable fertilizer.

Every year around Christmas, however, the water temperature along the coast rises, a phenomenon which the fishers call El Niño (translated as "the Christ child"). The appearance of El Niño marks the end of the fishing season as the fish migrate into cooler parts of the ocean. At irregular intervals, approximately once every four years, the rise in temperature is so pronounced that the fish shoals stay away even in spring, with disastrous consequences. At the same time, this induces massive changes in the weather conditions of large parts of the world, lasting for an entire year.

Over an area corresponding to one-fourth of the Earth's circumference, the Pacific water near the equator becomes warmer – above all directly off the South American coast, where the difference can amount to 5° C (41° F) above normal levels. The consequences are drought in Southeast Asia and Australia and torrential rains on the other side of South America. While Israeli farmers will enjoy more rain, Colombia will register an epidemic spreading of malaria, and the crop losses in Southeast Asia will induce a sharp rise in world market prices for coconut oil. Only in recent years have scientists found ways to predict a strong El Niño 18 months in advance so that the consequences can be anticipated.

Skerries in the South Pacific

● ● ● At the rim of the Antarctic Circumpolar Current south of New Zealand several small, mostly remote islands rise above sea level from the bottom of sub-marine plateaus. Stewart, the third largest island of New Zealand, is located on the Campbell Plateau, the submarine continuation of the South Island, merely 27 kilometers (17 mi.) off the south tip of the larger of the two main islands. Stewart Island is the southernmost inhabited island of New Zealand and is surrounded by numerous skerries, the Muttonbird Islands.

The six Auckland Islands lie 500 kilometers (310 mi.) further south of Stewart. They are of volcanic origin and serve as a habitat for countless birds – above all stormy petrels and penguins – but also for fur seals, sea lions, and elephant seals. There are even wild cattle to be found, the descendants of animals introduced by settlers in 1890 at the same time as they introduced sheep. The settlers gave up and the sheep became extinct, but the cattle managed to survive.

Some 200 kilometers (124 mi.) away, the rugged Campbell Island, located on the Rise of the same name, was discovered in 1810 by seal hunters who managed to deplete the extensive fur seal populations in a very short time. The introduction of sheep by settlers in 1896 came as the final blow to the island's ecosystem, as the animals devastated the vegetation so thoroughly that it has still not recovered.

Macquarie, Australia's southernmost island, is situated 1,500 kilometers (932 mi.) off Tasmania and represents the visible part of a mountain located in the middle of the Macquarie Ridge. The treeless island is the only known breeding ground of the royal penguin, and is currently home to some 1.7 million of the creatures. Furthermore, this is the only place on Earth where rock from the deep mantle 6 kilometers (3.73 mi.) below the ocean floor has been pushed above the water level.

The Macquarie Ridge is the border between the Indo-Australian Plate and the Pacific Plate, and at the same time separates the Indian from the Pacific deep-sea water. The geological processes taking place along the ridge are more complicated than those associated with other oceanic ridges. The Macquarie Ridge constitutes the rim of the Pacific Plate, which pushes westward against the Indo-Australian Plate, moving upward in the process.

Several sea miles further to the south, in the Hjort Trench, the more recent Indo-Australian Plate pushes eastward against the Pacific Plate, curving downward in the process. This is extraordinary insofar as older crust material normally sinks to the bottom because the rock is denser and therefore heavier.

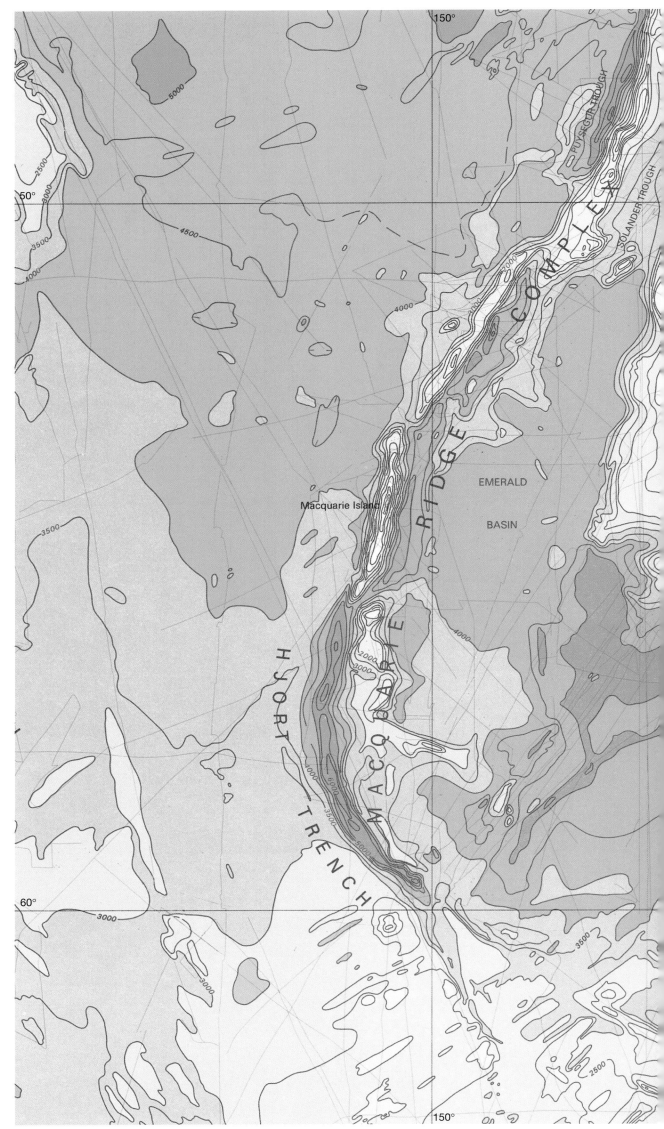

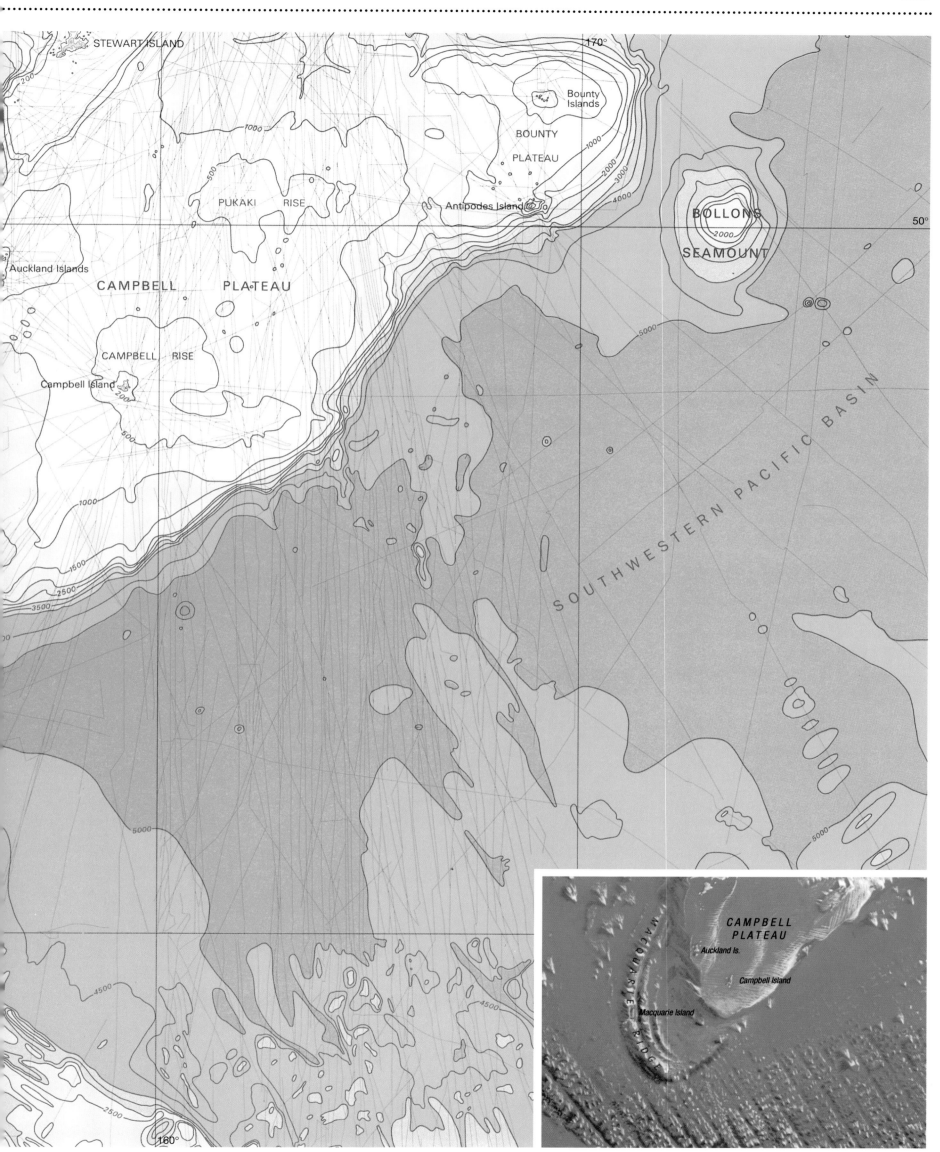

STEWART ISLAND

200

1000

500

PUKAKI RISE

Bounty Islands

BOUNTY

PLATEAU

1000

2000

3000

4000

Antipodes Island

50°

BOLLONS

2000

SEAMOUNT

5000

Auckland Islands

CAMPBELL PLATEAU

CAMPBELL RISE

Campbell Island

200

500

1000

1500

2500

3500

S O U T H W E S T E R N   P A C I F I C   B A S I N

5000

5000

5000

4500

4500

2500

160°

170°

CAMPBELL PLATEAU

Auckland Is.

Campbell Island

MACQUARIE RIDGE

Macquarie Island

Rough seas and stormy weather

●●● Cape Horn, a sheer rock on the island of Hornos, is the southernmost point of South America. Sailors passing the island on the coastal side sometimes mistake another rock for the Cape: the "False Cape Horn" on Hoste Island, which is 56 kilometers (35 mi.) further to the northwest.

By sailing around Cape Horn (and thus the southern tip of the American continent) in 1616, the Dutch seafarer Willem Schouten opened up the fastest sea route from the Atlantic to the Pacific. The English discoverer John Drake saw the Cape in 1578 when a storm drove his ship into the Drake Strait. But he decided to follow the route to the Pacific discovered by Magellan in 1520, even though it was far more difficult to navigate.

The Antarctic Circumpolar Current hitting the southern Chilean coast from the west pushes mainly through the 1,000-kilometer (620-mi.) wide Magellan Strait. In winter and spring, icebergs can be found floating around Cape Horn. Part of the water is diverted to the north and converges with the cold Humboldt Current flowing north off the South American coast of the Pacific. In years when the climatic phenomenon known as El Niño (an extraordinary warming of the Pacific) is particularly pronounced, the current moves away from the coast.

Due to the rough seas, the frequent storms, the low temperatures, and the tricky ice conditions, rounding Cape Horn is a merciless challenge to both ships and crews. Nevertheless, for most of the 19th and 20th century, until the inauguration of the Panama Canal in 1914, the Cape Horn route was of great importance in commercial terms. The over 13,000-kilometer (8,100-mi.) long route around Cape Horn was always faster than the arduous North American land route.

During the California gold rush, competition between the legendary clipper ships began. These slender boats were all built between 1850 and 1855. The *Flying Cloud*, for instance, made the route from New York to San Francisco in just 89 days at a maximum speed of over 13 knots – the traveling speed of modern freighters. For the ship owners, this was lucrative business, for the money earned with the freight of one single journey was often enough to cover the cost of the vessel's construction. Today, the route is taken only by supertankers too big to pass through the Panama Canal.

In 1945, crude oil was discovered in a bay near Manantiales not far from the eastern entrance to the Magellan Strait. It constitutes Chile's only oil field. The oil is pumped through pipelines along the Andes to the industrialized areas in central Chile.

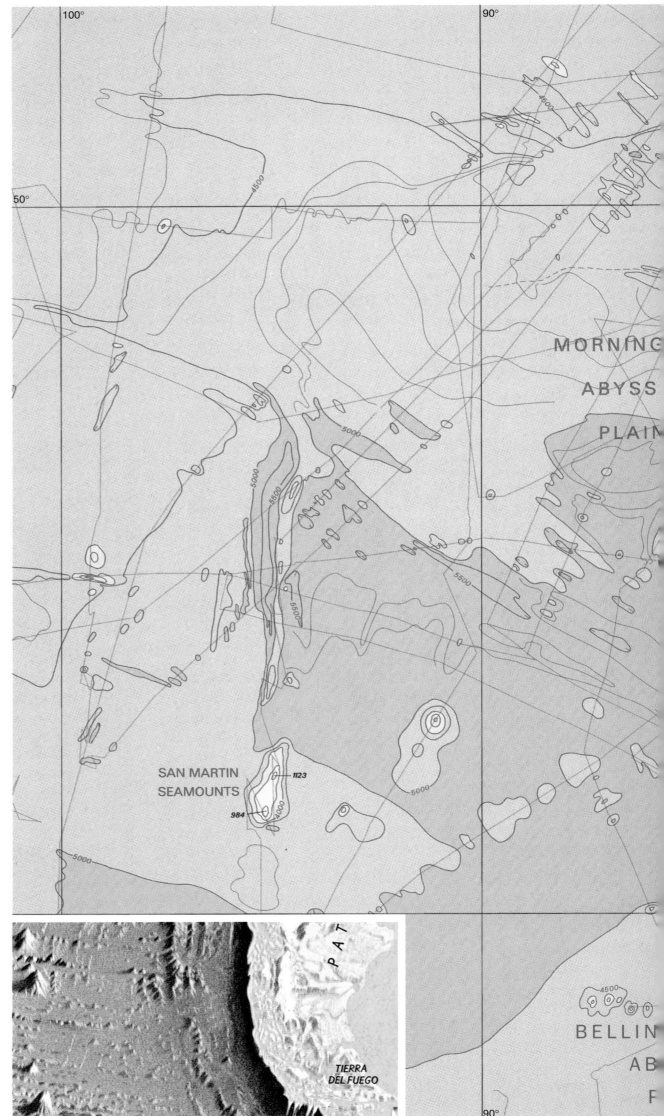

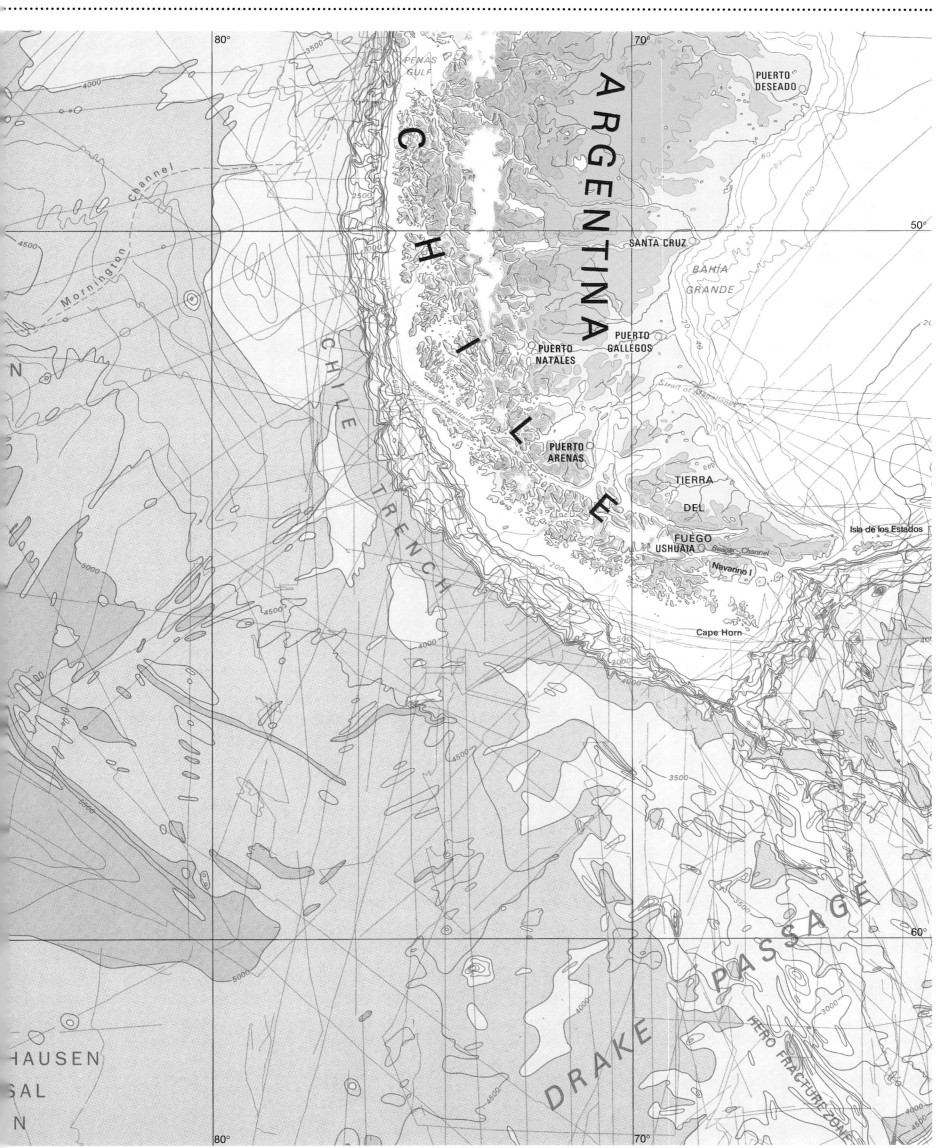

80°

70°

PENAS
GULF

PUERTO
DESEADO

A
R
G
E
N
T
I
N
A

C
H
I
L
E

Mornington Channel

Channel

SANTA CRUZ

50°

BAHÍA
GRANDE

4500

PUERTO
NATALES

PUERTO
GALLEGOS

Strait of Magallanes

C
H
I
L
E

T
R
E
N
C
H

PUERTO
ARENAS

TIERRA

DEL

5000

FUEGO
USHUAIA

Beagle Channel

Isla de los Estados

Navarino I

4500

Cape Horn

4000

5000

2000

4500

3500

4500

3500

60°

PASSAGE

5000

D
R
A
K
E

HERO FRACTURE ZONE

HAUSEN

SAL

3000

80°

70°

The Red Sea's colors

● ● ● In reality, the Red Sea is not red, but an intense blue-green. Its name derives from the blooming cyanobacterium *Trichodesmium erythraeum*, also called blue-green algae. In a calm sea, it sometimes reproduces in enormous numbers, forming a mile-wide slimy layer on the surface of the sea. After a couple of days, the algae die and stain the sea a reddish brown.

The Red Sea is approximately 2,000 kilometers (1,200 mi.) long, no more than 300 kilometers (190 mi.) wide and part of the enormous fracture zone between the African Plate and Arabian Plate, which extends over 6,000 kilometers (3,700 mi.) from the East African fracture system to the Jordan valley. It developed some 55 million years ago when Africa started drifting away from Arabia. Twenty-five million years ago, the Gulf of Suez and the northern part of the Red Sea emerged. The Gulf of Akaba to the north and the southern part of the Red Sea came into being only 3 million to 4 million years ago. Today, the two plates still drift away from each other at a rate of 15 millimeters to 16 millimeters (0.59 in. to 0.63 in.) per year.

At the deepest point of the marine trench, hot water escapes from a depth of some 3,000 meters (10,000 ft.). The water is loaded with minerals from the Earth's deeper layers. Thick layers of heavy metal mud cover the sea floor for miles around these hydrothermal vents, waiting to be used as raw material resources.

It takes 20 years for the Red Sea waters to complete a hydrological cycle. Oceanic surface water from the Gulf of Aden flows into the Red Sea via the western canal of the Mandeb Strait. The prevailing south wind drives it towards the Sinai Peninsula. In the Gulf of Suez, water evaporates to such an extent that the salt concentration rises sharply. This high-saline, heavy water descends to a depth of at least 400 meters (1,300 ft.), where it flows southward and back to the Indian Ocean via the eastern canal of the Mandeb Strait.

The fracture zone off East Africa and Arabia still exerts seismic activity in the surroundings of the Murray Ridge off the Gulf of Oman. To the west of it, the sea floor of the Oman Basin submerges under the continental plate.

The Persian and Arabian Gulf opening up behind the Strait of Hormuz is much older than the Red Sea trench. The northern part of the basin, the vast valley of Mesopotamia, was filled up with debris by the rivers. The Gulf is on average only 35 meters (115 ft.) deep – seldom more than 90 meters (300 ft.) deep – and is highly saline due to massive evaporation. Its floor consists of a several-hundred-meter-thick layer of mineral and organic sediments comprising abundant crude oil deposits.

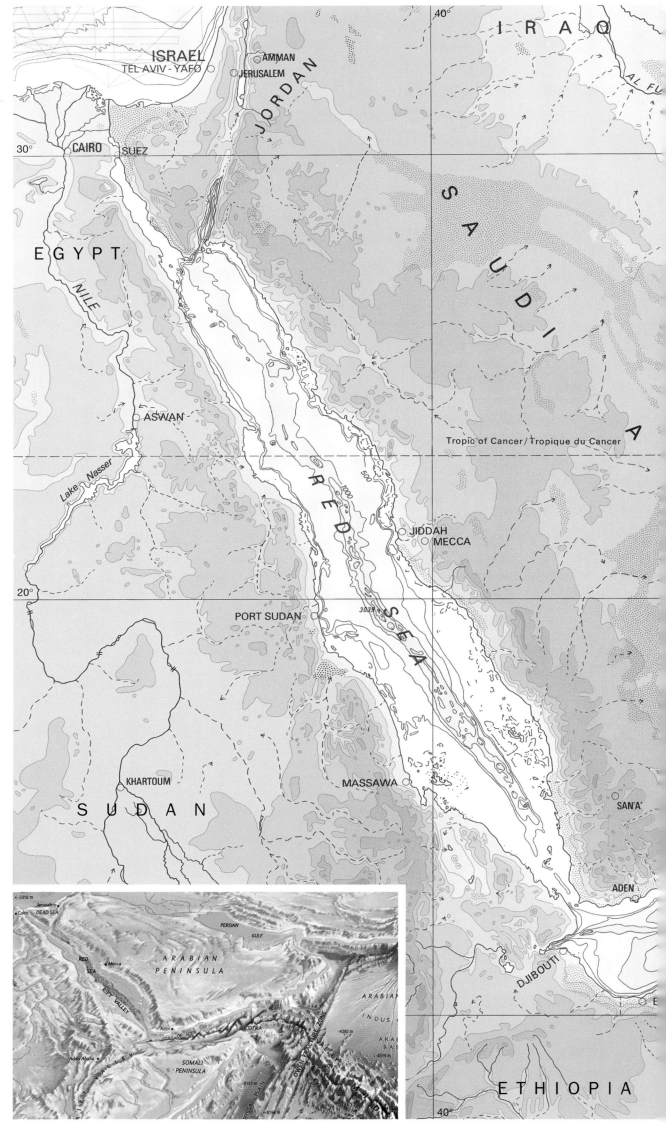

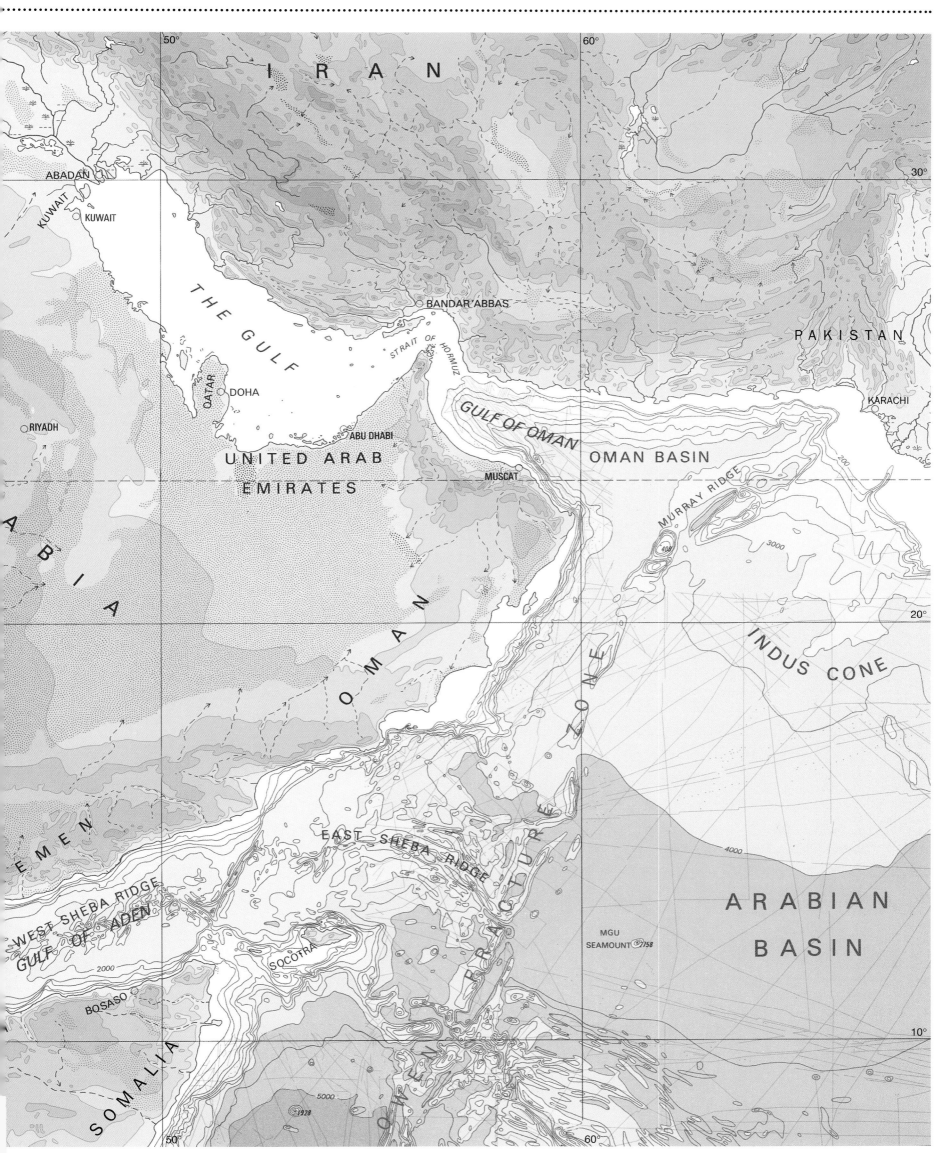

50°

60°

I R A N

ABADAN

30°

KUWAIT

KUWAIT

BANDAR'ABBAS

PAKISTAN

T H E   G U L F

Strait of Hormuz

KARACHI

QATAR

DOHA

GULF OF OMAN

OMAN BASIN

RIYADH

ABU DHABI

UNITED ARAB

EMIRATES

MUSCAT

MURRAY RIDGE

408

3000

A B I A

O M A N

20°

200

INDUS   CONE

F R A C T U R E   Z O N E

4000

E M E N

EAST SHEBA RIDGE

A R A B I A N

WEST SHEBA RIDGE

GULF OF ADEN

SOCOTRA

MGU
SEAMOUNT 2758

B A S I N

2000

BOSASO

O W E N

10°

S O M A L I A

5000

1928

50°

60°

Monsoons and fish graveyards

● ● ● The Indus River has carved a deep sub-marine canyon within the shelf border off Pakistan. During the annual rainy season from May to September, it washes enormous amounts of mud up to the deep-sea rim. Within the course of the Earth's history, a 860-kilometer (534-mi.) wide, 1,500-kilometer (932-mi.) long sediment cone has formed.

The southwestern monsoon brings summer rains from the open sea, and the monsoon winds shape the entire hydrological cycle in the Arabian Sea. The wind develops when the summers are particularly hot and the winters very cold on the Asian mainland. Due to the temperature differential between the land and the ocean, winds come from the northeast between December and February, and from the southwest between May and September.

The southwestern monsoon pushes the water masses of the Indian Ocean against the Arabian coastline, so that the "old" water drains into the open sea. It is replaced by cold, nutrient-rich deep-sea water which triggers an explosive algae growth that is even visible at a distance of 500 kilometers (310 mi.) offshore.

At the same time, the west wind drives sand from Arabia out to sea. Plankton organisms and bacteria adhere to the grains of sand from the deserts and to the mud particles from the rivers. Due to their increased weight, these particles sink to the bottom too quickly to be sufficiently consumed in the upper water layers. At the sea floor they rot, thereby drawing oxygen from the sea bed and generating hydrogen sulfide. Whenever a current drives this pungent deep-sea water to the surface, the fish die from lack of oxygen.

For this reason, the area off the easternmost tip of the Arabian Peninsula is also known as a "fish graveyard," since the remains of dead fish are found here in abundance. Yet massive death of fish also occurs in the open Arabian Sea. There, however, it is triggered by currents just below the surface which flow in directly from tropical areas and, from time to time, let warm, low-oxygen water rise into the upper layers.

The massive plankton boom, however, lays the basis for the rich fishing grounds off the Arabian coast, which are exploited mostly by individual fishers equipped with outriggers and dhows, although the big factory ships from India, Pakistan, Sri Lanka, and France are also frequently seen in this region.

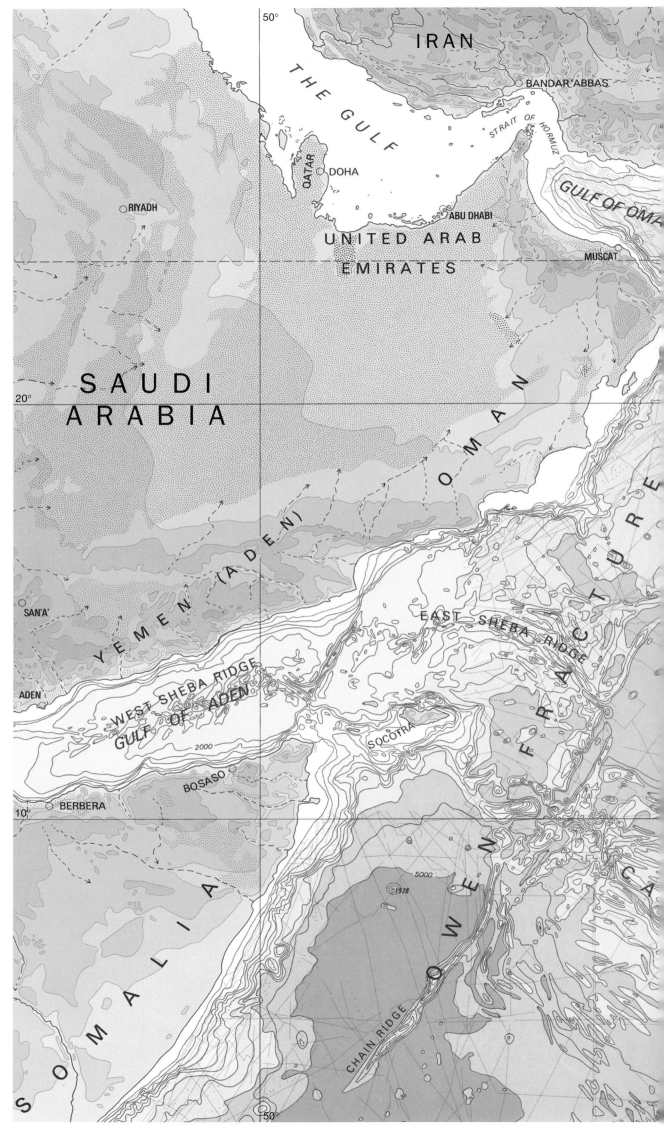

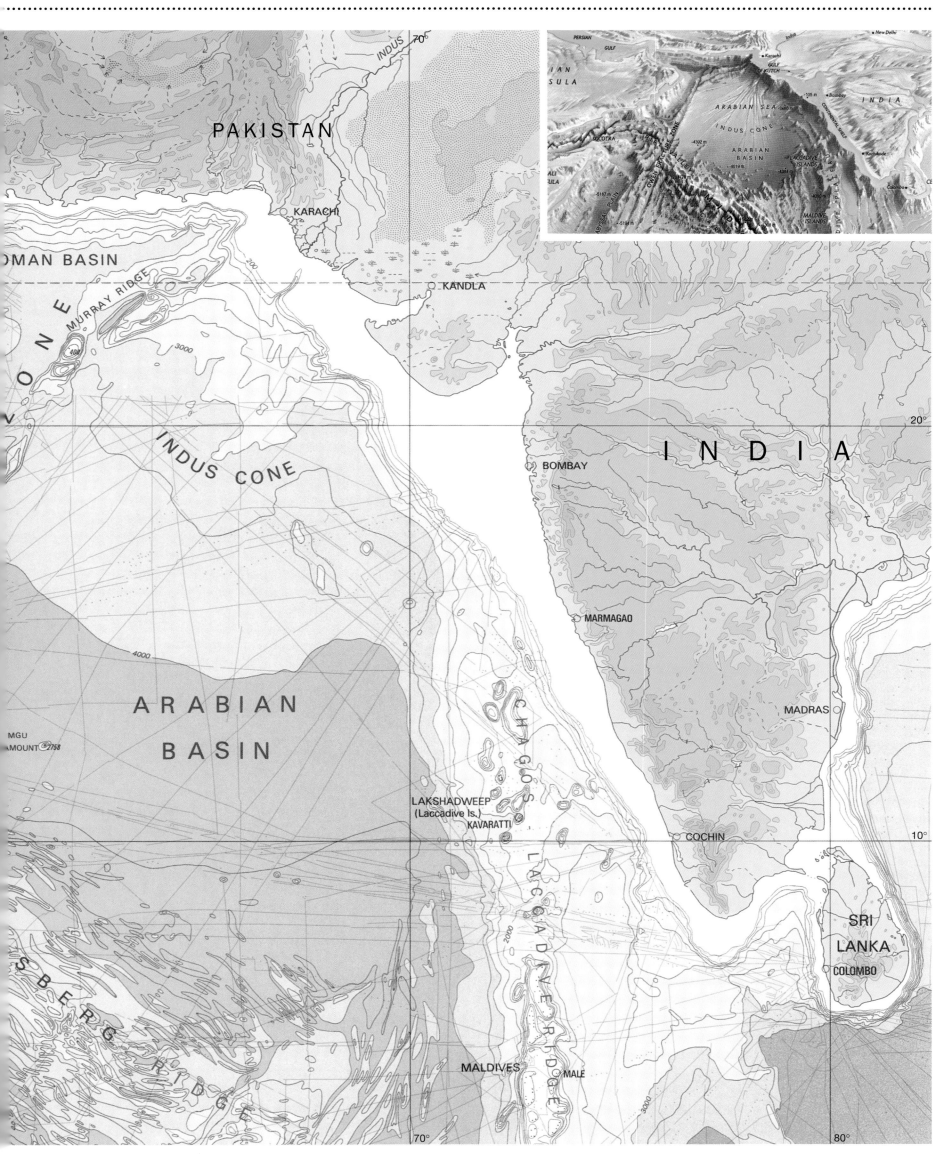

PAKISTAN

KARACHI

OMAN BASIN

MURRAY RIDGE

400

3000

ONE

INDUS CONE

KANDLA

70°

INDUS

20°

I N D I A

BOMBAY

MARMAGAO

4000

A R A B I A N

B A S I N

MGU
SEAMOUNT 2758

CHAGOS

LAKSHADWEEP
(Laccadive Is.)
KAVARATTI

LACCADIVE

MADRAS

COCHIN

10°

SBERG

RIDGE

2000

SRI
LANKA

COLOMBO

LACCADIVE RIDGE

3000

MALDIVES

MALE

70°

80°

The mud of the Ganges

●●● When India separated from Australia and collided with Asia some 150 million years ago, it created the Bay of Bengal in the process. With an average depth of 2,600 meters (8,500 ft.), the Bay of Bengal is relatively shallow. In its northern part, off the enormous delta marking the mouth of the River Ganges, there is a broad stretch of continental shelf which becomes narrower off the coasts of India and Myanmar (Burma). Its slopes towards the ocean are intersected by deep valleys: old river beds originating from a period when the shelf was not yet flooded.

The sediment cone washed by the River Ganges over the shelf rim before its delta, and piled up in the Bay of Bengal, represents the widest and thickest fluvial deposit on Earth. Over several millennia, the mud carried by the River Ganges on its 2,500-kilometer (1,500-mi.) long course has accumulated here. (The river drains one-fourth of the Indian mainland and also picks up the sediments carried in by the Brahmaputra River north of the delta.)

The mud originating from the numerous rivers serves as fertilizer to the vast wetlands that cover the coasts in marshes and mangrove swamps, offering ideal living conditions to coastal fish species. In this area, the opportunities for coastal fishing have not yet been fully exploited, because fishers typically still use small outriggers without sophisticated mechanical devices. Even when shrimp fishing was intensified for export, shrimp stocks remained stable.

On the high seas, there are some factory ships from the largest fishing nations – such as Japan, South Korea, and Taiwan – hunting for tuna. These fish avoid high-saline waters and prefer the open Indian Ocean. The reason is that the salt concentration of this sea is markedly influenced by massive amounts of fresh water. The normal saline concentration of 33 ppt to 34 ppt can drop to half the amount in autumn when the rivers are swollen by floods. The fresh water plume is still detectable further south in the open Indian Ocean.

To the east, the Andaman Islands and Nicobar Islands seal off the Andaman Sea against the Gulf of Bengal. Less than 5 percent of the Andaman Sea is deeper than 3,000 meters (9,900 ft.). Only in a valley system east of the Andaman-Nicobar Ridge does it reach a depth of more than 4,400 meters (14,400 ft.). While marine animals are scarce in the open Andaman Sea, fishers catch some 250 edible species of fish and various shells directly off the coast of the Malay Peninsula. West of the Nicobar Islands, the aseismic Ninetyeast Ridge emerges from the sediments of the gulf. It is the longest rise to be found in all oceans and follows a straight line southward for 4,500 kilometers (2,795 mi.).

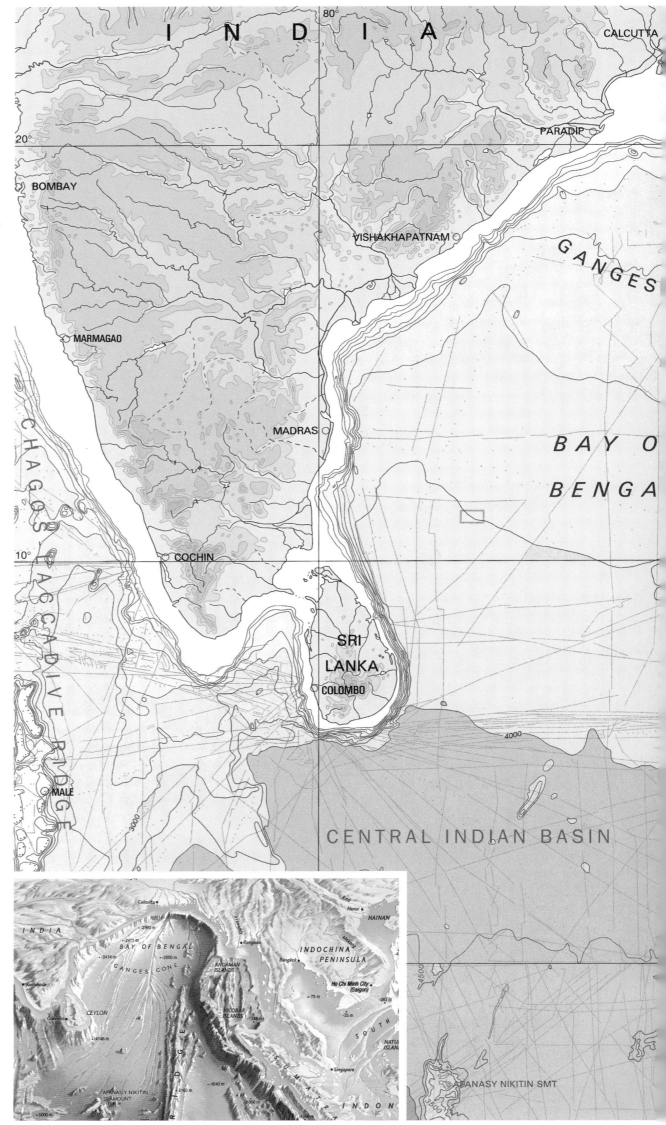

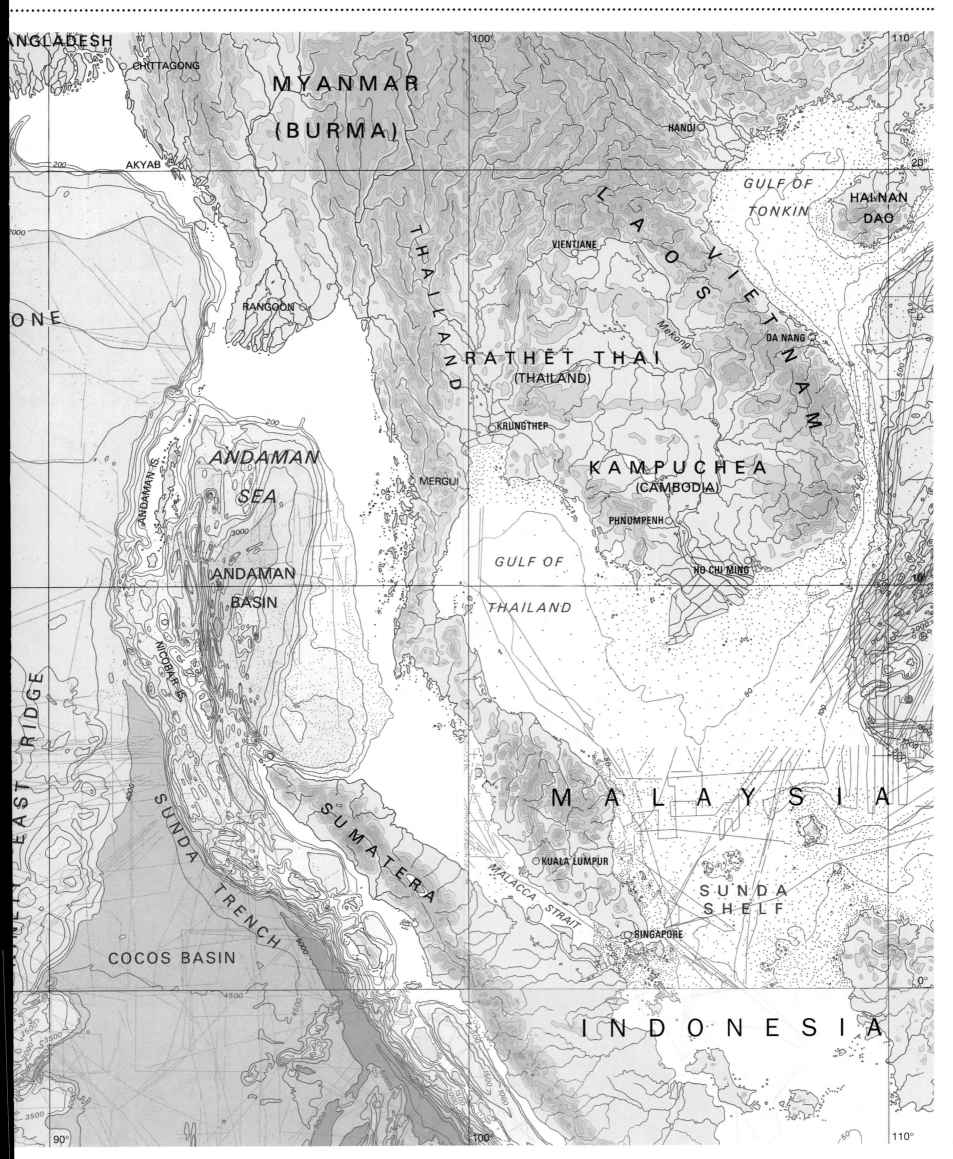

The ocean of many islands

●●● East of India is the largest group of islands on Earth. In addition to the 7,000 Philippine islands, more than 13,000 Indonesian islands are situated in the Sulu, Savu, Celebes, Molucca, Java, Banda, and Flores seas. The archipelago is separated from Asia by the Strait of Malacca and the South China Sea. The Timor Sea and Arafura Sea, as well as the Torres Strait, form the border towards Australia.

This rugged island and sea world is located directly on the equator at the boundary between the Pacific Ocean and the Indian Ocean. At this point, three large plates of the Earth's crust collide, forming a tight maze of shelf areas, volcanic mountain ranges, and deep-sea trenches.

The world's third largest island, Borneo, and the island arc formed by Sumatra, Java, Bali, and the Lesser Sunda Islands, are located on the Sunda Shelf, a southward extension of the Asian mainland. To the south and west, the shelf descends into deep-sea trenches like the 7,500-meter (24,600-ft.) deep Java Trench. New Guinea and the Molucca island of Halmahera belong to the Sahul Shelf, a northwestern extension of the Australian continental plate. The third big unit is formed by an extension of the mountain and trench belt extending from Japan over the Philippines and between Borneo and New Guinea. It is comprised of a number of volcanoes and deep-sea trenches surrounding Celebes and the almost one-thousand smaller Moluccas, also referred to as Spice Islands.

The Sulu Basin north of the Celebes Sea is a fault that was bent downwards like a bowl, breaking in the middle in the process. Today, two island chains protruding above sea level form its rim. The fault, which divides the sea floor from the northeast to the southwest, is visible above sea level as the Cagayan atolls and the volcanic Cagayan Sulu island group.

The Sulu islands, with their countless bays and secret passages, are a paradise for smugglers and modern pirates who still waylay cargo ships and use small speedboats to carry their loot and contraband goods to places of transshipment near the northeastern tip of Borneo. Their profit is considerable, for the most important shipping routes between Japan, India, Arabia, and Europe lead through the Malay Archipelago.

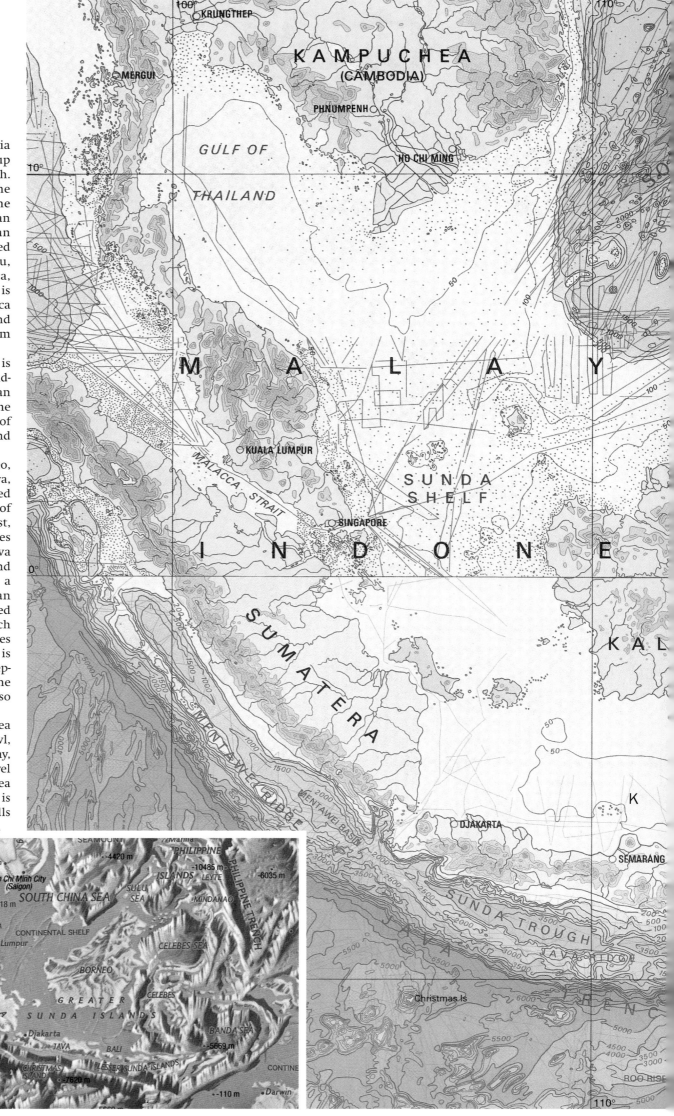

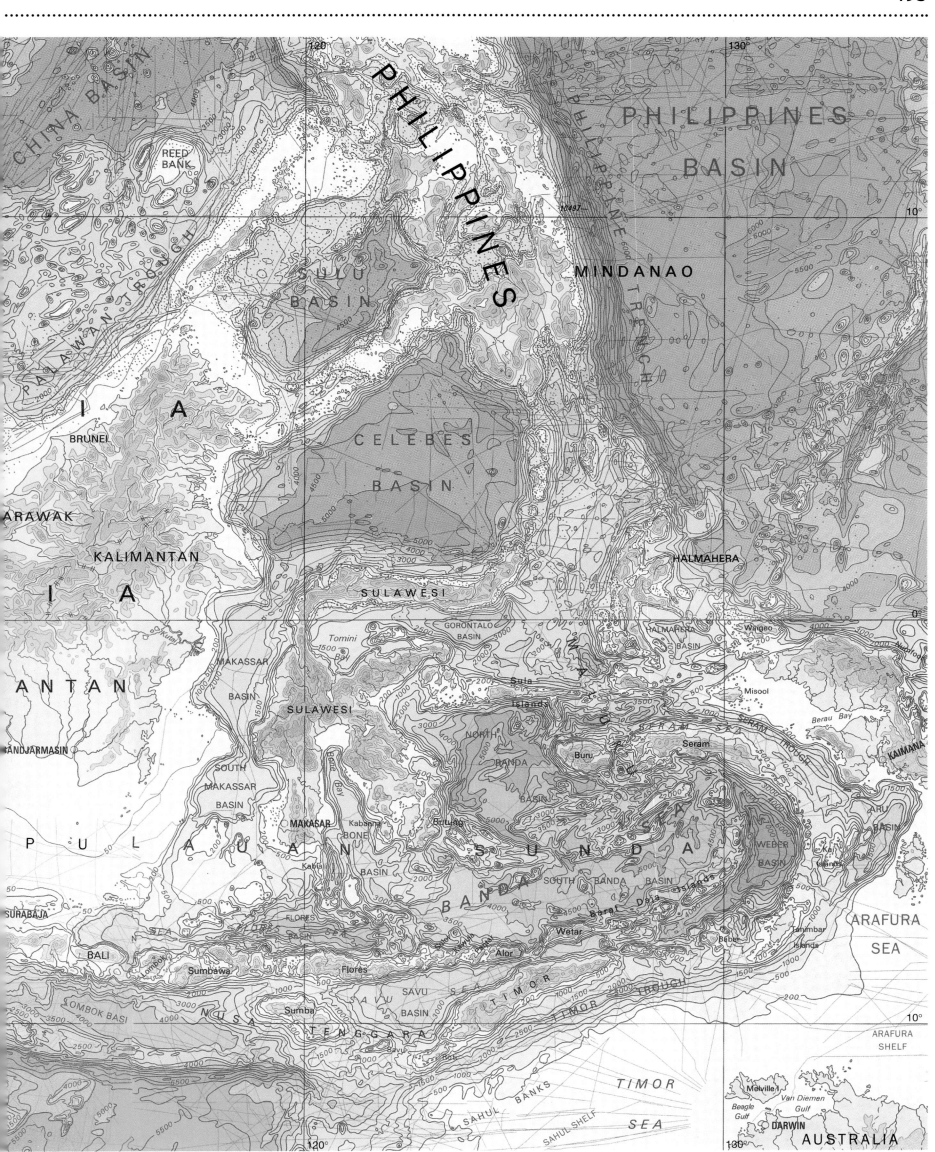

Home of a primeval fish

● ● ● Off the shores of Tanzania, the South Equatorial Current approaches the African coast. It is part of an enormous wind-driven water roll which continuously turns counterclockwise between Africa and Australia. Before reaching the African coast, the current divides into two branches. One of them is deviated northward and then immediately to the opposite direction where it converges with the Equatorial Counter Current. The other branch surrounds Madagascar on both sides. The strong, warm coastal Mozambique Current squeezes through the Mozambique Channel between Africa and Madagascar, which is the fourth largest island on the planet. Roughly 80 to 90 million years ago, Madagascar broke loose from India and settled down off the southeast African shore while India drifted further to the north.

The shallow, semicircular Mascarene Plain, located 640 kilometers to 800 kilometers (397 mi. to 497 mi.) to the northeast of Madagascar, was probably also left behind by the Indian subcontinent when it migrated towards Asia. Only 40 of the islands on or near the plateau are of continental origin, namely those located in the center of the Seychelles, while the remaining 75 Seychelles islands developed from coral reefs. The southern Mascarene Islands – Réunion, Mauritius, and Rodriguez – are of volcanic origin, just like the Comoros islands located between the northern tip of Madagascar and Africa.

For a long time, the waters surrounding the Comoros islands were believed to be the only habitat of the famous Crossopterygii, a fish species which has remained unchanged over the last 400 million years and is thus even older than the dinosaurs. When one of these animals was caught off East Africa in 1938, scientists realized that this primeval animal was part of a vertebrate evolutionary line which was then believed to have become extinct 65 million years ago. Despite these findings, the Crossopterygii are not the "missing link" between fish and four-legged land-dwelling animals that scientists had hoped it would be.

Since 1952, biologists have been aware that, over millions of years, the cool waters near the Comoros Islands have held a much larger population of these ancient fish at a depth of 200 meters to 300 meters (660 ft. to 990 ft.). Researchers from all over the world are now undertaking excursions in submersibles to investigate the life of these animals which are up to 2 meters (6.56 ft.) long and can weigh up to 100 kilograms (220 lb.). To date, it is still not known how old they get or when they reach sexual maturity. In the meantime, scientists have found another population of these primeval beings near Indonesia.

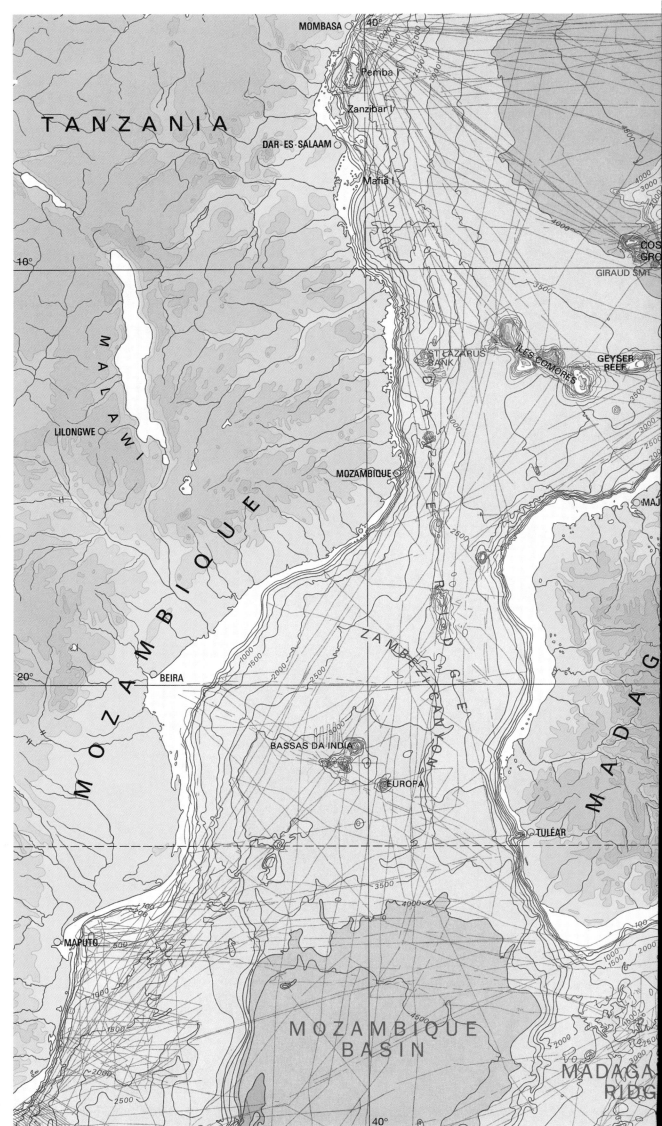

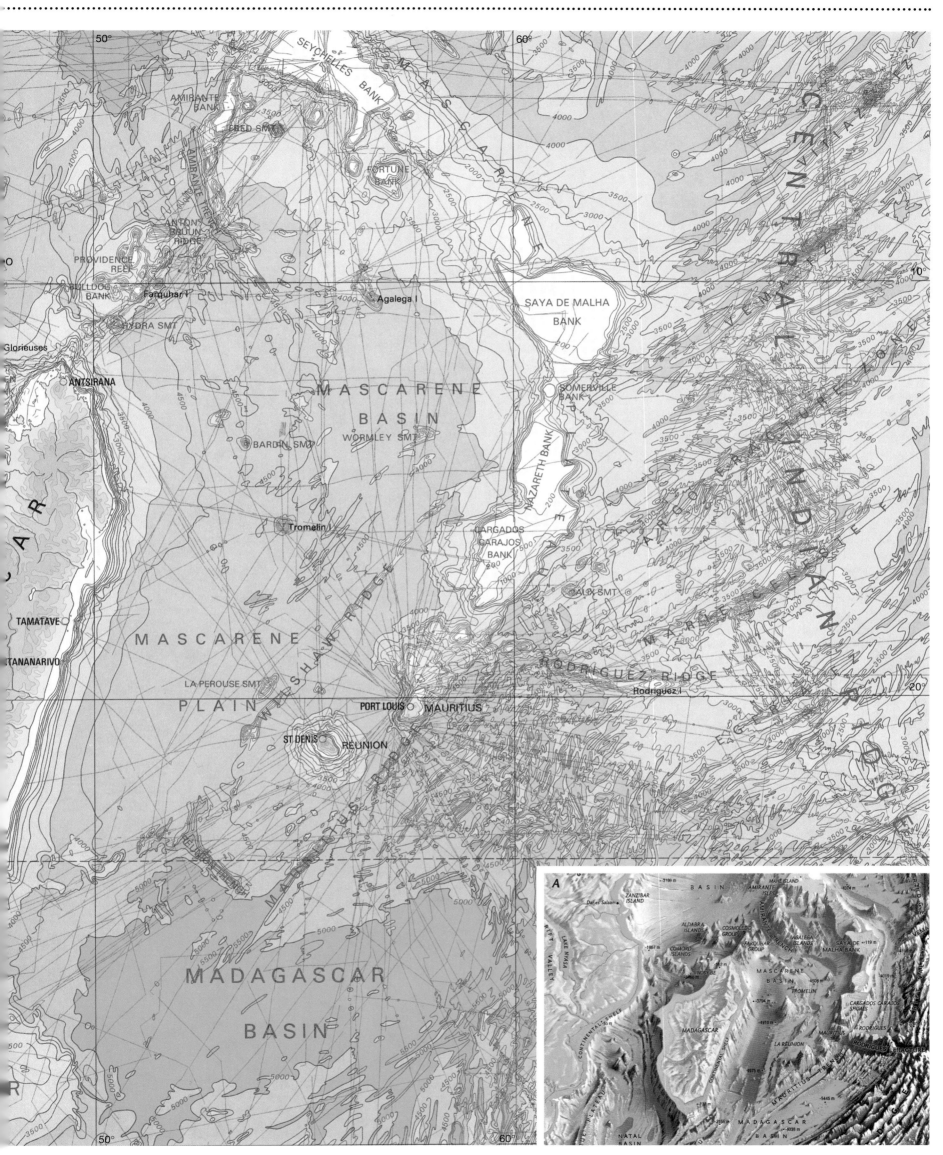

50°

60°

SEYCHELLES BANK

M A S C A R E N E

AMIRANTE BANK

FRED SMT

4000

4000

FORTUNE BANK

2000

2500

3000

3500

AMIRANTE TRENCH

ANTONS BRUUN RIDGE

PROVIDENCE REEF

10°

BULLDOG BANK

Farquhar I

Agalega I

SAYA DE MALHA BANK

4000

Glorieuses

HYDRA SMT

SOMERVILLE BANK

ANTSIRANA

M A S C A R E N E

NAZARETH BANK

B A S I N

BARDIN SMT

WORMLEY SMT

Tromelin I

CARGADOS CARAJOS BANK

ALIX SMT

TAMATAVE

M A S C A R E N E

RODRIGUEZ RIDGE

TANANARIVO

LA PEROUSE SMT

Rodriguez I

20°

P L A I N

PORT LOUIS

MAURITIUS

ST DENIS

RÉUNION

M A D A G A S C A R

B A S I N

5000

50°

60°

A

BASIN

MAHÉ ISLAND

AMIRANTE ISLES

ZANZIBAR ISLAND

Dar es Salaam

LAKE NYASA

RIFT VALLEY

ALDABRA ISLANDS

COSMOLEDO GROUP

COMORO ISLANDS

FARQUHAR GROUP

AGALEGA ISLANDS

SAYA DE MALHA BANK

NOSY BE

MASCARENE BASIN

TROMELIN

MADAGASCAR

CARGADOS CARAJOS SHOALS

RODRIGUES

CONTINENTAL SHELF

MAURITIUS

LA RÉUNION

MADAGASCAR BASIN

NATAL BASIN

A junction of ocean ridges

●●● Unlike those in the mid-oceanic ridges of the Atlantic and Pacific, the spreading centers in the Indian Ocean have hardly been investigated. The central ridge extends from the Gulf of Aden to the north, where it is called Carlsberg Ridge. It continues in a diagonal line through the ocean until reaching almost the southern end of the Macquarie Ridge. Here, between New Zealand and the Antarctic, it forms the Indian South Polar Ridge and converges with the South Pacific Ridge.

Southeast of the Rodriguez, Mauritius, and Réunion Islands, the Southwest Indian Ridge branches off at the Rodriguez Triple Junction towards the Bouvet Triple Junction located near Bouvet Island in the far south of Cape Agulhas. The ridge is located between the African Plate and the Antarctic Plate.

While the Bouvet Triple Junction is still very young and located on a stationary "hot spot," where molten rock emerges from the deeper layers of the Earth, the Rodriguez Triple Junction is older and actively migrating.

The Southwest Indian Ridge unfolds very slowly, pushing up no more than 13 millimeters to 18 millimeters (0.51 in. to 0.71 in.) of new ocean floor per year. Characteristic features of the ridge are its tightly folded crest and rugged flanks. Its crust is much thinner than that of other mid-oceanic ridges and indicates that this ridge is still rather young.

To the north, the Mid-Indian Ridge separates the Indo-Australian Plate from the African Plate. The southeastern continuation, which is designated as Southeast Indian Ridge from here on, is located between the Indo-Australian and the Antarctic Plates.

The relief of the Southeast Indian Ridge is much more supple than that of its Mid-Indian continuation or its southwest Indian counterpart. Atypically, the sea floor spreads to both sides at different speeds. Whereas an average of 58 millimeters (2.29 in.) of new sea floor are formed each year on both sides of the Rodriguez Triple Junction, the new sea floor amounts to 76 millimeters (3 in.) per year at the southeastern end near the Macquarie Ridge. Near the junction, the Mid-Indian Ridge is spreading at a rate of some 54 millimeters (2.13 in.) per year, as opposed to 30 millimeters (1.18 in.) per year north of the equator. The Mid-Indian and Southeast Indian Ridges therefore count among the oceanic ridges spreading at medium speed.

Chemical measurements in the areas of both triple junctions revealed increased sulfur and methane concentrations in the water. They point to hydrothermal vents which, so far, have not been investigated.

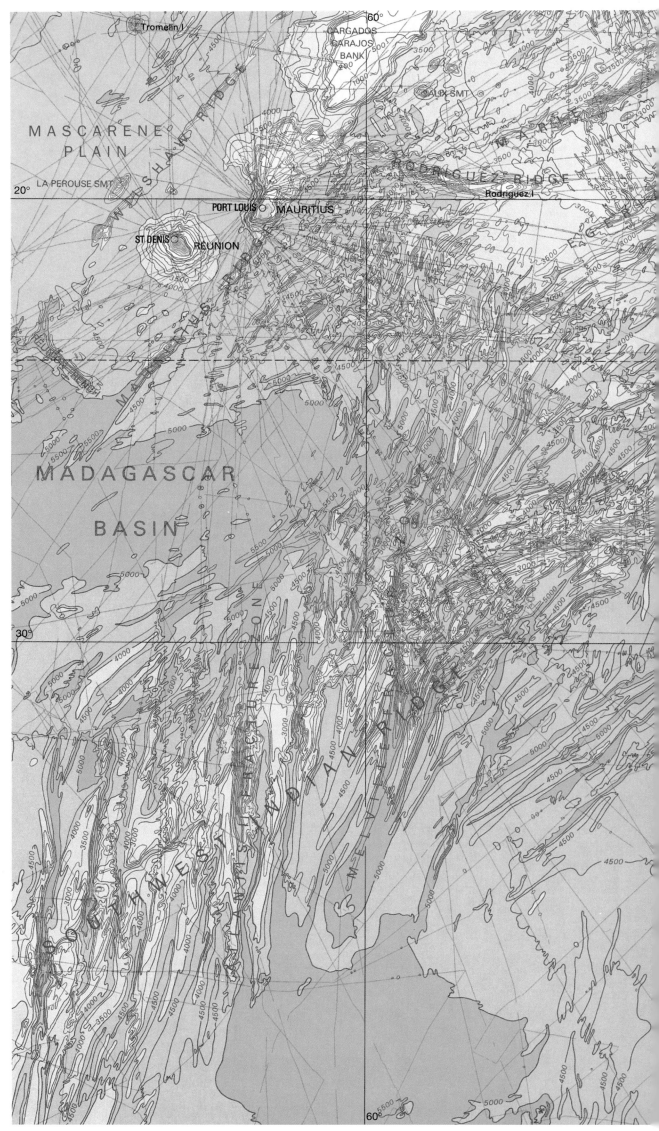

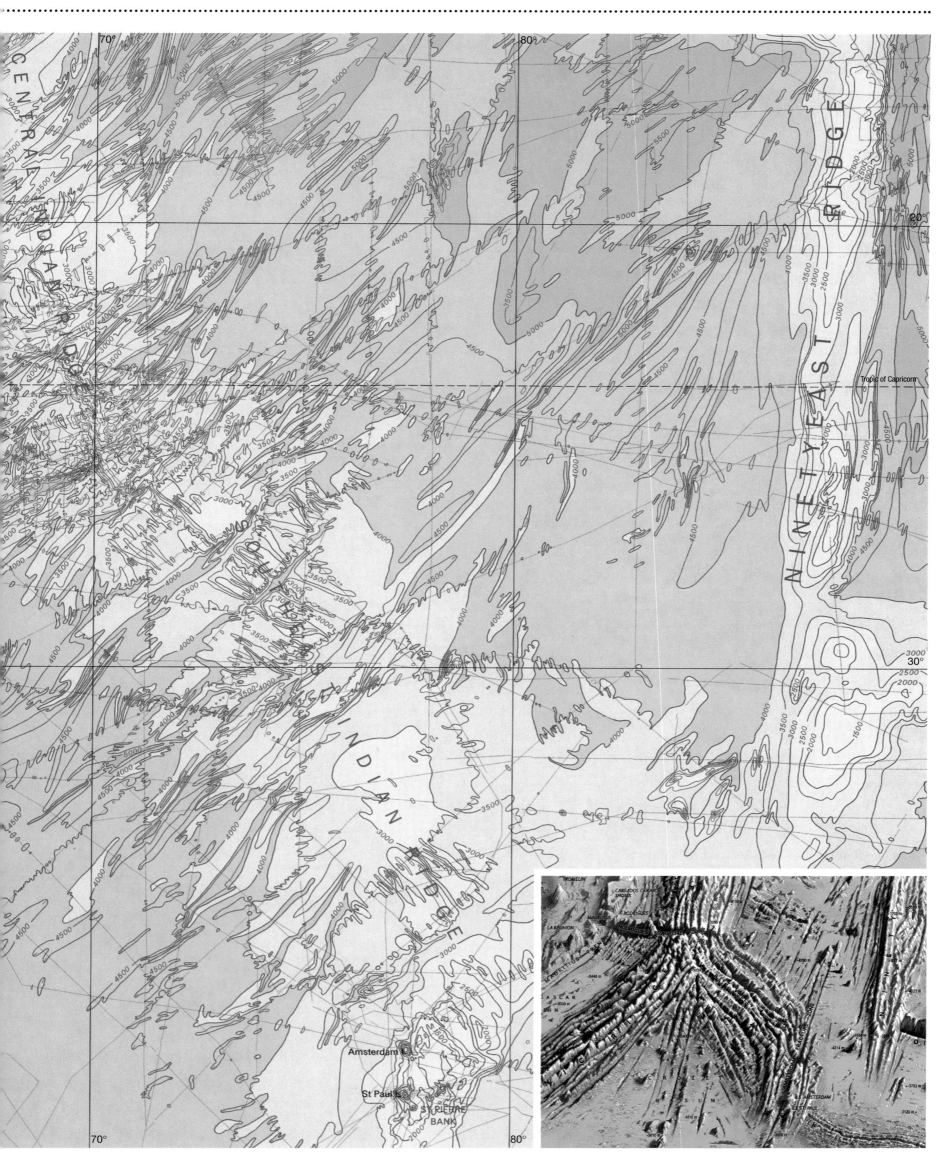

CENTRAL INDIAN RIDGE

NINETYEAST RIDGE

Tropic of Capricorn

INDIAN RIDGE

Amsterdam

St Paul Is

ST PIERRE
BANK

70°   80°

20°

30°

70°   80°

Where two ridges meet

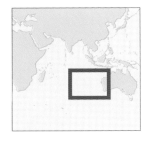

● ● ● West of Australia, the impressive Ninetyeast Ridge meets the West Australian Ridge. This sub-marine mountain range, extending in a straight line for 4,500 kilometers (2,800 mi.) parallel to 90° latitude, was only discovered in 1962. The mountains are still detectable under the sediment of the Gulf of Bengal.

Unlike the mid-oceanic ridges, the Ninetyeast Ridge neither exerts volcanic or seismic activity nor emits magma. It is presumably a fossil oceanic ridge, the activity of which has been dormant since the Tertiary Period some 1.5 million years ago.

The southern part of the Ninetyeast Ridge is barely 30 million years old, whereas the northern end must have existed some 80 million years ago. This means that it is one of the oldest structures of the Indic Ocean. Even though the ocean opened up 125 million years ago, nothing has yet been found to be older than 80 million years.

According to the uppermost sediment layers, the Ninetyeast Ridge protruded above sea level at the time of its emergence near the spreading center at the sea floor. While slowly sliding northward on the Indo-Australian Plate, the supporting plate gradually submerged.

Likewise, the West Australian Ridge shows no signs of seismic activity. It originally belonged to the Kerguelen Plateau at the rim of the Antarctic main plate, but broke off when Australia began to drift away from the Antarctic continent. This separation is evidenced to date by the deep Diamantina Fracture Zone extending between the West Australian Ridge and Australia's southwestern tip.

The cold West Australian Current moves along the Australian shore and forms the northward flowing part of the huge gyre, or eddy, which covers the entire southern part of the Indian Ocean. Unlike similar currents off the shores of other continents, this gyre is not strong enough to draw nutrient-rich deep-sea water to the surface. Therefore, the Australian west coast presents hardly any rewarding fishing grounds.

At the latitude of the Exmouth Plateau, which is part of the now-submerged Sahul Continental Plate, the current branches off. One branch remains near the coast and empties into the Timor Sea in the east, while the other part turns west to the open ocean and converges with the Indian South Equatorial Current heading towards Africa.

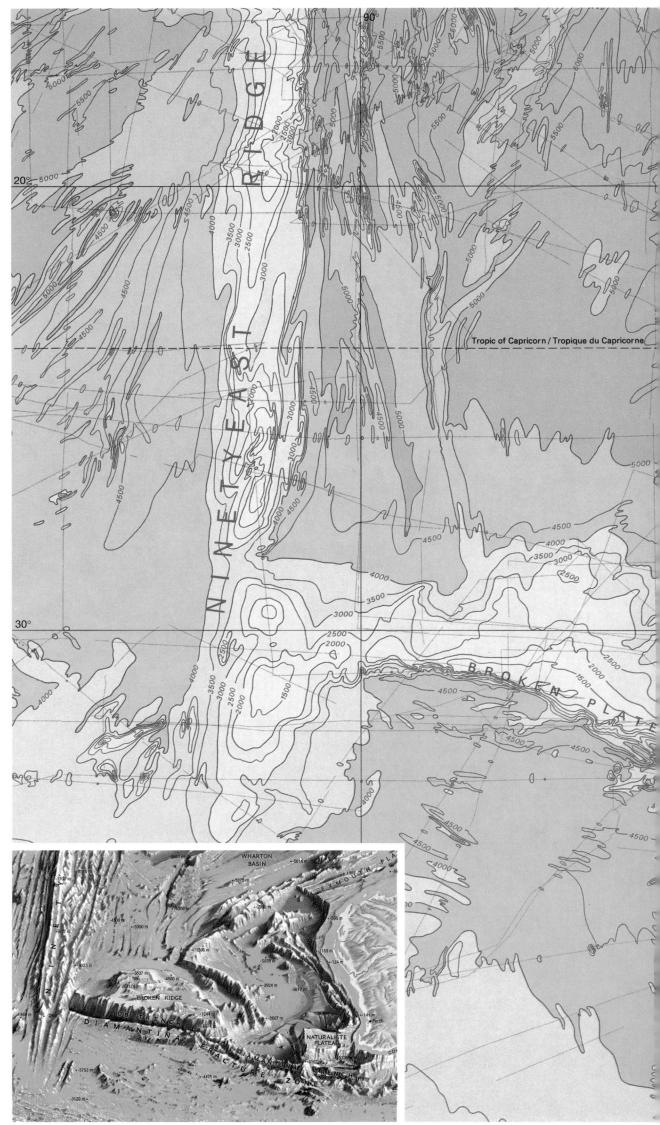

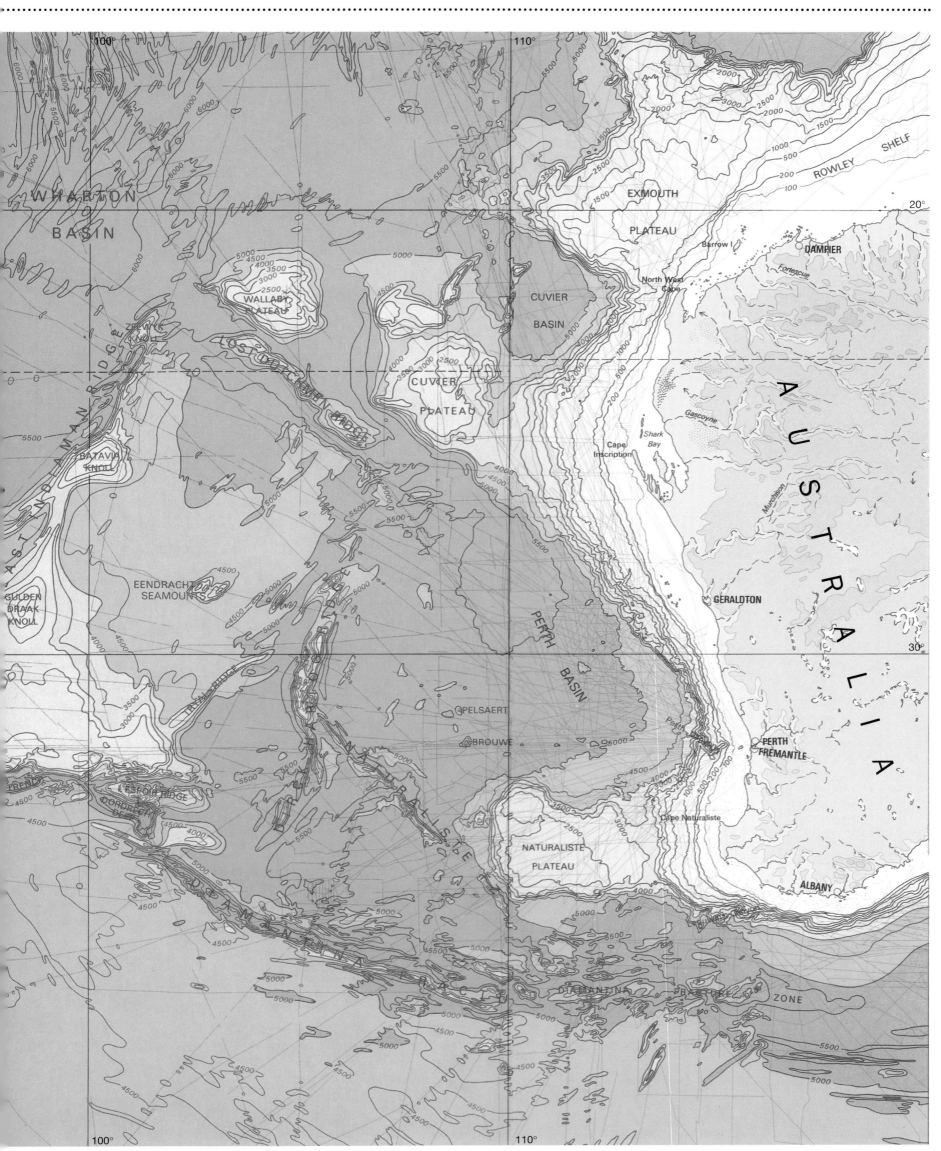

A cold and rapid current

●●● The torrential Agulhas Current flows along the southernmost coast of Africa. It drains the Indian South Equatorial Current which, north of Madagascar, drives its water westward. The African coast partially deflects this current to the south. One part flows around Madagascar, whereas another part, the Mozambique Current, passes south between Africa and Madagascar. Both branches eventually converge at the south tip of the island and form the 100-kilometer (62-mi.) wide Agulhas Current, one of the most rapid oceanic currents.

The current's speed depends on the seasonal pressure of the South Equatorial Current, but ranges on average between 0.75 kilometers per hour (0.47 mph) and 2.2 kilometers per hour (1.37 mph). Immediately off the South African coast, it reaches a maximum velocity of over 9 kilometers per hour (5.6 mph). Depending on the season, it pushes 80 million to 100 million cubic meters (2.8 billion to 3.5 billion cu. ft.) of water per second southward.

Since its water originates in low latitudes, it is a relatively warm 14° C to 26° C (57.2° F to 78.8° F). South of the Cape of Good Hope it collides with the cold Benguela Current (which carries water of Arctic origin), turns northward and flows along the South African west coast.

A small portion of the Agulhas waters mix with the Benguela Current and move into the Atlantic. The largest part, however, is abruptly diverted eastward and flows along the sharp frontiers bordering the Antarctic Circumpolar Current towards Australia.

The oceans around southern Africa are located in the zone of the "roaring forties" (at 40° S latitude), where strong west winds bring cold storms and rain. In earlier times, many vessels suffered shipwreck on the cliffs of the uninhabited Crozet Islands. The sea route around the Cape of Good Hope was the only way to Southeast Asia before the Suez Channel was opened. Today, the area is frequented only by large tankers unable to take the shortcut via Egypt.

Like the Prince Edward Islands, the Crozet archipelago is also of volcanic origin. Both groups of islands are located on the Del Caño Rise, a branch of the Southwest Indian Ridge stretching northeast from here in a straight line to the Mid-Indian Ridge. On the other side of this rise, the Madagascar Ridge, which carries the island of the same name, meets the oceanic ridge from the north.

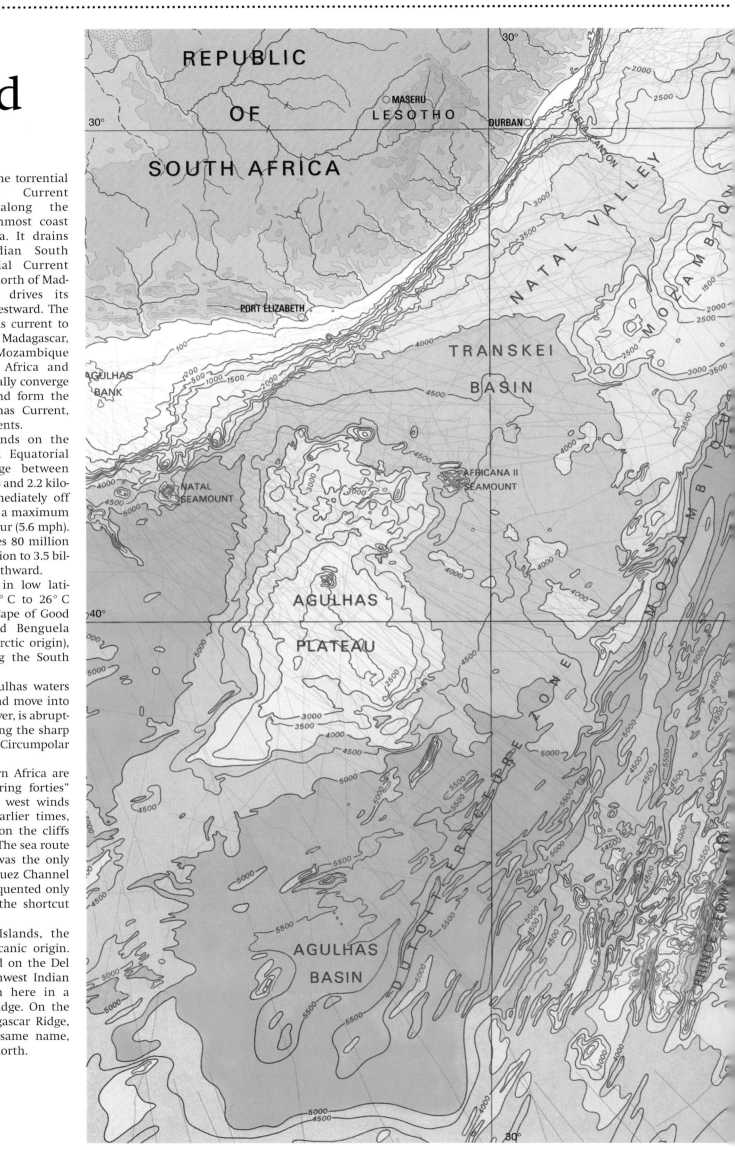

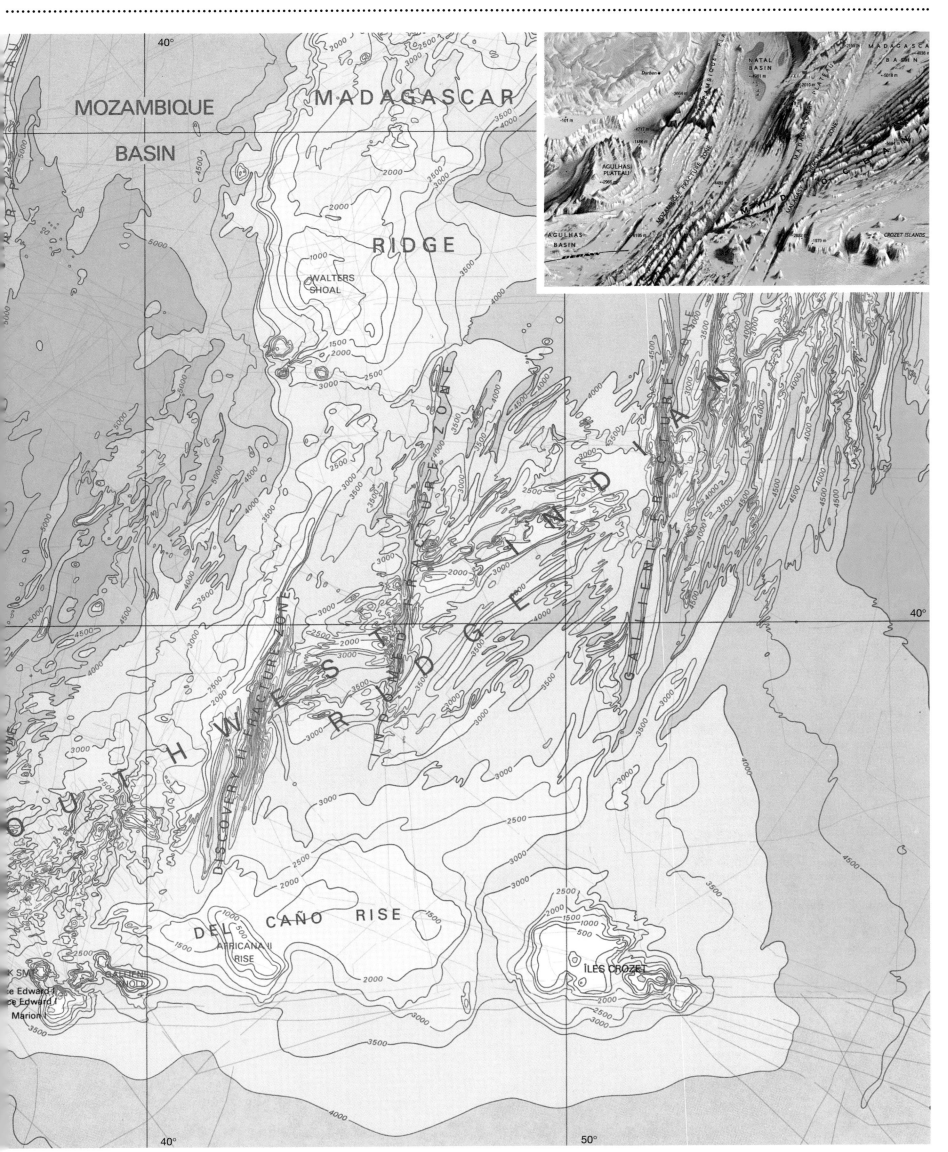

MOZAMBIQUE

BASIN

MADAGASCAR

RIDGE

WALTERS
SHOAL

40°

50°

40°

40°

DISCOVERY II FRACTURE ZONE

INDIEN

GALLIENI FRACTURE ZONE

DEL CAÑO RISE

AFRICANA II
RISE

ÎLES CROZET

Prince Edward I
Prince Edward I
Marion

Durban

NATAL
BASIN

AGULHAS
PLATEAU

AGULHAS
BASIN

MOZAMBIQUE FRACTURE ZONE

MADAGASCAR FRACTURE ZONE

CROZET ISLANDS

MADAGASCAR
BASIN

An island between two oceans

●●● Tasmania is an island between two oceans. While Pacific waves sweep against its east coast, the west coast offers a view of the Indian Ocean. The island is a continuation of the Australian mountain system called the Great Dividing Range. The 140-kilometer (87-mi.) wide connection between Australia and Tasmania, the Bass Strait, was flooded only some 10,000 to 15,000 years ago when the sea level began to rise at the end of the last ice age.

Natural gas was found there in 1965; two years later, crude oil was discovered. Production began in 1970. Besides the Timor Sea and the Northwest Australian Shelf, the Bass Strait is one of the most important Australian production areas for natural gas and oil. Other raw materials were discovered further down in the west of the South Australian Basin: manganese nodules containing valuable metals in pure form. So far, however, the technology is not yet advanced enough to collect the deep-sea nodules from their depth of 6,000 meters (19,700 ft.).

The Great Australia Basin extends over a 1,160-kilometers (720-mi.) stretch in the middle of the southern Australian coastline. This wide, shallow bay lies in the path of west winds with their frequent strong storms. High waves are probably the reason why only few factory ships cross this area.

This, however, could change in the near future. On the continental flank sloping down to the South Australia Basin, large populations of a valuable, very palatable deep-sea fish called orange roughy were discovered. As of the end of the 1970s, this species was caught mainly near the Pacific ocean cones near Tasmania where the fish rise from a depth of 800 meters (2,600 ft.) to 100 meters (330 ft.) in search of food. Fifty-thousand tons were caught by fishers in 1991, although the maximum quantity recommended by biologists is a mere 2,000 tons per year. Indeed, it was not rare for the fishers to haul in catches worth $225,000 US in only two days.

In the meantime, however, the populations have been depleted, which is not surprising considering that deep-sea fish develop slowly and enjoy a long life-span. The orange roughy can live to between 77 and 149 years of age and reach sexual maturity only after 20 to 30 years. This means that the species is particularly vulnerable to over-fishing. Marine biologists so far have not been successful in investigating exactly how this species lives.

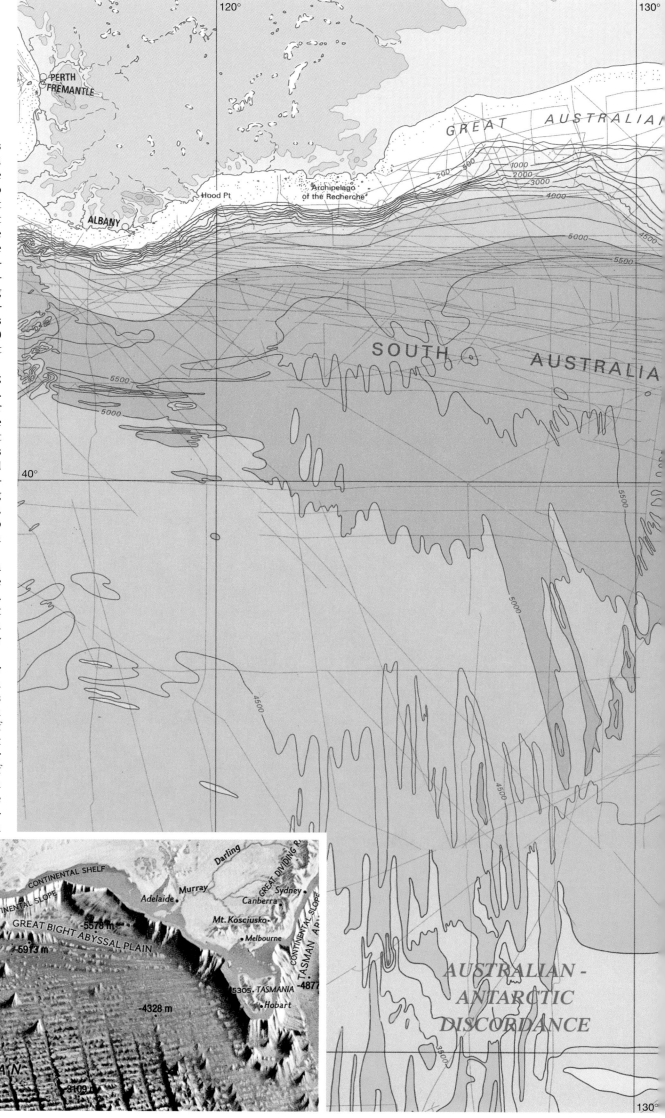

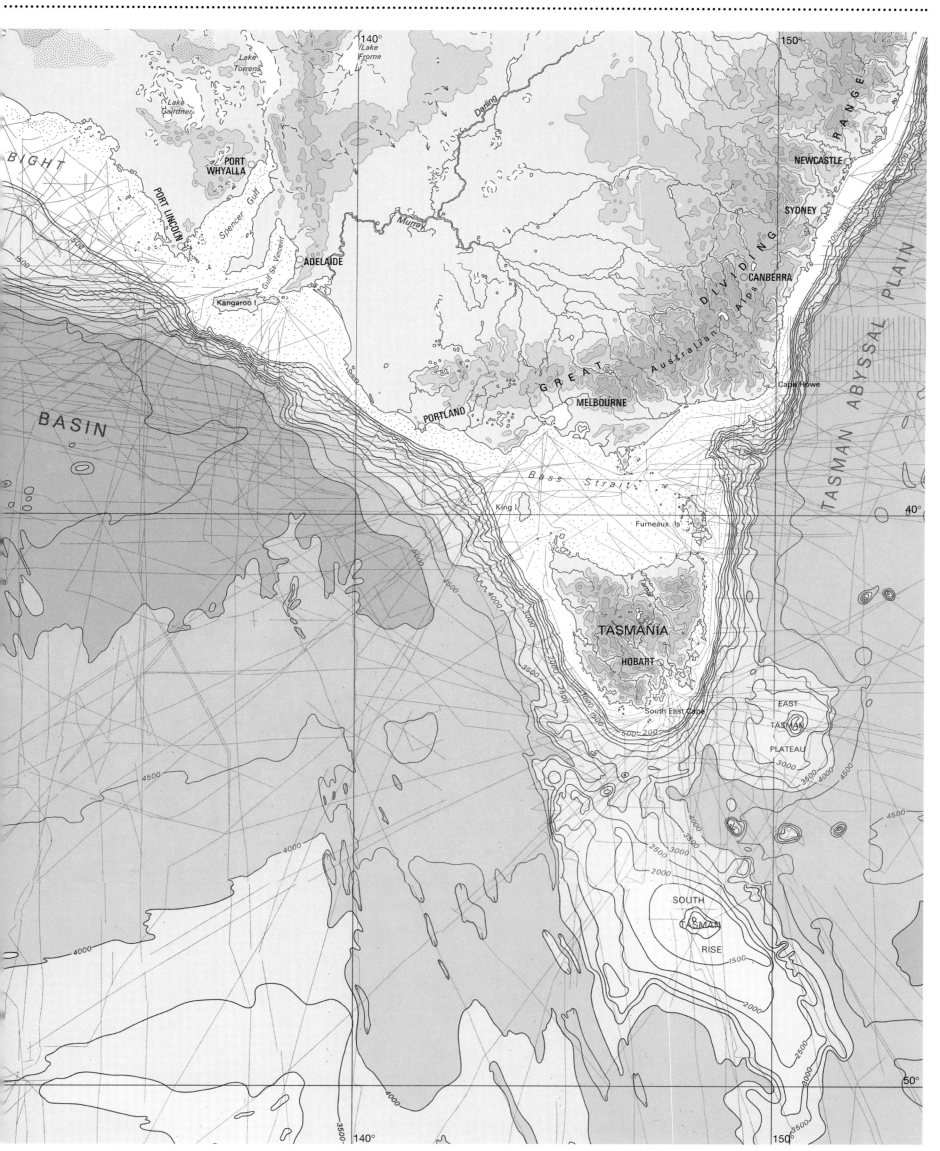

BIGHT

PORT
WHYALLA

PORT LINCOLN

Lake
Gairdner

Lake
Torrens

140°
Lake
Frome

Darling

Murray

NEWCASTLE

150°

RANGE

SYDNEY

Spencer Gulf

Gulf St. Vincent

ADELAIDE

Kangaroo I.

DIVIDING

CANBERRA

Australian Alps

GREAT

MELBOURNE

Cape Howe

TASMAN ABYSSAL PLAIN

BASIN

PORTLAND

Bass Strait

King I.

Furneaux Is.

40°

TASMANIA

HOBART

EAST

TASMAN

PLATEAU

South East Cape

SOUTH

TASMAN

RISE

50°

140°

150°

Remainder of a sunken continent

●●● The Kerguelen Plateau is the remainder of a sunken continent which was once located between the Indian Plate and the Australian Plate. Its size corresponded roughly to one-third of the Australian continent. The continent was formed during one of the tremendous volcano eruptions that took place some 110 million years ago. At that period, the Earth emitted enough magma to bury a surface the size of North America under a 3-kilometer (1.8-mi.) thick layer of rock.

The continent, however, had slowly grown from the sea floor even before the volcanic activity began. It was formed by basalt, a type of magma emerging slowly and inconspicuously from the sea bed. In drilling cores, scientists found not only the rock masses usually present on the continents, but also 90-million-year-old wood fragments, spores, and pollen. While the once timbered land cooled and shrunk, it slowly sank to the bottom of the ocean roughly 20 million years ago. Today, only the Kerguelen Archipelago as well as the Heard and McDonald Islands rise above sea level.

Around the largest of the "Desolation Islands" – as the Kerguelen Archipelago is also called – there are another 300 smaller islands. As of 1950, the only inhabitants of the 160-kilometer (100-mi.) long main island of the group, Port-aux-Français, with its majestic, up to 2,000-meter (6,600-ft.) high glacier mountains, are some 40 to 80 scientists.

Flowering plants thrive on the island group even though it is located in Antarctic waters. This is due to the Antarctic Convergence – the watershed surrounding the south continent between the Antarctic and the Kerguelen Islands – where cold polar water collides with warmer subantarctic water from the north. The cold water sinks to layers below the warm surface waters.

Kerguelen cabbage, a plant rich in vitamin C, was used by 19th-century explorers and whale and seal hunters as a welcome treatment against scurvy on their long journeys to the south. Today, the cabbage has been almost completely devoured by the rabbits that live on most of the islands. Together with reindeer and cats, the rabbits were introduced by settlers who tried in vain to make a living on the Kerguelen Islands in the early years of the 19th century. Even rats and mice were inadvertently brought onto the islands. On one island off Port-aux-Français there is still a herd of moufflons.

By contrast, the volcanic Heard and McDonald Islands, which are totally buried under ice and snow, are completely uninhabited. The volcano Mount Mawson on the Big Ben Mountain peninsula rises almost 2,750 meters (9,022 ft.) above sea level.

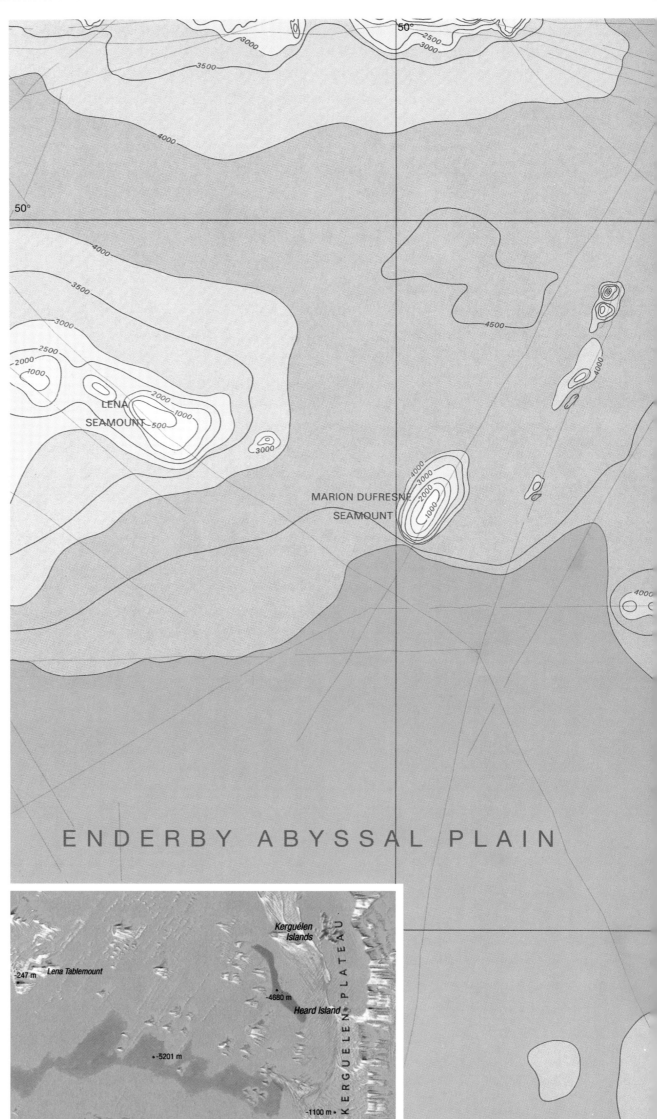

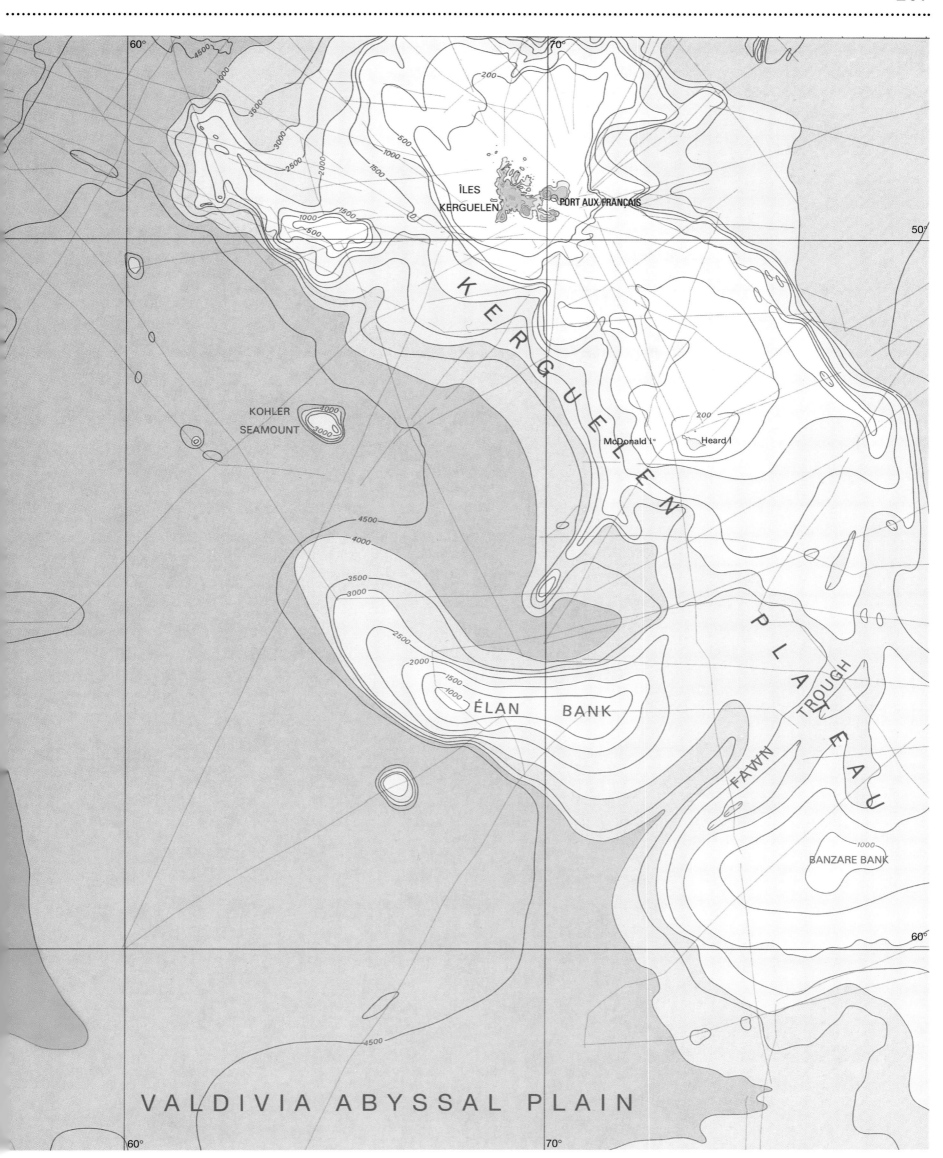

ÎLES
KERGUELEN

PORT AUX FRANÇAIS

K E R G U E L E N

P L A T E A U

McDonald I

Heard I

KOHLER
SEAMOUNT

ÉLAN   BANK

FAWN   TROUGH

BANZARE BANK

VALDIVIA   ABYSSAL   PLAIN

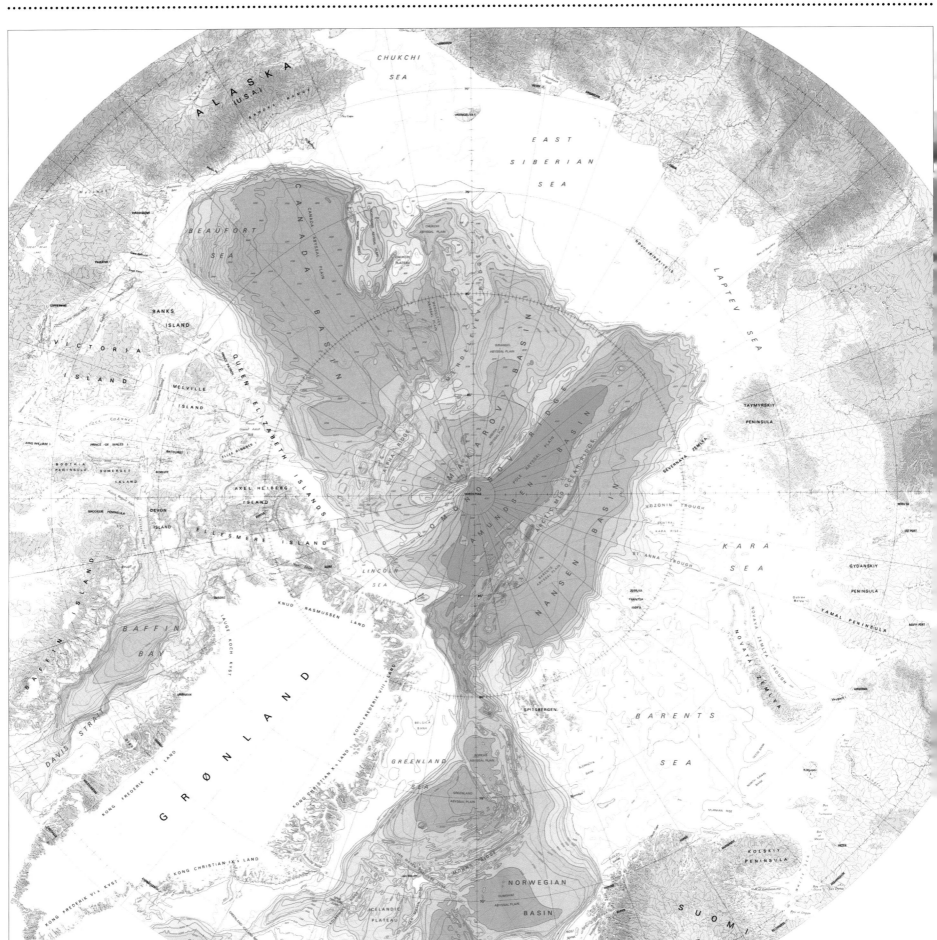

The Arctic and

Land masses and sea basins at

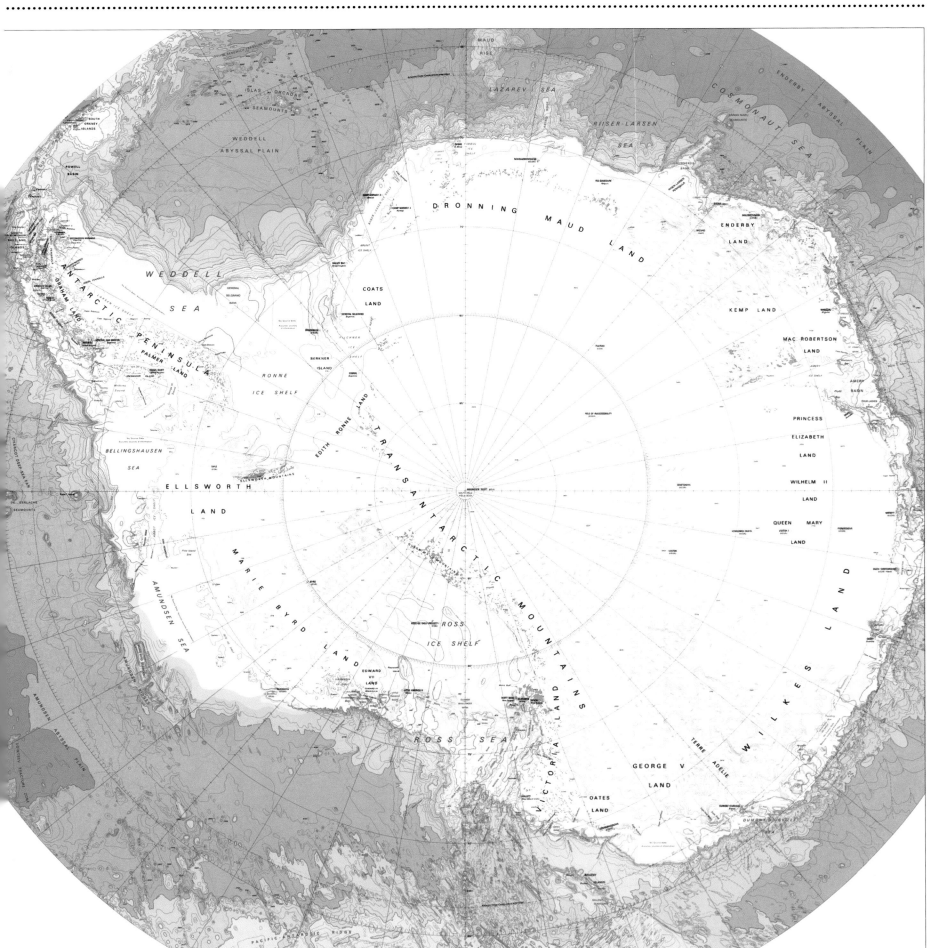

the Antarctic
the Poles

The oscillating North Pole

● ● ● A magnetic compass is useless in the icy maze of the Queen Elizabeth Islands. The northern tip points diagonally to the ground and changes direction almost on a daily basis. Somewhere southwest of Ellef Ringnes Island, the magnetic North Pole oscillates from day to day and even migrates northwestward by some 15 kilometers (9.3 mi.) per year.

These daily variations are caused by electrically charged particles emitted by the sun that disturb the planet's magnetic field when they reach the Earth. The long-term migration, and even reversal, of the magnetic field once in several million years, however, is caused by the liquid core of the Earth, which emits powerful electrical charges as it moves. The continuous changes in these currents induce changes in the direction and strength of the planet's magnetic field. For the purpose of navigation, continual adjustments must be made.

The Queen Elizabeth Islands are barely accessible because they are surrounded by ice all year long, while the Siberian coastline just opposite is not. When the sea water cools down to values below −2.2° C to −1.8° C (28.1° F to 28.8° F), depending on the saline concentration, ice crystals are formed and slowly converge into small sheets. The crystals themselves consist of pure water while the salt trapped in the brine pockets of the crystals is eliminated through capillary channels and cumulates in the water below the ice layer. After one year, the ice is already sufficiently salt-free to be melted and used as potable water.

The wind accumulates the icy pulp and condenses it into sheets 0.5 meters to 10 meters (1.6 ft. to 33 ft.) wide. The ocean waves push the sheets against each other until their rims arch upwards and the sheets look like huge pancakes. This "pancake ice" further coalesces and covers the Arctic Ocean with an icy layer some 15 to 20 million square kilometers (5.8 to 7.72 million sq. mi.) in size. A year-old ice sheet reaches an average thickness of 2 meters (6.6 ft.), whereas several-year-old ice layers grow to a thickness of 4 meters (13 ft.), which is sufficient to balance losses due to melting and the development of new ice.

The annual Arctic cycle of glaciation and thaw is an important motor for the oceanic currents. Cold, high-saline water, for instance, flows at the bottom of the Atlantic to the Newfoundland banks off the North American coast. At the same time, however, the fresh water generated in the summer through melted snow and ice can act as a barrier shutting off the warm surface currents flowing in from the south.

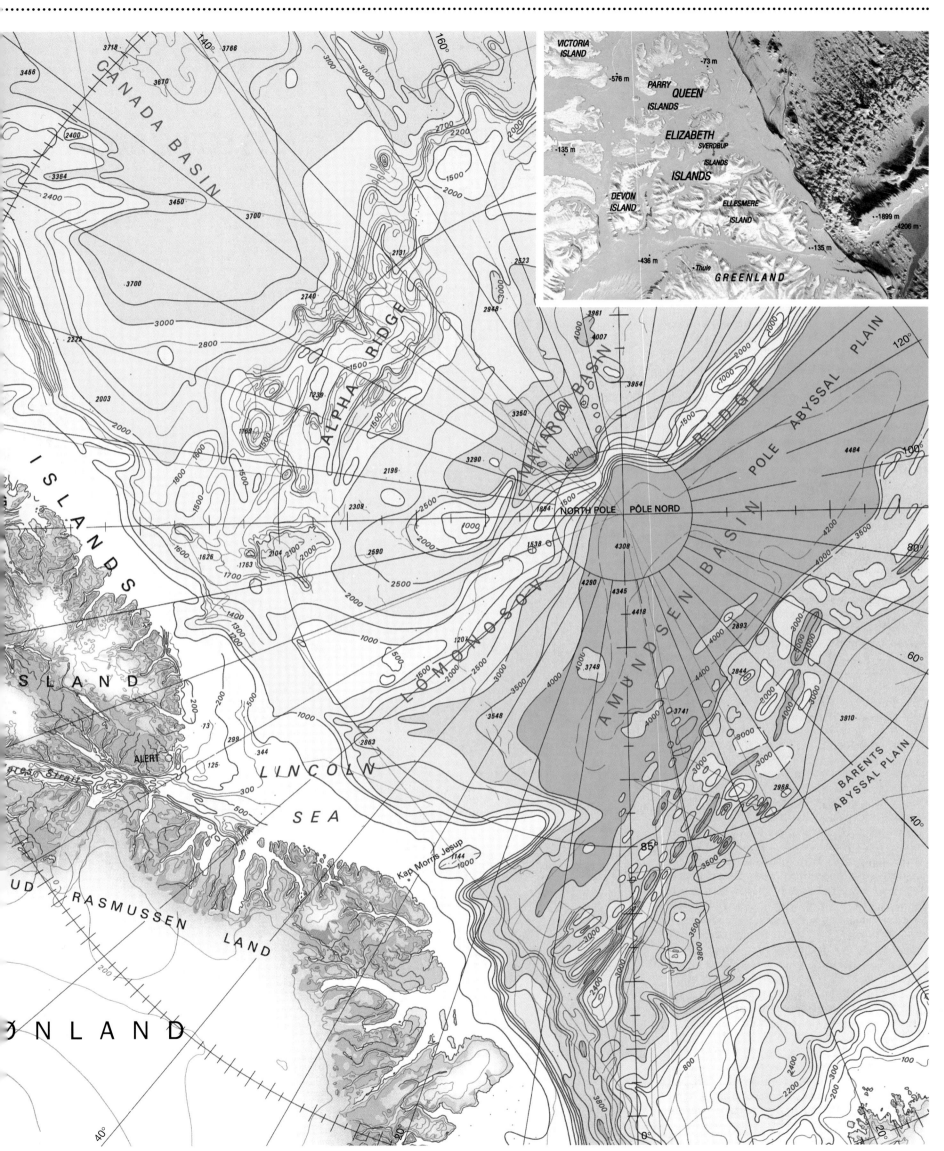

VICTORIA
ISLAND
−73 m
−576 m
PARRY
ISLANDS
QUEEN
ELIZABETH
SVERDRUP
−135 m
ISLANDS
ISLANDS
DEVON
ISLAND
ELLESMERE
ISLAND
−1899 m
−4206 m
−436 m
−135 m
Thule
GREENLAND

CANADA BASIN
3718
3766
140°
3456
3670
160°
3000
3364
2400
2700
2200
2400
3450
1500
3700
2000
2131
2523
3700
2740
3000
2948
2222
3000
2800
3000
2003
1500
1500
1239
1800
1500
1500
1169
1600
2196
2000
2308
2500
1600
1000
2104 2100
2000
1626
1700
2590
2000
1763
2500
1400
1300
1200
1000
1500
500
ISLANDS
ALPHA RIDGE
LOMONOSOV
120°
NORTH POLE PÔLE NORD
1500
1884
1538
4308
4290
4345
4418
3961
4007
MAKAROV BASIN
3954
3350
3290
POLE ABYSSAL PLAIN
120°
RIDGE
1500
100°
4484
80°
AMUNDSEN BASIN
2893
4200
3500
60°
2844
3749
3741
4400
3910
3000
4000
3548
2863
344
3000
3500
2968
2863
125
299
300
500
3000
3500
40°
BARENTS
ABYSSAL PLAIN
20°

ISLAND
S L A N D
ALERT
LINCOLN
SEA
Kap Morris Jesup
1144
1000
Robeson Strait
73
UD RASMUSSEN LAND
200
40°
INLAND
200
20°
0°
85°
2400
2200
3800
3600
100°
200

In the ice free Polar Sea

●●● The Kara Sea and the Barents Sea are two shallow shelf seas separated by the 1,000-kilometer (621-mi.) long double island of Novaya Zemlya, which is a continuation of the Ural Mountains. From 1955 to 1990, this icy island was used by the Soviet Union as a test area for nuclear weapons.

In total, the Soviet military detonated 132 nuclear explosives, including a 58-megaton hydrogen bomb, the most powerful ever detonated by humans. Satellite pictures show that radioactive gases are still escaping from subterranean cavities even today. In addition, more than 100,000 tons of radioactive waste were dumped below the north polar ice, including at least 15 nuclear reactors, as well as thousands of barrels and containers filled with radioactive waste that are now rapidly corroding in the high-saline Arctic waters.

The Barents Sea is a shelf sea, on average 230 meters (755 ft.) deep. In the Bear Island Trench, it reaches down to 600 meters (2,000 ft.). The North Cape and Spitsbergen Currents, final ramifications of the Gulf Stream system, wash warm water into the Barents Sea where it merges with cold polar water and rapidly cools. In winter, ice fields develop despite the high salinity of up to 34 ppt, although they are rather thin and recede far northward in summer. Murmansk and the Norwegian town of Vardø are accessible by ship all year long.

In the east, the Barents Sea merges into the Kara Sea which borders on Franz Josef Land in the northwest and on the Severnaya Zemlya islands in the east. The Kara Sea is a shallow shelf sea with almost half less than 50 meters (164 ft.) deep. Only 2 percent is deeper than 500 meters (1,609 ft.) – for instance, the deep-sea troughs of Saint Anna (max. 620 m /2,034 ft.) and Vozonin (450 m/1,476 ft.). The water is extremely cold with sharp boundaries between the individual layers. In winter, its temperature drops to −1.6° C (29.1° F), yet rises in the summer to 6° C (42.8° F) in the southwest and 2° C (35.6° F) in the north.

The Kara Sea first developed as the glaciers of the last ice age melted. Today the grooves carved by the glaciers are covered by a thin layer of alluvial sand. Rock deposits in the northeast, old sandbanks, and sandy coastlines were also shaped by glacial influences.

The border of the Kara Sea coincides with the Russian northern ship route, with Dikson serving as the major harbor. It connects great Siberian rivers like the Kara, the Ob, and the Yenisey. Timber, construction materials, furs, and foodstuffs are the most important goods for transshipment. Over the last years, the Kara Sea route has reassumed some of its former importance due to the detection of oil and gas deposits.

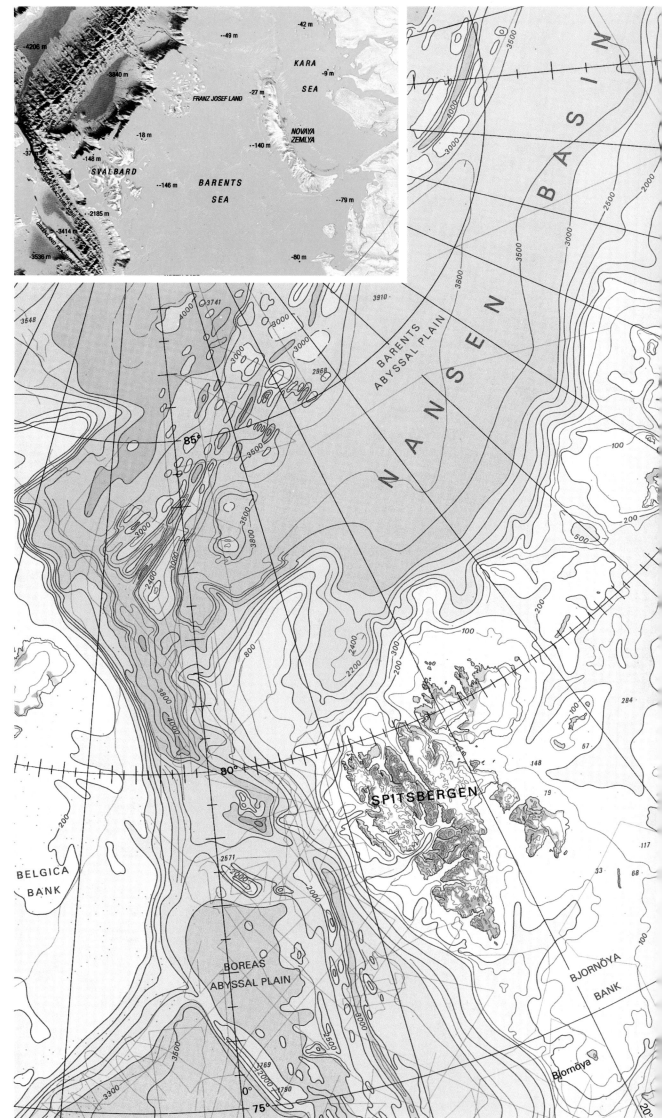

VOZONIN TROUGH

-229

-225

CENTRAL
30

KARA RISE

-500

ANNA TROUGH

K A R A

S E A

GYDANSKIY

PENINSULA

Ostrov
Belyy

Gulf of Ob

YAMAL PENINSULA

NOVAYA ZEMLYA

N O V A Y A   Z E M L Y A

NOVAYA ZEMLYA TROUGH

Bay of Kara

AMDERMA

Vaygach I.

ZEMLYA

NTSA

SIFA

B A R E N T S

S E A

GEESE BANK

NORTH KANIN
BANK

Kolguyev I.

Bay
of
Pechora

R O S S I Y S K A Y A   F E D E R A T S I Y A   (R U S S I A)

NORILSK

UST PORT

MURMAN RISE

Bay
of
Tscheskai

In the land of mighty rivers

●●● Sibiria's numerous rivers wash enormous amounts of fresh water into the sea, diluting the high-saline waters on the Eurasian side of the Arctic Ocean. The 3,500-kilometer (2,174-mi.) long Yenisey alone, fed by some 20,000 smaller rivers, brings 620 cubic kilometers (149 cu. mi.) of fresh water into the Kara Sea each year.

Almost all Siberian river water originates from rain or melted snow, with only a very small part of it being ground water or, in the case of the Ob River, glacial water stemming from the Altai Mountains.

In winter, the currents freeze down to the bottom of the river mouths and allow no more water to pass until the spring. The air temperature ranges between −20° C and −30° C (−4° F and −22° F) and drop to almost −60° C (−76° F) in the Altai Mountains. When the snow starts to thaw in early summer, the water level rises abruptly. While the ice fields break up, the ice floats are jammed together and dam up the water, or tear away entire embankments.

In northern Siberia, the soil is permanently frozen to a depth of 600 meters (2,000 ft.), with the exception of the coastlines and the continental shelf in the polar sea, which are free of ice. During the short two or three months of summer, when temperatures rise to 20° C (68° F), sometimes even 30° C (86° F), the uppermost soil layers thaw to a depth of 15 centimeters (6 in.) and transform the country into a vast swamp.

As permafrost prevents the surface water from seeping into the ground, numerous lakes appear in the summer all over Siberia. On the slopes, vast amounts of water drain from the soaked soil layers above the permafrost. Over time, the steep mountains were thus transformed into the long, flat hills typical of the Siberian tundra.

In summer, the great rivers are important commercial routes, especially the Ob and Yenisey, which are linked with international transport routes via the northern ship route (part of the Northeast Passage) and the trans-Siberian Railway. Around the oil and gas fields, which cover two thirds of the Russian power demand, large industrialized centers such as Omsk, Novosibirsk, Krasnoyarsk, and Yeniseysk have developed.

The area around the mouth of the River Ob contains 25 percent of the global oil deposits; to date, they are more or less unexploited because transport by ship is still too risky, particularly in winter. The alternative – use and maintenance of pipelines – is virtually impossible in the rough Siberian permafrost conditions.

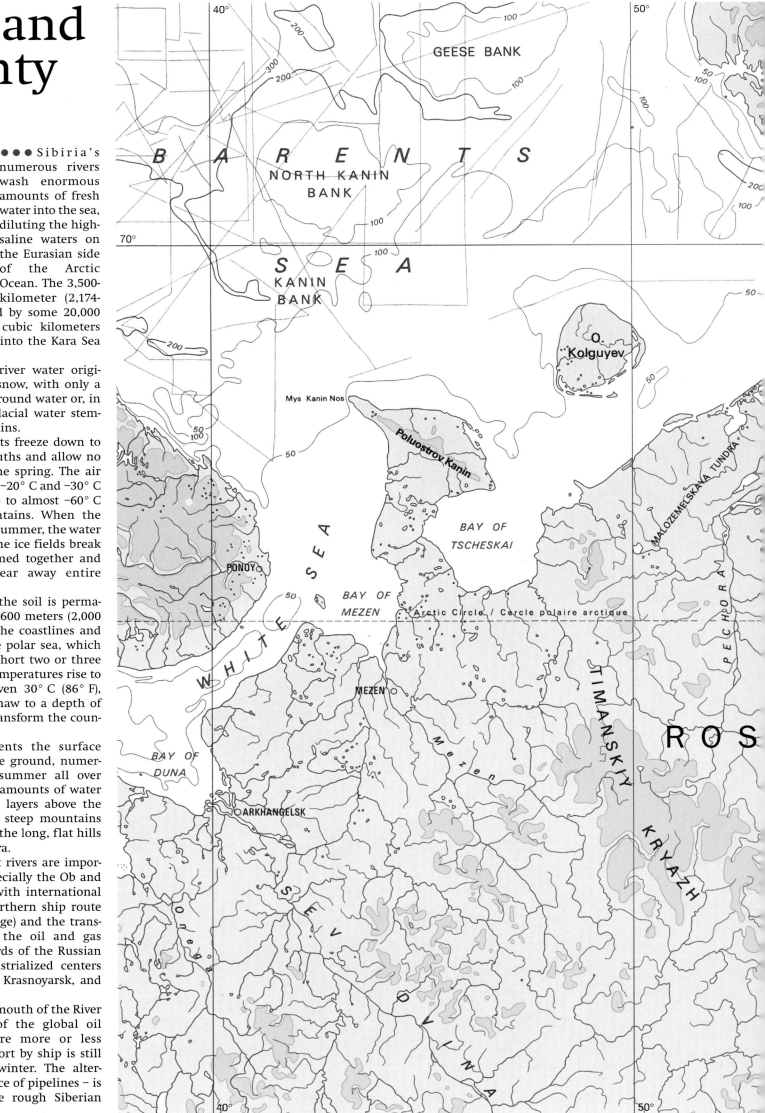

KARA SEA

60° 100

100

100

200

200

50

200

ZEMLYA

100

50

200

100

50

100

50

70°

POLUOSTROV
YAMAL

O. Vaygach

AMDERMA

Yugorskiy
P-ov.

Khr. pay Khoy

BAY OF KARA

GULF OF OB

70°

BAY OF
PECHORA

MELSKAYA TUNDRA

MAR

VORKUTA

POLYARNYY URAL

NOVYY PORT

KRYAZH CHERNYSHEVA

NYDA

BAY OF OB

I Y S K A Y A   F E D E R A T S I Y A

(R U S S I A)

60°

·-332 m

NOVAYA
ZEMLYA

YAMAL
PENINSULA

·-140 m

·-79 m

·-80 m

KOŁA
PENINSULA

·-13 m

TIMAN RIDGE

· Archangel

There is no relief chart available
for this segment of the map

Mountains at the North Pole

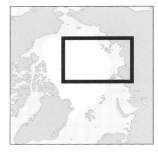

●●● Off the vast bays of the Siberian lowland, the Laptev Sea extends over the Eurasian shelf. Practically all year long, the sea lies under a cover of ice. Water temperatures in the north range between −0.8° C (30.6° F) and −1.6° C (29.1° F) during the cold season, but reach values just above 0° C (32° F) in summer.

Fresh water from numerous rivers drains into the sea and dilutes the salt water, especially near the coast. Salinity is low, even when the rivers are frozen in winter, and reaches just 20 to 25 ppt. In summer, when the rivers are swollen in flood, the value sinks to 5 to 10 ppt.

Starting at the New Siberian Islands, the Lomonosov Ridge extends from the bottom of the Arctic Ocean to past the North Pole. The enormous, 1,770-kilometer (1.099-mi.) long aseismic rise divides the ocean into two large basins. The ridge rises 1,800 meters to 3,400 meters (5,900 ft. to 11,200 ft.) above the sea floor, with its crest reaching almost 1,000 meters (3,300 ft.) below sea level. While the ridge was formerly believed to be a continuation of the Mid-Atlantic Ridge, it is now known that there is a seismically active stretch running 400 kilometers (248 mi.) nearer the Barents Sea.

The bottom of the Lena trench in the central cleft of the Nansen Cordillera holds pyrite blocks which develop only near hydrothermal vents. When the metal- and sulfur-containing solutions emerging from the hot vents at temperatures of 400° C (752° F) merge with the cold sea water, they trigger the formation of blocks consisting of metal and sulfur crystals. The Cordillera is now more accurately called the Arctic Mid-Oceanic Ridge.

The century-old dream of a sea route along the Siberian coast leading from the Atlantic to the Pacific – the Northwest Passage – is becoming more and more a reality. During the Second World War, the Soviet Union started to expand the shipping route, with icebreakers opening connections between the harbors along the polar sea during the brief summers.

As of 1991, gigantic nuclear-powered icebreakers have kept the northern passage ice-free throughout the year. Each year, they guide some 20 cargo ships and tankers designed especially for these icy waters in convoys through the pack ice. Owing to their powerful engines and their volume of approximately 20,000 gross register tons, the enormous ships are able to maneuver through the pack ice with ease. The sea route from Central Europe to Vladivostok is thus shortened from about 30 days to only 20 days.

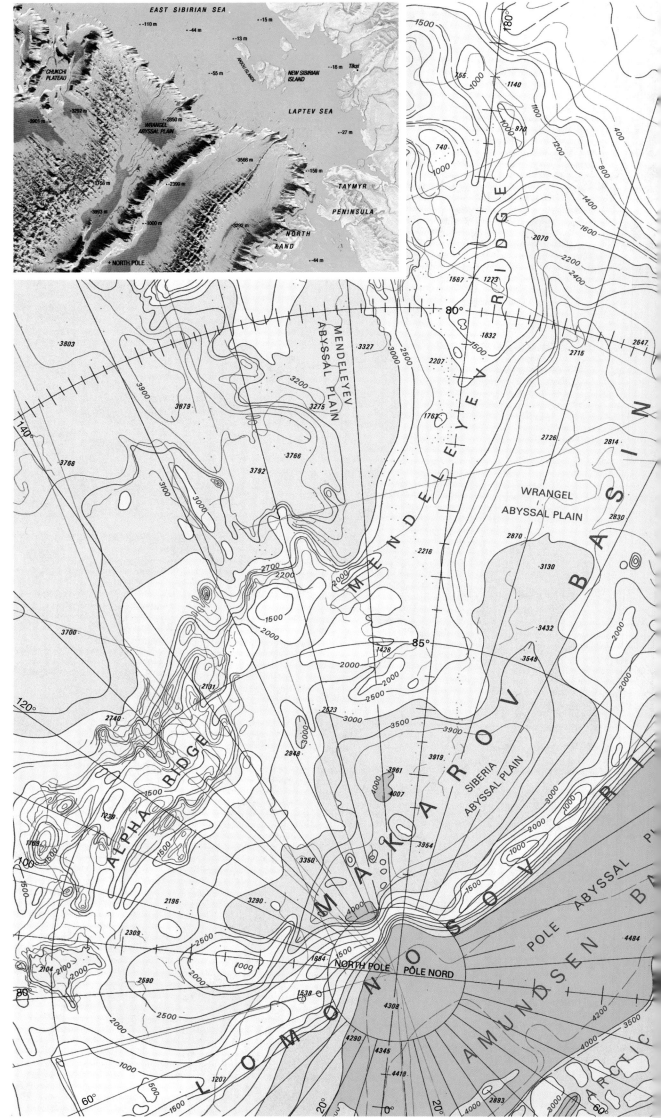

NOVOSIBIRSKIYE IS.

Bay of Buorkha

L A P T E V   S E A

ROSSIYSKAYA FEDERATSIYA (RUSSIA)

29
44
55
50
57
60
49
31
55
2879 2350
1398
360
TAYMYRSKIY

PENINSULA

ZEMLYA
110
SEVERNAYA
49
38
51
11
158
20
13
73
38

100
200
500
1000
1500
1600
2000
2400
2600
2800
2600
3200
3400
3449
3600
3800
3849
3500
3000
4000

2700
2600
2500
2000
1500
1600
1500
1000
2500
3000
3500
4000
3500
3000
3500

NANSEN BASIN

OCEAN RIDGE

VORONIN TROUGH

160°
140°
120°
100°
80°

A primary source of cold water

●●● The Weddell Sea and the Ross Sea form two bays cutting deep into the Antarctic continent and dividing it into East and West Antarctica. Both seas are iced up to an unusual extent, so that explorers blazed trails through the ice towards the eastern and southern coasts only in 1903 and 1917. Roughly 40 years passed before scientists established research bases along the southern and southeastern coasts, in 1956 and 1958, for the purposes of the worldwide International Geophysical Year.

The continental shelf surrounding the Antarctic is, in most parts, narrower than other shelves, even though the Weddell Sea broadens to 240 kilometers (149 mi.) along the Antarctic peninsula and to 480 kilometers (298 mi.) in the south. With a depth of 500 meters (1,640 ft.), it plunges much deeper than the shelves of any other continent which reach some 200 meters (660 ft.) at the most.

The Weddell Sea is probably the most important source of the cold water spreading at the bottom of the planet's oceans. More than half of this water is generated in the Antarctic, and most of that in the Weddell Sea, where the water circulates in a clockwise direction at the surface. At the tip of the Antarctic Peninsula, the cold water is picked up by the West Wind Drift circulating around the continent.

The interior of the bay is covered with floating shelf ice sheets originating from the Ronne and Filchner Ice Shelves, located on both sides of Berkner Island. These ice shelves never thaw, not even in summer. Numerous icebergs break off their seaward side – a process known as calving – and drift into the open Atlantic. The Ronne Ice Shelf is some 150 meters (500 ft.) thick and extends more than 800 kilometers (500 mi.) into the mainland. At 200 meters (660 ft.), the Filchner Ice Shelf is even thicker and extends 400 kilometers (248 mi.) into the Pensacola range in the Transantarctic Mountains on the eastern side of the bay.

In spring, the ice in the open Weddell Sea thaws and develops salt water channels populated by algae, small crustaceans, and young fish. As the sun becomes stronger, these animals reach the open sea where the algae bloom virtually explodes, providing a source of food for krill – 8-millimeter to 60-millimeter (0.3-in. to 2.4-in.) long, bioluminescent, shrimp-like animals which gather to form enormous dense shoals, sometimes reaching 1,800 meters (5,900 ft.) in diameter.

Krill serves as food to almost all of the Antarctic fauna. With its baleen, one single blue whale filters out 4 tons of krill per day, and all the whales in the southern oceans together consume 43 million tons of krill per year.

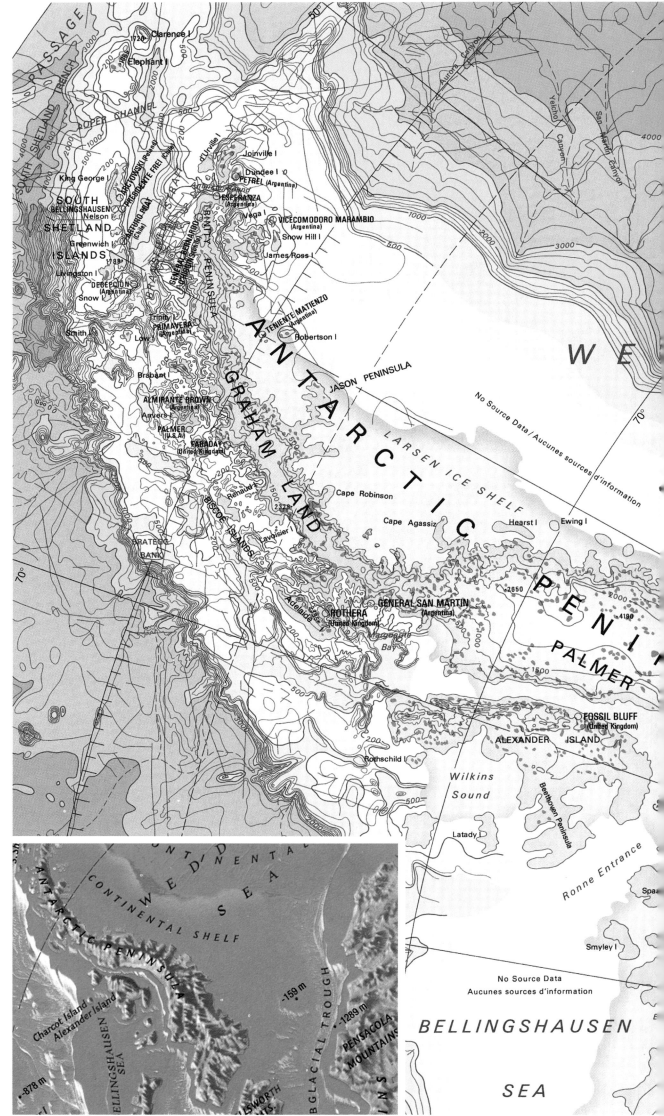

WEDDELL ABYSSAL
PLAIN

CAMP NORWAY 3 ○
(Norway)

○ CAMP NORWAY 4
(Norway)

RIISER-LARSEN ICE SHELF

Lyddan I

BRUNT
ICE SHELF

W E D D E L L

S E A

HALLEY BAY
(United Kingdom)

GENERAL

BELGRANO

BANK

C O A T S

L A N D

No Source Data

Aucunes sources
d'information

GENERAL BELGRANO ○
(Argentina)

DRUZHNAYA ○

F I L C H N E R

Kemp Peninsula

Cape Deacon

Cape Fiske

I C E

·3655

S U L A

S H E L F

BERKNER

ISLAND

976·

SOBRAL ○
(Argentina)

R O N N E

·1802

I C E   S H E L F

·224

·445

·400

T R A N S A N T A R C T I C   M O U N T A I N S

R O N N E   L A N D

·2070

·460

E D I T H

·461

○ SIPLE
(U.S.A.)

A meteorite and the tsunamis

●●● Scientists have known for a long time that the bottom of the Bellingshausen Sea is formed by a complete crustal plate which was still active 60 million years ago. This plate had gone missing in the "jigsaw puzzle" researchers had developed over decades to piece together the parts of the ancient supercontinent Gondwana.

Gondwana comprised mainly the modern southern continents of Australia, India, South America, and Antarctica. About 180 million years ago, it broke into pieces which then drifted apart. This affected not only the modern landmasses, but also numerous fragments which never developed into individual continents, but spread out on the sea floor instead – one of which was the Bellingshausen Plate. It was discovered only after modern surveying methods had become available – methods that were no longer impaired by the thick ice sheet permanently covering the ocean's surface.

Yet another secret lay hidden in the Bellingshausen Sea. Roughly 2.15 million years ago, the meteorite "Eltanin" – 1,000 meters (3,300 ft.) in diameter and traveling at a speed of 70,000 kilometers per hour (43,470 mph) – slammed into the bottom of this sea basin. With an explosive force equal to 100 gigatons of TNT, it destroyed 250 meters (820 ft.) thick sediment layer at the sea floor, scattering it over an area of more than 300 kilometers (190 mi.) around the impact site.

Eltanin is the largest meteorite known to have collided with the Earth. Its plunge into the Bellingshausen Sea provoked mile-high ripples spreading over every ocean of the world at a speed of 200 kilometers per hour (124 mph). Although the energy of the tidal waves was already subsiding when they hit the shores, they were still hundreds of feet high and likely to have planed down thousands of miles of coastlines.

Such tidal waves, or tsunamis, are also triggered by seaquakes, sub-marine volcano eruptions, and underwater coastal landslides. On the open ocean, they are seldom more than 1 meter (39 in.) high, but hundreds of miles long. Barely visible, they cross the oceans at an enormous speed. As the shallow coastal waters slow down the waves, they pile up to become powerful tsunamis which devastate large parts of the shoreline. If such tidal waves enter fjords, they may reach heights of up to 15 meters (50 ft.).

The northern and eastern coasts of the Pacific, where the continental and oceanic plates are subject to intense pressures that can trigger seaquakes, are particularly prone to this phenomenon.

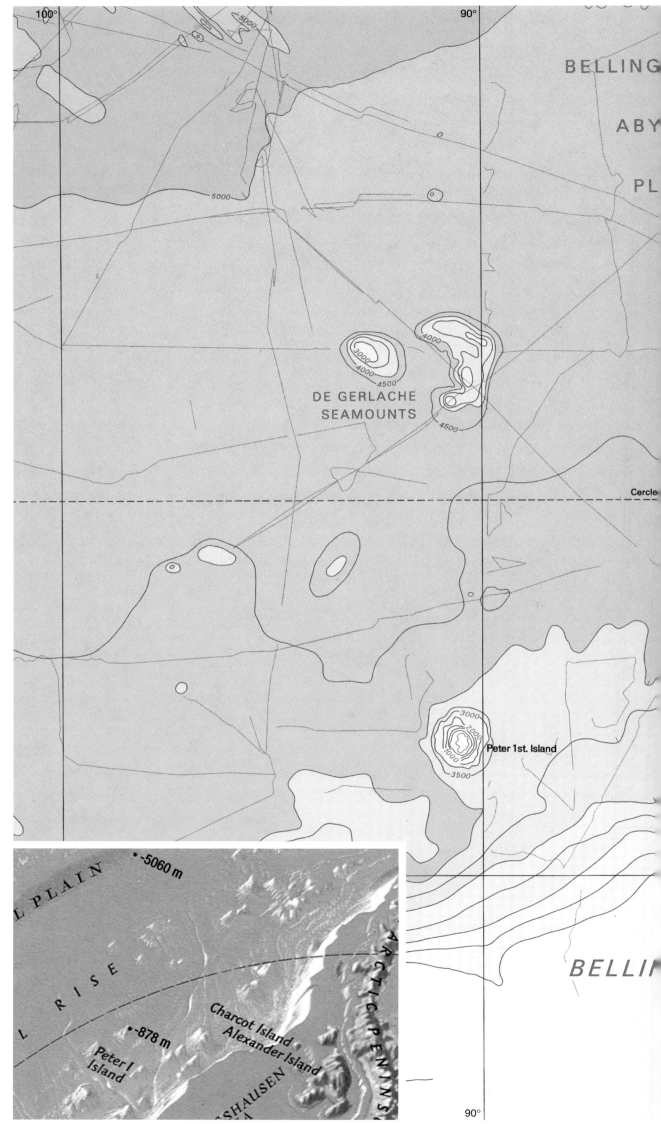

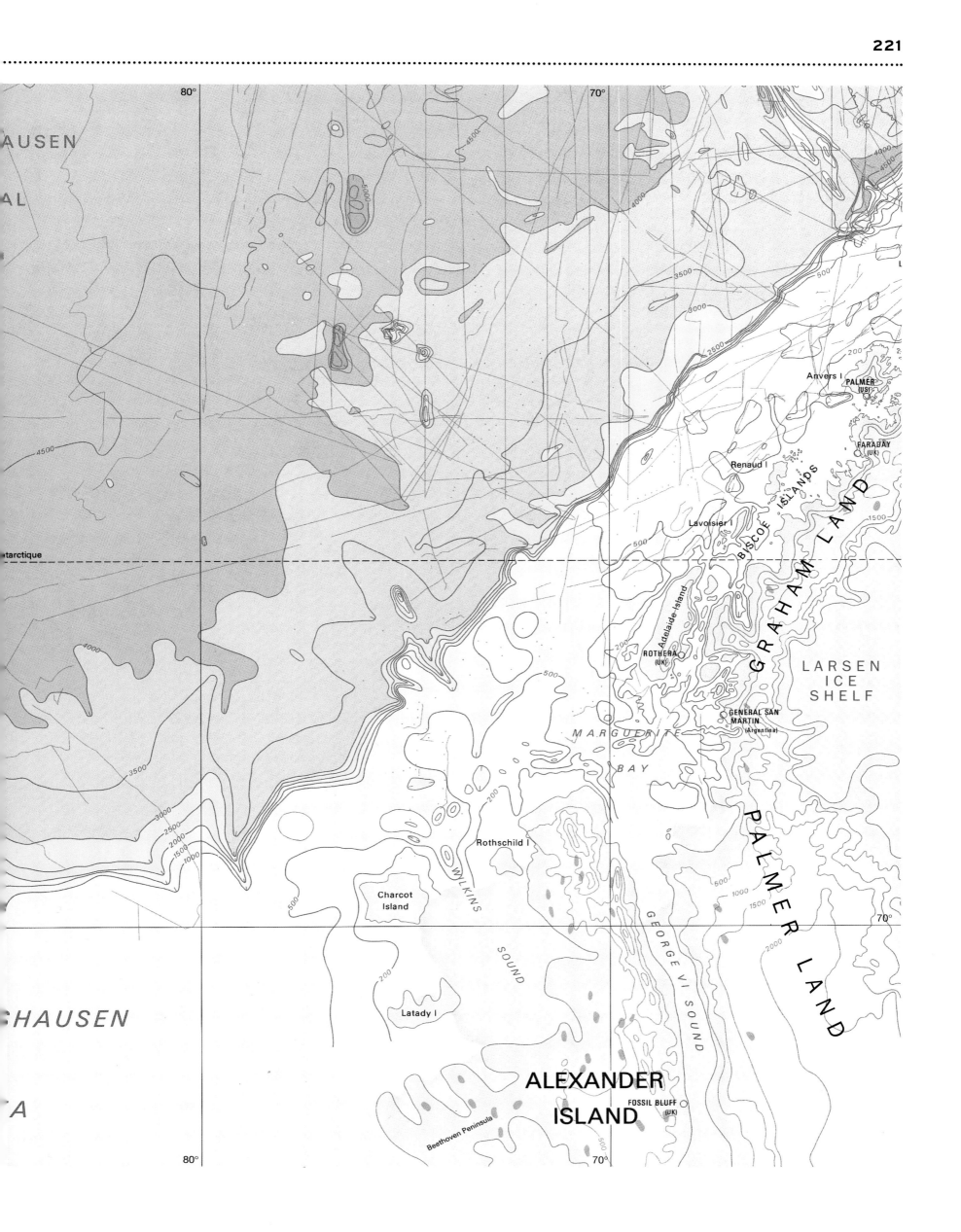

The pulsing Antarctic coast

●●● The Napier mountains in Enderby Land represent one of the oldest visible pieces of the Earth's crust. The Indo-Australian Plate came loose when the super-continent of Gondwana broke apart in the Paleozoic Era, 250 to 570 million years ago. Gondwana, which existed 2.5 billion years ago, was comprised of the modern southern continents.

The Antarctic is a "pulsating" continent insofar as its ice-covered coast shifts forward and backward to the rhythm of the seasons. In winter, the Antarctic Ocean is covered by an ice sheet 20 million square kilometers (7.7 mill. sq. mi.) in size which thaws down to 3 million square kilometers (1.2 mill. sq. mi.) in the summer. The seasonal decrease and increase of the Antarctic ice sheets is six times more pronounced than the variations in the pack ice extension around the North Pole. The ocean surrounding the Antarctic is, therefore, of vital importance for the heat exchange between ocean and atmosphere, thus influencing the global weather conditions.

The seas off the Antarctic coasts are among to the most stormy areas of the world. They are shaken not only by relentless, violent cyclones along the notorious "roaring forties" and "furious fifties" latitudes, but also by extremely cold, katabatic winds which rush down the high coastal mountains and blow over the sea in the "screaming sixties".

These winds originate in the cold, dense air emanating from the interior of the continent. Upon reaching a certain speed, they can turn into the much-feared Antarctic blizzards which whirl up loose snow and drive it through the valleys and out over pack ice and sea water at a speed of up to 150 kilometers per hour (92 mph).

On the coasts, enormous glaciers, sometimes as large as small countries, break off the inland ice. Due to their flat top they are also called table icebergs. The more they thaw, the more they lose their stability until they keel over, turning up their rugged bottoms. Off the coast, in the narrow East Wind Drift of the Polar Current, they float west along with the pack ice until they reach the Antarctic Circumpolar Current in the open sea and are deflected to the east.

Many icebergs drift on to the Subtropical Convergence located roughly on the 40th latitude. This invisible boundary where warm subarctic water collides with cold Antarctic surface water constitutes the northern border of the Antarctic Ocean. The water under the icebergs and the pack ice cools down and freezes, thereby releasing salt, especially in winter. This process makes the sea water heavier so that parts of it sink to the sea floor and merge with the oceanic bottom water.

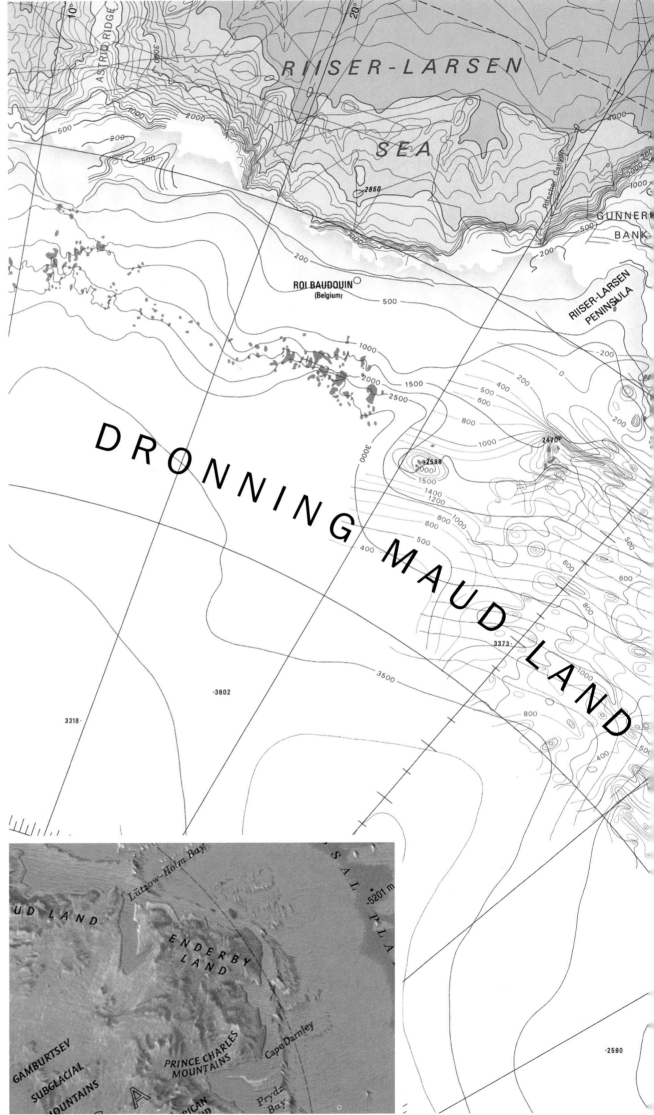

KAINAN MARU
SEAMOUNTS

COSMONAUT SEA

ENDERBY ABYSSAL PLAIN

40°

50°

60°

60°

1808

1580

360

- Holm

1216

SYOWA (Japan)

MOLODEZHNAYA

ENDERBY

LAND

200

200

200

500

500

500

1000

400

400

500

600

500

2400

2900

2879

2800

400

70°

KEMP LAND

400

500

600

800

1000

200

200

200

2225

3365

500

500

1000

1500

1000

500

1325

1000

1500

Casey
Bay

Amundsen

Cape Ann

1620

2300

Cape Boothby

1028

Edward VIII

1270

1942

1311

1781

Mawson Canyon

3420

3325

2200

MAWSON
(Australia)

STOREGG
BANK

1855

MAC. ROBERTSON

LAND

FRAM
BANK

Cape Darnley

Mackenzie
Bay

AMERY

ICE SHELF

Daly Canyon

Nylar Canyon

1864

3180

VALDIVIA ABYSSAL PLAIN

70°

Wilkins Canyon

Murray Canyon

3000

COOPERATION SEA

AMERY

BASIN

Prydz

Bay

Gateway to the Antarctic

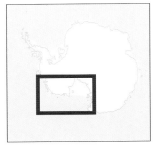

●●● The Ross Sea is the traditional gateway to the Antarctic. Of all the seas bordering the Antarctic continent, the Ross Sea is the least covered with ice and, therefore, the most accessible. Since James Ross discovered the Sea in 1841, numerous expeditions have taken the route via the Ross Ice Shelf into the interior of the Antarctic. The sea is relatively shallow, in most parts not deeper than 900 meters (2,950 ft.). Driven by the East Wind Drift near the continent, a large gyre circulates clockwise around the sea, whirling up nutrients from the sea floor which form the basis for the sea's rich flora and fauna. Branches of the gyre reaching Cape Adare in the western part of the bay are deviated by the West Wind Drift of the Antarctic Circumpolar Current and pushed eastward.

The Ross Ice Shelf, the "Great Ice Barrier," is the world's largest floating ice sheet – almost half the size of France. Like a wall 50 meters to 60 meters (164 ft. to 197 ft.) high and 800 kilometers (497 mi.) wide, it towers above the sea level; the 330-meter (1,083-ft.) thick ice float touches the floor only at the shores of the bay. The huge, softly curving ice surface reaches almost 1,000 kilometers (621 mi.) into the Antarctic and is therefore an excellent gateway for the exploration of the continent's interior.

Although the shelf's seaside border never seems to change, it gives rise to a number of huge icebergs which then float in the Antarctic Ocean for years. The glaciers in the Antarctic mountains are continually pushing new ice sheets towards the shelf at a rate of 110 meters to 1,100 meters (360 ft. to 3,600 ft.) per year.

Wildlife in the Antarctic Ocean is not restricted to the water and the coasts; the ice itself provides a habitat for numerous algae, bacteria, fungi, and animals.

When the ocean water starts to freeze at −1.8° C (28.8° F), it first forms even-shaped fresh water ice crystals, leaving behind a brine that accumulates in small channels within the growing ice floats. As further growth is confined to small, slowly increasing columns after the ice sheet has closed, this results in a dense network of small channels with diameters between fractions of a centimeter to several centimeters.

The channels are filled with brine, a solution which accommodates numerous algae, bacteria, and fungi. They, in turn, serve as food to ciliates, worms, and tiny crustaceans. These organisms are so efficiently adapted to their habitat within the ice that they quickly multiply. One cubic centimeter (0.06 cu. in.) can, therefore, contain a thousand times more microorganisms than the same amount of polar ocean water.

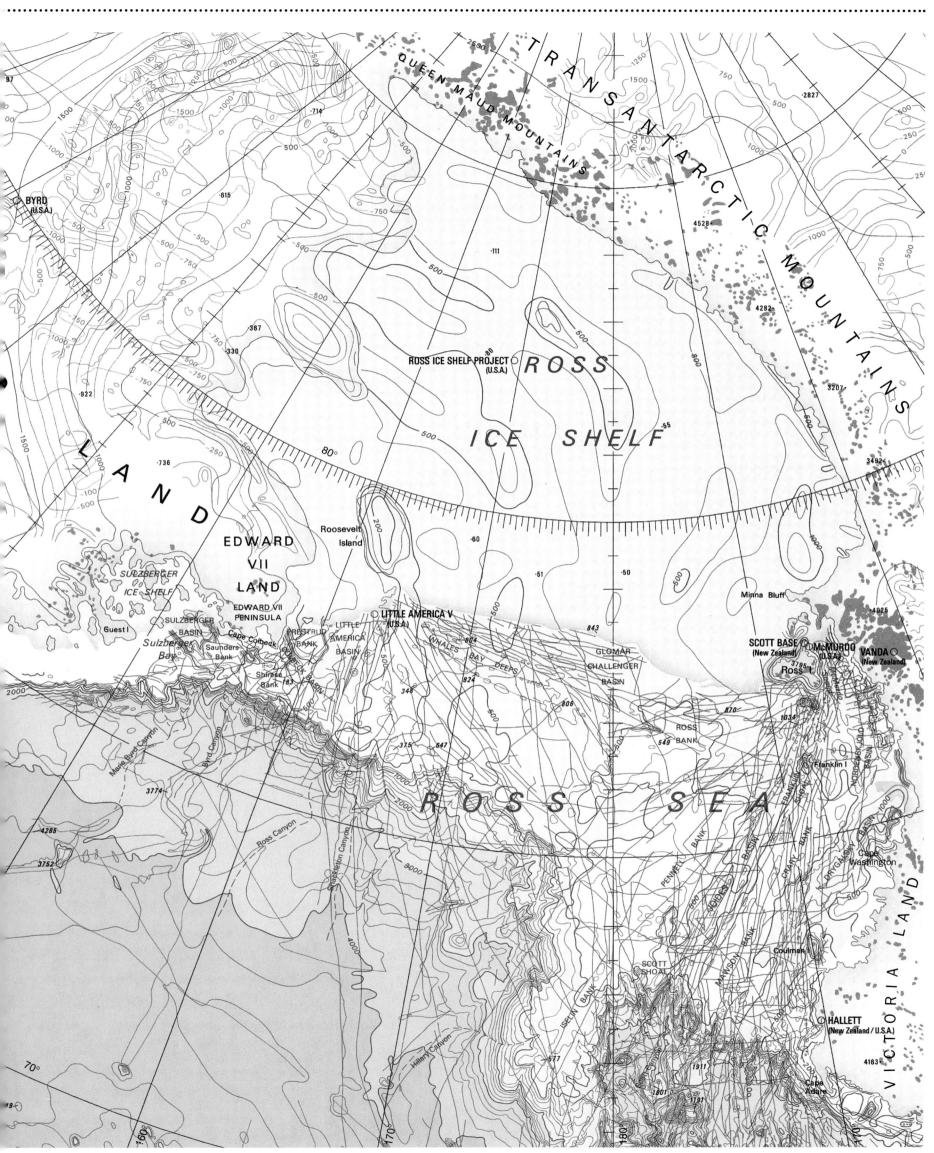

The Mediterran

Individual basins and their wat

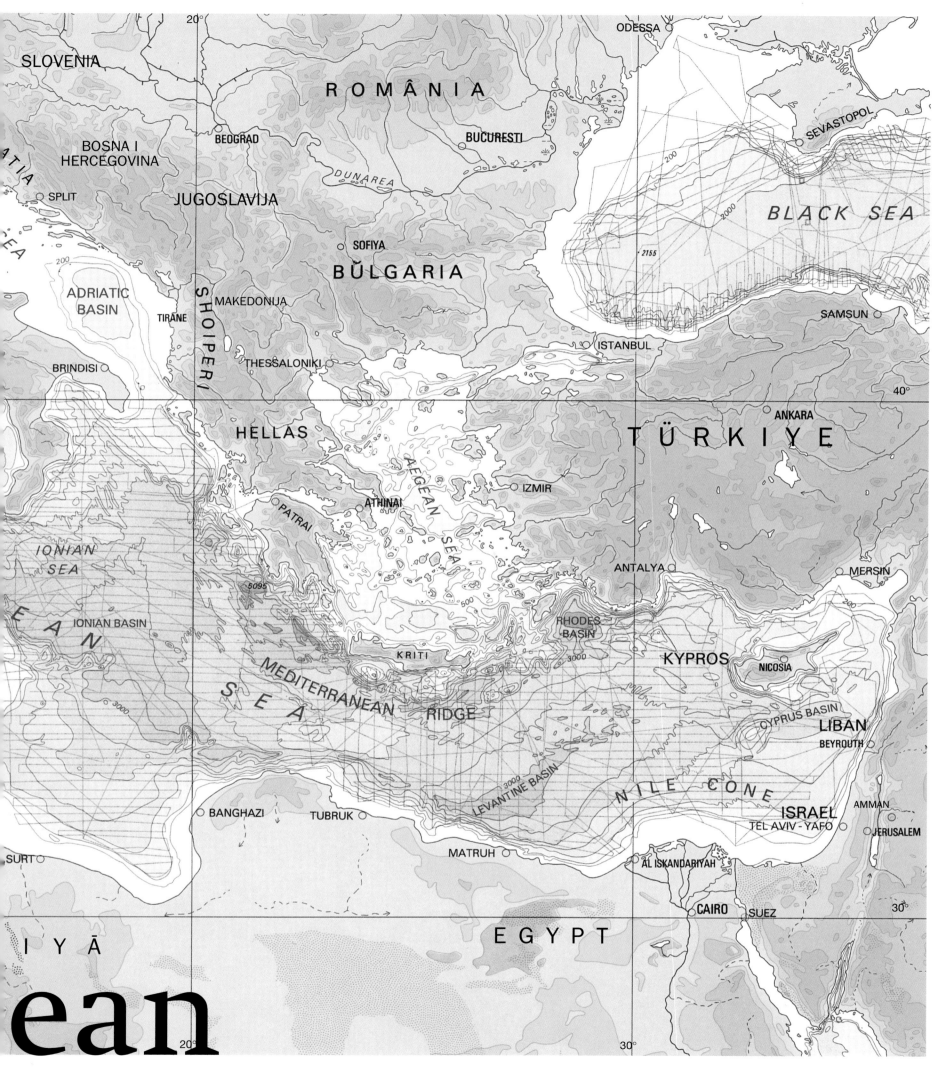

SLOVENIA

ROMÂNIA

BOSNA I HERCEGOVINA

BEOGRAD

BUCURESTI

DUNAREA

ODESSA

SEVASTOPOL

JUGOSLAVIJA

SPLIT

SOFIYA

BŬLGARIA

BLACK SEA

2155

SAMSUN

ADRIATIC BASIN

200

SHQIPËRI

MAKEDONIJA

TIRANE

THESSALONIKI

ISTANBUL

BRINDISI

40°

HELLAS

TÜRKIYE

ANKARA

AEGEAN SEA

ATHINAI

IZMIR

PATRAI

IONIAN SEA

5095

500

ANTALYA

MERSIN

IONIAN BASIN

RHODES BASIN

KYPROS

NICOSIA

KRITI

3000

MEDITERRANEAN RIDGE

SEA

CYPRUS BASIN

LIBAN

BEYROUTH

3000

LEVANTINE BASIN

NILE CONE

ISRAEL

AMMAN

BANGHAZI

TUBRUK

TEL AVIV - YAFO

JERUSALEM

SURT

MATRUH

AL ISKANDARIYAH

30°

CAIRO

SUEZ

IYĀ

EGYPT

ean

er depths

Deadly algae threatens the sea

●●● The Algero-Provençal Basin, or Balearic Basin, is the middle basin of the western Mediterranean. The relatively shallow Alborán Basin extends off the Strait of Gibraltar between Spain and Morocco. Surrounded by Corsica, Sardinia, and Sicily, the Tyrrhenian Sea borders Italy's west coast.

The Mediterranean and its surrounding mountain ranges were formed through continual collisions between the relatively solid European and African continental plates over the past 44 million years, which resulted in the plates drifting apart.

The Mediterranean basin was never dry. Five million years ago, when the Strait of Gibraltar opened up, the sea floor was already divided into several basins between 200 meters and 1,500 meters (660 ft. and 5,000 ft.) deep. These basins contained extraordinarily high-saline sea water, evidenced by the huge salt deposits discovered under the Mediterranean sea floor only around the mid-1970s.

The Balearic Islands are located in the center of the Algero-Provençal Basin on an underwater branch of the Baetic Cordillera, which runs along the coast of southern Spain and descends into the ocean at Cape Nao. The Balearic Islands include the major islands of Majorca, Minorca, and the smaller Cabrera. To their west lie Ibiza and Formentera, also called the Pitiusas.

In 1992, a lethal species of algae appeared on the east coast of Majorca. Native to the islands of the Caribbean and the Pacific, *Caulerpa taxifolia* escaped in 1984 from the aquarium of the Oceanographic Museum of Monaco. In a habitat devoid of enemies, which it found below the museum's windows, the algae soon became accustomed to the cooler temperatures and began multiplying without restraint. From Monaco, it migrated first to the Côte d'Azur, where it further multiplied and attached itself to the anchors of numerous leisure boats. These boats have since carried the microorganism to virtually every Mediterranean coastline, as the tiny plant can survive for 10 days even in tightly sealed anchor casings.

Shadowed by the algae overgrowth, Mediterranean seaweed is wilting. This plant, however, is crucial for the local ecosystem, as the Mediterranean contains few nutrient salts and thus little plankton. Seaweed is therefore the vital component at the basis of the food chain on which all other organisms depend.

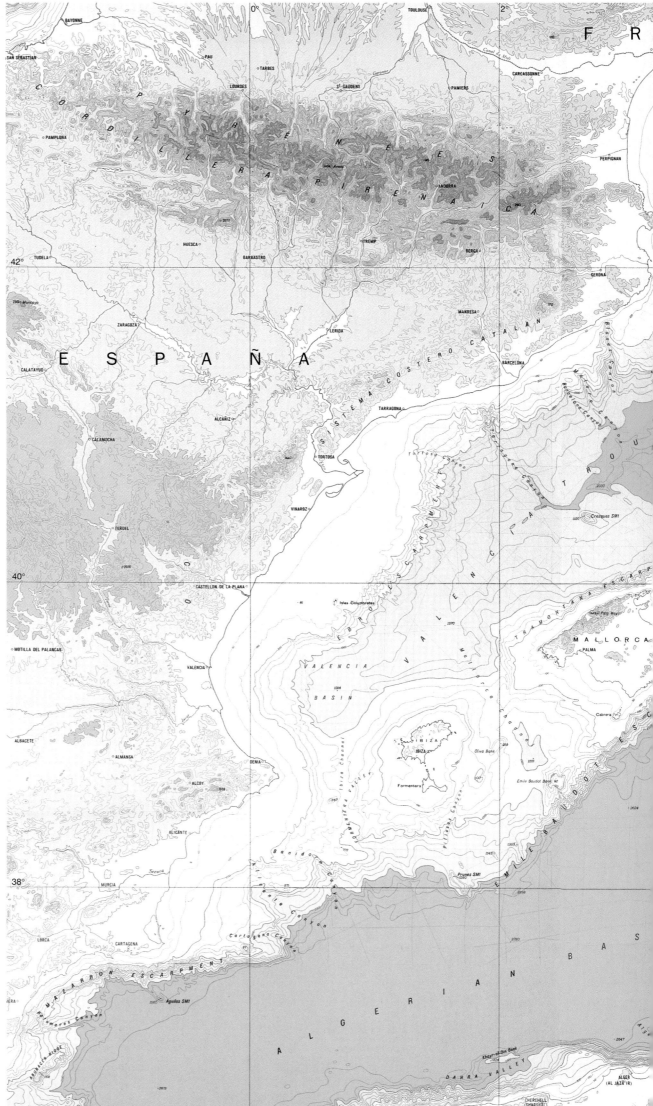

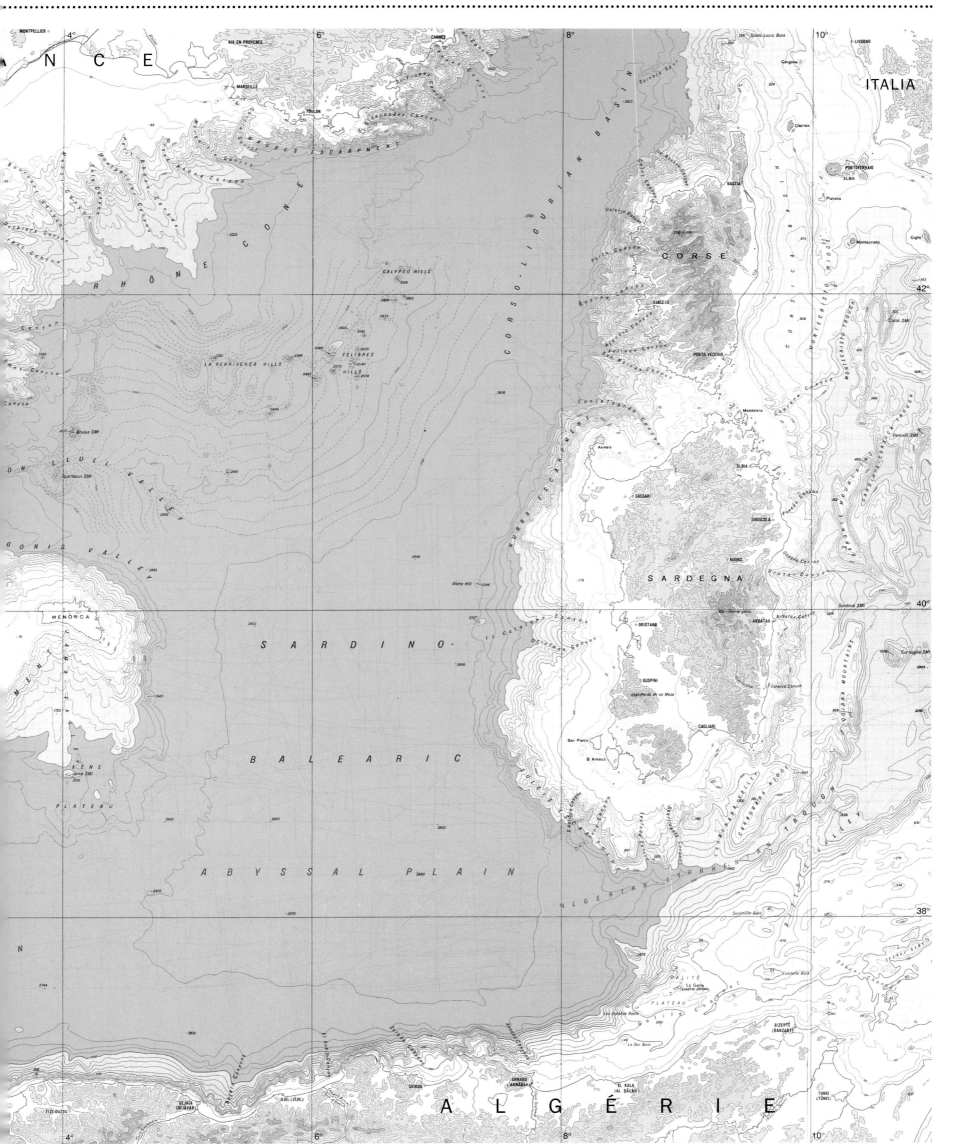

FRANCE

ITALIA

MARSEILLE

TOULON

CANNES

AIX-EN-PROVENCE

MONTPELLIER

RHÔNE CONE

MAURES ESCARPMENT

CALYPSO HILLS

LA RENAISSENÇA HILLS

FÉLIBRES HILLS

LLULL VALLEY

GONIS VALLEY

MENORCA

SARDINO-

BALEARIC

ABYSSAL PLAIN

ALGÉRIE

CORSE

BASTIA

AJACCIO

PORTO-VECCHIO

SASSARI

OLBIA

SINISCOLA

NUORO

SARDEGNA

ORISTANO

ARBATAX

GUSPINI

CAGLIARI

San Pietro

CORSO-LIGURIAN BASIN

CORSICA BASIN

MONTECRISTO TROUGH

MONTECRISTO RIDGE

PORTOFERRAIO
ELBA

Capraia

Montecristo

Gorgona

LIVORNO

NURRA ESCARPMENT

QUIRRA MOUNTAINS

BONIFACIO VALLEY

CARBONARA RIDGE

BIZERTE
(BANZART)

TUNIS
(TŪNIS)

ANNABA
(ʿANNĀBAH)

EL KALA
(AL QĀLAH)

SKIKDA

JIJEL (JĪJIL)

BÉJAÏA
(BIJĀYAH)

TIZI-OUZOU

ALGERIAN-PROVENÇAL TROUGH

The seas on either side of Italy

● ● ● The Italian "boot" and its continuation, a 360-meter (1,180-ft.) deep sub-marine ridge between Sicily and Africa, divide the Mediterranean in two parts.

The Strait of Otranto connects the Adriatic Sea with the Ionian Sea in the eastern basin. The surface currents are driven by the prevailing wind. The Bora, a strong northeastern katabatic wind, blows down from the mountains of the Balkans. In winter, it alternates with the less powerful Sirocco coming from the southeast.

The northern part of the Adriatic generates the majority of the Mediterranean's deep water, as water temperatures drop to 5° C (41° F) in winter. In very cold winters, there may even be ice on the Gulf of Trieste. The cold, heavy water sinks to the bottom, flows south, and crosses the Ionian Sea, eventually reaching the Levantine Basin.

Each summer, poorly oxygenated zones extend off the Italian coast of the northern Adriatic, killing any living matter which may exist. These zones are formed by the large deposits of nutrients washed into the sea by the Po River, which, in the normally nutrient-poor Mediterranean, triggers an explosive overgrowth of plankton that soon dies off and sinks to the sea floor. Bacteria decompose the remains, using up oxygen in the process.

The Ligurian and the Tyrrhenian Seas on either side of Italy are part of the western Mediterranean basin. The major islands of Corsica, Sardinia, and Sicily surround the Tyrrhenian Sea. They form obstacles, forcing the enormous clockwise gyre prevailing in this basin to dissolve into numerous smaller eddies and currents, some of which cross the narrow passages between the islands at break-neck speed.

The most striking features in the southern part of the Tyrrhenian Sea are the volcanoes – some still active, some extinct. The Lipari Islands, or Eolie Islands, for instance, represent the volcanic summits of a submerged mountain range west of the Italian boot tip. The volcano on Stromboli, the northernmost island of this group, is still active today.

Europe's greatest volcano, however, is located under the water. To the northwest of the Lipari Islands, the more than 2-million-year-old Mount Marsili rises 3,300 meters (10,827 ft.) above the bottom of the deep Tyrrhenian Basin.

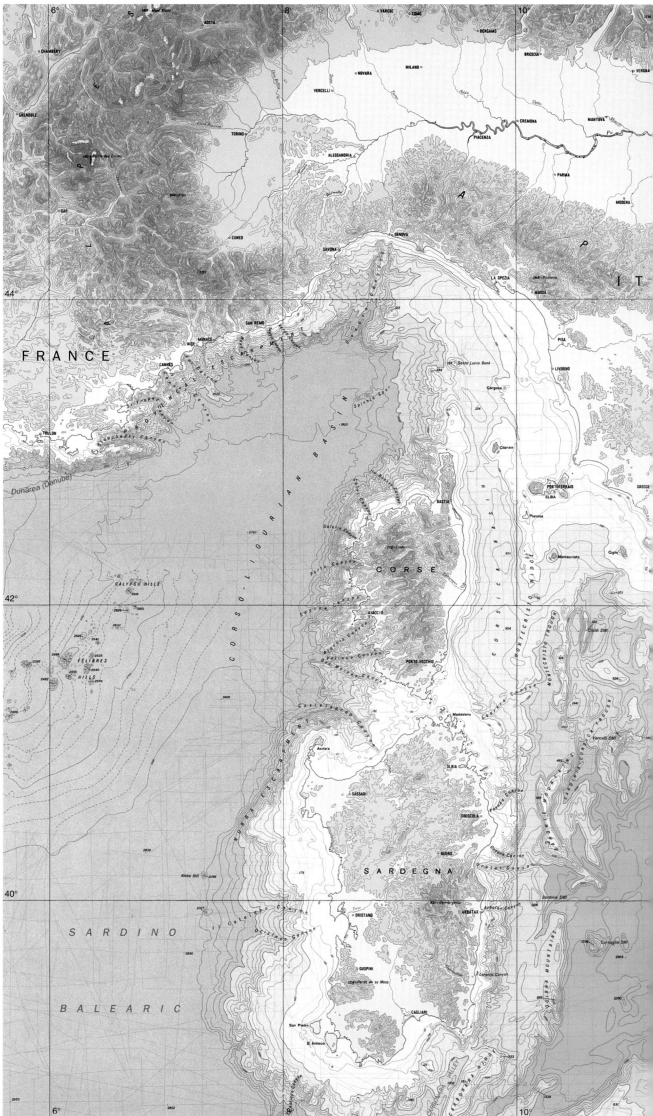

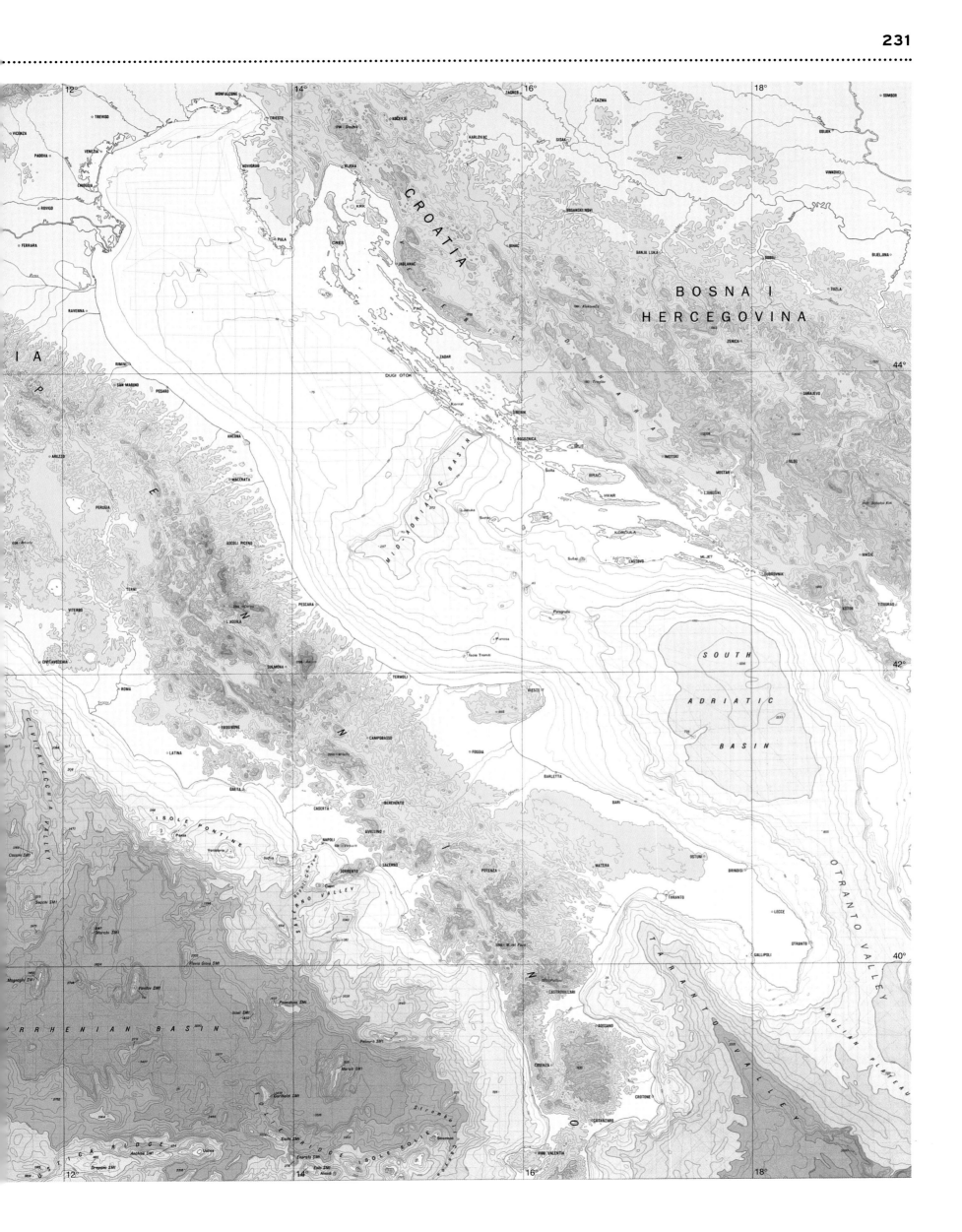

The Aegean Sea: a sunken land

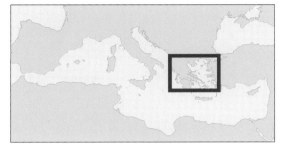

● ● ● The Aegean Sea in the eastern Mediterranean Basin is comparable to a large bay. The shipping lanes west and east of Crete connect it with the Levantine Basin, while the strait between Peloponnese and Crete provides access to the Ionian Sea. To the northeast of Crete, the deepest point in the Aegean sea lies 3,543 meters (11,625 ft.) below sea level.

The countless islands rising from the sea are the peaks of the Aegean Mountains, a now submerged land mass. This was still dry land 18,000 years ago, when the sea level was lower. The prevailing north winds, alternating in winter with mild southwestern winds, often spur strong currents between the islands, particularly the infamous, unpredictable, and often extremely violent currents near Euripus.

The strait between the Greek mainland and the Island of Euboea is, at its narrowest point near Chalcis, merely 40 meters (130 ft.) wide and 7 meters (23 ft.) deep. This is just sufficient for freight ships to pass. This natural channel can only be crossed if the current is not too strong, for it can change direction up to seven times a day. Aristotle tried to find an explanation for this phenomenon, which has still not been fully clarified.

Through the 61-kilometer (37.9-mi.) long and 1-kilometer to 6.5-kilometer (0.6-mi. to 4-mi.) wide Dardanelles, a swift surface current rushes from the Black Sea into the Aegean Sea. At the bottom of the 55-meter (180-ft.) deep trough, another powerful current flows into the Sea of Marmara. The Black Sea water carries small amounts of nutrient salts into the Aegean, which is one of the oceans on Earth with particularly low nutrient concentrations.

The southern Aegean is one of the areas of the Mediterranean where deep water is formed. After the saline concentration of the water has risen in summer, the water cools down in winter, becoming so heavy that it sinks to the sea floor and flows to the bottom of the Levantine Basin.

Africa meets Europe in a belt extending from the Dardanelles through the Sea of Marmara to the Black Sea. The Arabian Plate, part of the African Plate, shifts towards Europe at a rate of 2 centimeters to 3 centimeters (0.8 in. to 1.2 in.) per year (faster than the rest of the African Plate). Part of the plate, however, is jammed within the North Anatolian Fault, in the Pontic Mountains on the south shore of the Black Sea. Disastrous consequences would ensue if this part was ever abruptly pulled away by the Arabian Plate.

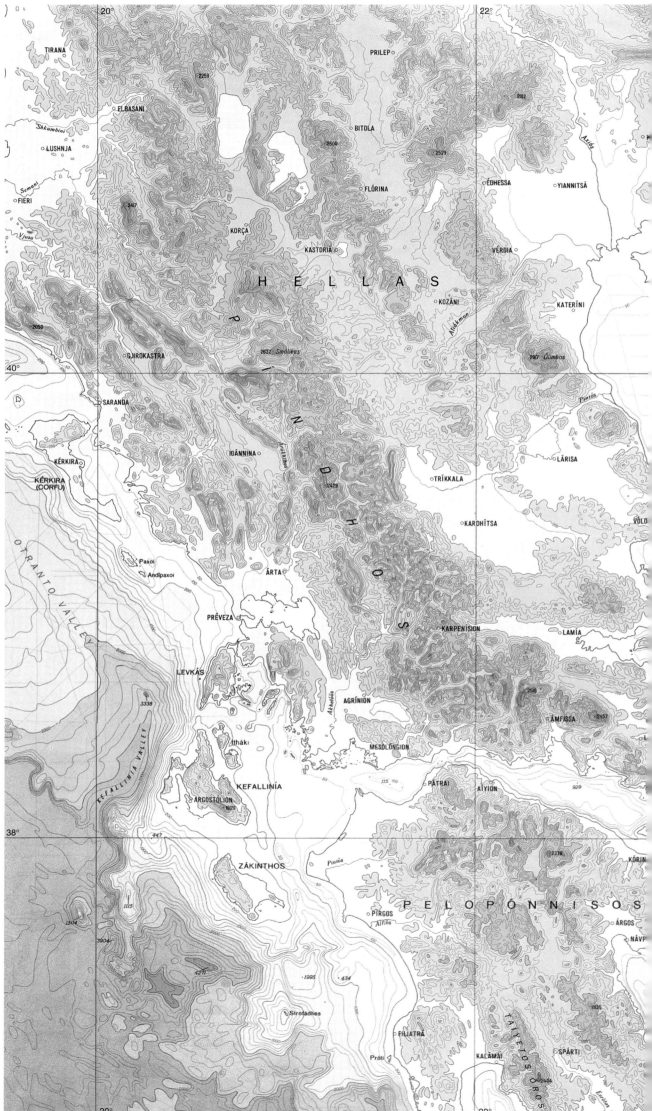

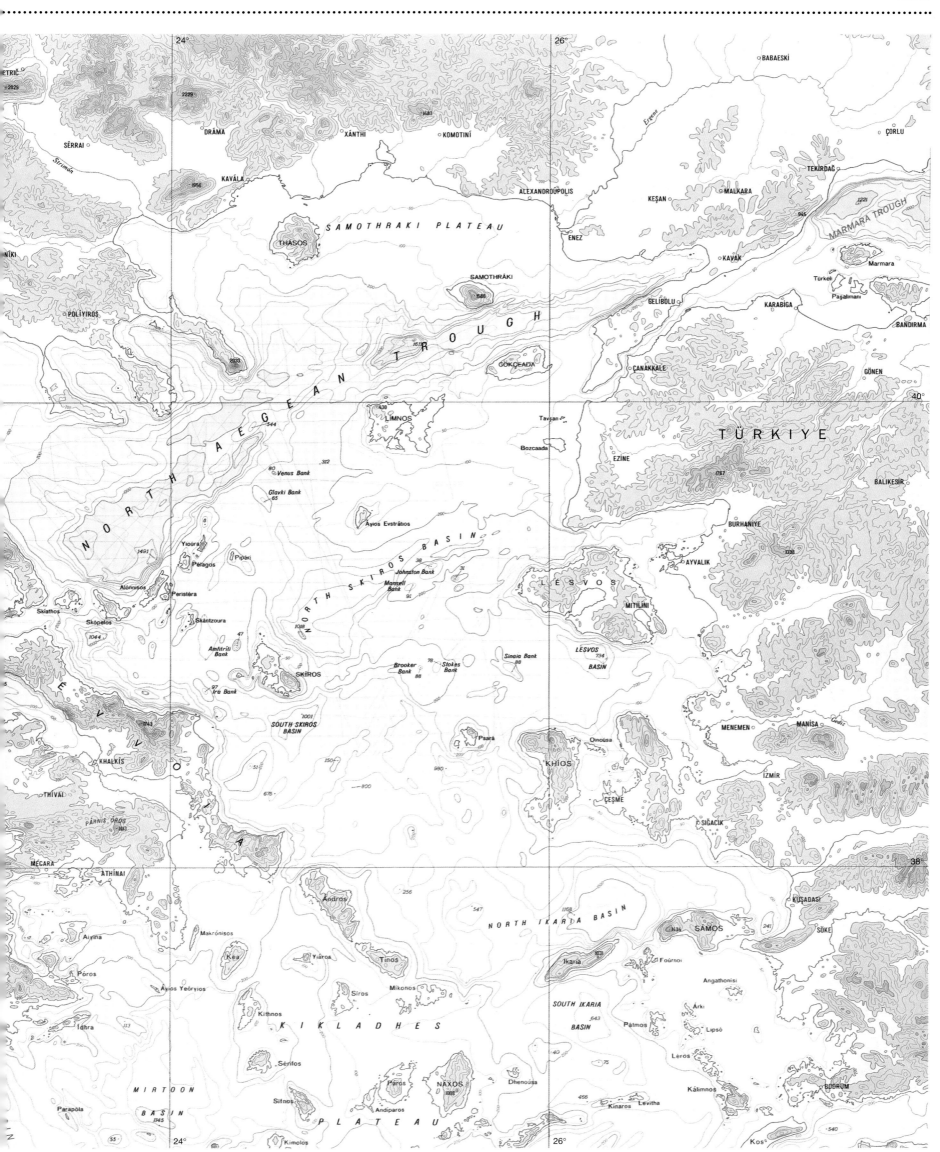

SÉRRAI
DRÁMA
XÁNTHI
KOMOTINÍ
BABAESKI
ÇORLU
Strimón
2029
2229
1483
KAVÁLA
1956
TEKIRDAĞ
1221
MARMARA TROUGH
ALEXANDROÚPOLIS
KEŞAN
MALKARA
945
THASOS
SAMOTHRAKI PLATEAU
ENEZ
KAVAK
Marmara
Türkeli
Paşalimanı
POLÍYIROS
SAMOTHRÁKI
1586
GELIBOLU
KARABIGA
BANDIRMA
NÍKI
ÇANAKKALE
GÖNEN
1673
GÖKÇEADA
2033

N   O   R   T   H   A   E   G   E   A   N   T   R   O   U   G   H

430
LÍMNOS
544
Tavşan
TÜRKIYE
40°
Bozcaada
80 Venus Bank   312
Glavki Bank 65
EZINE
1767
BALIKESIR
Áyios Evstrátios
BURHANIYE
1491
Yioúra
31
1038
AYVALIK
Pefagos   Pipéri
Johnston Bank   38
Peristéra
Mansell Bank   91
LÉSVOS
Skíathos
Skántzoura
MITILÍNI
Alónnisos
Skópelos
1044
1098
LÉSVOS   734
Amfitríti Bank   47
LÉSVOS
BASIN
SKÍROS
Sinaia Bank   88
Brooker Bank   88   78   Stokes Bank
97   Íra Bank
1001
SOUTH SKÍROS BASIN
1743
Psará
Onoúsa
KHALKÍS   51
980
KHÍOS
THÍVAI   150   800
675
İZMİR
PÁRNIS ÓROS   1413
ÇEŞME
SIĞACIK
MÉGARA
38°
ATHÍNAI
Ándros
256
KUŞADASI
547
NORTH IKARÍA BASIN   1168
SÁMOS   241
Aíyina
1434
SÖKE
Makrónisos
Ikaría   Foúrnoi
Kéa   Yiáros   Tínos
Póros
Ávios Yeóryios
Angathonísi
Síros   Mikonos
Árki
Lipsó
Kíthnos   SOUTH IKARÍA   643   Pátmos
Ídhra   113   BASIN
KÍKLADHES
Léros
Sérifos   40   75
NÁXOS   Kálimnos
MÍRTOON   Páros   1008   Dhenoúsa
BODRUM
Sífnos   456
BASIN   Andíparos   Kínaros   Levítha
1145
P   L   A   T   E   A   U
Parapóla
540
Kímolos   Kos
55
24°   26°

The Black Sea's death zone

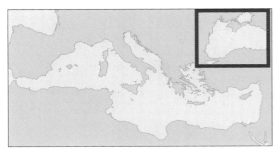

● ● ● Since the Turkish language refers to the Mediterranean as the "White Sea," the ocean off the northern coastline was consequently called the "Black Sea." It is a young sea which acquired its current appearance only 9,000 years ago.

Five to seven million years ago, the area between eastern Austria and the Aral Sea was covered by the vast Sarmatian Sea, with only the summits of the Carpathian Mountains and the Caucasus rising as islands above the sea level. When the land rose, the Sarmatian Basin divided into the Aral Basin, the Caspian Basin, and the Pontic Basin. Only 6,000 to 8,000 years ago, when the land bridge between Asia Minor and the Balkans tumbled, opening a passage towards the Mediterranean Sea, did the Pontic Sea develop into the modern Black Sea.

The Black Sea contains three different types of water. Each year, the rivers drain almost 340 cubic kilometers (82 cu. mi.) of fresh water into the sea, with the Danube alone contributing more than half of that quantity – 200 cubic kilometers (50 cu. mi.). When the Bosporus Rise collapsed, saline water flowed in from the Mediterranean. Today, more than 120 cubic kilometers (29 cu. mi.) of Mediterranean water are washed into the eastern part of the Black Sea each year.

But some of the ancient water from the era of the Pontic Sea can still be found. The 2,000-meter (6,600-ft.) deep Black Sea contains two overlying water layers showing remarkable differences. As there are practically no currents below about 200 meters (660 ft.), no oxygen reached the abyss for thousands of years. In a depth of 180 meters to 200 meters (590 ft. to 660 ft.) a sharply outlined layer divides the lifeless deep water with its toxic load of hydrogen sulfide from the surface water. This "death zone" comprises 87 percent of the overall water mass of the Black Sea.

Even the temperature distribution in the different water layers of the sea is extraordinary. The lowest temperature of 6° C to 7° C (42.8° F to 44.6° F) is already reached at a depth of 50 meters to 100 meters (164 ft. to 330 ft.). Further below, the temperature rises again until reaching 9° C (48.2° F) at the sea floor.

Being an inland sea that has little exchange with the world's oceans, the Black Sea is very sensitive to imbalance. For the last 30 years, eutrophy, or over-fertilization, has increased, especially in the western part. This has led to a deterioration of the ocean's flora and fauna. At the same time, foreign species brought in by ships have multiplied uncontrollably due to the lack of natural enemies.

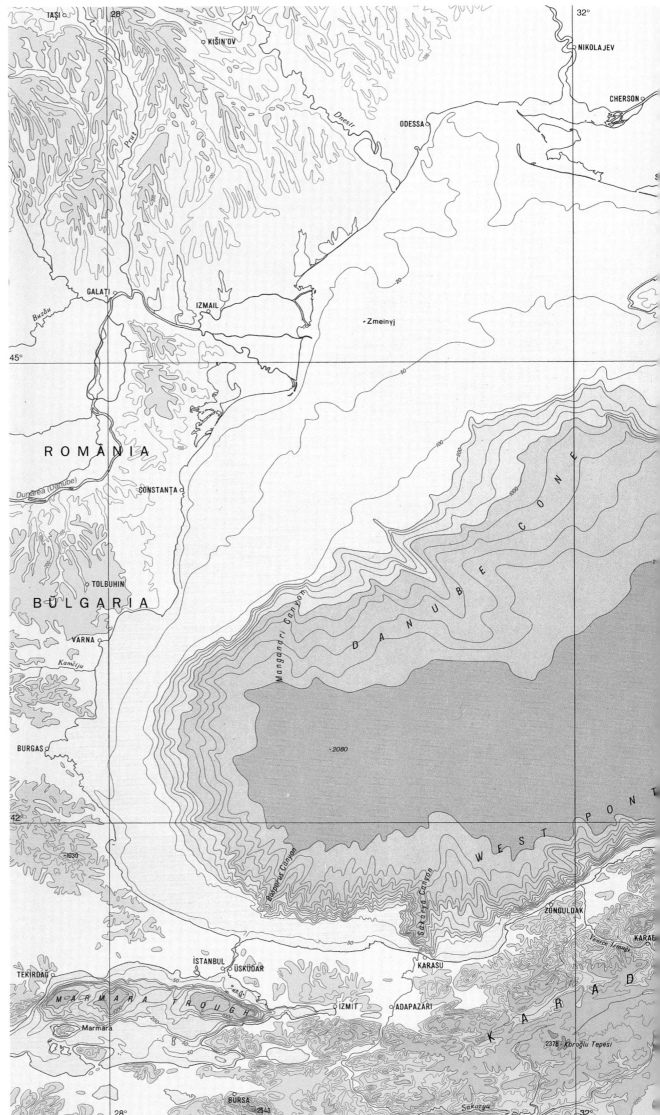

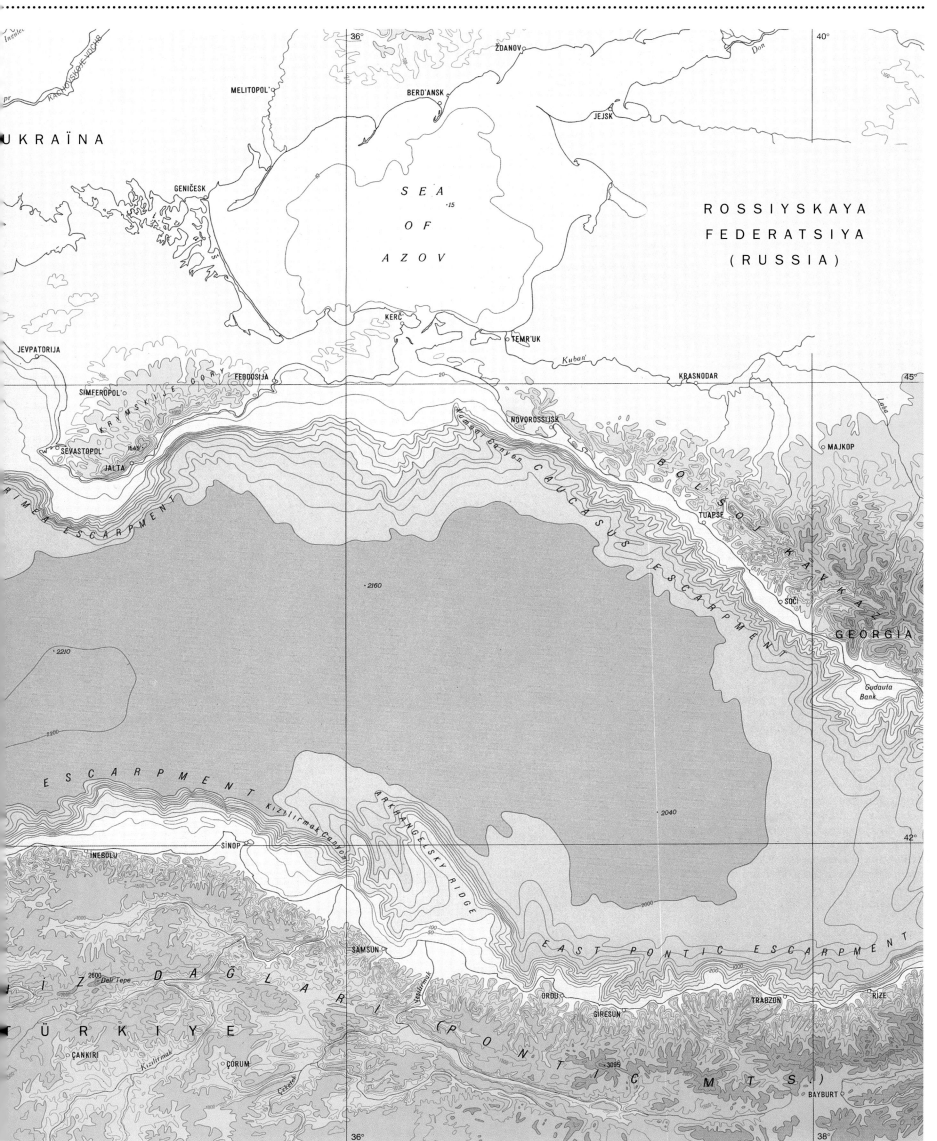

UKRAÏNA

ROSSIYSKAYA
FEDERATSIYA
(RUSSIA)

SEA
OF
AZOV

MELITOPOL'

ŽDANOV

BERD'ANSK

JEJSK

Don

·15

GENIČESK

KERČ

TEMR'UK

Kuban'

KRASNODAR

Laba

JEVPATORIJA

FEODOSIJA

45°

SIMFEROPOL'o

KRYMSKJJE GORY

NOVOROSSIJSK

BOL'ŠOJ

MAJKOP

SEVASTOPOL'

1545

JALTA

Pšada Canyon

CAUCASUS ESCARPMENT

TUAPSE

KAVKAZ

CRIMEA ESCARPMENT

·2160

SOČI

GEORGIA

·2210

Gudauta
Bank

·2200

ESCARPMENT

Kizilirmak Canyon

ARKHANGELSKY RIDGE

·2040

2000

INEBOLU

SINOP

42°

1000

100
50

SAMSUN

EAST PONTIC ESCARPMENT

2600

Deli Tepe

DAĞLARI

Yeşilirmak

ORDU

TRABZON

RIZE

İZ

GIRESUN

TÜRKIYE

(PONTIC MTS.)

ÇANKIRI

Kızılırmak

ÇORUM

Çekerek

·3095

BAYBURT

36°

38°

Gibraltar's currents and rises

●●● Between the "Pillars of Hercules" – the Rocks of Gibraltar on the Spanish and Moroccan side – the Strait of Gibraltar, some 60 kilometers (37 mi.) long and, at its narrowest point, 14 kilometers (8.7 mi.) wide, separates Europe from Africa. The opening towards the Atlantic prevents the Mediterranean from evaporating down to a salt sea. The inland sea is located in the Earth's dry climatic zone. Rain and fluvial water replace only one-third of the evaporating water; the remainder spills over from the Atlantic.

In the Strait of Gibraltar, the currents are impeded by two rises. The Tarifa Rise at the 23-kilometer (14.3-mi.) wide eastern end rises from a depth of 800 meters (2,600 ft.) to its saddle 280 meters (920 ft.) below sea level. It constitutes the barrier which prevents Mediterranean intermediate water from spilling over.

The Spartel Rise, on average 350 meters (1,150 ft.) deep, rises 21 kilometers (13 mi.) further to the west, its summits reaching up to 100 meters (330 ft.) below sea level. It constitutes the western end of the Mediterranean.

The oceanic deep water below the surface layer of the Mediterranean is surprisingly warm and salty, its temperature reaching 14.5° C (58.1° F) and its salinity ranging from 38.4 to 39 ppt. By means of comparison, the surface water of the North Atlantic shows a salinity of 36 ppt and a temperature around 13° C (55.4° F).

For this reason, the Atlantic water at the surface of the Strait of Gibraltar moves towards the Alborán Basin in a layer up to 200 meters (660 ft.) deep. Meanwhile, the Mediterranean intermediate water below it flows into the Atlantic after being formed in the sea's easternmost part, the Levantine Basin. Here, the surface water evaporates and becomes so heavy that it sinks to the bottom and moves back to Gibraltar in a 300-meter to 600-meter (990-ft. to 2,000-ft.) deep layer between the deep and surface water.

The velocity of flow of both currents can reach values of 2 to 3 kilometers per hour (1.2–1.9 mph) at the upper inlet and more than 1 kilometer per hour (0.6 mph) at the lower outlet, which generates turbulence tending to mix the two water layers. In the Atlantic, the water cascades down to the layers located in a depth of roughly 1,000 meters (3,300 ft.) and spreads westward with the Upper Atlantic Deep Water to the Bermuda Islands.

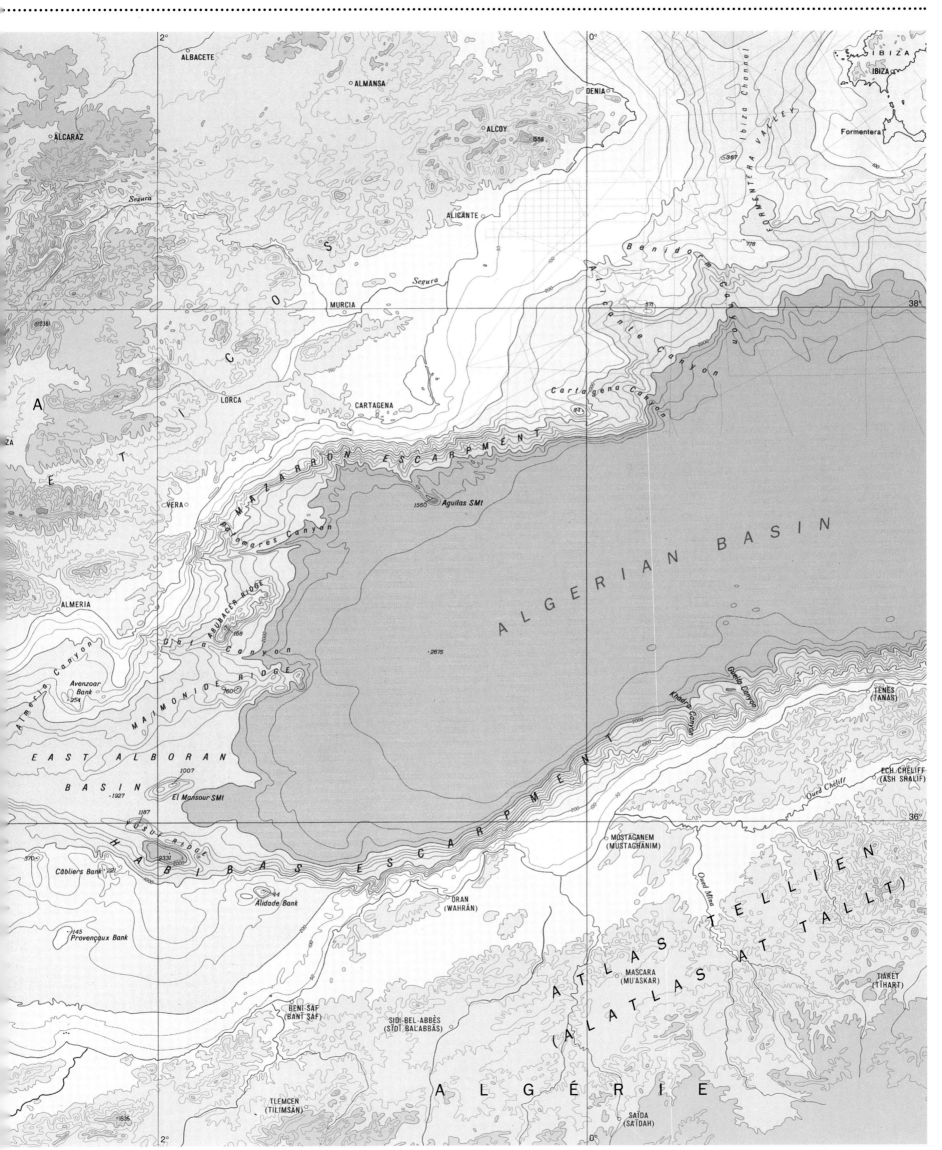

ALBACETE

ALMANSA

ÁLCARAZ

ALCOY

1558

DENIA

IBIZA

IBIZA

Formentera

Segura

367

Formentera Ibiza Channel

Formentera Valley

ALICANTE

Benidorm Canyon

100

778

COSTA

Segura

MURCIA

Alicante Canyon

38°

200

9238

LORCA

CARTAGENA

Cartagena Canyon

2000

83

MAZARRON ESCARPMENT

BÉTICA

VERA

Aguilas SMt

1560

Herradura Canyon

ALGERIAN BASIN

ABUBACER RIDGE

Gata Canyon

ALMERIA

168

Almeria Canyon

MAIMONIDE RIDGE

760

Avenzoar Bank
254

·2675

Chetta Canyon

TENÈS (TANÈS)

EAST ALBORAN

1007

El Mansour SMt

1927

BASIN

Khadra Canyon

600

ECH.CHÉLIFF (ASH SHALIF)

1187

Oued Chéliff

36°

YUSUF RIDGE

2331

MOSTAGANEM (MUSTAGHANIM)

570

Câbliers Bank 221

HABIBAS ESCARPMENT

44

Alidade Bank

ORAN (WAHRÀN)

Oued Mina

145

Provençaux Bank

ATLAS TELLIEN

MASCARA (MU'ASKAR)

TIARET (TIHART)

BENI-SAF (BANÌ SÀF)

SIDI-BEL-ABBÈS (SÌDÌ BAL'ABBÀS)

(AL ATLAS AT TALLÌ)

ALGÉRIE

TLEMCEN (TILIMSÀN)

SAÏDA (SA'ÌDAH)

1535

2°

Between Scylla and Charybdis

● ● ● Malta, Gozo, and Comino lie on a shelf extending from Sicily to the south. From the African coast, the Tunisian Plateau points towards Europe. Along its rim, there are the Lampedusa, Linosa, and Lampione Islands.

The threshold between these islands runs through the Strait of Sicily down to a depth of 350 meters (1,150 ft.) below sea level and divides the Mediterranean Sea into two large basins. Above the intermediate water, a layer of less salty, lighter Atlantic water flows slowly eastwards from the Strait of Gibraltar. In summer, when lots of water evaporates in the eastern Mediterranean, this current increases in volume to make up for the losses.

Ancient sailors dreaded the Strait of Messina between Italy and Sicily so much that it became a myth. Legends relate the story of Scylla and Charybdis, two female monsters that sat on either side of the narrow strait attempting to bring disaster upon ships and sailors.

The passage is 32 kilometers (20 mi.) long, 3 kilometers to 16 kilometers (1.9 mi. to 10 mi.) wide, and 90 meters (295 ft.) deep at its northern exit. A strong main current crosses it thrice daily at high speed from the south to the north, alternating with a less forceful current flowing in the opposite direction.

Triggered by the tides, normally hardly noticeable in the Mediterranean, this phenomenon provokes dangerous whirlpools. Sometimes the current is so violent that it rakes up seaweed from the sea floor or hurls deep-sea fish to the surface. While the main current is underway, the water level drops by 15 centimeters to 20 centimeters (5.9 in. to 7.9 in.).

Mainly in winter, a strong, cold wind blows from the northeast into the western and central Mediterranean. It is called Gregale, or Euraquilo, and is particularly pronounced on the island of Malta, where it can build up to the force of a hurricane and endanger ships out on the sea.

When cold air flows steadily from Central and Southern Europe to Libya, the Gregale prevails for four to five days. If a cyclone aproaches over the southern Mediterranean, the Gregale is broken down after one to two days.

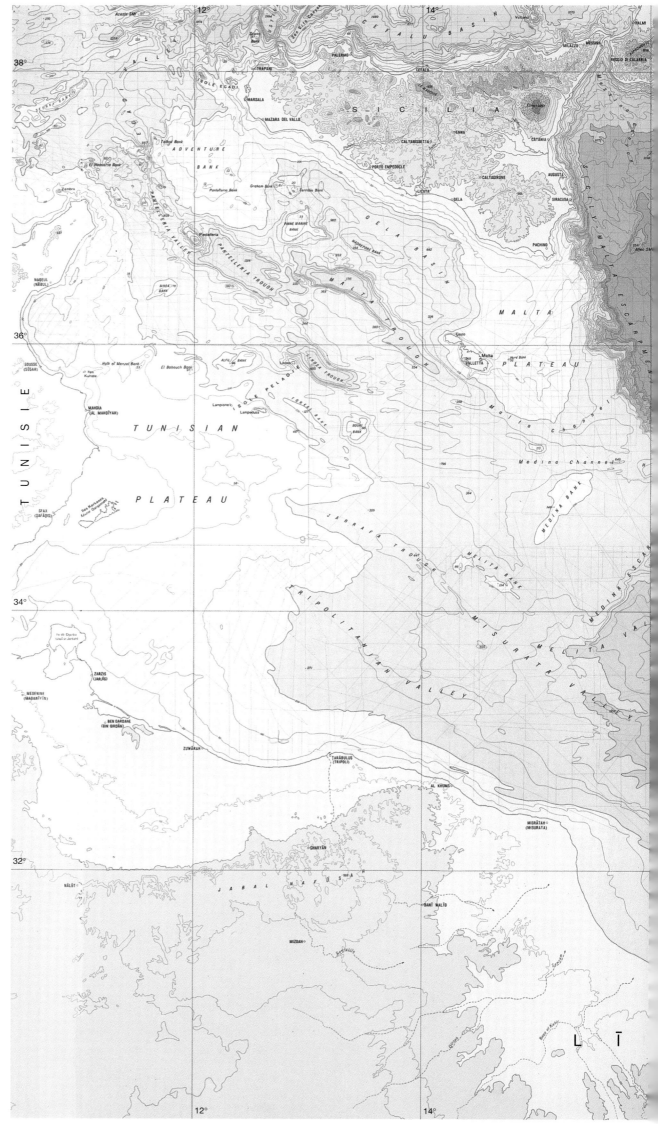

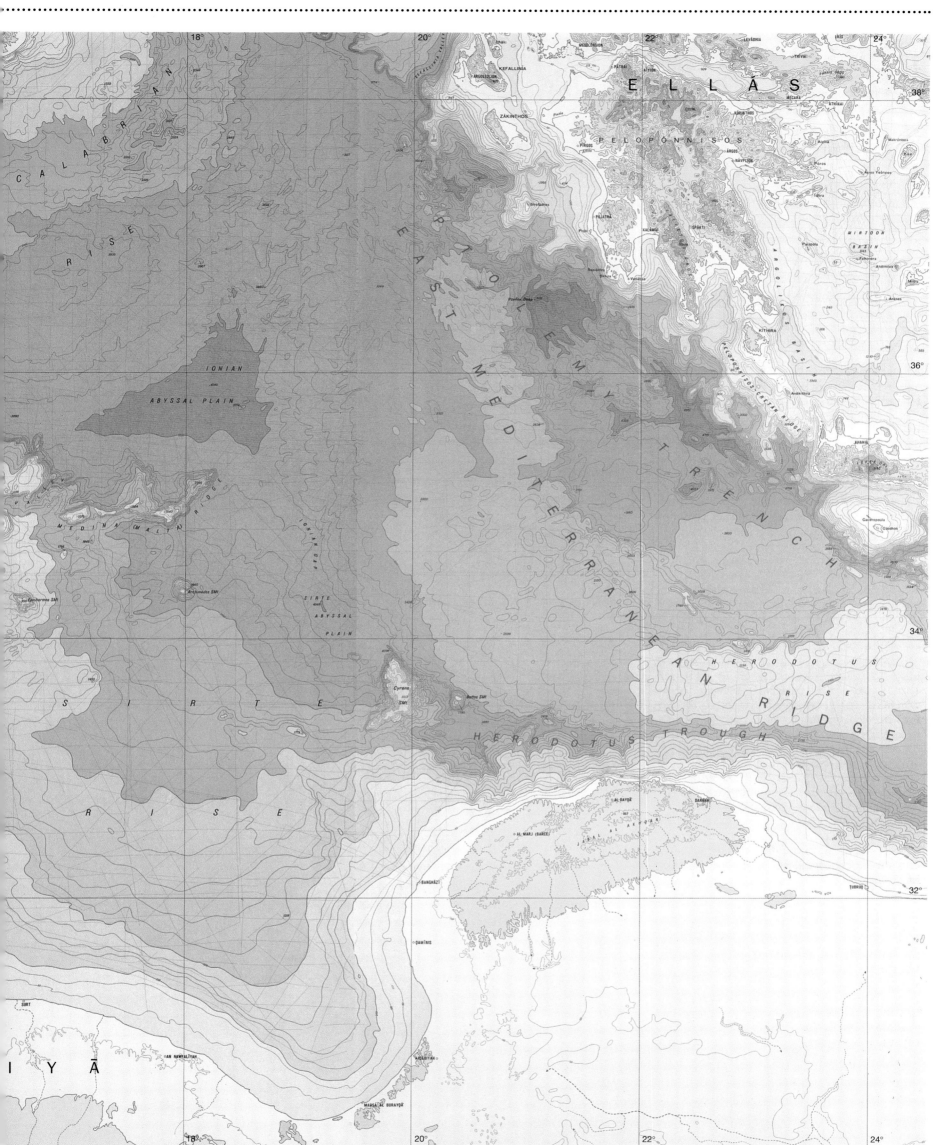

In the deep Levantine Basin

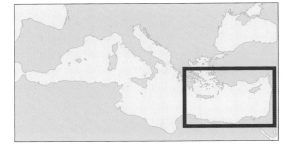

● ● ● The Levantine Basin is the easternmost of the two large, deep basins marking the bottom relief of the eastern Mediterranean. An underwater rise between the western end of Crete and the Libyan Al-Jabal Mountains separates the Levantine Basin from the Ionian Basin in the west. To the north, an island chain including Crete and Rhodes separates the basin from the shallower Aegean Sea.

In the Levantine Basin, the so-called "Levantine intermediate water" of the Mediterranean is produced. Below the surface layer, this water flows through the Strait of Gibraltar from the Mediterranean into the Atlantic. It is formed in late winter, especially on both side of Rhodes. As water evaporates in summer, the salinity of the eastern Mediterranean rises to 39 ppt. In the following winter, in cooling down from about 30° C (86° F) to 16° C (60.8° F), it becomes sufficiently heavy to sink, but not down to the deep water layer. This means that it accumulates at a depth of 300 meters to 600 meters (1,000 ft. to 2,000 ft.) below the surface, where it slowly flows westward. At this depth, it can easily overcome the underwater rises on its way to the Strait of Gibraltar.

Sea turtles, nowadays rare in the Mediterranean, nest on the beaches along the coasts of the Levantine Basin, but are threatened by the construction of new hotels. The turtles are unable to move to other, quieter beaches, since they always return to the place where they hatched. If that site is no longer available, the entire turtle colony becomes extinct.

With its length of 6,650 kilometers (4,130 mi.), the Nile is the longest river on Earth. Since primordial times, it has washed mud into the Mediterranean, forming an extensive delta reaching over 155 kilometers (96 mi.) from Alexandria to Port Said. Previously, the mud consisted mainly of fine-grained silt from the Ethiopian Plateau in Central Africa, one of the most fertile soils on the continent.

Since the completion of the Aswan dam in 1965, however, the ecosystem of the eastern Mediterranean has changed. The nutritious Nile water is no longer washed into the sea, leading to a breakdown in the once prospering sardine fishing industry. Likewise, the northern part of the Suez Canal is no longer supplied with fresh water from the Nile, preventing more than 120 new animal and plant species from migrating into the Mediterranean.

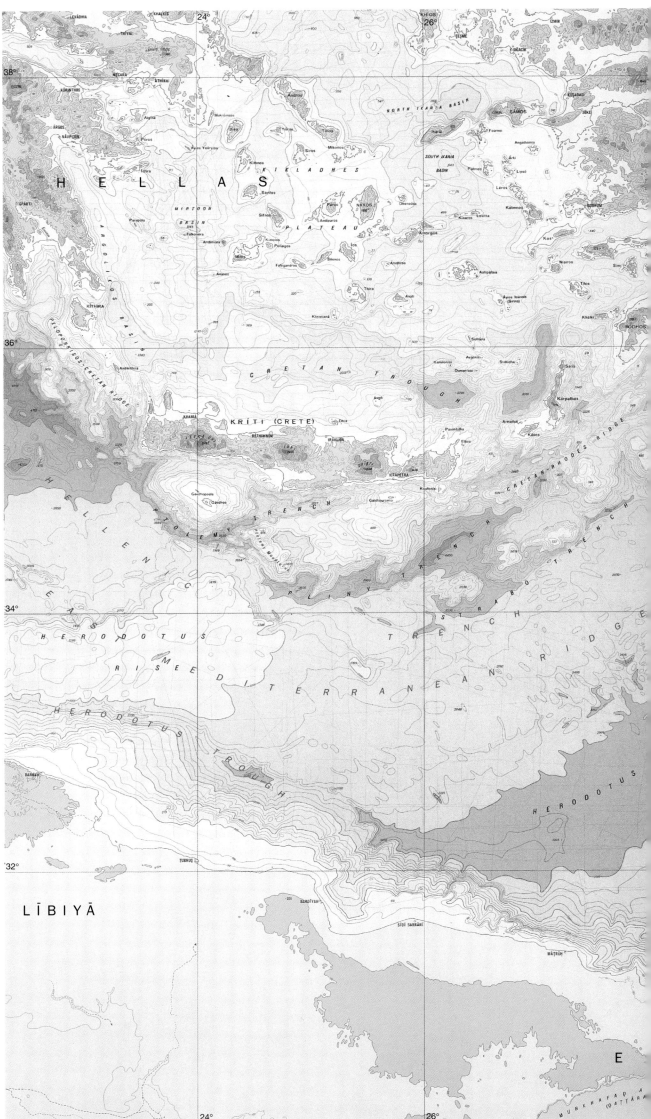

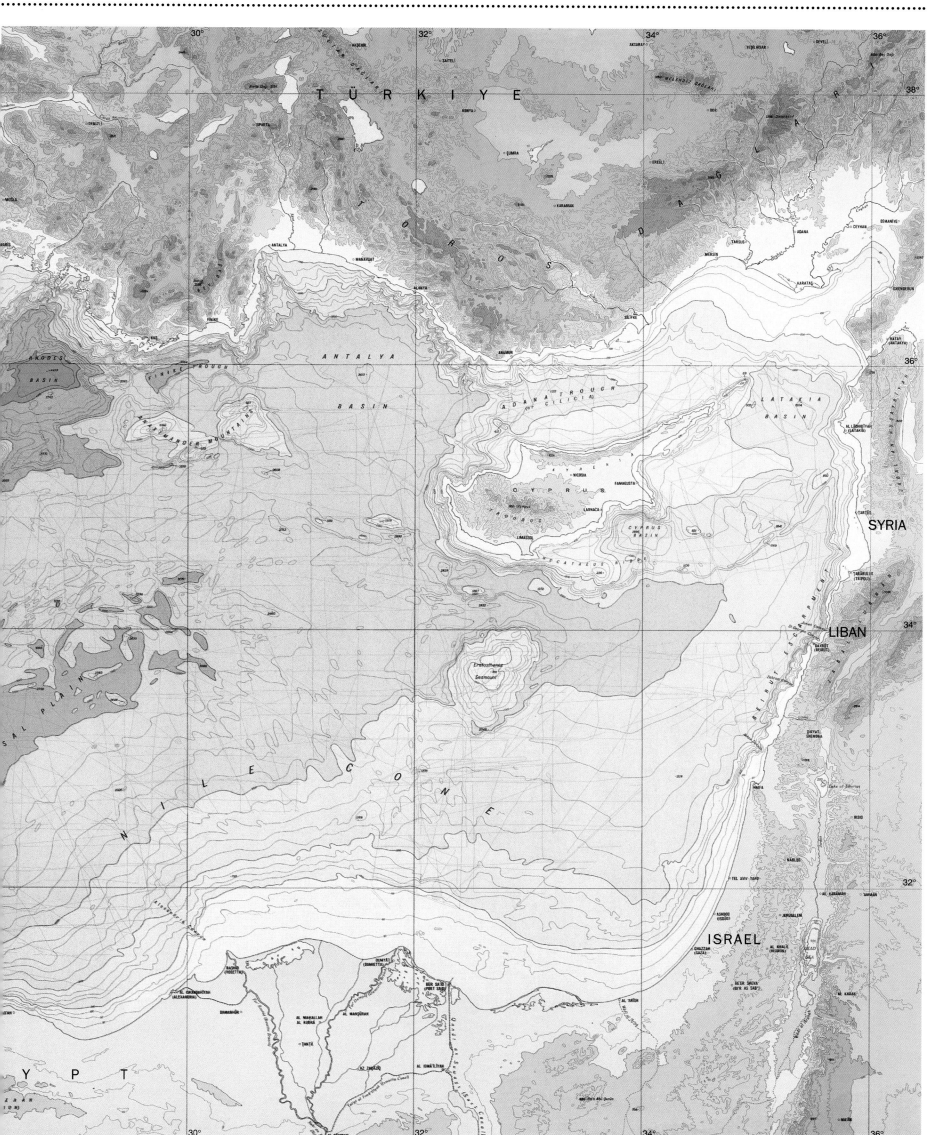

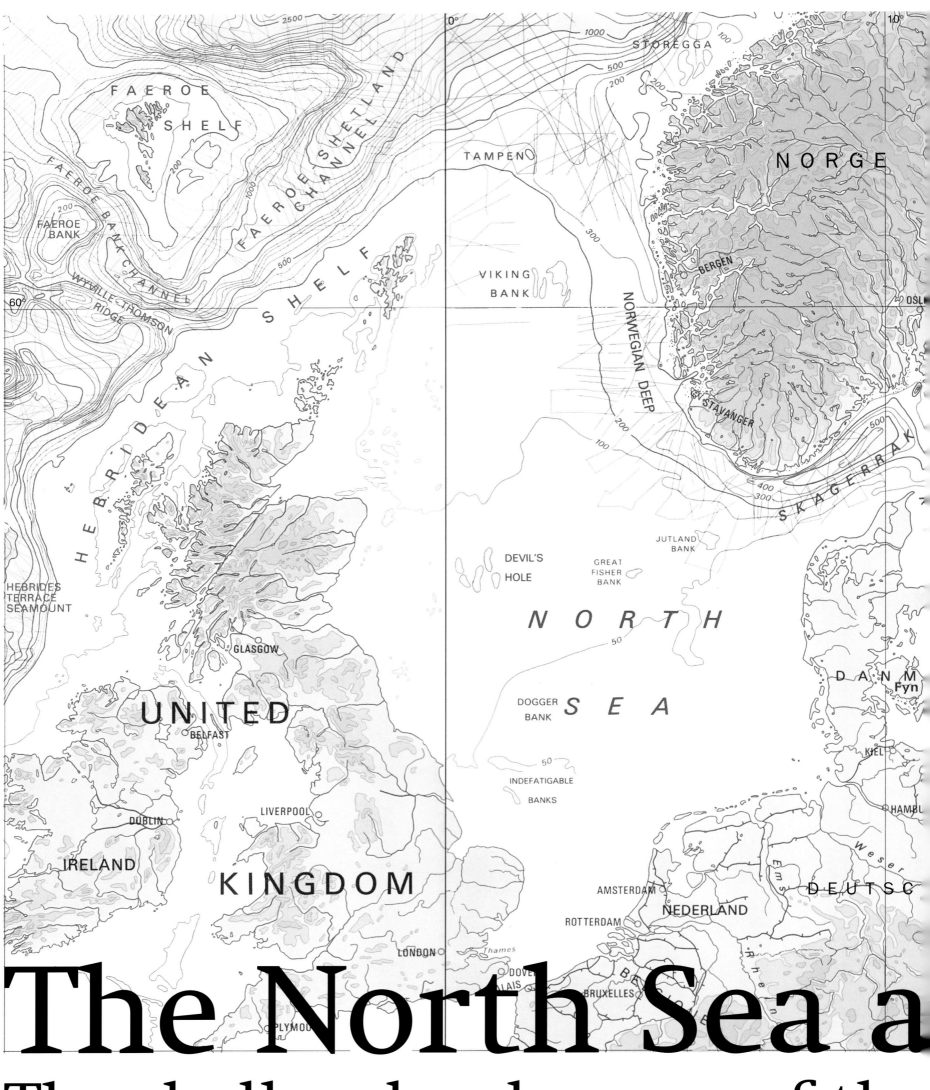

The North Sea a

The shallow border seas of the

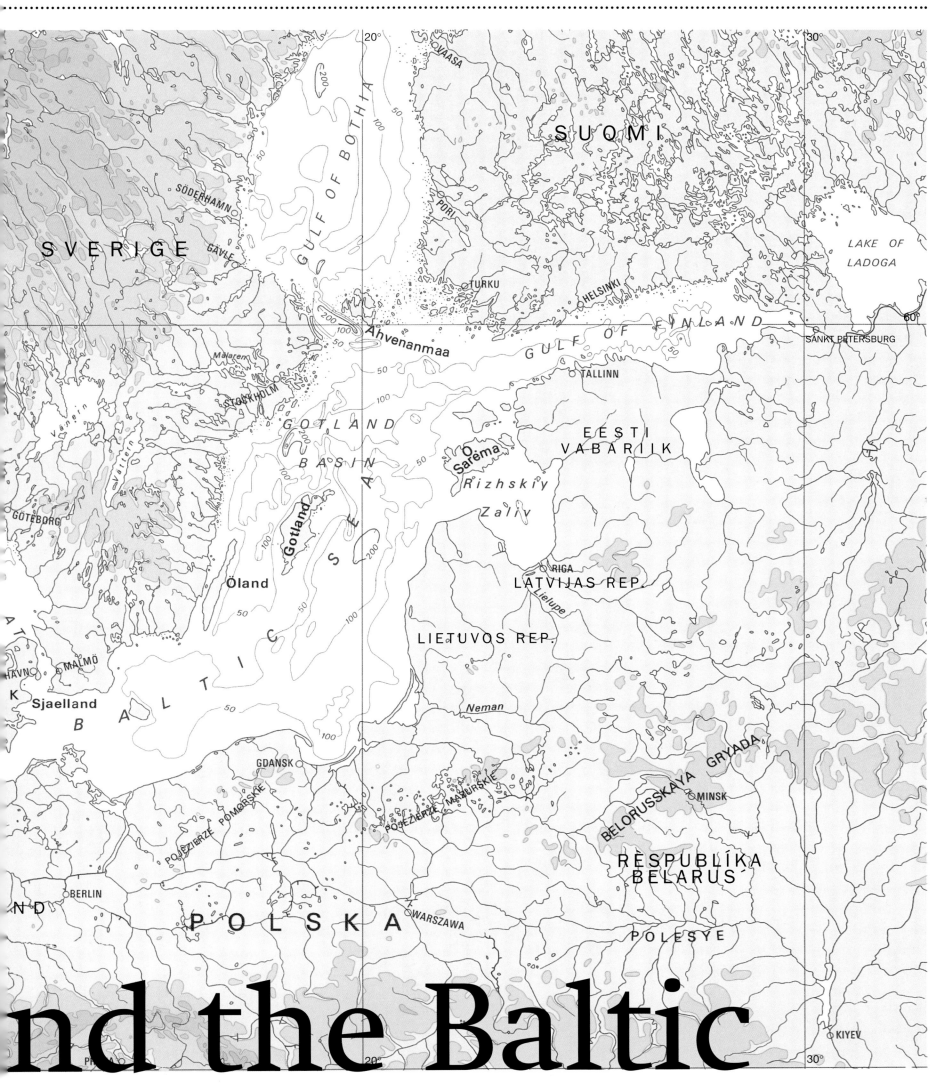

SVERIGE

SUOMI

GULF OF BOTHIA

SÖDERHAMN

GÄVLE

LAKE OF
LADOGA

VAASA

PORI

TURKU

HELSINKI

GULF OF FINLAND

60°

SANKT PETERSBURG

Ahvenanmaa

Mälaren

STOCKHOLM

Vättern

TALLINN

GOTLAND

BASIN

EESTI
VABARIIK

O.
Saréma

Rizhskiy

Zaliv

Vänern

BALTIC SEA

GÖTEBORG

Gotland

Öland

RIGA

LATVIJAS REP.

Lielupe

LIETUVOS REP.

HAVN

MALMÖ

Sjaelland

BALTIC

Neman

B

GDANSK

POJEZIERZE POMORSKIE

POJEZIERZE MAZURSKIE

BELORUSSKAYA GRYADA

MINSK

RÈSPUBLÍKA
BELARUS

BERLIN

ND

POLSKA

WARSZAWA

POLESYE

KIYEV

20°

30°

nd the Baltic

Atlantic

When the North Sea was formed

●●● When the ice receded during the last ice age 10,000 to 15,000 years ago, the southern part of the North Sea was dry land. Many of the modern sea bed formations, such as the Dogger Bank, are relics of that era. About 9,000 years ago, the coastline corresponded roughly to a line between the mouth of the Humber River in England and the Eiderstedt peninsula in the German land of Schleswig-Holstein.

Trawl nets are still bringing up mammal bones on the Dogger Bank that verify this date. When the water level rose and the North Sea Basin sagged some 7,000 to 8,000 years ago, the Dogger Bank became an island. On the island numerous species of animals sought refuge before the rising floods, eventually drowning along with the sand bank. Today, the Dogger Bank lies 13 meters (43 ft.) below sea level. The water depth of the North Sea is, on average, 40 meters (130 ft.), but can drop to 200 meters (660 ft.) in some places.

The southern connection between the North Sea and the Atlantic – the Strait of Dover, also called the English Channel – was formed only about 4,000 years ago. Today, 5,000 cubic kilometers (1,200 cu. mi.) of Atlantic water crosses it each year on the way to the southern North Sea.

The mud flats – Wadden Sea – constitute an ecologically unique amphibian landscape. In their current form, they are just a couple of centuries old. The islands and sandbanks have been continually shaped and modified by the waves and tidal currents over the years.

The tides are a result of the correlation between the attractive force of the moon and the centrifugal force of the Earth. The larger the water mass, the higher the tidal waves that it produces. The North Sea is much too small to accumulate its own tidal wave.

By contrast, the North Sea tides are accessory tides that depend on the situation in the Atlantic Ocean. One part of the tidal wave rolls in directly from the Atlantic through the Strait of Dover into the North Sea, while the other part comes from the north. The latter moves counterclockwise along the coasts and arrives with a 12-hour delay in the German Bay, where it produces a medium-sized tidal range of about 3 meters (10 ft.).

When the crest of a wave collides with that of another wave, the tides of both add up, as is the case in the German Bay. If, however, the crest of one wave collides with the trough of another, the tides neutralize each other. The combination of these two waves results in varying heights of low and high tide along the North Sea coast.

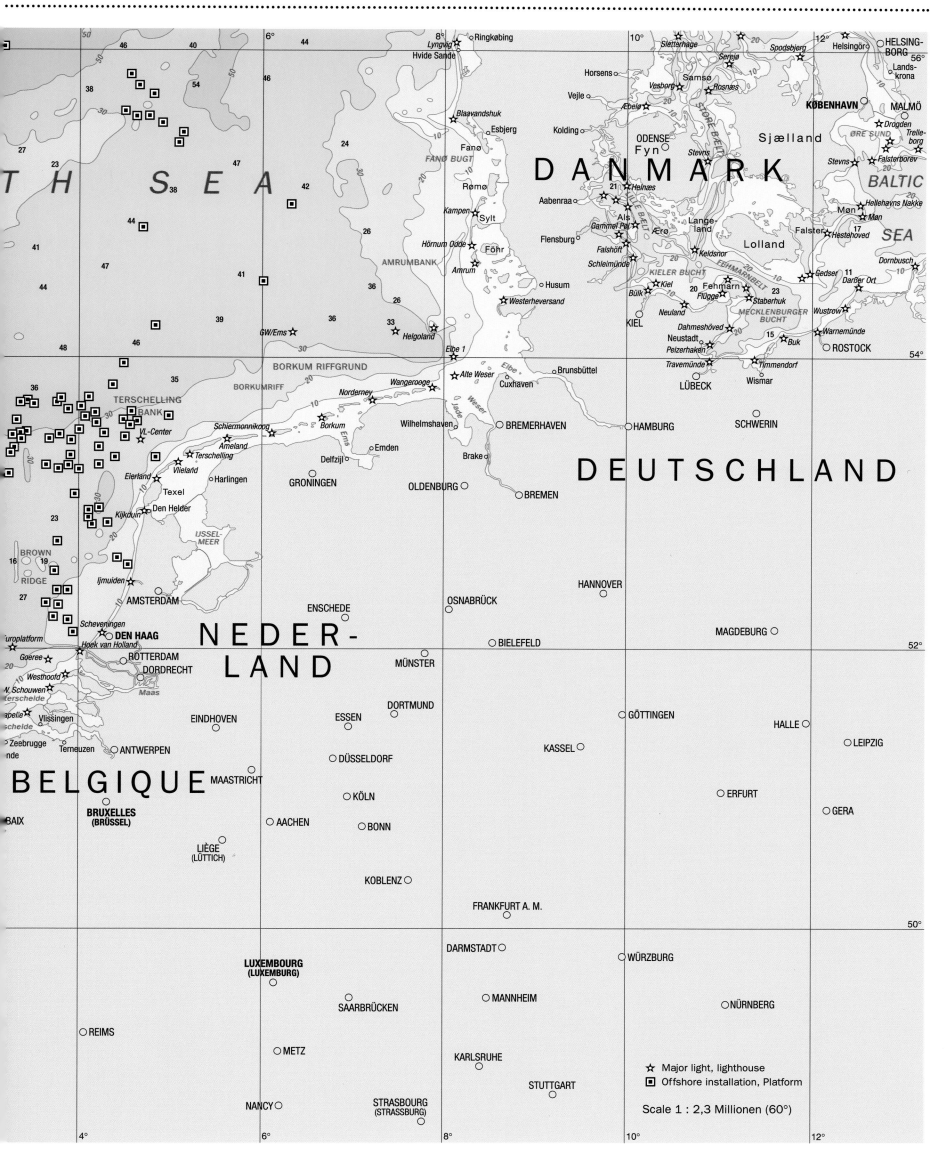

TH SEA

S E A

23

27

38

47

42

41

44

47

41

44

48

46

36

35

TERSCHELLING BANK

VL-Center

Ameland

Terschelling

Eierland

Texel

Kijkduin

Den Helder

23

BROWN

RIDGE

16 19

27

Europlatform

Scheveningen

Goeree

Westhoofd

N. Schouwen

terschelde

Capelle

schelde

Vlissingen

Zeebrugge

nde

Terneuzen

BAIX

Ringkøbing

Lyngvig

Hvide Sande

Blaavandshuk

Esbjerg

Fanø

FANØ BUGT

Rømø

Kampen

Sylt

Hörnum Odde

Amrum

AMRUMBANK

Husum

Westerheversand

GW/Ems

Helgoland

Elbe 1

BORKUM RIFFGRUND

BORKUMRIFF

Norderney

Wangerooge

Schiermonnikoog

Borkum

Vlieland

Harlingen

Ems

Delfzijl

Emden

IJSSEL-
MEER

Groningen

Amsterdam

Den Haag

Rotterdam

Dordrecht

Maas

Antwerpen

Maastricht

N E D E R -
L A N D

Enschede

Osnabrück

Bielefeld

Münster

Dortmund

Essen

Düsseldorf

Köln

Aachen

Bonn

Liège
(Lüttich)

Koblenz

Frankfurt a. M.

Hoek van Holland

Wilhelmshaven

Jade

Weser

Alte Weser

Cuxhaven

Brunsbüttel

Bremerhaven

Brake

Oldenburg

Bremen

Hamburg

Schwerin

Hannover

Magdeburg

Göttingen

Halle

Kassel

Leipzig

Erfurt

Gera

D E U T S C H L A N D

B E L G I Q U E

Bruxelles
(Brüssel)

Reims

Metz

Nancy

Luxembourg
(Luxemburg)

Saarbrücken

Strasbourg
(Strassburg)

Darmstadt

Mannheim

Karlsruhe

Stuttgart

Würzburg

Nürnberg

D A N M A R K

Sletterhage

Horsens

Vejle

Vesborg

Æbelø

Kolding

Odense

Fyn

Stevns

Aabenraa

Flensburg

Helnæs

Als

Gammel Pol

Falshöft

Schleimünde

Bülk

Kiel

Neuland

KIEL

Kieler Bucht

Fehmarn

Flügge

Dahmeshöved

Neustadt

Pelzerhaken

Travemünde

Lübeck

Wismar

Timmendorf

Spodsbjerg

Samsø

Serejø

Rosnæs

Lange-
land

Ærø

Lolland

Keldsnor

Staberhuk

Buk

Warnemünde

Rostock

Helsingör

HELSING-
BORG

Lands-
krona

KØBENHAVN

MALMÖ

Drogden

Trelle-
borg

ØRE SUND

Sjælland

Falsterborev

Stevns

Møn

Hellehavns Nakke

Møn

Falster

Hestehoved

Gedser

Darßer Ort

Dornbusch

Wustrow

BALTIC

SEA

MECKLENBURGER
BUCHT

FEHMARNBELT

STORE BÆLT

LILLE BÆLT

★ Major light, lighthouse
■ Offshore installation, Platform

Scale 1 : 2,3 Millionen (60°)

Gateway to the North Atlantic

● ● ● The broad passage between the Shetland Islands and Norway is the North Sea's main inlet for Atlantic water. Each year, some 40,000 cubic kilometers (10,000 cu. mi.) flow into the shallow shelf sea as branches of the relatively warm North Atlantic Current flow northward in the west of England and Ireland.

One-quarter of this water flows in between the Orkney and Shetland Islands, while about 1,000 cubic kilometers (240 cu. mi.) squeeze through the Pentland Firth. The only exiting current flows northward directly off the Norwegian coast in the vicinity of the Norwegian Trough, back to the North Atlantic Current, which later converges with the Norway Current.

The currents within the North Sea are a complicated matter. Variations of the North Atlantic currents influence them to the same extent as climatic and meteorological variations or the soil profile. On the whole, the water masses follow a clockwise circular current which carries them southward off the English east coast and northward off Jutland. North of Jutland, on the southern side of the Skagerrak, one branch of the current drains into the Baltic Sea where it meets its outlet in the north.

From April to September, the surface water heats up. In large parts of the North Sea, a temperature transition layer develops at a depth of 30 meters to 40 meters (100 ft. to 130 ft.). It separates the cover layer from the cooler deep water and prevents any exchange of water and nutrients between the two. The wind merely mixes the top layer, providing a thorough oxygenation and blending of nutrients and plankton organisms.

During the course of summer, however, most of the nutrients are lost as dead plankton and feces sink through the transition layer to the bottom water. The nutrients are thus unavailable for the plankton organisms, which are slowed down in their growth. In the deep water, however, the organic matter is decomposed by bacteria which use up the available oxygen in the process. Nutrients which are missing at the surface thus accumulate at the bottom where there is no flora.

Finally in autumn, when the surface water cools down and storms rage over the sea, the transition layer collapses and releases the nutrients along the entire water column. They can, however, be used only after the plankton algae receive sufficient light and warmth to bloom again during the next spring.

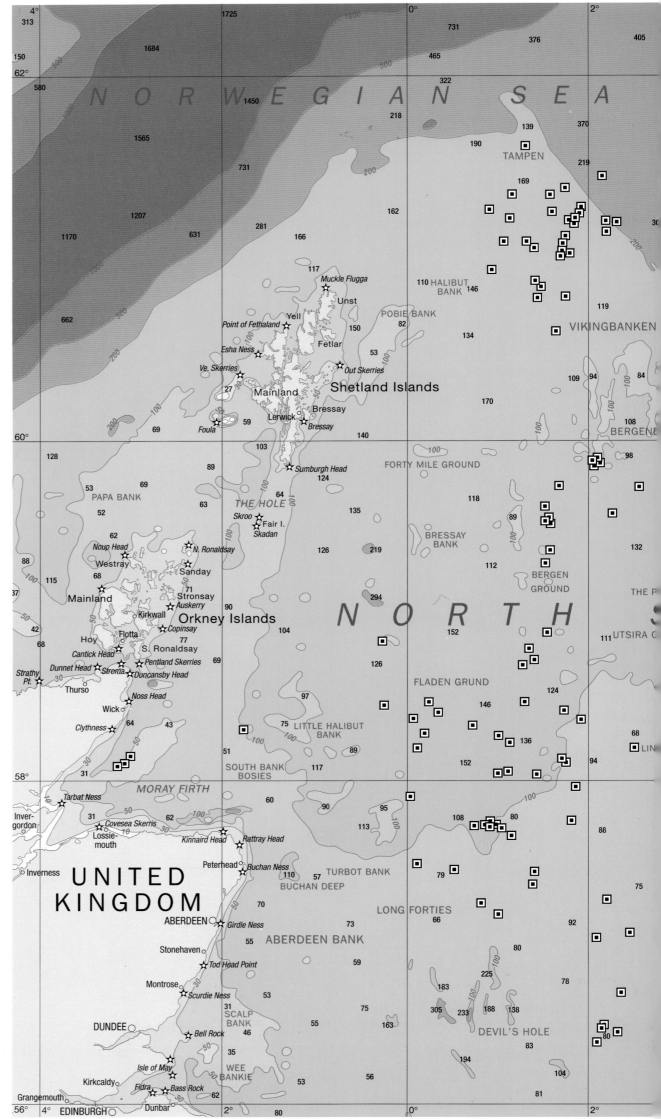

☆ Major light, lighthouse
▣ Offshore installation, Platform

Scale 1 : 2,3 Millionen (60°)

NORGE

STOR-FJORD

NORD-FJORD

Svinöy

Kråkenes

Måløy

Kvanhovden

Ytterøyane · Florö

SOGNEFJORDEN

Utvær

Holmengrå

Hellisöy

HARDANGER-FJORDEN

BERGEN

Sotra

Marstein

Slåtterøy · Stord

Bömlo

Haugesund

Utsira

Karmöy

BOKNA-FJORDEN

Kvitsöy

STAVANGER

Feistein · Sandnes

Obrestad

Eigerøy · Egersund

Flekkefjord

Farsund

Lista

Lindesnes · Ryvingen

EIGERSUNDS-BANK

REVET

OSLO

Drammen

Horten   Moss

Tönsberg

OSLOFJORDEN

Porsgrunn   Sandefjord   Fulehuk   Frederikstad
Larvik   Halden

Færder   Torbjörnskjär   Strömstad
Svenner

Jomfruland   248   Ursholmen

Risör   64
                         Väderöbod
Arendal   92
        Torungen   Hällö

Kristiansand   596   Hättan
                 445   Måseskär   Orust
Mandal   700
        Oksöy   SKAGERRAK   222
            619

SVERIGE

Vänern

Uddevalla   Vänersborg

Kungälv

Hätteberget   77   GÖTEBORG

Vinga

Trubaduren

Tistlarna

Nidingen

Fladen

NORSKERENNA

427
306
214
226
150
120
75
58

KATTEGAT

119   26   16

Hirtshals

Frederikshavn

Skagen

Hirsholm
N-Rönner

Læsö Repde

Læsö

Hals Barre

AALBORG

JAMMER-BUGTEN

LIMFJORDEN

Hanstholm

Lodbjerg

Mors

Thyborøn

Udbyhøj

Gjerrild

Randers

Grenaa   Fornæs

ÅLBORG BUGT

Anholt

Hesselø

DANMARK   ÅRHUS   Hjelm

Slettenhage

Lyngvig

Hvide Sande   Ringkøbing   Sjællands RevN

Spodsbjerg

Varberg
Subbeberget

Morups Tånge
Falkenberg

Halmstad

Tylögrund

Hallands Väderö

Kullen

Nakkehoved   Svinbådan

Helsingör   HELSING-BORG

JUTLAND BANK

Bovbjerg

LITTLE FISHER BANK

GREAT FISHER BANK

Ribgkøbing

The oily sea off Norway

●●● The modern face of the North Sea emerged only after the end of the last ice age some 10,000 to 15,000 years ago. The shelf sea, however, existed well before that era. Approximately 180 million years ago, the North Sea was already flooded. Since then, the ocean has receded time and time again, only to move forward a couple of million years later.

The rivers on both sides of the old shelf sea carried mud and the remains of animals and plants into the basin until a sediment layer 6 kilometers (3.7 mi.) thick developed over the course of millions of years. While layer deposited on layer, the pressure on the sediments at the bottom increased and compressed the material to sandstone and lime. At the same time, the temperatures in the depth rose, creating conditions favorable to the transformation of organic remains into crude oil and natural gas, some of which escaped through the porous rock to the sea floor and into the sea water.

The Norwegian bishop Erich Pontippidan noted as early as 1752 that the North Sea appeared to be oily in some places, suggesting that the sea, like the Earth, emanated "oily rivers." It was only 207 years later, in 1959, that oil companies detected an enormous gas field near the Dutch town of Groningen. It was soon discovered that parts of the North Sea Shelf contained huge deposits of gas and crude oil. For more than 10 years, geologists searched in vain for further oil fields. In 1969, they finally found oil in the Norwegian sector of the central North Sea at a depth of more than 1,600 meters (5,250 ft.).

In large parts of the North Sea floor, impermeable rock formations block the rise of oil and gases from the deeper layers of the sea bottom. Huge deposits could therefore continue to develop over the course of millions of years.

After Saudi Arabia, Norway possesses the second largest deposits of crude oil. The largest oil well discovered so far in the North Sea is the Statfjord Field in the Norwegian sector, merely a couple of miles away from the less productive Brent Field in the English sector.

The largest gas deposit is located below the Norwegian Troll Field in the middle of the Norwegian Trough, where the sea is 350 meters (1,150 ft.) deep. When the deposit was discovered in 1979, there was no technology available to collect gas from these depths in the rough North Sea conditions. In the course of a 10-year project by the Norwegians, dubbed "the Man on the Moon," engineers developed the heaviest floating platform (1.2 million tons) ever built. Ten enormous anchors hold the platform in place 90 kilometers (56 mi.) off Bergen. Production began in the autumn of 1996.

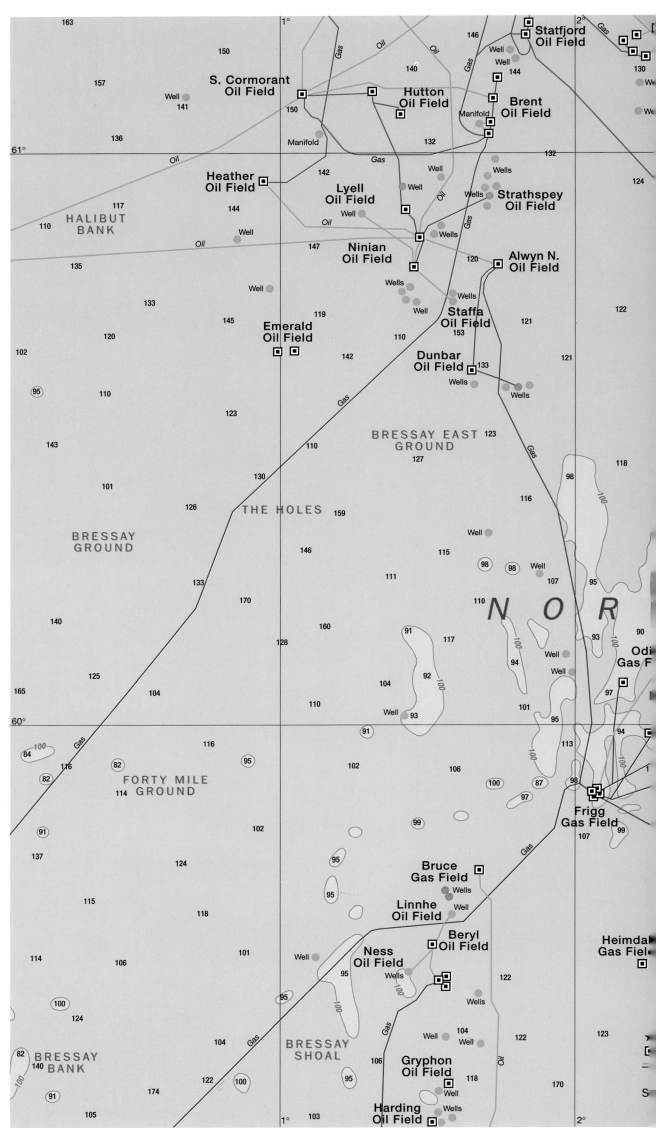

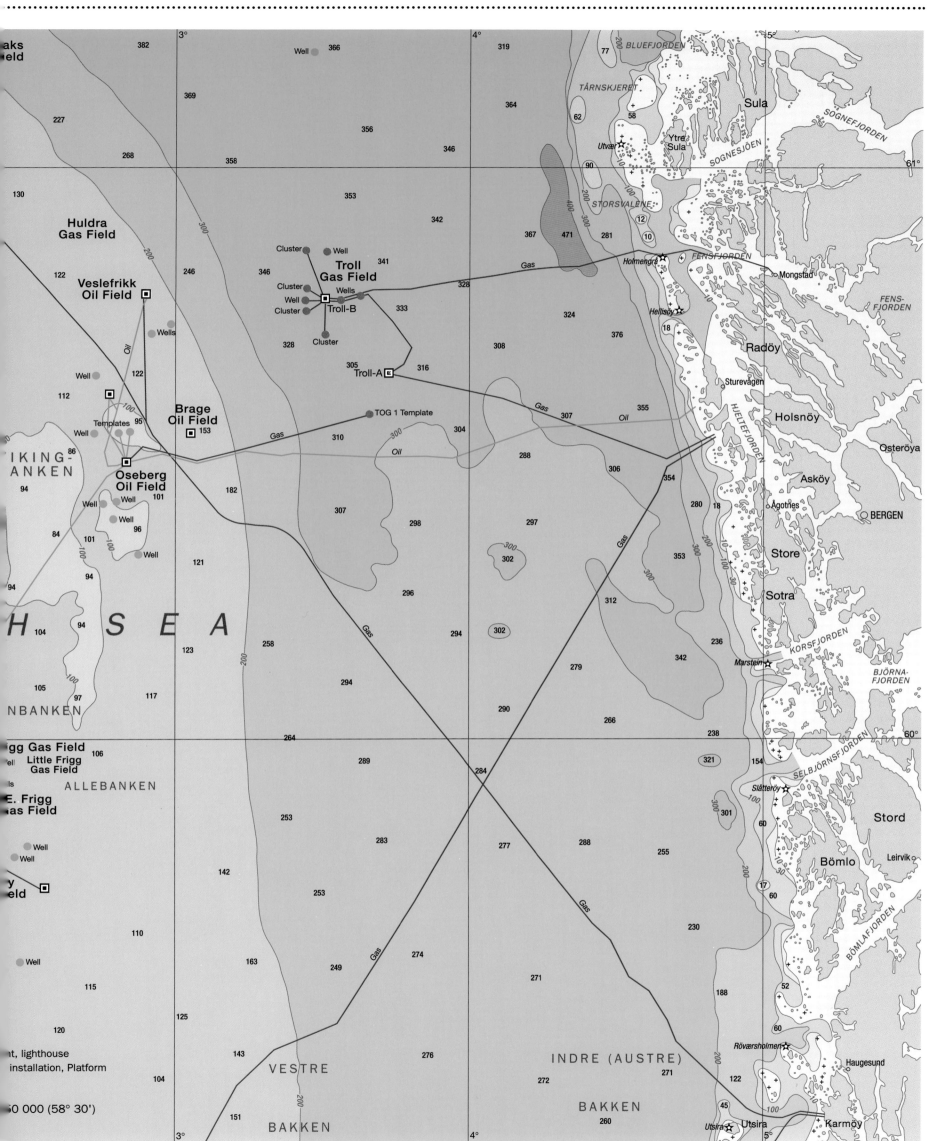

3°

Well 366

382

319

Well

BLUEFJORDEN

77

TÅRNSKJERET

Sula

369

364

62

58

Ytre
Sula

SOGNEFJORDEN

227

356

Utvær

268

358

346

90

SOGNESJØEN

61°

130

353

STORSVALENE

12

471

281

Huldra
Gas Field

342

367

10

Cluster

Well

Gas

Holmengrå

FENSFJORDEN

Mongstad

122

Veslefrikk
Oil Field

246

346

Troll
Gas Field

341

328

Wells

Troll-B

FENS-
FJORDEN

Cluster

Wells

Well

Cluster

333

324

Hellisøy

18

376

Radöy

Wells

Cluster

328

308

Sturevågen

Well

122

305

Troll-A

316

Holsnöy

112

Brage
Oil Field

TOG 1 Template

Gas

307

355

Österöya

Templates

95

Gas

310

Oil

304

Oil

Asköy

Well

86

153

288

306

Ågotnes

BERGEN

IKING-
ANKEN

94

182

354

280

18

Well

Well

101

307

298

297

Store

84

96

353

101

Well

302

296

Sotra

94

121

302

312

KORSFJORDEN

SEA

94

258

294

236

Marstein

123

294

279

BJÖRNA-
FJORDEN

104

105

290

266

238

60°

97

117

NBANKEN

264

321

154

gg Gas Field

106

289

284

SELBJÖRNSFJORDEN

Little Frigg
Gas Field

Slätterøy

ALLEBANKEN

253

283

277

288

255

301

Stord

E. Frigg
as Field

142

Bömlo

Leirvik

Well

253

60

Well

110

163

249

274

271

188

52

Well

115

125

Utsira

BAKKEN

60

120

143

276

INDRE (AUSTRE)

122

t, lighthouse

Haugesund

installation, Platform

104

272

271

45

50 000 (58° 30')

151

VESTRE

BAKKEN

260

Utsira

Utsira

Karmöy

3°

BAKKEN

4°

5°

Between sea and land

● ● ● The amphibian landscape of the mud flats – the Wadden Sea – extends to a width of 40 kilometers (25 mi.) off the Dutch, German, and south Danish coastline. The tides that rise and fall every 12 hours and 25 minutes have shaped this transition zone between land and sea.

Where the tidal range – the differential in sea levels between high and low tide – exceeds 1.35 meters (4.43 ft.), the closed dune coast in the north and west merges into a stretch of tidal mud flats and barrier islands called the West, East, and North Frisian Islands. Towards the interior of the German Bay, the islands become smaller and smaller. Where the tidal range exceeds 2.90 meters (9.5 ft.), there are no islands at all.

The landscape has been shaped, above all, by storm tides – although humans have reinforced their effects so thoroughly that large parts of the mainland have been lost to the sea. Diking and draining, the once widespread peat cutting, and the channeling of rivers have all contributed to the currents changing direction, or the more frequent or severe onslaught of storm tides.

The island barrier is still relatively young, although the first sandbanks were formed by the waves just after the last ice age. As soon as the islands emerged from the water, the wind began accumulating sand dunes. In their shadow, salt flats developed on the mainland flanks of the islands. Most of the dunes are just 600 to 900 years old. In North Friesian, they were still growing in the 17th century.

In the meantime, a dense thicket of vegetation has covered the islands' dunes, and the seaside bottom of the dunes is often protected by nets and walls. This means that the sand hills cannot be renewed, and no more wind-borne sand can reach the mud flats to solidify the mainland flanks. Nutrients are being leached out of old dunes, where the vegetation is becoming thinner and more vulnerable. After the Second World War, tourists walked through the dunes and damaged the vegetation so massively that the wind was able to carve vast troughs into the sand, thereby turning large dunes into irregular landscapes of many small sand hills.

One exception to this is the island of Helgoland, located in the open sea some 70 kilometers (43 mi.) off the German coast. The island is a sandstone block rising 61 meters (200 ft.) above sea level, consisting of age-old compressed sediments of ancient seas – a salt dome below the North Sea pushed upward 222 million years ago.

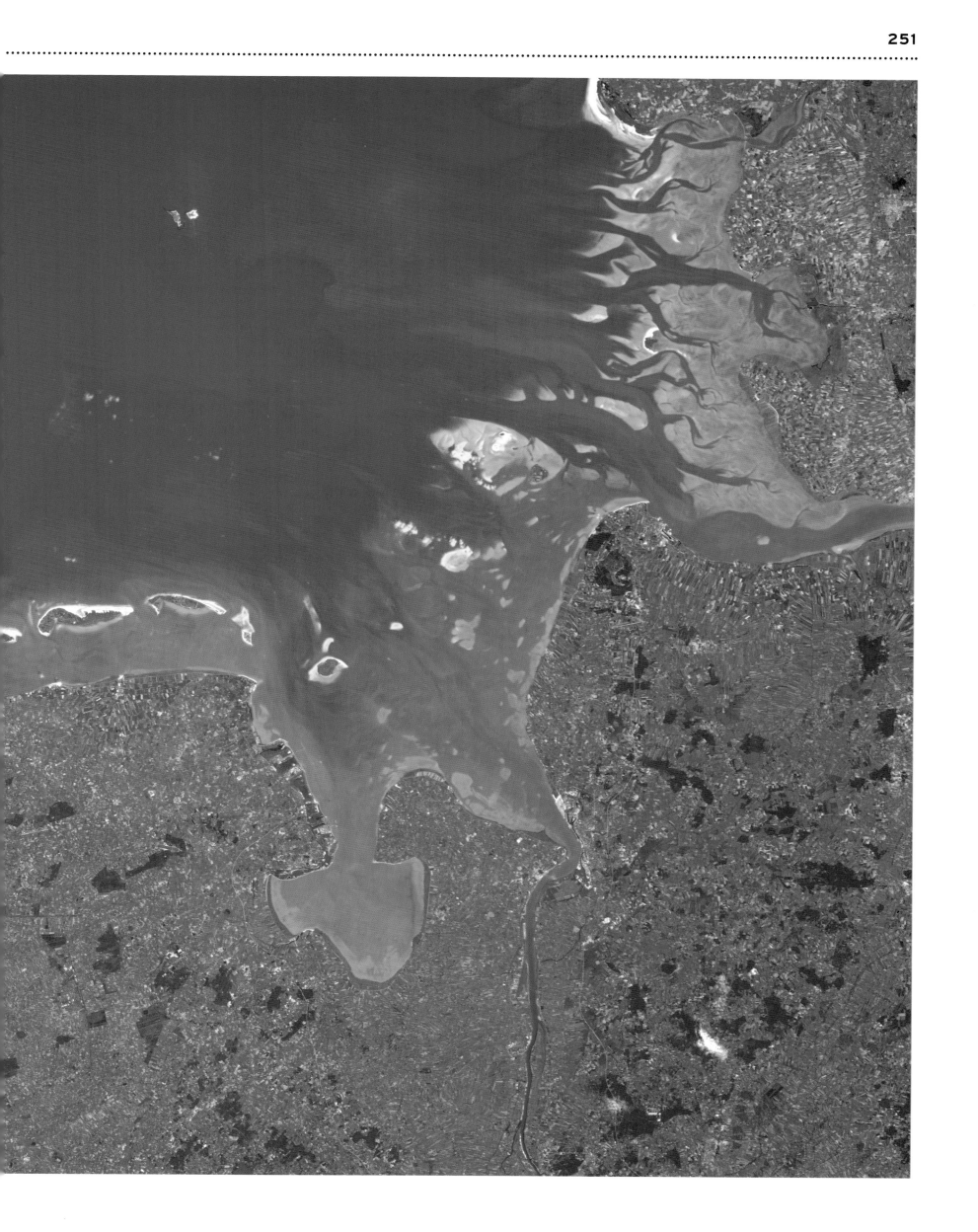

The narrow passage to the Baltic

●●● The south-western basins of the Baltic Sea – the Belt Sea and the Arkona Basin – are of vital importance for the water exchange between the North Sea and the Baltic Sea. They also contain important sea routes.

As old shipping lanes were no longer able to cope with increasingly complicated economic relationships, the 16-kilometer (10-mi.) long Sound connection was established between Denmark and Sweden in the year 2000. South of Copenhagen, a 3.5-kilometer (2.2-mi.) long tunnel leads to a 4-kilometer (2.5-mi.) long artificial island south of Saltholm. From there, the almost 8-kilometer (5-mi.) long bridge extends over The Sound to Lernacken near Malmö. Its center part, a viaduct of more than 1 kilometer (0.62 mi.), is suspended more than 60 meters (196 ft.). above The Sound on two pillars almost 200 meters (656 ft.) high. The construction of this bridge was preceded by one of the most meticulous environment impact statements ever made, as this major traffic artery is on a site that is vital to the water balance of the Baltic Sea and its entire ecosystem.

The Sound connects the Arkona Sea with the Kattegat, one of the two western basins of the Baltic Sea. The Great Belt joins the two halves of the Belt Sea which surround the island of Fyn. At the surface of the Sound and the Great Belt, low-saline water flows towards the Kattegat at a rate of some 1,370 cubic kilometers (329 cu. mi.) per year.

High-saline North Sea water flows along the bottom of the Baltic Sea. The 18-meter (59-ft.) deep Darss Rise between Falster and Darss, and the 7-meter (23-ft.) deep Drogden Rise between Amager and Sweden are the major obstacles hindering further spreading. Once every several years, the weather conditions are such that the ocean water spills over the rises and plunges deep into the Baltic Sea.

Special weather conditions on the coasts of the Belt Sea can induce storm tides with waves accumulating to 2 meters (6.6 ft.) and more. Storms blowing from the southeast for several days drive the waters of the Belt Sea eastward until the water level drops and the basin is refilled with North Sea water. When the storm subsides, the water masses accumulated in the east return to the Belt Sea. As the new water cannot flow back immediately, it dams up in front of the coastlines.

If, however, the storm moves further to the east, the wind shifts to the northeast and pushes even more water from the northeastern Baltic Sea into the Belt Sea, thus triggering even more violent storm tides.

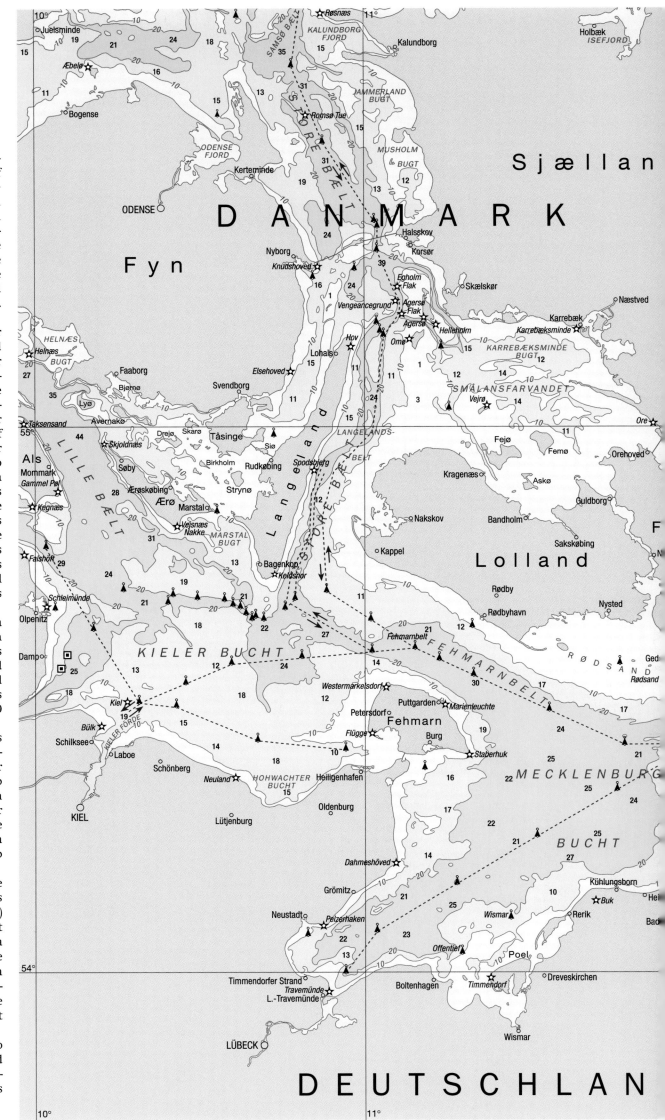

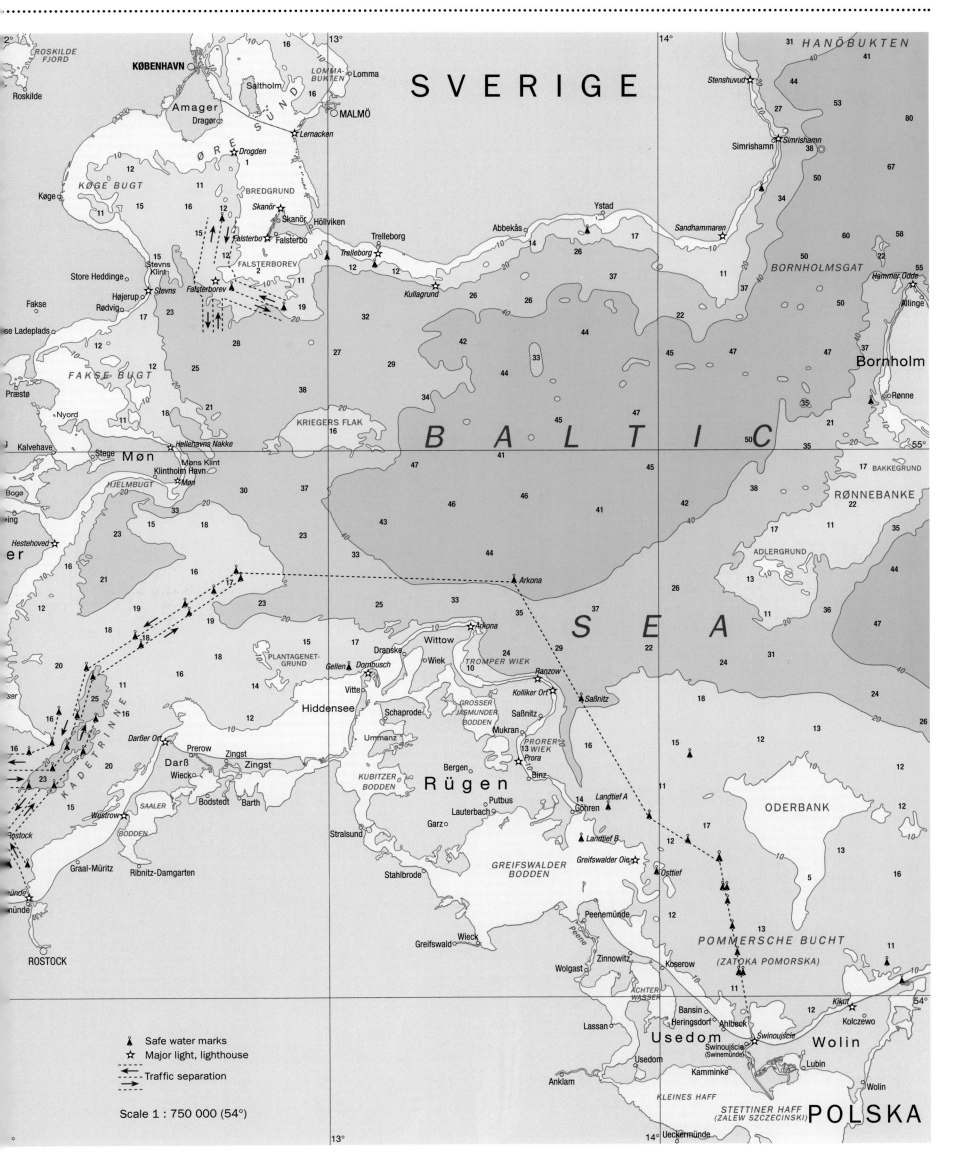

ROSKILDE
FJORD

KØBENHAVN

Saltholm

Amager
Dragør

Roskilde

Lernacken

MALMÖ

ØRESUND

Drogden
1

KØGE BUGT

Skanör

BREDGRUND

Køge

Skanör
Falsterbo   Höllviken

Falsterbo   Falsterbo

Store Heddinge
Stevns Klint

FALSTERBOREV
2

Trelleborg

Trelleborg

Ystad

Abbekås

SVERIGE

LOMMA-
BUKTEN   Lomma

Stenshuvud

Simrishamn   Simrishamn

Sandhammaren

HANÖBUKTEN

BORNHOLMSGAT

Hammer Odde
Allinge

Fakse

Højerup   Stevns
Rødvig

se Ladeplads

Præstø

Nyord

Kalvehave

Stege   Møn

Falsterborev

Kullagrund

Helnæhavns Nakke

Møns Klint
Klintholm Havn   Møn

FAKSE BUGT

KRIEGERS FLAK

BALTIC

Bornholm

Rønne

RØNNEBANKE

ADLERGRUND

BAKKEGRUND

Bogø

Hestehoved

HJELMBUGT

Arkona

Arkona

SEA

er

Wittow

Dranske   TROMPER WIEK

Wiek

Gellen   Dornbusch

Ranzow

PLANTAGENET-
GRUND

Vitte

Kolliker Ort

Saßnitz

Saßnitz

Hiddensee

Schaprode

GROSSER
JASMUNDER
BODDEN

Mukran

PRORER
WIEK   Prora

ODERBANK

Darßer Ort

Prerow   Zingst

Darß   Zingst
Wieck

Ummanz

KUBITZER
BODDEN

Bergen

Rügen   Binz

Putbus

Prora

KADETRINNE

SAALER
BODDEN

Wustrow

Bodstedt   Barth

Lauterbach

Garz

Göhren

Landtief A

Graal-Müritz

Stralsund

GREIFSWALDER
BODDEN

Greifswalder Oie

Landtief B

Osttief

Ribnitz-Damgarten

Stahlbrode

ROSTOCK

Peenemünde

POMMERSCHE BUCHT
(ZATOKA POMORSKA)

Greifswald   Wieck

Peene

Zinnowitz

Koserow

Wolgast

Kikut   Kolczewo

Bansin
Heringsdorf   Ahlbeck

ACHTER
WASSER

Lassan

Usedom   Wolin

Swinoujscie

Swinoujscie
(Swinemünde)

Lubin

Kamminke

Anklam

KLEINES HAFF

STETTINER HAFF
(ZALEW SZCZECINSKI)   POLSKA

Uckermünde

⚓ Safe water marks

☆ Major light, lighthouse

← → Traffic separation

Scale 1 : 750 000 (54°)

The Baltic's brackish water

● ● ● Less than 15,000 years ago, the Baltic Sea was covered by an ice shield 3,000 meters (9,843 ft.) thick. When the glacier receded, a fresh water lake formed between the terminal moraines, the mountains, and the glacier. Ten thousand years ago, the ice receded to behind the mid-Sweden terminal moraines, while salt water from the Skagerrak flooded in over the broad connection line running through what is now Sweden. Within a space of only 750 years, the land, now freed of the weight of the ice, rose so sharply that this connection closed again and the Baltic Sea turned into a fresh water lake once more.

While the Scandinavian Shield rose further, more and more fresh water flooded into the Baltic Sea, at first draining via mid-Sweden. Later, a broad river in the south emptied its water into the North Sea. Some 7,000 years ago, the post-glacial sea level of the oceans had risen so much that the Belt Sea was flooded and the Baltic Sea became the Earth's largest sea of brackish water.

The salinity of the surface water ranges between 15 to 25 ppt in the southwest, while it reaches only 6 to 8 ppt in the central Baltic Sea, and hardly 2 ppt at the point where the Gulf of Bothnia and the Gulf of Finland end.

With an average depth of 52 meters (171 ft.), the Baltic Sea is quite shallow, although its sea floor is clearly divided into individual basins separated from each other by high rises. The deepest point (459 m/1,506 ft.) is located in the Landsort Deep between Gotska Sandön and the Swedish east coast.

A typical feature of the inland sea is the stability of the water layers. In winter, the central Baltic Sea is covered by a 60-meter (197-ft.) deep, low-saline, cold cover on top of the high-saline, warmer deep water. Under the influence of warmer temperatures, a further barrier forms in summer at a depth of 20 meters to 30 meters (66 ft. to 98 ft.) within the top layer, separating the warm surface water from the colder intermediate water which maintains its cool wintry temperature. These clearly outlined transition layers thoroughly reduce the deep water exchange. Once every couple of years, in certain weather conditions, high-saline, nutrient-rich North Sea water enters the bottom of the Baltic Sea. Most of the time, however, it remains in the southern basins and seldom reaches the central parts of the Baltic Sea.

As brackish water is not frequently found on our planet, evolutionary forces have developed only a few types of organisms adapted to that kind of habitat. Most of the plants and animals present in the Baltic Sea are marine species hardly able to survive in these conditions.

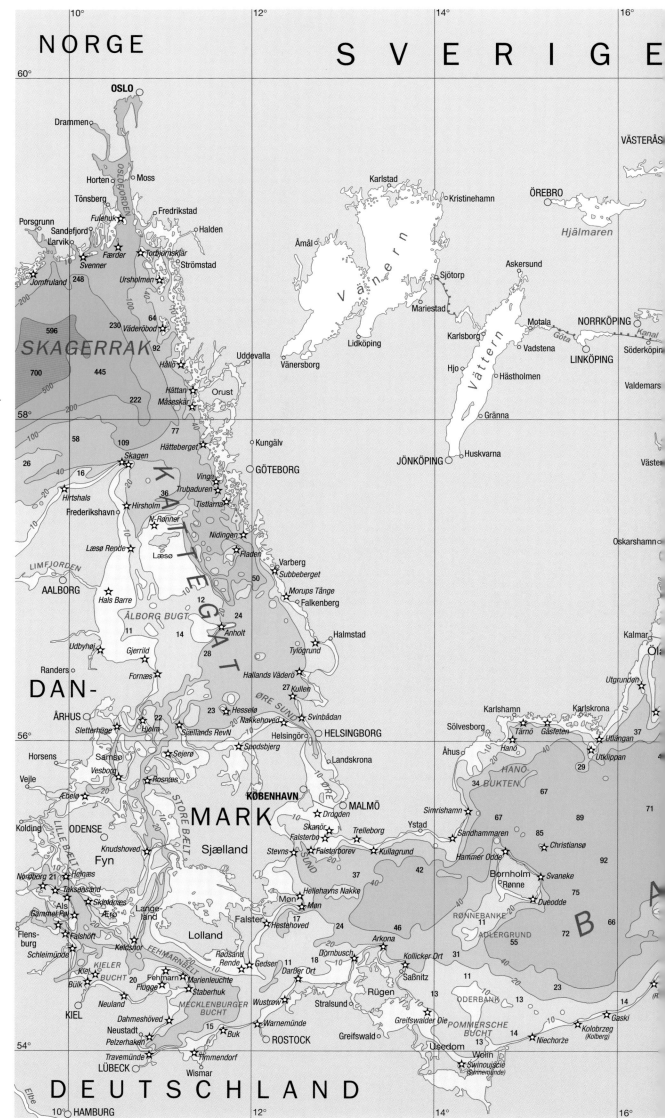

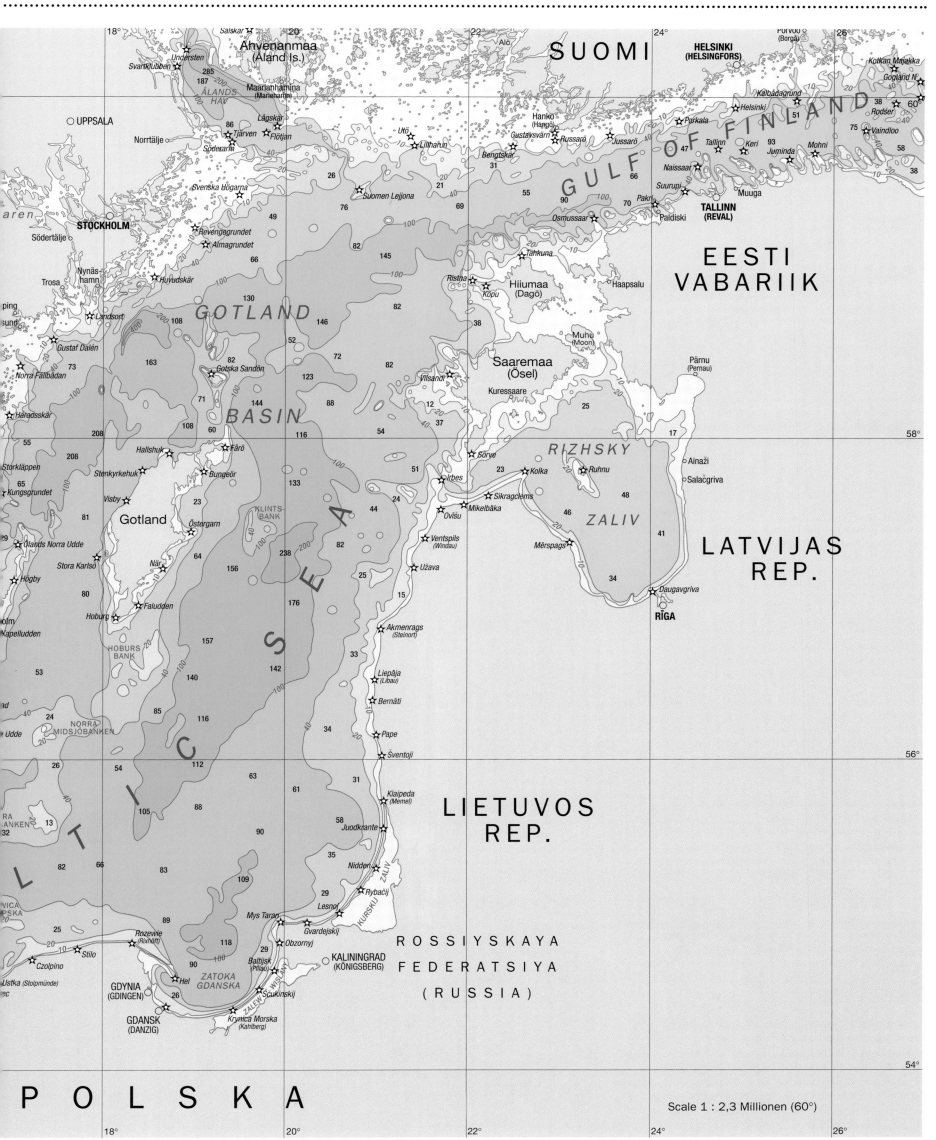

18°   20°   22°   24°   26°

S U O M I   HELSINKI
                      (HELSINGFORS)

Salskar ☆   Porvoo
                                          Alö   (Borgå)   Kotkan Majakka
Ahvenanmaa   Gogland N?
(Åland Is.)   38
Understen ☆   Kalbådagrund   Rödser
Svartklubben ☆   Helsinki   51   60°
285   Porkala ☆   75 Vaindloo
187   Hanko   Tallinn
ÅLANDS   Maarianhamina   (Hangö)   Russarö   Jussarö   Keri 93 Mohni 58
HAV   (Mariehamn)   Gustavsvärn ☆   ☆   ☆   ☆   Juminda
○ UPPSALA   Naissaar 38
86   Lågskär   Utö   Bengtskär   Suurupi 66 Muuga
Norrtälje ☆ ☆ Tjärven ☆ Flötjan   ☆ Lillharun   31   Osmussaar ☆ 90 70 Pakri TALLINN
Söderarm   Paldiski   (REVAL)
                    26   Suomen Lejjona   55
Svenska Högarna   76   69   Tahkuna ☆
                    49   ☆ Ristna   Haapsalu   EESTI
STOCKHOLM   82   Hiiumaa   VABARIIK
Södertälje   ☆ Revengegrundet   145   Köpu   (Dagö)
                    ☆ Almagrundet   100   82   38
Nynäs- 66   Muhu
hamn Huvudskär ☆ 130   146   82   (Moon)
Trosa   Saaremaa   Pärnu
ping   108   52   Vilsandi ☆   (Ösel)   (Pernau)
        73 Landsort ☆   72   82   12   Kuressaare   17   58°
sund   163 Gotska Sandön ☆ 123   37   25
        71   144   88   54   Sörve ☆   RIZHSKY Ainaži
208   108 60 BASIN 116   23 ☆ Kolka Ruhno Salacgriva
55   Fårö ☆   51 ☆ Irbes   48
Storkläppen 208 Hallshuk ☆   133   ☆ Sikragciems 46 ZALIV 41 LATVIJAS
65 Stenkyrkehuk ☆ 23   44   Ovišu ☆ Mikelbåka   34   REP.
Kungsgrundet Visby ☆ Gotland ☆ Östergarn KLINTS-   82   Mērspags ☆   Daugavgriva ☆
81   BANK 238 200   Ventspils   RIGA
Ölands Norra Udde ☆ 64   156   82   (Windau) 25
Stora Karlsö ☆ När ☆ 176   25   Užava ☆ 15
Högby 80   ☆ Akmenrags
Hoburg ☆ ☆ Faludden 157   (Steinort)
Kapelludden HOBURS 142   33   Liepāja
53   BANK 140   34   (Libau) ☆ Bernäti ☆
24   85 116   ☆ Pape
Udde NORRA   ☆ Šventoji   56°
MIDSJÖBANKEN 112   63   31
26 54   88 61   Klaipeda
105   90   (Memel)   LIETUVOS
13   58   REP.
32   66 83   35 Juodkrante
82   109   Nidden
        89 90   29 ☆ Rybačij
25 Rozewie   118   29 Lesnoj
(Rixhöft)   90   Obzornyj Mys Taran Gvardejskij
Stilo ☆   29 ☆   ROSSIYSKAYA
Czolpino ☆   Baltijsk ☆ Ščukinskij FEDERATSIYA
Ustka (Stolpmünde) GDYNIA 26 (Pillau) KALININGRAD (RUSSIA)
(GDINGEN) Hel   (KÖNIGSBERG)
GDANSK Krynica Morska
(DANZIG) (Kahlberg)   54°

P O L S K A

18°   20°   22°   24°   26°

Scale 1 : 2,3 Millionen (60°)

The island from the Ice Age

●●● Countless small and tiny islands, the skerries, line the southern and southwestern coasts of Finland. They emerged from an age-old, softly declining trunk of the Baltic Shield. About 2.3 million to 10,000 years ago, alluvial glaciers ground off all traces of erosion and soft rock from between the hard granite layers, polished the surfaces, and left behind a landscape of smooth humps.

When the ice melted, the landscape was at first flooded by a fresh water sea trapped between the terminal moraines and the ice shield. As the Baltic Shield rose, the numerous humps emerged from the water and turned into islands.

In the belt of skerries, the islands become lower and smaller with increasing distance between the coast and the sea. At the beginning of the open sea, only flat, bare rock humps rise above the water level.

In some places – for instance, in the skerries area around Hanko – several 10-kilometer (6.2-mi.) wide groups of skerries emerge from the Baltic Sea. The inner belt is formed by the rockbound mainland coast and the mostly timbered, tightly packed islands near the mainland. The outer skerries, often no more than bare rocks, are shaped by the wind and the sea.

Nowadays, there are only few permanent residents left on the skerries, which are instead becoming more and more popular as holiday resorts. Holiday homes can be found on virtually every tiny island today.

The islands constitute an amphibian border between the land and the sea where plants and animals find relatively favorable living conditions. The calm, shallow water can reach considerably high temperatures near the shorelines. Although life virtually explodes during the brief, bright summer months, only a few species are able to cope with the brackish water and its maximum salinity of 5 ppt.

Of the approximately 150 firmly installed algae indigenous to the Kattegat in the far west of the Baltic Sea, only 25 can survive in the brackish waters of the skerries area in southwestern Finland. The lack in variety cannot be balanced by fresh water species, as they tolerate not even the slightest degree of salinity.

The Bay of Finland is believed to be the most polluted region of the Baltic Sea. Almost 80 percent of the phosphate and 60 percent of the nitrogen contained in the plant nutrients within the bay are washed into the inlet by the Neva River. The Neva is only 74 kilometers (46 mi.) long, but it is the largest river to empty into the Baltic Sea. Its lower reaches collect waste waters from the Saint Petersburg area.

M I

Hamina
(Frederikshamn)

Loiviisa
(Lovisa)

Porvoo
(Borgå)

Kotka

Munapirtti

Kirkonmaa
6

29

Vahterpää

Kaunissaari
(1)

Emäsalo

Sårvsalo

Vatskär

Kejvsalö

27

Ristisaari

ORRENGRUND
36

Veltkari
31

47

46

Tainio

9

4

9

9

Suur Pellinki

Tiiskeri

38

38

21

9

Kotkan Majakka
2

8

26

50

65

28

35

46

27

29

9

9

62

32

8

Gogland N
5

30

Gogland

HELSINKI
(HELSINGFORS)

Porkkalan-
niemi

24

9

47

33

25

8

3

37

49

50

Gogland S

62

60°

31

Helsinki

26

26

Kålbådagrund

27

27

38

50

Rodser

Virginy

29

Porkala

35

64

58

27

53

25

36

22

Bol'šoj Tjuters
91

63

22

46

31

38

42

43

57

63

27

68

84

93

75

57

104

Vaindlo
2

66

Malyj
Tjuters
68

65

5

54

81

77

88

93

84

76

68

79

83

5

27

Tallinn

60
Keri
4

92

PÄRISPEA

NAGAEVA

KALK-
GRUND

81

58

62

NEU-
GRUND
27

92

81

4

85

Prangli N

102

Aksi

Mohni

84

3

67

1

28

4

5

NARVA LAHT

82

7

83

Aegna

Leesi

Juminda

77

27

40

1

3

28

38

40

47

33

Naissaar

Aegna

76

16

Malusi

86

5

37

Vainupea

8

Letipea

25

39

40

37

61

65

Naissaar

27
Keipsi

Rammusaar

TALLINNA

39

LAHT

Muuga

Kohtla-Järve

34

Suurupi

TALLINN
(REVAL)

Kiperort

29°

ROSSIYSKAYA

Rondo

FEDERATSIYA

Primorsk

(RUSSIA)

Zap.
Berëzovyj

Bol.
Berëzovyj

8

Stirsudden

Zelenogorsk

21

GREKOVA

Flotskij

20

29

22

Sestroreck

8

AGAMEMNON

28

27

22

24

24

GULF OF FINLAND

Tolbuchin

EESTI

22

22

29

28

BARIIK

Pen-Cheta-Stor

22

31

20

Kotlin

60°

22

DEMAN-
STEJNSKIE

5

Sepelevskij

Kronštadt

NEVSKAJA

PROVODNIK

Krasnaå Gorka

SANKT PETERSBURG

ZAPAL

22

23

Ustinskij

GUBA

8

Lomonosov

Nevа

31

20

KOPORSKAJA
GUBA

Petrodvorec

Gorki

29°

+ Dangerous underwater rock

☆ Major light, lighthouse

-◄--- Traffic separation

--►--

Scale 1 : 750 000 (60°)

When the Baltic Sea freezes up

●●● The Gulf of Bothnia is composed of two smaller basins, the Bothnia Sea in the south and the Bothnian Wiek in the north. Almost exactly in the middle stands the Kvarken Rise with its skerries that cut into both sides of the bay. Not far to the west of Kvarken, the Scandinavian Shield rises by approximately 1 centimeter (0.4 in.) per year, faster than any other part of the Baltic region.

Immediately after the last ice age, when the ice had just about melted, the shield rose from the water at a rate of some 3 centimeters (1.2 in.) per year. Despite the worldwide postglacial rise in water level that neutralized part of the land rise, remains of the former coastline have been preserved in heights of 300 meters (948 ft.).

The Baltic Sea is located in the southern border zone of a climatic region where seas can freeze up. In extremely cold winters, the Baltic Sea is buried completely under an ice cover, but even in warmer winters, there is an ice sheet at least over the Bothnian wiek, most of the time over the entire Bay of Bothnia. Due to the low salinity which remains permanently below 6 parts per thousand, sometimes dropping to as little as 2 parts per thousand, the frost limit of the ocean water is raised. Unlike polar ice, this ice does not contain capillary channels for frozen brine. In the northern Baltic Sea, the water freezes completely to form a clear, transparent, and very hard ice.

Near Kemiles at the northern end of the Bay of Bothnia, the bay is buried under a closed ice sheet for 170 to 190 days a year, while the Åland Islands at the southern end of the bay are covered with ice only for 4 to 50 days per year.

In the north of the Bothnian Wiek, glaciation usually begins in early November. In the last two weeks of January, the entire bay is buried under permanent ice which reaches its maximum thickness by the end of March. In the skerries region off Kemi, the ice sheet can be 80 centimeters to 120 centimeters (32 in. to 47 in.) deep, near the Kvarken Islands on average 50 centimeters (20 in.), and near the Åland Islands still about 40 centimeters (16 in.).

The Bay of Bothnia is usually ice-free in the second half of May. After extremely cold winters, however, there may still be ice floats on the water in June.

The biggest problem for ships are the ice ridges that form when the wind pushes the ice floats against each other at the beginning and end of the icy period. These ridges can rise 3 meters to 4 meters (9.8 ft. to 13 ft.) above sea level, and reach 15 meters to 28 meters (49 ft. to 92 ft.) below the water surface.

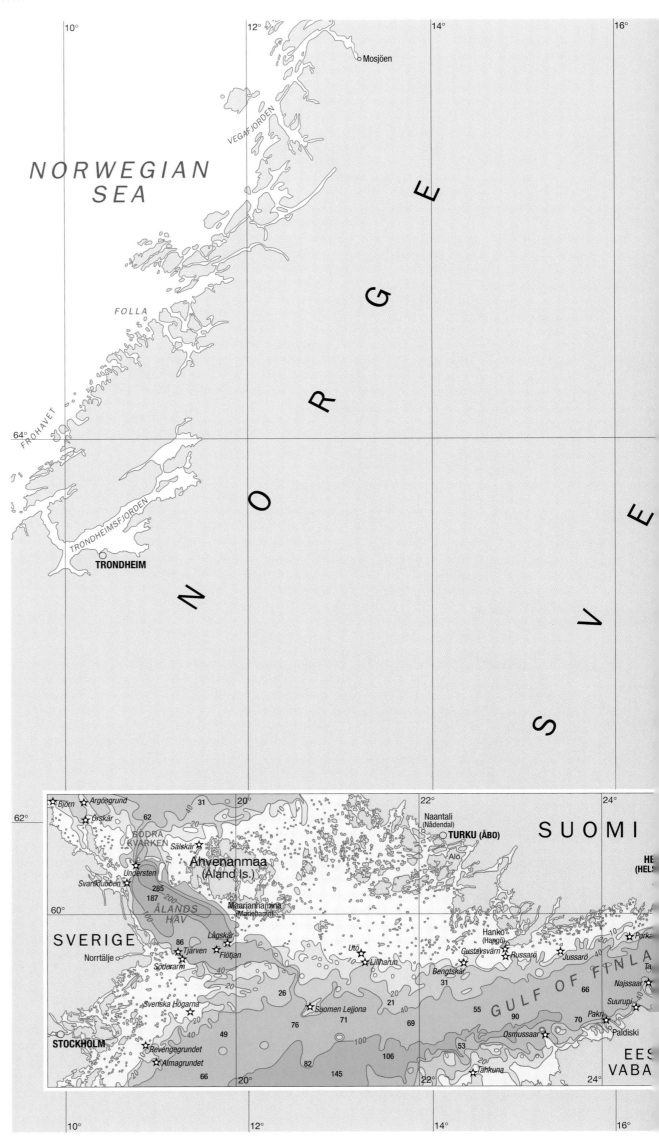

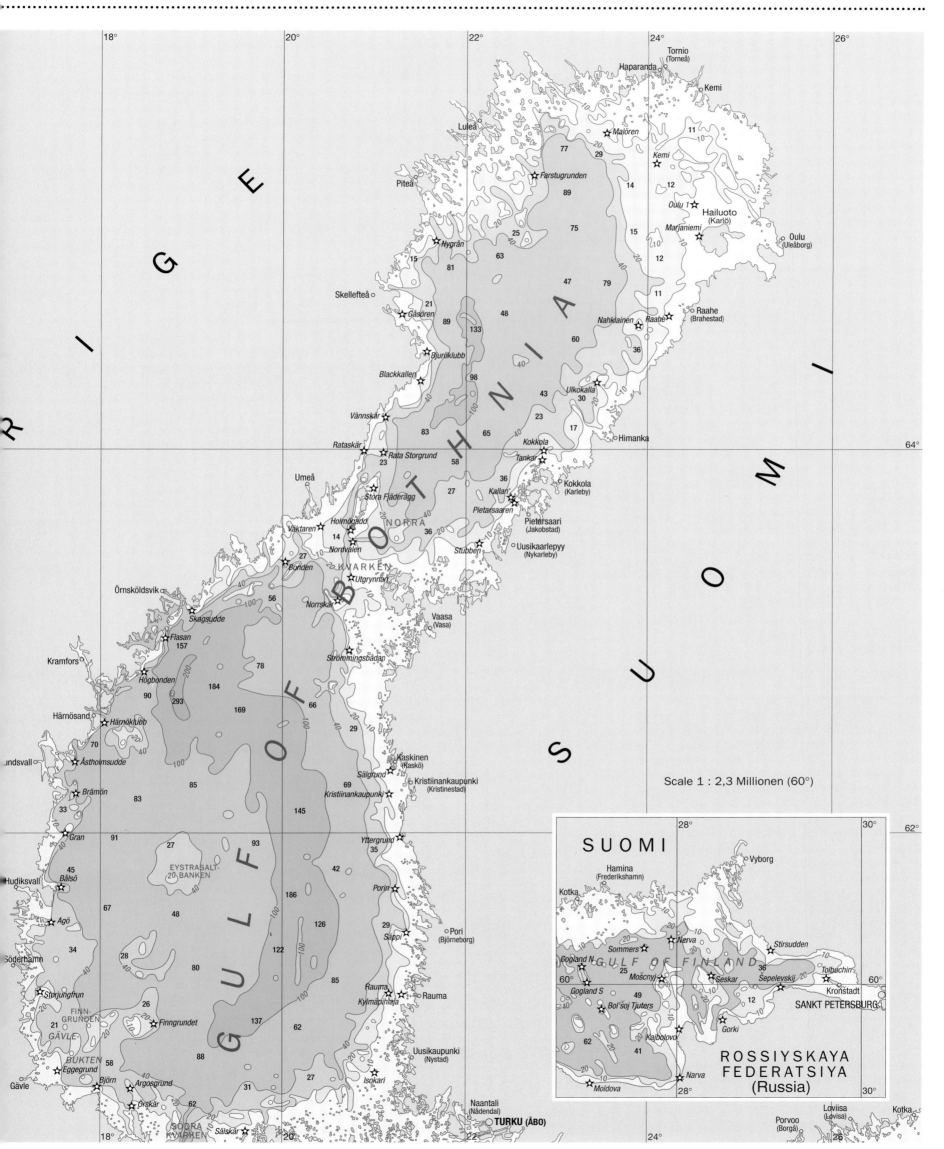

GULF OF BOTHNIA

NORRA

KVARKEN

Scale 1 : 2,3 Millionen (60°)

SUOMI

GULF OF FINLAND

ROSSIYSKAYA
FEDERATSIYA
(Russia)

Tornio
(Torneå)
Haparanda
Kemi
Luleå
Malören
Kemi
77
29
Piteå
Farstugrunden
Oulu 1
Hailuoto
(Karlö)
89
14
12
25
75
15
Marjaniemi
Oulu
(Uleåborg)
Nygrån
81
63
12
15
47
79
Skellefteå
11
21
48
Raahe
(Brahestad)
Gåsören
89
133
Nahkiainen
Raahe
60
36
Bjuröklubb
98
Blackkallen
43
Ulkokalla
30
23
17
Vännskär
83
65
Kokkola
Rataskär
58
Tankar
Rata Storgrund
23
Umeå
27
36
Kokkola
(Karleby)
Stora Fläderägg
Kallan
Holmögadd
NORRA
36
Pietarsaaren
Vaktaren
14
Pietarsaari
(Jakobstad)
Nordvalen
27
Stubben
Uusikaarlepyy
(Nykarleby)
Bonden
Utgrynnan
Örnsköldsvik
56
KVARKEN
Norrskär
Skagsudde
100
Vaasa
(Vasa)
Flasan
157
Strömmingsbådan
Kramfors
78
Högbonden
200
184
Härnösand
90
66
Härnöklubb
293
169
70
29
Åstholmsudde
40
Kaskinen
(Kaskö)
Brämön
85
Sälgrund
Kristiinankaupunki
(Kristinestad)
33
83
69
Kristiinankaupunki
Gran
91
145
Yttergrund
45
93
35
Bålsö
27
42
EYSTRASALT-
BANKEN
20
Porin
67
186
Porin
48
126
Agö
29
Pori
(Björneborg)
34
122
Säppi
28
80
85
Storjungfrun
26
Rauma
FINN-
GRUNDEN
137
Kylmäpihlaja
Rauma
21
62
GÄVLE
Finngrundet
88
BUKTEN
58
Uusikaupunki
(Nystad)
Eggegrund
31
27
Isokari
Gävle
Björn
Argosgrund
Örskär
62
SÖDRA
KVARKEN
Sälskär
Naantali
(Nådendal)
TURKU (ÅBO)

SUOMI
Vyborg
Hamina
(Frederikshamn)
Kotka
Stirsudden
Nerva
Gogland N
Sommers
25
Moščnyj
36
Tolbuchin
Seskar
Šepelevskij
Kronstadt
Gogland S
49
SANKT PETERSBURG
Bol'šoj Tjuters
12
62
Gorki
Kajbolovo
41
Narva
Moldova
Porvoo
(Borgå)
Loviisa
(Lovisa)
Kotka

INDEX

This index focuses on the oceanographic information contained in the nautical charts. Geographic indications relating to the continents are included only to a minor extent.

Abbreviations:
F. Z. = Fracture Zone
I. = Island
Is. = Islands (group)
Mt. = Mountain
SMt. = Seamount
Ri. = River

PHOTO CREDITS

Flyleaf AKG;
2-3 Emil Luider/ RAPHO/Focus;
4-5 Klaus Bossemeyer/ Bilderberg; 6-7 IFA-Bilderteam;
8-9 Fred Bavendam/Save-Bild;
10-11 Brad Lewis/ Science Photo Library/Focus;
12-13 Jan Stromme/ FOTEX/Picturesque;
14-15 Elichi Kurasawa/Focus;
22 AKG; 23 Sylvain Cazenave/ Vandystadt/Focus; 24 AKG;
25 Simon Fraser/Science Photo Library/Focus, Dorling Kindersley; 26 The Natural History Museum-London;
27 AKG; 28 Woodfin Camp/Kenneth Garrett/Focus;
29 AKG; 44-47 AKG;
48 Dr. Johannes Kinzer;
48-49 Hila Küpper/GEO;
51 Hila Küpper/GEO;
52 Daniel J.Cox/Wildlife, Jeff Rotman/Save-Bild;
53 D.Perrine/ Wildlife,Dorling Kindersley;55 J. M. La Roque/ Auscape/Save-Bild,Jahr Verlag Wale+Delphine;
56 Dr. Friedrich Krügler;
57 Anne Benthues; 58 Dorling Kindersley; 59 Friedrich Stark/Das Fotoarchiv;
60 IFA-Bilderteam; 61 Herbert H.Böhm; 62 NASA/Science Photo Library/Focus;
63 Bettmann/Corbis/Picture Press; 64 BuddyMays/Travel Stock; 65 DPA, aus"Planet der Meere"; 66 Dorling Kindersley;
67 Elichi Kurasawa/PPS/Focus, IFA-Bilderteam, J. Freund/ Wildlife; 69 Simon Fraser/ Science Photo Library/Focus, Dorling Kindersley; 70 Dorling Kindersley, Simon Fraser/ Science Photo Library/Focus;
71 Walter Mayr/Focus;
72 Maersk Sealand, Georg Fischer/Bilderberg; 74 Rolf Nobel/Visum; 75 Dirk Eisermann/Das Fotoarchiv; 76 DPA, Till Leser/Bilderberg; 77 DPA, Miquel González/Laif; 78 DPA, Christopher Pillitz/Network/ Focus; 79 Wolfgang Volz/ Bilderberg; 80 Dana Press, Visum; 80 Schweden-Werbung, DPA; 82 IFA-Bilderteam, Peter Kullmann/ Focus;
83 IFA-Bilderteam, O.Jossen/ action press; 84 Rainer Drexel/ Bilderberg, Dole; 85 Hahn/ Laif; 86 Andreas Hub/Laif;
87 Jochen Tack/Das Fotoarchiv, IFA-Bilderteam;
88 National Maritime Museum-London; 88-89 ©1991 Mel Fisher Maritime Heritage Society-Key West FL, Dylan Kibler; 90 REX Features, DPA (2); 91 Illustration by Ken Marschall © 1992 from Titanic: An Illustrated History, a Viking studio/ Madison Press Book, Rudolf Gillmann;
92 Simon Fraser/Science Photo Library/ Focus, DPA; 93 Robert Visser/ Greenpeace, Michael Yamashita/Focus, Dorling Kindersley; 94 Klaus-D. Francke/ Bilderberg;
94-95 Dorling Kindersley;
96 Corbis/Picture Press;
96-97 Dorling Kindersley;
98 M. Kirchgessner/Bilderberg;
99 Drewa/Fotex, IFA-Bilderteam; 100 Drewa/Fotex;
101 DPA, Arno Gasteiger/ Bilderberg; 102 David A.Hardy/

Science Photo Library/Focus, Prof. Dr. Peter Halbach, Gunter Grzesik/GEO; 103 IFA-Bilderteam; 104 DPA;
105 Wisniewski/Silvestris;
106 AKG; 107 Fahrbach;
108 Kurt Amsler/Vandystadt/ Focus; 109 Silvestris (2), Dorling Kindersley; 110 IFA-Bilderteam (2), Michael Peukert/ Focus; 111 Barry Lewis/ Network/Focus, IFA-Bilderteam (2);
112 IFA-Bilderteam;
113 Stange/action press, IFA-Bilderteam, Dorling Kindersley; 114 IFA-Bilderteam, Morgan/Greenpeace;
115 IFA Bilderteam; 116 Dirk Eisermann/Das Fotoarchiv, National Maritime Museum Picture Library-London;
117 Hartmut Schwarzbach/ Argus; 118 Nik Wheeler/ Monaco Oceanographic Museum/Das Fotoarchiv;
119 Rolf Nobel/Visum, Collection du Musée océanographique de Monaco;
bookend AKG

Diagrams and charts:
26 Harald Blanck;
50 Melanie Wolter;
54 Rainer Droste/GEO;
56, 57, 58 Harald Blanck;
61, 62 Rainer Droste/GEO;
63, 64, 65 Melanie Wolter;
68, 74, 75, 79 Harald Blanck;
84, 86 Günther Edelmann/ GEO; 88 Harald Blanck;
98, 103 Günther Edelmann/ GEO; 105 Harald Blanck;
106 Rainer Droste/GEO;
107 Melanie Wolter;
115 Harald Blanck

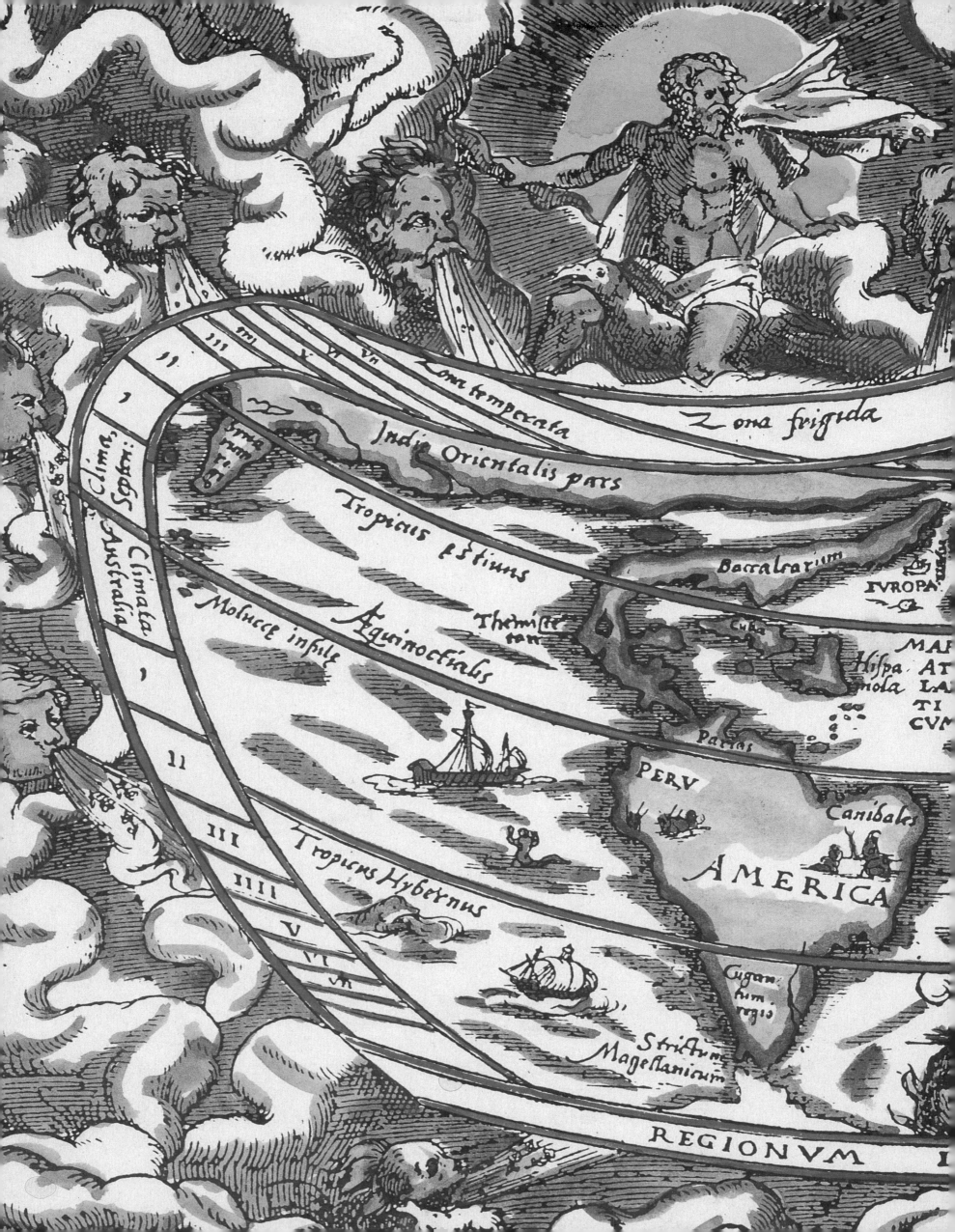